Prodromal or Residual Symptoms:

(1) marked social isolation or withdrawal
(2) marked impairment in role functioning as wage-earner, student, or homemaker
(3) markedly peculiar behavior (e.g., collecting garbage, talking to self in public, hoarding food)
(4) marked impairment in personal hygiene and grooming
(5) blunted or inappropriate affect
(6) digressive, vague, overelaborate, or circumstantial speech, or poverty of speech, or poverty of content of speech
(7) odd beliefs or magical thinking, influencing behavior and inconsistent with cultural norms, e.g., superstitiousness, belief in clairvoyance, telepathy, "sixth sense," "others can feel my feelings," overvalued ideas, ideas of reference
(8) unusual perceptual experiences, e.g., recurrent illusions, sensing the presence of a force or person not actually present
(9) marked lack of initiative, interests, or energy

Examples: Six months of prodromal symptoms with one week of symptoms from A; no prodromal symptoms with six months of symptoms from A; no prodromal symptoms with one week of symptoms from A and six months of residual symptoms.

E. It cannot be established that an organic factor initiated and maintained the disturbance.

F. If there is a history of Autistic Disorder, the additional diagnosis of Schizophrenia is made only if prominent delusions or hallucinations are also present.

Schizophrenic Disorders

Sense and Nonsense in Conceptualization, Assessment, and Treatment

PERSPECTIVES ON INDIVIDUAL DIFFERENCES

CECIL R. REYNOLDS, *Texas A&M University, College Station*
ROBERT T. BROWN, *University of North Carolina, Wilmington*

Current volumes in the series

EXPLORATIONS IN TEMPERAMENT
International Perspectives on Theory and Measurement
Edited by Jan Strelau and Alois Angleitner

HANDBOOK OF CREATIVITY
Assessment, Research, and Theory
Edited by John A. Glover, Royce R. Ronning, and Cecil R. Reynolds

HANDBOOK OF MULTIVARIATE EXPERIMENTAL PSYCHOLOGY
Second Edition
Edited by John R. Nesselroade and Raymond B. Cattell

HISTORICAL FOUNDATIONS OF EDUCATIONAL PSYCHOLOGY
Edited by John A. Glover and Royce R. Ronning

INDIVIDUAL DIFFERENCES IN CARDIOVASCULAR RESPONSE TO STRESS
Edited by J. Rick Turner, Andrew Sherwood, and Kathleen C. Light

THE INDIVIDUAL SUBJECT AND SCIENTIFIC PSYCHOLOGY
Edited by Jaan Valsiner

LEARNING STRATEGIES AND LEARNING STYLES
Edited by Ronald R. Schmeck

PERSONALITY DIMENSIONS AND AROUSAL
Edited by Jan Strelau and Hans J. Eysenck

PERSONALITY, SOCIAL SKILLS, AND PSYCHOPATHOLOGY
An Individual Differences Approach
Edited by David G. Gilbert and James J. Connolly

SCHIZOPHRENIC DISORDERS
Sense and Nonsense in Conceptualization, Assessment, and Treatment
Leighton C. Whitaker

THEORETICAL FOUNDATIONS OF BEHAVIOR THERAPY
Edited by Hans J. Eysenck and Irene Martin

A Continuation Order Plan is available for this series. A continuation order will bring delivery of each new volume immediately upon publication. Volumes are billed only upon actual shipment. For further information please contact the publisher.

Schizophrenic Disorders

Sense and Nonsense in Conceptualization, Assessment, and Treatment

Leighton C. Whitaker

Swarthmore College
Swarthmore, Pennsylvania

With a chapter by

Antonio E. Puente

University of North Carolina at Wilmington
Wilmington, North Carolina

Plenum Press • New York and London

Library of Congress Cataloging-in-Publication Data

Whitaker, Leighton C.
Schizophrenic disorders : sense and nonsense in conceptualization, assessment, and treatment / Leighton C. Whitaker ; with a contribution by Antonio E. Puente.
p. cm. -- (Perspectives on individual differences)
Includes bibliographical references and index.
ISBN 0-306-44156-X
1. Schizophrenia. 2. Schizophrenia--Diagnosis. I. Puente, Antonio E. II. Title. III. Series.
[DNLM: 1. Schizophrenia--diagnosis. 2. Schizophrenia--therapy. 3. Schizophrenic Psychology. WM 203 W577s]
RC514.W433 1992
616.89'82--dc20
DNLM/DLC
for Library of Congress 92-17021
CIP

ISBN 0-306-44156-X

A Division of Plenum Publishing Corporation
233 Spring Street, New York, N.Y. 10013

Printed in the United States of America

For
Suzanne, Corinne, Priscilla, and Benjamin

Preface

No diagnosis of mental disorder is more important or more disputable than that of "schizophrenia." The 1982 case of John Hinckley, who shot President Reagan, brought both aspects of this diagnostic dilemma to the forefront of national attention. It became evident to the general public that the experts engaged to study him exhaustively could not agree on whether Hinckley was schizophrenic. General public outrage ensued, as schizophrenia, "the sacred symbol of psychiatry," in the words of Thomas Szasz (1976), emerged as a king of Alice in Wonderland travesty. Schizophrenia seemed not to be a legitimate diagnostic entity but some sort of facade erected to protect the guilty.

In 1973, David Rosenhan had already shown the readers of *Science* that *schizophrenia* was a label that could be given to normal people presenting with a supposed auditory hallucination on even one occasion. In Rosenhan's studies, mental health professionals were outclassed by the regular psychiatric hospital patients, who correctly saw the false schizophrenics as imposters while the professional diagnosticians continued to fool themselves.

These events are not isolated. Despite the many claims to diagnostic certainty, universally accepted criteria for calling someone a schizophrenic do not exist. At most, a high rate of agreement occurs only when a group of mental health professionals in the same institution are trained rigorously to use certain diagnostic criteria to rate information obtained in a certain way. However, so many systems are used for diagnosis that, although one group of experts may agree substantially among themselves, no two groups are likely to agree with each other. A patient clearly defined as schizophrenic by the experts at one institution may easily be diagnosed differently at another institution. Our confidence falls still more when, as usually happens in ordinary practice, diagnoses are generally made quickly, often by someone in training who sees the patient for perhaps 15 minutes in an emergency room. Once made, the diagnosis tends to stick, or if changed, it may be changed, for example, to "manic-depressive illness" just as arbitrarily as the original diagnosis was given. The unwittingly primitive nature of much ordinary diagnostic practice results in little or no information about the degree of disorder, its position on the dimension of acute to chronic, motivational and situational considerations, or the patient's strengths, though all of these individual differences are crucial to meaningful assessment and treatment. Although there are notable exceptions to these all-too-typical practices, vagueness of definition makes possible many varieties of uses and misuses of the label *schizophrenia.*

Many experiences have led to my writing this book, including various clinical and research undertakings at six psychiatric hospitals over a period of 15 years, plus many years of outpatient work with severely disturbed persons. One of my first experiences was with a 23-year-old woman who had two children and was in the process of a divorce, and who was accurately diagnosed as having Hodgkin's disease in the fourth or terminal stage back when no cure existed. She was expected to live for less than two years. Her only "skill' was dancing, which she had to give up because of her disease. She became severely withdrawn; was admitted to a psychiatric hospital, where she was diagnosed as "schizophrenic"; and was told by the chief psychiatrist—trained at an elite psychiatric institution—that she would always be schizophrenic. But her psychotherapist, who agreed that she had become schizophrenic, predicted a successful outcome. Her hope and hard work enabled her to become quite normal psychologically, according to independent observation, until more than 11 years later, when she finally died of Hodgkin's disease. Her physician, a hematologist, ascribed her surprising longevity to her great will to live. He said that she was the most normal person he had ever known, and he credited her with keeping up his morale and that of his colleagues, and of other terminal patients, for whom she had begun a group support program. He refused to believe, at first, that she had ever been diagnosed as schizophrenic or had ever been in a mental hospital. This case and many others impressed on me the need to go far beyond the simple diagnostic label *schizophrenia,* with its stereotyped connotations.

Whereas, traditionally, "schizophrenics" have been grouped together as if they were a homogeneous lot of creatures vastly different from "normals," I know of no other diagnostic group in which the individuals are more different, both intraindividually and interindividually. Careful observational studies show that the intraindividual differences are enormous, as exemplified in changes within the individual over time—sometimes from one day to another as well as over the years. As Silvano Arieti (1974), the late psychiatrist who devoted most of his life to trying to understand and help schizophrenics, said, "A striking characteristic of schizophrenia is the great variability of its course" (p. 49).

Interindividual differences are also marked. A diagnosis of schizophrenia may be distinguished, ironically, from other psychiatric diagnoses by the heterogeneity of the people given that label. As Arieti (1974) stated, "The symptomatology of schizophrenia assumes a large number of clinical forms" (p. 30). Psychiatrists Strauss and Carpenter (1981) declared that

> Heterogeneity of patients classified as schizophrenic is almost the hallmark of the disorder; yet, the modal schizophrenic patient is often processed through the health care system with surprisingly little attention paid to him or her as an individual and with unwarranted assumptions that the individual represents primarily one case in a homogeneous group phenomenon (p. 208).

Professional opinions about the concept of schizophrenia tend to fall into two schools: The first opinion, of believers in schizophrenia as a meaningful diagnostic category, is that "schizophrenics" have enough in common to be addressed adequately by nomothetic science; the second is that they do not. Some members of the first school tend to overemphasize the sameness among people called schizophrenic, whereas members of the second school tend to disdain the term altogether in favor of emphasizing individual differences. I propose that both nomothetic science and idiographic science should be used, and that these two approaches must be integrated if the concept of schizophrenic disorders is to make sense.

The result, politically, of emphasizing the nomothetic approach to the virtual exclusion of the idiographic is to homogenize "schizophrenics," usually for purposes of biological theory and treatment, as if they literally have physical diseases of the mind. Single-minded emphasis on the individual differences, however, has often enabled professionals and society at large to deny responsibility for providing any treatment or care. The deinstitutionalization movement in the United States, which emphasizes freedom and deemphasizes care and treatment, has left most patients without any viable care—whether inpatient or outpatient—quite as if the patients have no really disabling deficits and can essentially take care of themselves. Despite claims to the contrary, there is little evidence that the care and treatment that society provides people called schizophrenic is much better today than that provided in previous eras.

I decided, after reading much of the literature, doing research, working directly with schizophrenic persons for many years, and teaching courses on schizophrenic disorders, to write a book that would present a primarily psychosocial perspective on schizophrenic disorders, emphasizing an evaluation of both the assessed and the assessors. What follows is an attempt to take into account the personal, economic, and political pressures that (on one hand) segregate schizophrenic persons into disease entities having little or no kinship with the rest of us in terms of our deeply human emotions, personal relationships, and ways of thinking, and that (on the other hand) deny the seriousness of these disorders and their substantial commonality.

This book attempts to delineate the sense and nonsense of how schizophrenic disorders are conceptualized and assessed and how persons labeled *schizophrenic* are treated, as well as the sense and nonsense of schizophrenic modes of being.

LEIGHTON C. WHITAKER

Swarthmore, Pennsylvania

Acknowledgments

Many persons have contributed to whatever merit this book may have. Robert Brown and Antonio Puente, both of the psychology department faculty at the University of North Carolina at Wilmington, encouraged me to begin this book eight years ago. I am indebted to Professor Brown for his patience, support, and editorial assistance, and to Professor Puente for his contributing Chapter 8, "Assessment of Possible Neural Substrates."

Three other publishers granted me permission to publish excerpts from their books: Vintage Books, Random House, New York, for Susan Sheehan's 1983 book *Is There No Place on Earth for Me;* Pocket Books, Simon & Schuster, New York, for Romola Nijinsky's *Nijinsky* (1972); and the *Diagnostic and Statistical Manual of Mental Disorders* (Third Edition—Revised), copyright © 1987 American Psychiatric Association, Washington, D.C.

Many colleagues have contributed their encouragement and ideas. In particular, I wish to thank Arthur Deikman, M.D. and Bertram Karon, Ph.D., who have been especially helpful. My son Benjamin Whitaker deserves many thanks for dragging his father, kicking and screaming, into the computer age and for providing considerable help with the format of this book. Birgitte Haselgrove was quite helpful in preparing the final manuscript.

Contents

1

Introduction to the Phenomena and Their Conceptualization

Schizophrenic Experiences

To study and to help schizophrenic persons is to explore the range and depth of the human condition. As a group of people, those persons called schizophrenic represent every nationality, religion, ethnic origin, socioeconomic status, variety of intellectual endowment, emotional experience, and value system that may be encountered. None of their mental or emotional experiences are truly outside the capacity of other human beings, though our fear of them is often so great that we would deny any similarity between ourselves and people labeled *schizophrenic.* Ironically, the fear that we have in common with schizophrenic persons leads us to deny our similarities with them and makes us unable, therefore, to ascertain the true variations in the human condition that can be meaningfully assessed and how we can be of genuine help.

Our tendency to regard schizophrenic persons as alien creatures is promoted by bizarre and alienating behavior that may forcefully distance us even when we would ordinarily be friendly and caring:

> Jim, a young man dressed only in pants and shirt on a cold day, enters a psychotherapist's office smiling but averting his gaze. He sits down still smiling and still avoiding looking at the therapist. On the one hand, he seems to want to be with a fellow human being, and on the other hand, he looks like a wild animal ready to bolt out of the room at a moment's notice. He confirms this impression of extreme ambivalence as he says he wanted very much to come but almost decided not to. As he dares to look at the therapist for the first time, he conveys a feeling of terror, immediately generating a feeling of terror in the therapist himself. It is a gut terror, so basic and obliterating of any rational thoughts that the therapist himself is momentarily possessed by it. A minute goes by before the therapist can put this situation in any kind of perspective; he realizes then that the patient is terrified of him and of the cataclysmic possibility of rejection on the one hand and hurtful intrusion on the other.

The therapist kept on seeing Jim despite a momentary inclination to stop seeing him or at least to avoid the all-too-meaningful and threatening kind of emotional communication that had struck the therapist almost as soon as Jim entered the room. Jim became able, with his nondistancing therapist's help, to avoid a further acute breakdown, although he had had a severe schizophrenic breakdown two years earlier in high school.

Another young man was not so fortunate:

> Joe had survived a difficult family situation well enough to attend college, but he experimented frequently with the drug lysergic acid (LSD) and claimed greatly expanded mental powers that carried beyond the days when he was actually ingesting LSD. College became quite difficult for him, and he dropped out. He insisted that he was quite different from other human beings in that he had extraordinary powers. Matters took an even more serious turn when he "discovered" that other people were "broadcasting" their thoughts into his mind and reading his mind as well. Joe had some realization that he needed professional help and allowed himself to be psychiatrically hospitalized for a couple of weeks, but he then left the hospital, against medical advice, and his condition worsened. He continued to refuse both prescribed drug treatment and psychotherapy but continued to take LSD and used other illicit drugs also. His condition further deteriorated, and he died of a self-inflicted overdose of illicit drugs.

In this case, the treatment challenge was greatly complicated by illicit drug use, which apparently both facilitated and furthered a schizophrenic-like psychosis. Joe's ambivalence about getting close to other humans was expressed in his avoiding their help while insisting that they were very close in terms of the thought broadcasting and mind reading. His alienation persisted and even worsened, as magical, irrational means of communion with other humans were fantasized in place of real communion. His schizophrenic-like state was expressed in his pervasive mistaking of fantasy for reality.

The cases of Jim and Joe illustrate three primary characteristics of schizophrenic disorders: extreme fear, lack of communion with others, and a pervasive inability to distinguish fantasy from reality. These primary characteristics may be flagrant or quite well disguised, and mild or severe, so that the identification of a schizophrenic disorder often requires considerable skill, especially if one is to understand the degree of disorder, its acuteness or chronicity, its particular form, the factors producing and maintaining the disorder, and ways to help the person. We must address another kind of qualification also. Jim was said to be in a "schizophrenic-like" state because his condition was at least precipitated by an organic cause, in this case the drug LSD. A diagnosis of schizophrenic disorder is made only when a specific organic insult cannot be established as initiating and maintaining the disorder. Thus, schizophrenic disorders are characterized by the combination of extreme fear, lack of communion with others, an inability to distinguish fantasy from reality, and the absence of organic causation.

The fear characteristic of schizophrenic disorders is so extreme that perhaps a better word is *terror* (Karon & Vandenbos, 1981; Strauss & Carpenter, 1981). This terror is usually quite obvious during the acute phase of a schizophrenic breakdown. For example, dilated pupils, a racing heart, and a conviction that one's death is imminent signal an extreme emergency. When the person reacts to such panic with bizarre and grossly implausible "explanations," such as delusions of mind control and persecution, he or she is beginning to have a schizophrenic breakdown. Typically, the bizarre explanations express a fear-produced inability to communicate with other people and a substitution of fantasy for the reality that terrifies the person. This substitution is outside conscious awareness or control of the person; it is unwitting. The bizarre explanations reflect the illogicality, impairment, and unwittingness that characterize the cognitive dysfunction called *schizophrenic thought disorder.* If the explanations become crystallized into delusions, one may observe an apparent lessening of the fear. But what is happening is a transformation from overt to covert fear, or from manifest into latent fear (a transformation analogous to the conversion of kinetic into potential energy observed in physics). The delusional transformation serves to dam up otherwise wild, rampaging terror. If this transformation persists over months and years, the person becomes chronically schizophrenic. In such a defended state of mind, marked by a retreat from emotions, the person may seldom express strong emotion of any kind, but the lack of expression of emotion—or *affect,* as it is called—should not be confused with an actual lack of affect. Just as manifest fear may be transformed into latent or dammed-up fear, so may latent fear burst the dam and become wild, chaotic, and clearly manifest:

> John, a 35-year-old chronically schizophrenic man, had been hospitalized for a few months and then discharged while apparently apathetic and listless. He was sent to a psychotherapist who related to him in a calm, accepting way and encouraged him in life's simpler tasks, including obtaining an undemanding maintenance job and becoming able to write checks to pay household bills. As the therapy advanced, ever so cautiously, John learned also to balance his checkbook (though the same cannot be said for the therapist). During the year of this highly supportive psychotherapy, the patient progressed to the point of getting a promotion to a maintenance-supervisor position after writing a maintenance manual that had impressed his boss and fellow workers. The therapist then left the state to accept another professional position, and a new therapist took over. At first, the new therapist was supportive and gently encouraging, essentially following the treatment plan of the first therapist and seeing the patient make further slow progress. But deciding that the treatment was moving too slowly and that the patient should become more active and expressive, the new therapist offered John the interpretation that he was too passive and that this passivity was due to latent homosexuality. Though only of medium build and seemingly quite limited vitality, John responded immediately by destroying a large roomful of furniture and requiring four policemen to subdue him. John's previous lack of affective expression did not mean that he lacked affect or that his affect was "flat."

Schizophrenic persons may appear quite passive and withdrawn, especially in more advanced and severe forms of the disorder, such as John's chronic condition, but also in some relatively acute conditions in which the person has become so terrified as to become immobilized in a *catatonic* state of utter muteness and apparently lifeless immobility:

> A man of about age 30, name and address unknown, was brought by police to a state mental hospital. The police said they had found the man lying in a gutter on the street,

> and observers said he had been totally unresponsive. Thinking that the man might be in a coma, hospital authorities ordered an electroencephalogram (EEG), commonly known as a *brain wave test.* While administering the EEG and attaching objectively nonpainful electrodes to the man's scalp, the chief technician observed him to be slightly resistant and became convinced that the man was scared stiff rather than brain-damaged. As testing was concluding and the EEG record proved normal, the technicians again observed the man slightly resisting their touching him as they removed the electrodes. The chief technician then said to his assistant "Mr. What's-His-Name thinks these electrodes are dangerous, but they're not dangerous at all." The man then struggled to talk and stammered out his name in an unintelligible form, which the chief technician repeated in the same form and which the man then corrected with some sense of indignation. Both technicians then introduced themselves in a friendly fashion and reassured him that the electrodes were not dangerous, to which the patient replied, "Everything is dangerous!" The patient was further reassured, whereupon he sat up and was introduced to the unit chief, who was quite startled at the man's sudden recovery from his "coma."

The fear of dying plays a great role in many if not all schizophrenic breakdowns (Karon & Vandenbos, 1981; Searles, 1965). The patient just described—like the animals of many species, including humans—had sought to protect himself from death by appearing as if he had already died; he was in a *catatonic stupor.* The opposite phenomenon, extreme activity, may be displayed in an agitated attempt to stave off death. Thus, so-called *catatonic excitement,* a frantic and wild binge of activity, is the other side of the coin from catatonic stupor. These catatonic conditions are somewhat similar to so-called *schizoaffective conditions,* in which either heightened responsiveness or depression appears, the former being an active attempt to stave off death, and the latter serving to avoid being attacked by "lying low." These two sides of the coin are never far apart, and the coin may flip quickly, or over a period of several months as in the following case:

> Jerry had joined a religious cult and felt a strong communion with the cult members, which was disrupted as the cult leaders made increasing demands on the members to renounce all worldly pleasures. Jerry, far from home and in his middle 20s, left the cult and went to live on his own in a strange town for a few months; then he went home to establish himself again in a familiar community. He maintained a highly technical, impersonal job of the kind he had held in the previous city, but he found himself losing interest. Jerry was persuaded to see a therapist but resisted therapy on the grounds that it might promote in him further involvement in earthly pleasures like enjoying food and relationships with women. By then, he had begun to feel that he had a kind of extrasensory communication with an older man who lived next door. He dropped out of psychotherapy after a couple of sessions and gradually showed more signs of a full-blown schizophrenic breakdown, which culminated in his stopping cars on the street and telling them about his lawn. Jerry would tell each driver that his lawn now had all weeds except for a few blades of grass. Some of the drivers offered words of encouragement, saying that they hoped his lawn would prosper, but Jerry was not reassured.
>
> Having become flagrantly delusional, Jerry was placed in a psychiatric hospital. After his discharge from the hospital, he resumed psychotherapy and realized that his lawn was a metaphor for himself and that his hope for himself, his spirit, had dwindled

to just a few fragile strands. He knew that his frequent thoughts of death represented his fear of his own and others' dying. At this point, he was no longer clearly psychotic but had lapsed into the defensive depression and apathy that often follow what is often called the active phase of a schizophrenic disorder.

As Zigler and Glick (1988) proposed, the active or excited phase of a paranoid schizophrenic disorder is behaviorally and motivationally similar to manic states of excitement, and in this way, at least some forms of paranoid schizophrenic disorder are a kind of camouflaged depression. Like the manic person who lapses into depression after desperate attempts at denial and warding off, the paranoid schizophrenic person may go through an excited phase while trying to ward off depression and low self-esteem.

The frenzied excitement that Jerry showed when he stopped drivers on the streets to seek help with his "dying lawn" was a kind of protest against his own death, ostensibly physical death but, in the case of a schizophrenic breakdown, the death of the spirit or the desire to live. Thus Jerry was also trying to communicate with others, though he was doing so "inappropriately" in terms of social norms. He would have reached out more appropriately had he not been so afraid of other people and what they might do to him. Each of his bids for help was to a stranger with whom he would have only the briefest contact. He made contact with each driver on his own terms, knowing that none of them would stop long enough to hurt him. In this way, he expressed the extreme *ambivalence* toward getting help and communicating with others that has traditionally been regarded as another hallmark of schizophrenic disorders.

Some Common Related Conditions

The three primary characteristics of schizophrenic disorders that were noted and illustrated in the previous section of this chapter—extreme fear, lack of communion with others, and an inability to distinguish fantasy from reality—do not distinguish schizophrenic disorders from other disorders unless all three are present and organic causation is absent. People with organic brain syndromes—actual diseases or physical defects of the central nervous system—may display seemingly similar kinds of characteristics, though their impairment is of neurological capacity rather than functional ability. Schizophrenic persons, by definition, have functional rather than physical disorders. Inconsistency of functioning ability is a hallmark of schizophrenic disorders, whereas consistency of limitation is a hallmark of central nervous system impairment:

A 40-year-old man was tentatively diagnosed as schizophrenic and was referred for psychological test evaluation. His direct and friendly manner and lack of fear and the ease of communicating with him immediately impressed the examining psychologist. The patient had great difficulty on certain of the psychological tests, especially on tasks involving geometric designs. Overall, the test results and his manner suggested an organic brain syndrome and not a schizophrenic disorder. Subsequent extensive neurological evaluation revealed brain atrophy, evidently related to prolonged inhalation of noxious gases while he was working in a ditch at an oil refinery.

Schizophrenic persons are distinguished in many ways by their inconsistencies over time and in terms of emotional and intellectual challenges. For example, a schizophrenic person's overall intelligence corresponds little to the severity of that person's thought disorder. Thus, on the *Whitaker Index of Schizophrenic Thinking* (WIST; Whitaker, 1980), many of the very highest indexes have been obtained from persons with very superior overall intelligence as measured by the Wechsler Adult Intelligence Scale—Revised (WAIS-R; Wechsler, 1981).

We may also observe, even in quite extreme form, one or two of the three primary characteristics of schizophrenic disorders in many other people who are not schizophrenic. The phenomenon of bigotry is a good example. Bigotry, according to Webster's *New Third International Dictionary,* is "the state of mind of a bigot; obstinate and unreasoning attachment to one's own belief and opinions with intolerance of beliefs opposed to them." Bigots, in their obstinate resistance to reason that would help them to distinguish their fantasies from reality, show at least one characteristic of a schizophrenic disorder. And the delusional intensity that bigotry often attains would suggest that, like the schizophrenic person who has "explained" his or her fear, the intensely bigoted person is also extremely afraid, although in a latent or covert way. Challenges to bigotry tend to activate the fear and may even intensify the bigot's beliefs. But if the bigot's beliefs are in harmony with a substantial number of other people's beliefs, the bigot is in communion with others and is not regarded as schizophrenic. Thus, the millions of Nazis who promulgated extremely irrational and refutable beliefs about Jews would not be diagnosed schizophrenic on that account, however odious their beliefs and however grossly out of touch they were with reality.

A person who has an irrational belief of delusional intensity that is not shared by others but who, apart from this belief, is not obviously odd or bizarre would be diagnosed according to the revised third edition of the *Diagnostic and Statistical Manual* (DSM-III-R; American Psychiatric Association, 1987), as having a "Delusional (Paranoid) Disorder." The fact that the person stands alone distinguishes him or her from many persons who are bigoted to the point of delusional intensity but who receive support for their beliefs from other persons.

Like severely bigoted persons, the person with a delusional disorder may exhibit grandiose and persecutory convictions; these convictions are two sides of the same coin. The person says in effect that he or she is, or at least would be, great if it were not for someone's persecuting him or her. This phenomenon of grandiose-persecutory fantasies of delusional intensity is familiar on a broad scale in the propaganda of bigoted groups, for example, the Nazis or the Ku Klux Klan. The Nazis were supposedly destined for greatness because of their pure Aryan blood but were thwarted and threatened with contamination by the Jews. Similarly, Ku Klux Klan members fancy that they will rise to greatness if they can exterminate blacks, Catholics, and Jews, who they believe have contaminated society and them.

Common to schizophrenic, bigoted, and paranoid conditions are extreme problems with self-esteem or self-worth. Paranoid and bigoted orientations are ways to raise oneself, no matter how irrationally, from a condition of devastatingly low self-esteem. Schizophrenic persons differ from groups of bigoted people in that they have not established a consensus or communion with others with whom they can share their beliefs; they are unable to convince others of the correctness of their beliefs. Schizophrenic persons are exceedingly individual, or idiosyncratic. Persons with delusional (paranoid) disorder are just as solitary in their beliefs but have contained their oddness enough so that it is not, at least obviously, greatly at variance with the beliefs of every other person, except in the area of a single delusion. But most schizophrenic persons have paranoid features, and the degree of their containment of their oddness is an important assessment issue:

> Students in an abnormal psychology class visited a mental hospital, where they spent an hour walking around the grounds with four patients. Three of these patients seemed easily identifiable. The young man who talked a mile a minute and kept doing cartwheels was obviously manic. Another patient was obviously depressed. Yet another seemed to be brain-damaged, as suggested by her speech limitations. But the fourth patient remained a mystery until the hour was almost up; he seemed entirely normal. One of the students then happened to mention something about a toothache. At that point, the patient was seized with excitement as he reached into his pocket and grabbed a handful of newspaper clippings, which he said revealed how he had been prevented by the FBI from becoming a dentist.

Although the breakdowns in rational thinking observed in various forms of what we might call group madness, exemplified by bigotry, are closely similar to those individual forms of breakdown exemplified by delusional paranoid disorders and schizophrenic disorders, the schizophrenic disorders are sometimes romanticized as creative. But being schizophrenic is quite different from being creative, except that both involve an individuality of mind.

The person in a schizophrenic state of mind has difficulty bringing thoughts and feelings into logical order and communicating with others. The creative person is able to organize the *primary process* of unorganized impressions—that is, establish a *secondary process*—and then reach even further to a third, or creative, organizational level. Silvano Arieti (1976), who made extensive comparisons of schizophrenic and creative cognitive phenomena, calls the creative level a "tertiary process." In essence, the schizophrenic state of mind is especially far removed from the creative state of mind in terms of cognitive level. Creativity is characterized by a level of awareness and control (i.e., wittingness) that not only shows mastery of certain ideas from the standpoint of consensual belief and usage but has gone beyond these ideas in various ingenious ways. The creative person may appear "mad," however, when that person's ideas seem "far out" and have not yet been tested so as to achieve *consensual validation,* the acceptance of ideas or opinions by others.

The creative person and the schizophrenic person may also appear quite similar if others do not agree with their beliefs. But lack of agreement or consensus, by itself, does not make a delusion, unless the beliefs have been adequately subjected to *reality testing* and found to be invalid. The question is whether the beliefs can stand up to observational or experimental inquiry. Therefore, our ultimate concern should be with the truth of assertions rather than with deviance from social norms. Einstein's theory of relativity lacked consensual validation for many years because certain needed astronomical observations could not yet be made. Meanwhile, because of the Nazi persecution, Einstein went into exile, and a hundred Nazi professors published a book condemning his theory of relativity. Unconcerned, Einstein said, "If I were wrong, one professor would have been enough" (Fadiman, 1985, p. 187). In contrast to the creative person's discovery or invention, the schizophrenic person's delusion cannot be validated by means of an impartial test.

Schizophrenic thinking disorder also has its counterpart in the way advertising may get us to accept grossly illogical equations. Advertisements for the leading damaging drugs in our culture, cigarettes and alcohol, often rely on a form of short-circuited cognition that is quite similar to schizophrenic thinking (Whitaker, 1989). For example, television ads appearing during breaks in athletic events try to equate beer drinking with athletic prowess. A television commercial shown often during major league baseball games shows a baseball and a bottle of beer side by side while we are told both visually and aurally that they go together. This vivid visual and auditory imagery that correlates alcohol and America's favorite sport suggests that beer enhances one's athletic prowess. The ad is powerfully sensory, has an autistic or wish-fulfilling component, and, of course, does not invite critical thinking. Given the absence of the time or the inclination to do the work that thinking requires, the passive recipient of the ad tends to equate two behaviors that are actually contradictory in combination. By sponsoring an arm-wrestling contest, another beer company suggests that muscular strength is increased with alcohol use. This schizophrenic-like equation is contradicted by the seldom-attended-to fact that alcohol use diminishes muscle strength both immediately and cumulatively over one's lifetime.

Similarly, advertisers tell young women who want to have radiant complexions, brilliantly white teeth, and beautiful figures that they can attain these features, as well as suave sophistication, by smoking cigarettes. These grossly illogical implications, which are direct opposites of the truth, are conveyed powerfully by wish-fulfilling appeals mediated by pictures of women with these desirable features smoking cigarettes. Such advertising relies on short-circuiting thinking per se and, when successful, yields a product very similar to schizophrenic inability to think logically. When we are influenced by these forms of advertising, we are engaged in what might well be called the schizophrenic thinking of everyday life.

Incidence, Prevalence, and Costs of Schizophrenic Disorders

The dilemma of how exactly to define schizophrenic disorders shows itself especially clearly when epidemiologists attempt to estimate these disorders' incidence and prevalence. Even the incidence of schizophrenic disorders, the rate at which new cases occur each year, is difficult to estimate because of marked variations in diagnostic practice as well as possible underreporting due to the stigma attached to the label *schizophrenic.* For example, the higher incidences reported for the United States are partly, at least, a function of a broader definition of schizophrenic disorders, especially before the adoption of the third edition of the *Diagnostic and Statistical Manual* (DSM-III; American Psychiatric Association, 1980) and the DSM-III-R (American Psychiatric Association, 1987). Most other countries have used a narrower definition of schizophrenic disorders. Furthermore, estimating the incidence and prevalence of schizophrenic disorders is made quite difficult because epidemiology, the science of the estimation of disease incidence and prevalence, is designed to address phenomena that have more readily definable disease characteristics, including etiology, course, prognosis, and evidence of cellular morbidity. Schizophrenic disorders have unknown etiology, course, and prognosis from the standpoint of the usual physical criteria for diagnosis, and they have no firmly established physical pathology or cellular morbidity. Nor is there the kind of highly agreed-upon and reliable definition for *schizophrenia* that there is for most diseases. Thus, estimates of the incidence, prevalence, and costs of schizophrenic disorders rest on shaky bases. The figures are really predicated on certain ways of looking at behavioral phenomena to represent a group of disorders that are certainly not definable as diseases and are even difficult to define as syndromes.

Karno and Norquist (1989) indicated just how basic this dilemma is and how important it is to achieve meaningful classification:

> During the 90 years that it has been a recognized syndrome, schizophrenia, with its protean manifestations and lifelong course, has been the classical refractory mental disorder—refractory to consensual conceptualization, definition, and identification of etiology, and tragically refractory to prevention and treatment. Schizophrenia has epitomized the axiom that classification is essential to scientific understanding. A basic process in understanding it is a program of epidemiological studies of the disorder (viz., assessments of its distribution among populations and of factors associated with its occurrence). (p. 699)

Keeping in mind the limitations of representing schizophrenic disorders as diseases with reliable and accurate diagnoses and counting only those people who present for treatment, I note here some of the commonly cited figures for incidence, prevalence, and cost.

In terms of incidence, Babigian (1985), for example, noted that between 100,000 and 200,000 Americans "develop schizophrenia" each year. In other words, many new cases present for care each year in the United States, and perhaps about 1 person per 2,000 in this country is seen by mental health practitioners who report that person as schizophrenic for the first time during that reporting year. Noting that reported variations in prevalence rates for schizophrenia are even greater than variations in incidence rates, Babigian (1985) cited estimates of 0.6%–3.0% of the U.S. population as being schizophrenic at some time in their lives, and estimates of 0.19%–0.90% in European studies, and from 0.21% to 0.38% in Asian studies. Strauss and Carpenter (1981) noted that reported lifetime prevalences, taking into account all of the individuals diagnosable as schizophrenic sometime during their lives, range internationally from about 2 per 1,000, or 0.2%, to nearly 10 per 1,000, or 1.0%, and that at any one time (point prevalence), according to community surveys in various countries, some 0.5%–3.0% of the population are schizophrenic.

The cost of schizophrenic disorders has been calculated in the United States in terms of direct treatment and also in terms of many less obvious indirect costs, including law enforcement, maintenance and transfer of patients, burden on families, and lost productivity. For example, Strauss and Carpenter (1981) noted that the direct treatment cost is perhaps $17 billion per year:

> Indirect costs, staggering when one estimates the years of unemployment, required support for housing, food and necessities, training, facilities development, supplemental and other hidden expenses, probably raises the monetary burden of schizophrenic illness close to $40 billion per year. (p. 71)

According to Talbott, Goldman, and Ross (1987), persons diagnosed schizophrenic in the United States occupy 25% of all hospital beds and account for 40% of all long-term care days (although they are only 1% of the population at any one time), and 85% of the total cost of "chronic mental illness" is accounted for by chronic schizophrenic patients.

The task of elaborating epidemiological categories for schizophrenic disorders is greatly complicated by the social stigma attached to the diagnosis or label. Although it is commonly reported that "Schizophrenia is more prevalent in certain population groups, such as those of lower socioeconomic status" (Strauss & Carpenter, 1981, p. 73), the social stigma casts doubt on the validity of the reported figures. Schizophrenic disorders, like suicide, may be underreported in the face of political, religious, and social influence. For example, prominent families may pressure mental health professionals to avoid diagnoses of schizophrenia. But schizophrenic disorders may be more common among poor people even after underreporting influences are taken into account. An early hypothesis (Faris & Dunham, 1939) posited downward socioeconomic drift for persons who were becoming and continuing to be schizophrenic, based on the notion that disability leads to poverty. A more recent explanation (Karon & VandenBos, 1981) is that poverty itself is a major stressor that drives people schizophrenic.

All investigators appear to agree that the vast majority of schizophrenic disorders have an early onset, typically in adolescence or early adulthood. The challenges to youth to become autonomous without having become emotionally secure in early life, and without having learned the socialization skills required in adult life, may be critical.

Investigators do not disagree much about the distribution between the sexes; male and female incidence and prevalence seem not to differ except possibly for age of onset. Strauss and Carpenter (1981) state that

> The peak age for first admission to hospital in males is between ages 15 and 24, and for females, between ages 25 and 34. This implies that there are important differences in biological, psychological, and/or social factors by sex that affect the occurrence of schizophrenia. (p. 73).

Perhaps men become schizophrenic earlier and have much higher suicide rates because of the cultural emphasis on a macho orientation and the consequent greater reluctance to seek psychotherapy or other help with emotional problems (Whitaker, 1987).

Problems with the Disease Concept of Schizophrenia

The label *schizophrenia* is highly suggestive of a disease in terms of the history of the concept of schizophrenia and the overwhelming emphasis on discovering disease properties. But neither the specific concept of *schizophrenia* as a disease nor the general concept of *mental diseases* has ever met the criteria for physical disease. Actual central nervous system diseases—for example Alzheimer's disease, in which there are histopathological changes in brain tissue—and diseases originating elsewhere in the body that then impinge on the nervous system do not, of course, meet the definitional criteria for schizophrenic disorders. The notion of disease, outside these realms of demonstrable physical pathology, applied to mental disorders has the status of a mere metaphor. Scientifically, it has little to recommend it any more than a "sick economy" needs the special attention of physicians. Furthermore, schizophrenic disorders are by definition functional rather than organic. The possibility that there are important biological and genetic substrates that may predispose individuals to develop schizophrenic disorders must, of course, be considered. But such substrates as may exist have not thus far appeared to play major causal roles, as will be discussed later in this book.

Sometimes the fact that "schizophrenia" and other "mental illnesses" are treated medically gives the impression that they must be diseases: Why else would they be treated medically? The answer to this question may be found in the history of social and political influences forming the concepts of mental illness and schizophrenia, and not in the medical laboratory. Given the continuing and even increasing tendency to reduce the concept of a group of psychological disorders to a physical disease, it is not surprising that the term *schizophrenia* inspires the most violent attacks in terms of the label's connotation of disease. Many, if not most, of these attacks have come from physicians, including psychiatrists, who, by reason of their medical education, have pointed out that the medical model of disease has been extremely valuable in the realm of physical disease but has been of great disservice in the field of mental disorder.

Psychiatrist Thomas Szasz is perhaps the best known critic of the disease model for mental disorders generally, beginning with his book *The Myth of Mental Illness* (Szasz, 1961), and for schizophrenic disorders particularly, in his book *Schizophrenia: The Sacred Symbol of Psychiatry* (1976):

> The psychiatrists have borrowed the disease model from medicine and, on the strength of it, declared psychiatry to be a branch of medicine—a specialty based on the combination of a medical metaphor and the police power of the state. (Szasz, 1976, pp. 79–80)

He has claimed that "the phenomenon psychiatrists call 'schizophrenia is not a demonstrable medical disease but the name of certain kinds of social deviance (or of behavior unacceptable to the speaker)" (1976, p. 67).

Szasz (1976) may appear, on casual reading, to have been denying the existence of any such human condition as 'schizophrenia,' but he did not deny that there are conditions of alienation and impaired mental and social functioning, and that great suffering may be involved for people called schizophrenic. He summarized his position as follows:

> There is, in short, no such thing as schizophrenia. Schizophrenia is not a disease, but only the name of an alleged disease. Although there is no schizophrenia, there are, of course, countless individuals who are called "schizophrenic." Many (though by no means all) of these persons often behave and speak in ways that differ from the behavior and speech of many (though by no means all) other people in their environment. The differences in behavior and speech may, moreover, be gravely disturbing either to the so-called schizophrenic person, or to those around him, or to all concerned. (p. 191)

Szasz would remove these human conditions of deviance and impairment from the medical disease model that prevails in psychiatry and would not allow such persons to be made "patients" and treated against their wills. He suggested that we refuse to support "coercive psychiatry" and develop a better paradigm for addressing the phenomenon of impairment, on the one hand, and deviance, on the other. I suggest distinguishing the impairment phenomena by objectively measuring the types and degrees of impairment of psychological and social functioning, thus distinguishing true impairment from mere social deviance.

Psychiatrist Karl Menninger and clinical psychologists Martin Mayman and Paul Pruyser, all of the Menninger Foundation, linked the simplistic use of the label *schizophrenia* to other vague terms in psychiatry and law that lend themselves to vicious stigmatization and bigotry:

> Such witch-hunting designations as "schizophrenia," "neurosis," "insanity," and "psychopathic personality" are not really understood . . . by anyone. . . . Their use only disguises essential ignorance or incompleteness of knowledge. (Menninger, Mayman, & Pruyser, 1963, p. 322)

These authors, like many others, have stayed within a medical model but have relinquished the definiteness of the concept *disease* for the medical concept *syndrome.* A syndrome is defined as "a set of symptoms which occur together; the sum of signs of any morbid state, a symptom complex" (*Dorland's Illustrated Medical Dictionary,* 1988, p. 1629). Menninger *et al.* (1963) asserted:

> Current nosologies and diagnostic nomenclature are not only useless but restrictive and obstructive. *This does not mean the discarding of useful terminology or syndrome appellations.* To refer to a constellation of symptoms as constituting a schizophrenic picture is very different from referring to the individual presenting these symptoms as a victim of "schizophrenia" or as "a schizophrenic." Some *symptoms* are by definition "schizophrenic," but no patient is. The same patient may present another syndrome tomorrow. (p. 33)

One may still wonder why, if schizophrenic persons are so diverse, changeable, and stigmatized by their labels, they should be labeled even in terms of a syndrome. Psychiatrist Leopold Bellak, who conceptualized the phenomena as *Disorders of the Schizophrenic Syndrome* (1979), explained:

> I have based my use of the nomothetic label "schizophrenic syndrome" on the fact that, however diverse individuals may appear, they share enough intragroup similarities and intergroup differences to make that label useful. I agree that, regrettably, labeling leads to stereotypes, to self-fulfilling prophesies, and to social abuse, and I am in favor of doing everything possible to minimize these effects of diagnostic labeling. (p. 588)

The concept of a syndrome for schizophrenic disorders is certainly less presumptuous than the disease concept, but is it adequate? Psychiatrist Silvano Arieti, who has considered the matter from many points of view, noted in his book *Interpretation of Schizophrenia* (1974):

> Some authors consider schizophrenia an illness, others a syndrome, still others a mental mechanism or even a way of living. There is some truth in each of these views, and yet at closer analysis all of them prove unsatisfactory. The understanding or the clarity that they seem to offer reflect the facility of approaches that take into consideration only one or a few aspects of a complicated problem. (p. 3)

Rejecting the utility of both the traditional medical model of disease and the more modest medical concept of a syndrome, psychologists John Neale and Thomas Oltmanns (1980) argued that even

> the syndrome approach tends to emphasize the use of symptoms in defining the disorder to the exclusion of other potential referents (e.g., treatment response). There is also a simultaneous tendency to believe that there is agreement on the primary symptoms of the disorder. This is clearly not the case in schizophrenia. (p. 18)

They asked:

> If schizophrenia is not a disease, or a syndrome, or a label, what is it? We believe that it is most usefully thought of as being an open *scientific construct*. . . . A hypothetical construct is simply an abstract, explanatory device or concept. In the case of behavioral disorders, a hypothetical construct is an internal event whose existence is inferred on the basis of observable behaviors and the context in which they occur. (p. 19)

Like Neale and Oltmanns, who proposed a model that is open and broad, psychiatrists John Strauss and William Carpenter (1981) chose not to use either the traditional medical disease model or the psychoanalytic model, on the assumption that both are inadequate. They advocate "an interactive developmental systems model of schizophrenia" that is "a socio-psycho-biomedical approach," explaining their choice as follows:

> We choose a medical model, but one broadly defined. Scientific and sociopolitical factors, as well as our professional backgrounds and experience, dictate this choice. Scientifically, it is our view that the possible alternative nonmedical models do not possess sufficient

> breadth to incorporate the range of biological, psychological and sociological data relevant to understanding and treating the schizophrenic patient. (p. 9)

They acknowledged that the psychoanalytic viewpoint—and, for that matter, the entire psychological meaningfulness of the "patient's experience of schizophrenia"—has been hampered by the assumption, held by Sigmund Freud himself, who himself was remote from schizophrenic persons,

> that such persons could not be investigated psychoanalytically because they were unable to establish a transference relationship. This view has discouraged two generations of clinicians and investigators from intensive explorations of the experiences of persons with schizophrenia. (p. 43)

Clinical psychologists Bertram Karon and Gary VandenBos (1981) made evidently quite effective use of the psychoanalytic orientation in doing psychotherapy with schizophrenic persons, but their work and careful documentation of results are fairly exceptional. They explained:

> It is one of the anomalies of psychotherapy in our society that the best trained and most experienced psychotherapists, the fully trained psychoanalysts, typically treat neurotic patients possessing social and economic resources sufficient to receive treatment three to five times per week, while the least trained and most inexperienced therapists are apt to be assigned the most severely disturbed psychotic patients, who often have little by way of social or economic resources. The latter psychotherapists are expected to carry out treatment in very restricted periods of time, so it is no wonder that they so frequently feel overwhelmed.
>
> The inexperienced therapist becomes aware of the conflicting mass of scientific literature which presents many contradictory theories, none of which are entirely convincing. Most of these theories do not recommend psychotherapy with such patients. (p. 5)

Furthermore, the lack of a "transference" relationship applies only to positive transference, the generalization that patients make to their therapist that brings into therapy positive expectations that they have formed previously in life. It is true that schizophrenic persons seldom bring strong feelings of positive transference to the therapy situation, but there is no lack of transference if one includes negative feelings, that is, negative transference: "The patient may seem insensitive to everything except the therapist's weak spots. He may be fiendishly adept at arousing anxiety, guilt, anger, or feelings of incompetence" (Karon & VandenBos, 1981, p. 6). It is no wonder, given this kind of greeting, that most therapists do not choose to do psychotherapy with schizophrenic persons. Thus, when treatments of schizophrenic disorders are offered, they are nearly always of kinds that do not make emotional demands on the treaters but are restricted to doing something to, rather than with, the patient. Accordingly, when "treatment response" is made a criterion for diagnosis, the treatment is nearly always drugs, shock treatment, or psychosurgery; treatment responses in terms of psychotherapy of significant duration or meaningfulness are seldom ascertainable. In terms of the physical disease or syndrome models, therefore, there is a kind of circularity: "schizophrenia is defined as a medical phenomenon because it is treated medically."

Recent Definitions of Schizophrenic Disorders

Just as concepts of schizophrenic disorders have been at variance with one another over the years, so have the "official" definitional criteria used for diagnosis. European definitions have been narrower than those used by the American Psychiatric Association, though the gap was reduced considerably by the introduction in 1980 of the third edition of the *Diagnostic and Statistical Manual* by the American Psychiatric Association and its successor, the DSM-III-R (1987). The earlier DSM-II gave a relatively broad definition:

> This large category includes a group of disorders manifested by characteristic disturbances of thinking, mood and behavior. Disturbances in thinking are marked by alterations of concept formation which may lead to misinterpretation of reality and sometimes to delusions and hallucinations, which frequently appear psychologically self-protective. Corollary mood changes include ambivalent, constricted and inappropriate emotional responsiveness and loss of empathy with others. Behavior may be withdrawn, regressive and bizarre. The schizophrenias, in which the mental state is attributable primarily to a thought disorder, are to be distinguished from the Major affective illnesses (q.v.) which are dominated by a mood disorder. The Paranoid states (q.v.) are distinguished from schizophrenia by narrowness of their distortions of reality and by the absence of other psychic symptoms. (American Psychiatric Association, 1968, p. 33)

This definition emphasizes the primary importance of the thought disorder in distinguishing the "schizophrenias" from related disorders and is more specific in this regard than the definition offered in the previous edition of the manual. But, like the previous edition, it does not define the thinking disturbance, or thought disorder, per se.

The DSM-III (1980) and the DSM-III-R (1987) do give some definition to the content and form of thought regarded as disordered. They also restrict the definition of a schizophrenic disorder by reserving the term for an "illness" having continuous signs for at least six months, while designating shorter duration illnesses of a quite similar nature "schizophreniform disorder." The term *schizoaffective disorder,* as cited in the DSM-III-R, designates "those instances in which the clinician is unable to make a differential diagnosis with any degree of certainty between Affective Disorder and either Schizophreniform Disorder or Schizophrenia" (American Psychiatric Association, 1987, pp. 208–210).

The DSM-III introduced multiaxial evaluation as an officially approved method of classification intended to provide a more comprehensive diagnostic picture. Each person is evaluated on each of five axes. Briefly, the system is as follows, as reported in the DSM-III-R (American Psychiatric Association, 1987):

> Axis I Clinical Syndromes and V Codes (Codes label conditions not attributable to a mental disorder that are a focus of attention or treatment.)
>
> Axis II Developmental Disorders and Personality Disorders (including specific personality traits or the habitual use of particular defense mechanisms.)
>
> Axis III Physical Disorders and Conditions (that are potentially relevant to understanding or managing the case.)

Axis IV Severity of Psychosocial Stressors (that have occurred in the year preceding the current evaluation that may have contributed to the development of a new mental disorder, recurrence of a prior mental disorder, or the exacerbation of an already existing mental disorder.)

Axis V Global Assessment of Functioning (the clinician's overall judgment of a person's psychological, social, and occupational functioning on the Global Assessment of Functioning Scale that assesses mental health-illness.) (pp. 15–21)

The DSM-III-R (American Psychiatric Association, 1987) "diagnostic criteria for a schizophrenic disorder" still leave great latitude for labeling someone schizophrenic. Only the first set of stipulations (A) states any signs (1), (2), or (3) that are relatively characteristic of schizophrenic disorders, and only one of these signs has to be present in the active phase. These criteria give considerable latitude for confusion with many other conditions. The endpapers display the DSM-III-R criteria.

To illustrate the room for error, all of the signs under A that are said to characterize schizophrenic disorders may be found also in some other common disorders, for example, paranoid psychoses as well as paranoid schizophrenic psychoses for signs (1), (2), and (3). Criterion B also does not distinguish schizophrenia from other disorders. The emphasis on deterioration of functioning (in such areas as work, social relations, and self-care) shows that people are regarded as *becoming* schizophrenic—that is, regressing in psychological functioning—rather than merely being fixated at or never having developed beyond an immature level.

The concept of deteriorated functioning has long been a part of the definition of schizophrenic disorders. But the extent to which fixation rather than regression (deteriorated functioning) is characteristic of the inadequate functioning varies. Where regression to, rather than fixation at, a deteriorated level of functioning is marked, the behavior is likely to be bizarre because of the juxtaposition of inadequate with still relatively adequate levels of functioning abilities. But quite fixated individuals may also show considerable deficits in functioning ability, and it is not apparent from these criteria whether or to what degree such long-standing impairment should be designated schizophrenic. Criterion D, specifying "Continuous signs of the disturbance for at least six months," which must include "an active phase," emphasizes the regressive characteristic because "positive" signs of disorder are virtually all of the psychotic symptoms in the active phase (symptoms in A) that are clearly both disturbed and disturbing. In contrast, negative symptoms, such as apathy and other signs of decreased ability to function, are usually not so disturbing to others but have great significance for long-term outcome because they tend to predominate in the most deteriorated, chronic schizophrenic disorders.

Summary

Schizophrenic experiences may be characterized as states of terror that force changes in behavior and personality so that a sense of communion with other persons is lost and there is an extreme inability to distinguish fantasy from reality. The terror motivates both the person and would-be proximate others toward alienation. Case examples were given illustrating both the patient's terror and its psychologically infectious nature.

Schizophrenic disorders are similar in certain ways to some other common conditions, including bigotry, which also features extreme irrationality but is consensually supported by others. Lack of consensual validation or supportive agreement is part of the definition of psychoses generally and of schizophrenic disorders particularly.

There have been many studies of incidence, prevalence, and cost, all complicated by definitional disagreement, diagnostic unreliability, and relying necessarily on that cases presenting for treatment. Estimates of newly developed cases (incidence) range from 100,000 to 200,000 per year for the United States. Estimated rates of the percentage of people who are schizophrenic at any time in their lives (prevalence) vary even more. U.S. prevalence estimates range from 0.6% to 3.0%. International prevalence estimates range from 0.19% to 0.9%. The costs of schizophrenic disorders include not only direct treatment costs but a host of expenses due to nonproductivity and special supportive financial arrangements.

The disease-entity concept of schizophrenia does not meet the classical definition of disease in terms of cellular pathology. No designation, whether disease, disorder, or syndrome, fully grasps the characteristics of schizophrenic disorders.

Recent definitions of schizophrenic disorders include, perhaps most importantly, the 1980 and 1987 revisions of the *Diagnostic and Statistical Manual of the American Psychiatric Association,* known as the DSM-III and the DSM-III-R, respectively, which represent a narrowing of the traditionally very broad American definition and bring the United States more into line with European definitions. There remains considerable definitional disagreement internationally, however, and there are major definition problems in the DSM-III and the DSM-III-R.

2

Historical Overview
Myths and Fact

The Hospital and the Three Revolutions in Psychiatry

Historically, persons diagnosed as schizophrenic have had little to say about their treatment choices, especially if they were poor and quite disturbed in their ability to function. Relatively affluent and self-possessed persons have generally been given more and better treatment choices. Typically, schizophrenic persons in this century were placed in hospitals remote from population centers, the effect being a kind of segregation from "normal society" that, while protecting others from being disturbed, was usually harmful to the patients themselves. Even "modern" hospitals have not generally provided the treatments of choice.

Charles Kiesler (1982) showed that all 10 studies of alternatives to hospitalization for mental patients treated in the recent years before his study indicated superior results for nonhospital treatment, and 9 out of the 10 alternatives were definitely less expensive. These findings are easy to understand, given the poor quality of diagnosis and treatment in most hospitals admitting mental patients. Hospitals have not diminished either the overall expense of caring for mental patients or the numbers of patients who "need to be hospitalized."

There has been a shift, however, of mental patients from psychiatric to nonpsychiatric hospitals, including general hospitals. According to Kiesler, "The site of mental hospitalization has changed dramatically in recent years. More inpatient episodes (almost 60% of the total) occur in general hospitals than in any other setting" (p. 1328). This trend is consonant with the "deinstitutionalization" of state mental hospitals and with the concurrent trend toward further "biologizing" or "medicalizing" psychiatry.

The first revolution in psychiatry was called "moral treatment" by the physician Phillipe Pinel (1745–1826), who removed the chains of mental patients in France. Actually, as Bassoe (1945) pointed out, it was not Pinel but physicians in Valencia, Spain, in 1409 who were the first to remove the chains of patients and to institute moral treatment. But more distancing, objectifying, unempathic, and even cruel physical methods of custody and treatment replaced moral treatment. In Spain, "With the advent of the inquisition and the hunt for heretics charity was largely lost sight of, and, as usual, the insane were the first to be neglected" (Bassoe, 1945, p. 738).

The second revolution in psychiatry, associated with the development of psychoanalysis, was quickly medicalized, especially in the United States, despite the many vigorous objections of the founder of psychoanalysis, Sigmund Freud (1856–1939), for example, in his book *The Question of Lay Analysis* (1926/1950). Psychoanalysis was reduced to a medical specialty rather than opening up broad vistas of inquiry, as had been intended. Bruno Bettelheim, in his book *Freud and Man's Soul* (1984), documented eloquently how even the "standard" or official translations of Freud's writings transformed them into the framework of medicine and distanced them from the emotional impact of what Freud was saying. For example, the word *psychoanalysis,* which Freud coined,

> combines two words of Greek origin, but few are conscious of the fact that the two words refer to strongly contrasting phenomena. "Psyche" is the soul—a term full of the richest meaning, endowed with emotion, comprehensively human and unscientific. "Analysis" implies a taking apart, a scientific examination. English readers of Freud are further thrown off by the fact that in English the accent in "psychoanalysis" is on "analysis," thus emphasizing the part of the word that has scientific connotations. With the German word Psychoanalyse, on the other hand, the accent is on the first syllable—on "psyche," the "soul." (Bettelheim, 1984, pp. 11, 12)

> When Freud appears to be either more abstruse or more dogmatic in English translation than in the original German, to speak about abstract concepts rather than about the reader himself, and about man's mind rather than about his soul, the probable explanation isn't mischievousness or carelessness on the translators' part but a deliberate wish to perceive Freud strictly within the framework of medicine, and, possibly, an unconscious tendency to distance themselves from the emotional impact of what Freud tried to convey. (Bettelheim, 1984, p. 32)

Thus, the second revolution, like the first, came to be commanded by the very forces of emotional distancing they were intended to correct. Meanwhile, "medical scientists" gained what seems in retrospect outrageous latitude to destroy human brains that they claimed, without any neurological evidence whatever, were diseased.

Egas Moniz (1874–1955) was a clinical professor of neurology at the University of Lisbon, Portugal, who believed that "morbid" ideas stimulated and restimulated the neurons, though no pathological changes could be detected in the synapses or in the nerve cells of patients with functional psychoses. The already possibly damaging procedure of electroshock treatment was then replaced in many cases with the absolutely certain and irrevocable damage of prefrontal lobotomy. Alexander and Selesnick (1966) noted that "during the 1940's psychosurgery was often advocated for patients with intractable psychoses resistant to shock treatments. . . . Anxiety was relieved, but at the price of a loss of self-respect and of empathy with others" (p. 285). One is struck by the nonsense and destructiveness of this "therapeutic treatment," which won Moniz the Nobel Prize in 1949. Ironically, the destruction of self-respect and the ability to be empathic, so notable in the lobotomized patients, seems to have been matched by the lack of respect and empathy in the practitioners, who, unlike the patients, were able to engage in pseudoscientific rationalizations.

Psychiatrist E. Fuller Torrey illustrated this folly in the words of Dr. Walter Freeman, a professor of neurology at George Washington University, Washington, D.C., who advocated lobotomy for psychotic persons and claimed to produce excellent results:

> Disturbed patients often become friendly, quiet, and cooperative. They retain their basic psychotic dissociation and often their delusional ideas, but they no longer react to them so vigorously. Hallucinations are reduced or suppressed in about half the cases . . . the results are usually quite good, especially from an administrative point of view. (quoted in Torrey, 1988, pp. 106–107)

As Torrey (1988) also noted, this folly was brought home to the family of Joseph Kennedy, Sr., father of President Kennedy, who agreed to have his mildly retarded daughter, Rosemary, undergo lobotomy in 1941. The disastrous results included her no longer realizing who she was and having her capacity to speak almost completely destroyed. She was usually confined thereafter to a nursing home.

The so-called third revolution in psychiatry occurred in the 1950s, when the phenothiazines, or "major tranquilizers," were introduced. Problems of patient management were reduced as the vast majority of patients diagnosed schizophrenic, and also many patients with other diagnoses, were administered doses of these drugs, which changed their actively disturbed appearance. The drugs were thought to be miraculous in their effects. There was an expectation in many quarters that the "disease" would be cured. Greater manageability and the hope instilled in the staff did appear to make more patients "dischargeable," though not necessarily functional. Certainly the positive or outwardly disturbing symptoms were reduced, though heavily drugged patients usually had a zombielike appearance and manner, as if chemically straitjacketed or functionally lobotomized. Supposedly, it was easy to diagnose patients by assuming that, if the patient "improved" with administration of Thorazine or another phenothiazine, the diagnosis of schizophrenia was confirmed. Like the vast majority of mental health practitioners observing this "revolution," I assumed that the phenothiazines accounted for the apparent improvements in manageability and dischargeability of otherwise severely disturbed patients. But the following unsettling experience stimulated skepticism and a critical attitude.

In 1960, the superintendent of a public mental hospital housing 2,000 "schizophrenics" gave an after-dinner presentation to the hospital staff. The mood of staff was pleasant, seemingly the product not only of a good dinner but a good year, in which patient manageability and dischargeability had improved greatly. The superintendent—by training, an internal medicine specialist—elaborated with the aid of charts just how great these improvements had been, and he noted that they coincided with the hospital's introduction of phenothiazine treatment. By now, his audience was quite comfortable, assuming that this correlation signified that the phenothiazines were responsible for the improvement.

But Dr. J. noted that, in his capacity as overseer of medical supplies, he had seen to it that, at random, one half of the patients had been given phenothiazines and the other half had been given placebos. He reported that the discharge rates for the two groups were the same. He went on to attribute the results to the change in staff attitudes and expectations about patient hopelessness or curability, based on knowing that the patients were being given the new "miracle drugs." Unfortunately, Dr. J. died the following year, and his findings were not published.

Almost two decades later, sober scientific evaluation of the effects of the phenothiazines suggested further cautions because of the limitations in "improvement" and both the short- and the long-term "side effects," which may produce permanent impairment. Psychiatrist Leopold Bellak (1979) summarized some of the limitations:

> Regrettably, pharmacotherapy has not proven itself to be a cure for the schizophrenic syndrome. In most instances it affects prominently what Eugen Bleuler calls the secondary symptoms—that is, delusions, hallucinations, and possibly thought disorders—but it does not affect the personality structure of schizophrenics. . . . The patient often remains withdrawn, peculiar, etc., or what we might call a "silent schizophrenic." (pp. 17, 18)

But careful assessment of schizophrenic and related disorders, let alone careful assessment of the persons so impaired, became preempted by the supposed ease of diagnosis which can be confirmed, so it is assumed, by response to the drugs. Psychiatrists Carpenter and Strauss (1979) highlighted the problem:

> The current proclivity to rapid diagnosis based on a few conspicuous psychopathological manifestations, followed (or often preceded) by narrowly and automatically derived treatment decisions, is a reprehensive model for the psychiatric clinician and serves the needs of none but the third-party payer. A symptom orientation has pragmatic advantages in classification, but it is sorely abused when our clinical concepts and maneuvers become preoccupied only with flagrant psychotic symptoms. We have reached the low point where virtually every patient receiving a diagnosis of schizophrenia is urged to accept long-term drug therapy as the only rational basis for treatment (since antipsychotic drugs modify symptom status) while ignoring the intrapsychic and interpersonal consequences of the illness so familiar to Kraepelin and Bleuler. (p. 317)

In this light it is not difficult to understand how the studies of David Rosenhan (1973), published in *Science,* could have obtained results so devastating to confidence in the psychiatric diagnosis of "schizophrenia." In essence, Rosenhan placed several normal persons in a variety of psychiatric hospitals. He showed that *schizophrenia* was a label quickly given to any person who presented with just one possible auditory hallucination—a hallucination by no means actually typical of schizophrenic persons—on just one occasion. Without exception, the psychiatrists attached the schizophrenia label, without any other evidence than that the pseudopatients exhibited some "concomitant nervousness," and they continued to apply it to all of the pseudopatients throughout their relatively lengthy hospital stays. The real patients discovered readily, through their own observations, that these pseudopatients were not mentally disturbed persons. The pseudopatients observed that, although lots of drugs were prescribed for real patients and pseudopatients alike, very little staff time was spent talking to any of the patients. They found that doctors and nurses had little to say to them or hear from them.

Though Rosenhan's study drew considerable criticism (Crown, 1975; Farber, 1975; Millon, 1975; Spitzer, 1975; Weiner, 1975), the study left little latitude for arguing against his basic conclusion: "Thus set and setting, the contexts of mind and environment, heavily determine psychiatric diagnosis" (Rosenhan, 1975, p. 465). Clearly, the availability of the drugs and the myth of easy diagnosis and treatment had preempted both real science and humane concern.

Ample evidence exists now to show that both the abominable conditions of most mental hospitals and their distancing of patients from their families, communities, work ties, and the hospital staffs themselves have in large measure contributed to the "deteriorating course" assumed for so long to be characteristic and even clearly diagnostic of "schizophrenia." Empirically, it could be seen that patients in mental hospitals did tend to deteriorate. But the danger of this, and many other instances of simple empiricism, is that the context is not taken into account. As Bellak (1979) put it:

> what used to be considered pathognomonic of "schizophrenic regression" is probably largely "iatrogenic." Patients were often sent to state hospitals as far away as thirty miles from their family and from the community in which they had lived. They lived isolated existences on the wards in conditions approximating perceptual isolation and sensory deprivation, and they suffered from disuse atrophy of their ego functions. Under these circumstances bizarre regressions were not at all surprising. The utter sense of hopelessness fostered in institutions run in very poor and dictatorial fashion by an ill-trained staff was often hardly better than that described in *One Flew Over the Cuckoo's Nest.* Acts of sadism were tolerated, if not encouraged. (pp. 4, 5)

The psychiatrist Peter Breggin (1983) greatly extended the argument that psychiatric treatment using the phenothiazines and other powerful psychiatric drugs has had iatrogenic consequences. He stated that all of these drugs disable the brain and that this disabling influence is not merely a "side effect" but the entire effect, including the so-called main effect that is intended. He explained that the intended therapeutic effect is actually iatrogenic or harmful:

> The apparent improvement that patients show is actually a disability, a loss of mental capacity inflicted by the drugs. By rendering the patients less able to think, to feel, or to determine the course of their conduct, these drugs make the patients less troublesome to others, and sometimes less troublesome to themselves. (p. 2)

Breggin noted that the powerful major tranquilizers, including those that go by the trade names Thorazine, Mellaril, Prolixin, Stelazine, and Haldol, as well as the "mood" drugs lithium and Elavil, are often prescribed not just for 90%–100% of patients in hospitals or just by psychiatrists. They are also prescribed in private practice by almost any physician who deals directly with individual patients. At least several million people a year are receiving these drugs. Having reviewed considerable evidence, Breggin concluded that

> The widespread use of the most potent psychiatric drugs—the major tranquilizers—has created a public health menace of great proportions. These drugs are known to produce a permanent, disfiguring neurologic disease, tardive dyskinesia, in a large percentage of cases. Still more ominous, the same drugs permanently damage the higher centers of the

> brain, producing irreversible psychoses, apathy, generalized brain dysfunction, dementia and other effects similar to those resulting from lobotomy. (p. 2)

Why the vast evidence of the harmful effects of psychiatric drugs goes relatively unheeded must be understood as a failing of our society in general and not merely of physicians in particular. Given the unprecedented rates of divorce, drug use, migration, and youth suicide in the United States, there is a societal theme of alienation conducive to schizophrenic and related disorders and to morbid dependency on drugs rather than constructive interdependency among people. These two major forces, societal alienation and the power of institutionalized medicine, appear to be having a synergistically potent effect. The drugging of America is especially evident in physicians' drug-prescribing habits and patients' acceptance of and even eagerness for drugs.

By 1982, according to the National Survey on Drug Abuse by the National Institute of Drug Abuse, per capita use of prescription drugs in the United States had become 10 times greater than in the next seven most developed nations combined; physicians in the United States were writing over 60 million prescriptions for Valium alone each year. Meanwhile, the rate of suicide among younger people in the United States increased greatly from 1950 to 1980, and by the 1980s the preferred suicide method in actually dangerous and near-lethal attempts in the general population had become prescription drugs, especially and ironically the so-called antidepressants (Kathol & Henn, 1983).

Ambiguity in the definitions of "schizophrenia," the treatment of "schizophrenics" as if they are diseased, and political pressures may readily combine to create a gross perversion of the enabling and self-determination functions of the mental health enterprise. In Soviet psychiatry, the ostensibly dispassionate objective listing of symptoms played ever-compliant host to the unrestrained passion of politics. Political dissidents, by their very dissent, were known absolutely to have "sluggish schizophrenia" and "creeping schizophrenia." And how was it known that there was a creeping toward "schizophrenia"? Diagnosis was determined by prognosis, and if someone was moving in a deviant direction, he or she had a bad prognosis, and a bad prognosis was grounds enough for a bad diagnosis. Thus, the tautology was complete. A tautological argument survives if its false premise cannot be contested. In the case of Soviet psychiatry, the false premise was that political deviance equals morbidity. In their book on repression by psychiatry in the Soviet Union, Zhores Medvedev and Roy Medvedev (1979) noted how Zhores became psychiatrically imprisoned, in the words of a letter of protest by Aleksandr Solzhenitsyn, who exposed the Gulag archipelago:

> Because of the very diversity of his talents, he is charged with being abnormal, a "split personality." His very sensitivity to injustice, to stupidity, is presented as a "morbid deviation," "poor adaptation to the social environment." Apparently to harbor thoughts other than those which are prescribed means that you are abnormal. Well-adjusted people all think alike. (Medvedev & Medvedev, 1979, p. 135)

Ludmilla Thorne (1977), a writer who specializes in Russian subjects, documented the assessment and treatment practices used on Soviet dissidents, for example, on the leading mathematician Leonid Plyushch:

> After a year in prison, he was examined not by one but by three psychiatric commissions. The first found him to be suffering from "reformist delusions," "Messianic elements" and that old favorite, "sluggish schizophrenia." The third examination, held five months after the first, was chaired by none other than Dr. Andrei Snezhnevsky, director of the Institute of Psychiatry of the Academy of Medical Sciences and the moving spirit of the "Moscow school of psychiatry," which is known for its extremely loose definition of schizophrenia. The entire session lasted 20 minutes. (p. 62)

On the basis of this commission's report, Plyushch was committed to the Special Psychiatric Hospital at Dnepropetrovsk, which was regarded in dissident circles as the worst of the lot.

There are many tautologies in the literature on schizophrenia and in actual diagnostic and treatment practices in countries everywhere. In his book *Psychiatric Slavery* (1977), psychiatrist Thomas Szasz argued that the criterion of deviance is also used in American psychiatry to confine and coercively treat persons who are deviant, sometimes criminally deviant, but who are not suffering from a psychiatric "disease" or "illness" and whose civil rights are violated by involuntary commitment and forced treatment. Szasz called this approach "quasi-medical." He especially scorned any attempt

> to justify depriving an innocent person of liberty on the grounds that he is mentally ill and that he will receive treatment for it, a reasoning that implies—as essentially unchallengeable—that the subject has, in fact, an illness; that it is treatable; that the treatment will be forthcoming; and that it will be effective. Actually each of these premises may be false. (p. 122)

The whole sociopolitical context of assessment of schizophrenic and related disorders is not merely important but of the essence if we are ever to engage successfully in understanding ourselves well enough to understand our patients. Practices arising out of treatment of people labeled schizophrenic often beg the question of assessment; treatment often determines assessment findings. More broadly, assuming that there is such a thing or entity as schizophrenia and that it is a disease has continued to bias research and treatment approaches, as well as assessments of individuals, toward biological explanations and treatment.

The Theme of Alienation: Segregation, Emigration, and Prejudice

Whereas "schizophrenia" has received enormous attention as a kind of circumscribed disease entity, the contribution of psychosocial influences has received relatively little attention. However, there have been a number of noteworthy studies of schizophrenic phenomena within various social contexts. Judging by the results, factors such as segregation, emigration, and prejudice play important roles in the incidence and prevalence of schizophrenic disorders in given populations. It would appear that these factors, and any others that contribute to an individual's sense of alienation or sense of not "belonging" to a socially esteemed group, are significant predisposing elements in the causation, the perpetuation, and even the worsening of schizophrenic impairment.

Arieti (1974) provided a concise account of several important studies. As in all studies relying heavily on diagnoses with low reliability and relying on correlational methods as well, the epidemiological statistics are subject to various interpretations other than simple cause and effect. In some cases, for example, one may ask whether the presumed cause was, at least in part, an effect. What appears to be most significant is the pattern of these findings and the general theme they suggest.

The studies, as summarized, show that "bachelorhood, separation, divorce, and widowhood are poor risk in comparison to marriage" (Arieti, 1974, p. 493), and that immigration and migration are associated with greater risk, as are living in cities and industrial areas, being black or Puerto Rican in the United States, and being poor. All of these conditions relate to being alien in the sense of either losing or not having close and esteemed social relatedness. Poverty per se, though tending to be associated with most of the other variables, may not always be critical itself. Torrey (1979) noted that

> in Norway there is a relationship between schizophrenia and lower socioeconomic class . . . that . . . remained relatively unchanged between 1926 and 1965. . . . On the other hand, much evidence has come to light that the opposite is true in India, and that schizophrenia in that country is most prevalent among the upper socioeconomic classes. (p. 26)

In essence, it appears that being alienated, both prehospital and in-hospital, can have major effects in terms of the development and worsening of schizophrenic conditions and that the opposite is also true, that acceptance helps.

The degree to which the person is alienated from rather than esteemed by others has important implications in assessment. In general, longitudinal assessment should take into account the psychosocial context of the development and course of schizophrenic and related disorders. In particular, the place and the social context of the assessment processes, as well as the person(s) doing the assessment, may be critical. For example, I found that my own research assistants, assigned to test schizophrenic patients, had extremely varying rates of success in obtaining "testable" patients. Whereas most found many "untestable" individuals, one assistant in particular found virtually all patients, no matter how regressed, "testable." Similarly, I had occasion to visit a hospital where the director of research had to withdraw one particular assistant from testing duties because she had a powerful and immediately elevating effect on the patients and so "spoiled the standardizing" of testers. Neither of these assistants administered the tests incorrectly; in fact, they were both superior in testing ability. But both were powerful therapeutic presences and thus were able to gain more cooperation and to test many more subjects.

Similarly, the personalities and techniques of various interviewers may have greatly ameliorating effects on the "pathology" of patients. For example, students of Harvard psychiatrist Elvin Semrad have remarked that patients appeared to stop being schizophrenic while he sat talking with them. Thus, there is a kind of "assesso that should be taken into account in terms of assessing the assessment meth results. Assessors, as well as therapists, who are not too terrified to identify with patients, and who are empathic with and accepting of them as persons, may affect the results in a positive direction.

Like people generally, psychiatrists, psychologists, social workers, and other "mental health professionals" tend to disidentify with the mentally disturbed person (Deikman, 1971). The certain hallmarks of this prejudicial orientation, which can be so readily mistaken for "science," are assuming that patients are not fully human and that doing something to them instead of with them is therefore appropriate. This orientation, which flourishes among professionals as well as laypersons in authoritarian cultures and subcultures, contrasts with real science, which, while bold in its effort, is humble in its admission of doubt, and which eschews prejudice.

The nature of the assessment of schizophrenic and related disorders depends on what assumptions are held about them. If one brings all of the common assumptions into the assessment situation, there is no apparent need for assessment except to make a quick judgment based on merely a single apparent symptom, just as it happened in the Rosenhan (1973) studies. On the other hand, if one wishes to do truly helpful assessment, one must explicitly eliminate the common assumptions from the task. These assumptions are often so widely accepted and promulgated that it is necessary to become aware of each assumption so as to avoid being influenced by it and allowing it to limit and determine the parameters of investigation. Some false assumptions have been exposed and one should be aware of their proven incorrectness, and others, although seemingly substantiated, need further study. In general, there is very little that can be taken for granted about persons labeled schizophrenic because, as a group, they are an extremely heterogeneous and changeable lot of people, not unlike "normals" both in their complexity and in their sharing of basic human qualities.

Myths about Schizophrenia and Its Assessment

The most common myths about "schizophrenia" are expressed in favorite slogans that are as popular today in many quarters, both professional and lay, as when they were first proclaimed and accepted. They are essentially statements of heart-felt prejudice and, as such, are extremely difficult to counter, even with genuine scientific evidence. Each of these myths is designated here by its slogan, after which both its origin and its scientific contradiction are discussed.

"Once a Schizophrenic, Always a Schizophrenic"

The term *dementia praecox* was coined by the French psychiatrist Benoit Morel, who observed "dementia" beginning in a 14-year-old boy. Morel used the word *praecox* to denote that the apparent dementia began early in life, in contrast to senile dementia. The so-called dementia was not similar to the progressive and inevitable deterioration found in senile dementia or to other forms of organically caused dementia, such as in general paresis, the advanced stage of syphilitic deterioration of the brain. Yet the notion of an inevitable progressive deterioration in dementia praecox, later called *schizophrenia* by Eugen Bleuler, persisted, abetted by the conditions of "treatment" to which "schizophrenics" were subjected. Even Eugen Bleuler thought that the schizophrenic person had an inevitable downhill course, as discussed later in Chapter 4 in terms of his handling of the case of the famous dancer Vaslav Nijinsky.

Many modern and otherwise more sophisticated practitioners and institutions retain this obsolete assumption, so they are uninterested in seeing if the patient has changed for the better and are content with "treatment" that merely subdues rather than rehabilitates. For example, at one prestigious psychiatric institute, psychiatrists proclaim on seeing a "schizophrenic" person who is clearly no longer schizophrenic that the patient could not have been schizophrenic in the first place, because real schizophrenics remain schizophrenic.

At another prestigious psychiatric teaching center, a psychiatric colleague and I decided to contradict this prejudice by selecting a patient who was, by ward staff consensus, grossly and classically schizophrenic, complete with the delusion that she was the Virgin Mary. Following several months of quite successful psychotherapy, she was presented by her psychotherapist, a psychiatric resident, to a supervising psychiatrist, who was also a highly esteemed training psychoanalyst. The occasion for this presentation and a prolonged in-depth interview of the patient with the psychoanalyst was consideration of the patient for an analysis with a psychoanalyst in training, which required that the patient be quite strong psychologically and essentially normal. The supervisory or training psychoanalyst concluded firmly that the "prospective psychoanalytic patient" was "quite normal" and therefore an ideal candidate. The psychiatric resident then revealed for the first time that the patient had recently been hospitalized for a couple of months when she was schizophrenic, with classical symptoms. The psychoanalyst then stated that the patient could not have been schizophrenic and that perhaps there had been a mistake in identity. The resident then produced the hospital records documenting the symptoms and the patient's identity. Follow-up of this patient 10 years later continued to show that the psychoanalyst's judgment, based on the patient's normality in terms of interview evidence, was quite right, as the patient did not become schizophrenic again.

Fortunately, in recent years there has emerged abundant evidence from several studies showing not only that the prejudice "once a schizophrenic, always a schizophrenic" is wrong but that generally, if anything, having been schizophrenic presages recovery (M. Bleuler, 1978; Ciompi, 1980; Harding, Brooks, Ashikagawa, Strauss, & Breier, 1987a, 1987b; Harding, Zubin, & Strauss, 1987c; Huber, Gross, & Schuttler, 1975). For example, Manfred Bleuler, the psychiatrist son of Eugen Bleuler, detailed his findings of generally positive change in his book *The Schizophrenic Disorders: Long-Term Patient and Family Studies* (1978). Summarizing "My Sixty Years with Schizophrenics" (M. Bleuler, 1979), he concluded from his careful studies of large numbers of patients that a full 50% of severely schizophrenic persons were "completely or socially recovered some years after the onset of psychosis, and a substantive percentage of the rest are at least improved" (p. ix). Only 10% were actually found to be chronically schizophrenic on long-term follow-up.

As another example, Ciompi (1980) and Ciompi and Muller (1976) studied the long-term course of patients diagnosed as schizophrenic in terms of the stricter European definition of those disorders. Their large-scale study, done in Italy, also showed that, by and large, schizophrenic individuals tended to become more functional and able, not less so, as has been and is still believed by most practitioners, as well as laypersons. They noted that, even in advanced age, the schizophrenic individuals they studied did not take on features of an organic disorder. Their schizophrenics not only tended not to deteriorate but they showed improvement on the whole.

Whereas it has now been established that people labeled schizophrenic tend as a group to improve over their life spans, it must be emphasized that there is, of course, enormous variety. Thus, instead of there being a certain predictable course, as is characteristic of most physical diseases, actual observation shows, as Arieti (1974) stated, that "A striking characteristic of schizophrenia is the great variability of its course" (p. 49) and that, as Strauss and Carpenter (1981) noted, "Every imaginable variation between full recovery and devastation occurs" (p. 67). In essence, then, the simple diagnostic label *schizophrenia* gives no information about the individual's course or prognosis, even when and where that label is applied in accordance with rigorous diagnostic practice. Therefore, the prejudice "once a schizophrenic, always a schizophrenic" has no basis whatever in reality.

"Anyone Can Identify a Schizophrenic"

Frequently, one hears among mental health professionals that there is no need for any assessment procedures in order to tell who is schizophrenic because any professional, if not layperson, can tell right away. One of the dangers of this assumption is that, where adequate assessment methods are lacking, being superstitious and having hostility toward someone have always made it easy to "tell on" someone, and the label *schizophrenic* is therefore easily applied to religious or political deviants.

There are two crucial false assumptions in this prejudice. The first, as we have seen, is that the real challenge of assessment is not met simply by calling people schizophrenic, because that label by itself reveals little of predictive value. Second, professionals actually have a very low rate of agreement among themselves about who is schizophrenic unless highly specific criteria and methods are used by mental health professionals trained especially to use them. Yet there are mental health professionals who claim, for example, as one psychologist did, to be able to tell immediately by the way the person smells or, as another psychologist claimed, simply by the way the person walks. The latter claim was bolstered by simply looking for a zombielike appearance, as any patient at his institution was immediately begun on large doses of Thorazine following a psychiatric resident's cursory examination. One had only to observe who walked like a zombie to tell who was "schizophrenic." Thus, without realizing it, this psychologist was begging the question of who was schizophrenic.

Essentially, the question hinges on the reliability of the diagnosis of "schizophrenia." In plain language, people do not know what they are talking about if they do not, in fact, agree on what are actual cases of schizophrenic disorder. The reliability of ordinary diagnostic practice generally falls far below the reliability achieved in formal studies, in which the professionals are given specific definitions and procedures to follow in a reliability study. Even then, if high reliabilities are achieved, one discovers that other groups of diagnosticians achieving relatively high reliabilities are usually not "talking about the same thing." There is generally some overlap in operational definitions, but seldom very high congruence, between groups of diagnosticians.

As will be discussed more fully later in this chapter, even achieving high reliability in the designation or naming of something does not guarantee that the designation will have validity or usefulness. Reliability is a necessary but not sufficient condition for reaching the scientific aims of prediction and control of the phenomena in question. It is conceivable, therefore, that we could achieve quite high reliabilities in our use of the term *schizophrenia* and yet be saying nothing helpful toward the goals of predictability and control. The message for now is that modesty and doubt are appropriate once again. These qualities would seem to promote a meaningful expansion of knowledge, whereas arrogance helps to reduce the field of inquiry. For example, in a study done by a psychologist abroad (Yaroush, 1982), psychiatrists were asked to label various hospital patients schizophrenic or not schizophrenic. The psychiatrists all predicted that the task would be quite easy and that they would agree at a high rate, especially as they all worked together in the same hospital. Actually, however, their "blind" ratings showed them to be so much at variance with one another that there could be little possible validity in their ratings, as low reliability places a very low limit on possible validity.

In contrast, Bilett, Jones, and Whitaker (1982) studied the confidence and reliability of a group of 10 especially highly trained and experienced clinical psychologists who were given psychological test protocols on 12 difficult-to-diagnose adolescents (ages 16–19) whom they then categorized blindly. The psychologists as a group expressed considerable doubt about their ability both to agree among themselves and to distinguish hospitalized schizophrenic, nonschizophrenic hospitalized, and relatively "normal" adolescents from one another. These professionals, however, showed both a very high agreement among themselves and a high ability to distinguish the three categories of adolescents.

"Crazies Are Completely Different from Us"

This slogan and its close relative, "He's completely crazy," are untrue. No one is "completely crazy" or psychotic, and no schizophrenic person is completely different from "normal" people. Whatever aspect of human behavior or cognition is measured, the results show a continuum, not a dichotomy. Even such seemingly "far-out" phenomena as hallucinations and delusions occur as a matter of degree in "normals," and hallucinations and delusions come in all shades of severity (Strauss, 1969). Prejudice segregates "crazies," thus creating rigid categorical differences that deny the similarities between "us and them." Accepting the fact of degree and rejecting simple categories have threatening implications, however. If they, the "crazies," are not so different from us, then we, too, may become crazy. The prejudiced person said, implicitly at least, "I could never become crazy." Yet we know definitely that there are situations that can and do drive anyone exposed to them "crazy," for example, schizophrenic. Karon and Vandenbos (1981) cited such a situation:

> In World War II, every soldier who underwent a particular battlefield experience developed schizophrenic symptoms. The precipitating situation was very simple. The soldier was under fire and in danger of being killed. He dug a foxhole under fire as quickly as he could, one just barely big enough to get into. He crawled into it and stayed there. He didn't eat or drink. He urinated and defecated on himself, because there was no other place to urinate or defecate without being killed. If the situation lasted for several days, every soldier appeared classically schizophrenic when the shooting stopped, and his buddies came up to him. That is, when these patients were finally rescued, they exhibited Bleuler's primary symptoms, plus hallucinations, delusions and/or catatonic symptoms. (p. 43)

Although many soldiers recovered with rest, provided they were relatively strong psychologically before the trauma, one can all too readily imagine more than a temporary or schizophreniform psychosis (in the nomenclature of the DSM-III-R) developing if the stress were to continue. Even soldiers who did recover from a schizophrenic state were often afflicted chronically with posttraumatic stress disorders. Fortunately, some folk wisdom may allow us to know our own limits when we say, though often half-jokingly, "This situation is driving me crazy!"

"Not Giving Phenothiazines to Schizophrenics Is Malpractice"

This prejudice, so rigorously enforced by the majority of psychiatrists and so often endorsed by other mental health professionals, is not shared by well-informed practitioners. Psychiatrists Strauss and Carpenter (1981, p. 202) noted that, although some clinicians and administrators fear that they will be vulnerable to charges of withholding treatment unless drugs are used, multiple modalities are available and it is intellectually indefensible to define the treatment of schizophrenic persons so narrowly.

Most patients, perhaps two thirds of hospitalized patients for whom phenothiazines are prescribed, do not take their drugs if they can possibly avoid them. Many who do take them do so out of actual or threatened coercion. On the whole, patients seem not to believe that these drugs are good for them. There is ample evidence now to support patients in their distaste for the so-called antipsychotic drugs. Some patients, though certainly not enough, know that permanent disablement may later become apparent.

Contrary to earlier expectations, tardive dyskinesia, an extreme form of permanent disablement, can develop even in short-term, low-dose drug treatment, as Breggin (1983) noted. Tardive dyskinesia is an almost always irreversible disease that appears obviously in a small percentage of cases but, in fact, develops in a very large percentage of patients given the major tranquilizers. For example, Korcyzn and Goldberg (1976) found Parkinsonism, with general motor retardation and a stiffened facial expression being among the more subtle signs, in more than 60% of patients receiving a variety of major tranquilizers, and they observed that the newer drugs tended to produce a higher incidence of the disease. Besides the grotesque appearance of involuntary motor movements of the facial muscles and the limbs, patients are impaired mentally, usually for life.

Scientists are beginning to recognize that, as Breggin (1983) stated, the harmful effects of the neuroleptic drugs are not just due to "side effects" but are the main effects or, putting the matter most straightforwardly, are all of the physical effects. Estimates of the numbers of people who become diseased in terms of tardive dyskinesia keep increasing because the disabling effects of the drugs are cumulative and therefore delayed in clear manifestation, so that long-term clinical observation of the effects at least over a 20-year period is needed. By 1979 the most systematic studies had estimated that 24%–56% of patients had already developed tardive dyskinesia (Breggin, 1983). By 1991, it was estimated that there were two million cases of tardive dyskinesia cases in the United States and about forty million cases worldwide (Breggin, 1991). Many other forms of damage are becoming evident in countless other patients. For example, a study reported in 1989 found akathisia—a symptom of extrapyramidal malfunctioning associated with jitteriness—in 71 percent of 110 patients at Boston's McLean Hospital (Breggin, 1991, p. 72). The upshot of the accumulating evidence is that these "medications" are turning "schizophrenics" and many other people into cases of actual mental disease because the drugs damage the nervous system, including the brain. What has been defined as a condition without brain damage, according to the *Diagnostic and Statistical Manual* of the American Psychiatric Association in all of its last three editions (1968, 1980, 1987), increasingly comprises cases of iatrogenically determined brain disease.

The seriousness of the brain-disabling effects of psychiatric drugs is still denied even by some prominent professionals and even though the American Psychiatric Association's Committee on Tardive Dyskinesia has estimated that 40% of patients with long-term use of "antipsychotic" drugs develop tardive dyskinesia (Karon, 1989). Clearly, only the most prejudiced can deny that the "antipsychotic" drugs can produce but cannot cure a disease. We may arrive at the realization sometime in the 1990s that to administer phenothiazines in nonemergency circumstances should be considered malpractice because of the very harmful effects of these drugs, especially in comparison to the extreme limitations in their possibly helpful effects. As Bellak (1979) noted:

> Whatever role the biological matrix may play in some sufferers of the schizophrenic syndrome, currently available drugs are unable to reverse the lack of cognitive development and psychological structure which seem to play such a critical role in the syndrome's pathogenesis. (p. 18)

Furthermore, there are methods of psychological care and humane orientations that would increase rather than decrease the abilities and powers of self-determination of people called mental patients. Although it is extremely difficult to find facilities where one is allowed to work with schizophrenic and related patients without drugs, there are clear examples, from both historical analyses and experimental programs, of superior treatment without drugs. Most notably, Karon and VandenBos (1981) showed that psychotherapy is the treatment of choice for schizophrenic persons in terms of strengthening their abilities. Unlike drug treatment, these authors' psychotherapeutic approach enabled patients to think better, in other words, to have less thinking disorder, the most important and primary of the disabilities characteristic of schizophrenic disorders. Thinking ability enables adaptive living, not merely vegetative survival. Deikman and Whitaker (1979) showed that the "management" and therapeutic dilemmas anticipated, if drugs were not used, were either nonexistent or quite solvable with psychological approaches, though hospital staff generally predicted great difficulty and were highly resistant initially. Furthermore, there is now evidence that treatment after the "third revolution" in psychiatry that emphasizes drugs is not superior, as is commonly assumed. Bockhoven and Solomon (1975) compared two five-year follow-up studies and got surprising results:

> The finding of no substantial change in the outcome of schizophrenic patients was not expected in view of the absence of psychotropic drugs during the entire 5 years of the Boston Psychopathic Hospital follow-up period, compared with the extensive use of psychotropic drugs at Solomon Center for both initial treatment on admission and the entire period of aftercare. This finding suggests that the attitudes of personnel toward patients, the socioenvironmental setting, and community helpfulness guided by citizen organizations may be more important in tipping the balance in favor of social recovery than are psychotropic drugs. The distinctive value of the drugs may be limited in most instances to their capacity to alleviate the distress of acute emotional decompensation. (p. 800)

The date from this study showed that, although the drug-era patients had initially shorter hospital stays (32 weeks compared to 47 weeks), they also showed greater relapse rates (7 in 10). The authors concluded:

> Rather unexpectedly, these data also suggest that psychotropic drugs may not be indispensable to the success of community-based mental health services and that their extended use in aftercare may prolong the social dependency of many discharged patients. (p. 801)

Other studies, comparing drug treatment with psychosocial and psychotherapeutic approaches, show the latter to be definitely superior to drug treatment. For example, Carpenter, McGlashan, and Strauss (1977) demonstrated a significantly superior outcome for acutely schizophrenic patients who were given psychosocial treatment and only sharply limited drugs as opposed to the outcome for patients who received the usual treatment emphasizing drugs. Karon and VandenBos (1975) showed that psychotherapy, instead of medication, for schizophrenic patients saved at least 22% of total treatment costs because the psychotherapy patients had shorter hospital stays.

The common practice of automatically administering phenothiazines to every person labeled schizophrenic before a careful assessment can be accomplished creates several quite serious problems:

1. Failure to recognize the need for even moderately thorough assessment.
2. Contamination of the presenting symptoms, signs, and personality assets with drug effects.
3. The mistaken clinical impression that actual drug-damage symptoms are signs of inherent biological deficit or central nervous system damage.
4. A worsening of the already classically difficult task of distinguishing previously brain-damaged schizophrenic persons from those who are phenothiazine–brain-damaged patients.
5. Possible slowing down or stoppage of improvement in thinking ability and social skills, due to the drugs, making impossible a longitudinal assessment of improvement otherwise ascribable to psychological or social treatment.
6. Since a high percentage of patients manage not to ingest the drugs, inability to distinguish drug-induced effects from other effects.

For purposes of adequate assessment, patients should not be started on drugs first, and if a drug regimen is instituted later, they should be provided with a "drug holiday." The usual practice of giving anyone quickly and superficially labeled schizophrenic neuroleptic drugs results in many nonschizophrenic persons' being damaged for nothing, as well as obliterating opportunities for adequate assessment and alternative methods of treatment.

There is no evidence, despite claims to the contrary, that the drugs improve the thinking disorder that Eugen Bleuler (1911/1950) considered the primary and central disturbance "in the schizophrenics." The drugs' apparent effectiveness is often related to certain illusory phenomena. Because virtually all "schizophrenic" persons are placed on phenothiazines as soon as they are diagnosed (often instantaneously, after only a cursory emergency-room interview by a psychiatric resident), any "improvement" that occurs, however defined, may be attributed to the drugs, though it is well established that even rapid improvements may occur because of many other influences. And because improvement is usually defined as a reduction in disturbing behavior, and the phenothiazines do reduce much motor activity and emotional expressiveness and language use that may be considered disturbing, the resulting reduction of bizarre or otherwise frightening behavior and language may be seen as improvement. Furthermore, once made dependent on the drugs, both physically and psychologically, and then taken off drugs, schizophrenic persons may again exhibit bizarre behavior, an effect seeming to imply that the drugs have helped. In fact, dependence on the drugs, together with the lost opportunity to develop mastery and competence of one's own, may lessen functioning abilities, even to the point of tardive psychosis, which occurs after drug withdrawal in reaction to the brain damage done by brain accommodation to the drugs. Thus, one need not be surprised that, when adaptive ability is the criterion for improvement, the results of drug treatment per se are no better than the treatment results before the advent of the phenothiazines (Bockhoven & Solomon, 1975).

Surely there are many other myths about "schizophrenia" that are perpetuated out of fear and prejudice. The myths discussed above were selected because they all deny or minimize the need for careful assessment. Any one of them, if left unchallenged, may make a mockery, though an unrecognized mockery, of any assessment procedure. Defining a problem well may go a long way toward solving the problem, whereas definitions predicated on false assumptions distract us from finding genuine solutions.

Science versus the Trappings of Science

The word *science* brings to mind knowledge that we can rely on. Scientific knowledge is knowledge that, having been subjected to rigorous tests of validity and usefulness in predicting and/or controlling certain phenomena, provides us with a degree of certainty. Its methods both generate hypotheses and test them against reasonable doubts so that we develop convictions about the truth or falseness of various propositions. We stand ready to support convictions based on scientific evidence and to contradict convictions that do not stand the tests of science. Not all propositions are testable—for example, the existence of God—but so many propositions can be generated and so many can be made testable that the scientific method and scientific knowledge keep growing.

"Scientific" knowledge that proves to be false should be disregarded as a distraction, and other propositions should then be pursued. Human desire, however, has kept many false and propositions scientifically proven to be false alive and guiding social and professional practice. Rationalizing the surgical procedure of lobotomy won the Nobel Prize for the neurologist Egas Moniz, which seemed to guarantee the validity and usefulness of lobotomy, but it turned out to be useful only to those who would diminish the disturbing behavior of people designated as patients. Whereas schizophrenic disorders generally follow a favorable course on the whole, the irreversible damage done by lobotomy not only prevented possible improvement but guaranteed that the person so "treated" would be reduced to a vegetative existence. This example shows that mere theory, a terribly mistaken rationalization in this instance, should not be allowed to stand by itself but should be subjected to scientific proof wherever and whenever possible. But proof may require many decades of work, as did the proof of Copernicus's proposition that the sun, and not the earth, is the center of our particular system. Professional practice often does not wait for scientifically established truth but tends to proceed largely on the bases of theory and empirical "evidence," the latter often meaning that, whatever it is, it is acceptable if it seems to work. Lobotomy, like leeches, seemed to work. Because it is not always possible to wait for rigorous scientific evidence, one must look to other safeguards, among these knowledge of our own human proclivities to protect ourselves from psychological as well as physical threats.

Truly scientific advances may make us feel less important, perhaps less important in the universe or less superior to other creatures, than we had believed or wanted to believe ourselves to be. Copernicus's supporter Galileo was punished for removing us from the center of the universe, as it were. Darwin made us feel like monkeys and brought wrath as well as recognition on himself. Freud made us uncomfortably aware of our unawareness and was widely condemned, mistranslated, and misinterpreted. All of these discoverers brought us sobering news that greatly threatened our self-esteem. In each case, the knowledge they gave us, which could put us in greater real instead of illusory control, told us how very little we had known and how much more there was to know than we had ever imagined. Science, especially in its major advances, has disquieting effects that shake our confidence and security by showing us how very little we know and how very ignorant we are. Therefore, it takes great tolerance to abide real science; intolerance promotes pseudoscience.

When we think of science, it is easiest to focus on its more tangible aspects, that is, the resultant knowledge and the particular methods, the latter often conceived of as the technology of science. Real science, including scientific method, is not predicated on technology, however. Rather, technology should serve scientific methods of inquiry. Neither technology nor merely the coldly deductive or inductive processes formalized to rationalize scientific method are adequate. Scientific journal articles usually present an artificially ordered rationalization of a study, not its actual process. The actual process of successful scientific inquiry requires familiarity with the subject matter, imagination, and intuitive understanding, often in disorderly procession. We have seen that people, including professionals, have strong proclivities to distance themselves from "schizophrenics," rather than to closely observe and imaginatively interact with them, so as to develop greater familiarity with and a direct sense of their subjects. This kind of distancing, by itself, results in a kind of pseudoscientific objectifying of the subject; it dehumanizes the subject rather than objectifies it, in the scientific sense of bringing observation-based propositions to objective testing. A tendency to distance the subject matter at the outset, and not just when writing an article, precludes real scientific understanding. In fact, it keeps mental health professionals more ignorant than the patients, as Rosenhan (1973) showed.

The combination of the distancing proclivity, the tendency to make political concerns a part of the purview and practice of medicine, and the vaunting of technology for technology's sake has produced many destructive methods of treatment. If one has surgical means at one's disposal, try them on patients; if one has access to drugs, try them on patients. This approach to treatment can be presented as empiricism: It "works" because it "works." Or more insidiously, whatever is done may be rationalized by a theory that does violence to the legitimate aims of the mental health enterprise by weakening people instead of making them stronger. One of the most reliable signs of such rationalizations is that a given treatment method makes patients "more manageable." Lobotomy certainly made patients more manageable. Similarly, we may hear that a treatment successfully "targets symptoms." Typically, such "targeting" does something to patients to reduce secondary-level symptoms while ignoring and perhaps disguising the need for help with primary difficulties. Sometimes, it is the cry for help that is successfully targeted and reduced. So we must eschew technology per se, accepting it only if good and effective uses are made of it.

What happens if we use technology simply because "it's there" or even because it is useful in another field of inquiry? We produce something like the "mad scientist," though the phenomenon may not be recognized as such for many years; for example, it took many years to stop the practice of lobotomy. Today, drugs have replaced lobotomy and some forms of shock treatment, and the drugs are venerated, just as lobotomy and shock were, because they are part of "medical science," in other words, because drugs or "medicine" is a part of medical technology and because we live in a drug culture.

The entire concept of *mental illness* itself needs to be questioned. It is unlikely that we can dismiss the phenomena of human psychological impairment that are thus categorized; in this sense, mental illness is not a myth, as Szasz (1961) claimed. But we should regard "mental illness" as a metaphor, as Sigmund Freud did, and not mistake it for a real illness, as Bettelheim (1984) emphasized:

> Of all the metaphors that Freud used, probably none had more far-reaching consequences than the metaphor of mental illness, and—derived from it—the metaphor of psychoanalysis as the treatment and cure of mental illness. Freud evoked the image of illness and its treatment to enable us to comprehend how certain disturbances influence the psyche, what causes them, and how they may be dealt with. If this metaphor is not recognized as such but, rather, taken as referring to objective facts, we forfeit a real understanding of the unconscious and its workings. (p. 39)

Psychological impairment and physical illness are merely analogous as far as we know at present. Taking the metaphor literally leads directly to reliance on physical assessment and treatment. No one responds literally when it is said that we have a "sick economy," though it may be a useful metaphor. Economists do not recommend that surgeons and druggists be employed to treat the "sick economy."

As noted by Strauss and Carpenter (1981), "Most estimates suggest that about 20% of variance (a statistical measure of variability) of outcome of schizophrenic disorders from the worst possible to the best possible can be predicted by the most effective measures available" (pp. 64–65). This extreme limitation in predicting the outcome of "schizophrenia" may be due in large part to the fact that most of the "science" of schizophrenic disorders is limited to nomothetic science or generalization about characteristics common across individuals. Science should, of course, attempt to generalize across individuals, but adequate systematization comprises both the nomothetic and the idiographic approaches.

Bettelheim (1984) emphasized that the idiographic approach, a historical method of studying singular events, is a major productive method, particularly for understanding psychodynamic influences; it allows us to consider the entire complexity of individual human personality, a rich composite and integration of a conflictual gestalt changing over time and situation. This approach may seem like opening Pandora's box, which indeed it is. But while introducing more variables—rather idiosyncratic variables, at that—may seem to dispel any hope of systematization that would enable us to achieve the scientific aims of prediction and control, the fact is that individual human personality is likely to be of quite great significance in determining susceptibility to schizophrenic impairment. Idiographic science has a particularizing effect that, together with the generalizations of nomothetic theory, can greatly enrich our scientific knowledge.

The extreme limitations on predictive efficacy may also be politically determined. Traditionally, the task of assessment by means of testing procedures was mostly given over to clinical psychologists, who began their work as a junior profession in relation to psychiatry during World War II, when there was an urgent need for mental health professionals. As Sargent and Mayman (1959) documented, clinical psychology itself grew out of both academic psychology and psychiatry. Psychologists were trained in scientific method, experimentation, and measurement. The ideal of the clinical psychologist was to be a "scientist-practitioner" according to the so-called Boulder Model. But their testing functions were viewed generally as the work of "tester-technicians" who were ancillary, like other technicians. Furthermore, as clinical psychologists were gradually allowed treatment functions and proved themselves equally good psychotherapists, their testing and measurement functions came to be neglected, partly, perhaps, because these functions were an embarrassing reminder to some of a limited and quite ancillary past.

The ancillary and low-status role of the "tester-technician" has tended to keep "psychiatric diagnosis" in the forefront as the criterion for testers to agree with. Even when quite prominent psychiatrists, such as Robert Knight (1952) or Silvano Arieti (1974), extolled the value of psychological test evaluation, especially in explicating the evidence of a thinking disorder, few listened so seriously as to give psychological test evaluation any claim over even unstructured interviews. Less scientifically sound methods could prevail on political grounds alone.

Thus, not only was psychological test evaluation often poorly done and therefore often poorly received, but the very criteria for the diagnosis of "schizophrenia" were handed down, however unintelligibly and dogmatically, by psychiatrists whose diagnoses often had little reliability or validity. Most unscientifically, clinical psychologists tested "schizophrenics," as labeled by one or another psychiatrist, and correlated their test findings with this poorly defined category, to tell what "schizophrenia" was. The primary emphasis on psychiatrists' diagnoses has tended to limit the field of professional assessment to correlating test results with these diagnoses and overlooking other criteria and the many important parameters of schizophrenic disorders.

Summary

Psychiatry is generally conceived of as having gone through three revolutions, marked by "moral treatment," which actually began in Spain early in the 15th century, when the chains of mental patients were removed, thoug associated with Philippe Pinel's removing the chains of patients in F 18th century; the development of psychoanalysis early in the 20th centu. advent of the major psychotropic drugs in the mid-20th century. Psychiatric hospit by and large, even in the modern era, have not proved superior either to the moral treatment era or to the less expensive nonhospital programs of the modern era. The standard, nearly universal administration of neuroleptic drugs to patients diagnosed schizophrenic has led to many problems, both physical and psychosocial, that have only begun to be recognized.

Alienation is a central theme in schizophrenic disorders, as experienced by patients within themselves and in relation to other people. Segregation from society, emigration from place to place, and prejudice against schizophrenic persons serve to increase the incidence of schizophrenic disorders. Treatment itself has often been alienating, as it has fallen in line with management goals emphasizing quelling disturbing behavior more than helping the disturbed.

Myths about "schizophrenia" and its assessment include "Once a schizophrenic, always a schizophrenic"; "Anyone can tell a schizophrenic"; "Crazies are completely different from us"; and "Not giving phenothiazines to schizophrenics is malpractice." These myths are not supported by evidence, but they are nevertheless staunchly held beliefs not only in society generally but even among many mental health professionals. Assessment is usually short-circuited by the majority practice of assuming diagnoses after only a brief interview and beginning to administer neuroleptics before there is time for truly adequate assessment.

Much of the extreme reduction of psychiatry to reliance on not only the knowledge but the physical procedures of a narrow medical model has resulted in a pseudoscientific orientation in which "mental illness" is treated almost entirely by somatic means instead of as a metaphor. The result is often real disease, such as tardive dyskinesia, rather than effective treatment of what are—in the main, probably—severe psychosocial problems.

3

The Parameters of Assessment

Simply attaching the label *schizophrenia* to a person may have little predictive power except to stigmatize and damage the person, whether the diagnosis is "correct" or not. Strauss and Carpenter (1981) noted their "belief that labeling an individual as schizophrenic and the social consequences of many of the behaviors of schizophrenic patients induce reactions and expectations which are antitherapeutic in nature" (p. 4).

Ordinary diagnostic labeling may lack other predictive efficacy otherwise because

1. The assessment of the person is typically brief and superficial and thus not sufficiently precise and complete to make it scientifically and practically useful.
2. The person's life circumstances and the social and interpersonal influences affecting the person are not assessed and/or cannot be predicted or controlled.
3. Treatment possibilities are limited or unknown.

All of these deficiencies must be resolved if we are to achieve appreciable predictability of outcome. This chapter delineates what needs to be assessed and notes some basic deficiencies that characterized most assessment studies, at least up to the advent of the DSM-III (American Psychiatric Association, 1980).

In addition to setting criteria for reliability, validity, and generalizability, we must specify several dimensions of schizophrenic disorders to provide sufficient conditions for assessment formulations to achieve enough refinement even to begin meaningful measurement. Of course, we must also have adequate measurement methods to make prediction and control a reality. Primarily, this chapter depicts the several dimensions of schizophrenic disorders that must be considered if we are to differentiate schizophrenic from related disorders and from the "normal," to differentiate one schizophrenic individual from another, and to differentiate the schizophrenic person over time. The process of specification, including a precise characterization of individual schizophrenic persons and both the nomothetic and idiosyncratic approaches, provides a basis for understanding commonalities and differences among schizophrenic disorders and, most critically for practical purposes, profiles of status and change. This chapter concludes with an examination of the adequacy of traditional subject-selection procedures and diagnostic interviews through the 1970s.

The Basic Dimensions

Degree of Disorder

The nominalistic approach by itself (simply labeling an individual schizophrenic or not schizophrenic) has extreme limitations that, if not taken into account, can result in gross mistakes in treatment as well as diagnosis. Though one can claim, with some justification, that a kind of crystallization takes place when an apprehension or opinion becomes a delusion, or when talking to oneself becomes hearing voices, close examination shows a continuum of symptomatology, that is, precursors and determinants that will reveal the apparently "brand-new" schizophrenic symptom to be one of several stages in a process and not simply a discrete all-or-none phenomenon. For example, Strauss (1969) demonstrated with rating-scale evidence that hallucinations and delusions are best conceptualized as points on continua rather than all-or-none phenomena. Furthermore, there are hierarchies specifiable within a developmental model that characterize levels of delusions or levels of hallucinations, as well as the relationship of delusions to hallucinations or of loose associations to reference ideas. For example, Zigler and Levine (1983) showed that patients who manifested delusions were at a higher developmental level than those with hallucinations. So we must aim at least for an ordinal scale of measurement and not simply a nominalism. Specifying the degree as well as the type of symptom or inability is essential.

When one considers the degree of a schizophrenic disorder overall, it becomes apparent that both the severity of particular symptoms and inabilities and the extent to which they pervade a person's functioning are at issue. Some persons have extreme degrees of particular symptoms, such as firmly fixed delusions, but their symptoms are so circumscribed that we would not call them schizophrenic, though isolated symptoms may easily pass for "schizophrenia," as Rosenhan (1973) demonstrated, even when the symptom is not of the schizophrenic type. By definition, schizophrenic disorders are characterized by the extensity as well as the intensity of certain types of symptoms and inabilities.

A developmental hierarchy model suggests that the most recently acquired and most difficult-to-achieve mental faculty is the first to show disturbance when an individual becomes schizophrenic. Thus, a disturbance in the thinking abilities, especially the ability to think actively in the here and now, tends to occur first. And in schizophrenic disorders generally, one would expect considerably more difficulty in thinking than in perception and more difficulty with perception than with sensation.

Specifically, the ability to think logically and abstractly represents a high level of cognitive development acquired relatively late in the individual developmental process. In general, abstract thinking ability is considered due after about 10 years of age and seldom before. There is no exact age of demarcation, but adolescents are normally expected to have acquired the rudiments, at least, of the ability to organize symbolic representations of concepts. One would expect to find evidence of a fairly pervasive thinking disorder in a late adolescent, or an adult, if the individual is to be considered schizophrenic at all. A severe thinking disorder may take the form of delusions or a marked blocking of thought processes.

Further down the developmental hierarchy, one would expect disturbances of perceptual ability, including hallucinations, starting with the auditory mode because it is more advanced than the visual mode, which, in turn, is more advanced developmentally than the olfactory mode.

Thus, it is common in persons who are relatively mildly schizophrenic overall to find evidence only of a "thinking disorder." If other factors are held constant, the presence of delusions suggests a severe thought disorder, especially if they are firmly fixed or quite pervasive. Hallucinations are signs, on the whole, or a still deeper disturbance than delusions (Zigler & Levine, 1983), and within the range of hallucinations, olfactory hallucinations signal very severe disturbance. At the most extreme levels of developmental fixation and/or regression, there are disturbances even of the ability to take in sense impressions.

As one considers the rich complexity introduced by the specification of types and degrees of symptoms and inabilities ranging along the developmental hierarchy or continuum, together with the myriad combinations and permutations possible, it becomes clear that no two nominalistic systems of diagnosis need agree very substantially even on the general nominalistic diagnostic label. Furthermore, some systems are quite exclusive and narrow in the definition of "schizophrenia," and others are quite inclusive. European diagnostic systems have usually included fewer people in the schizophrenic category than systems prevalent in the United States, although formally, at least, the discrepancy has lessened with the introduction of the DSM-III (American Psychiatric Association, 1980) and the DSM-III-R (American Psychiatric Association, 1987), which are much more exclusive than DSM-II (American Psychiatric Association, 1968).

Still further disagreement arises from the significance given the types of signs or symptoms, as well as their degree, in various combinations. Finally, the typically informal diagnostic approaches that are common in actual diagnostic practice produce massive confusion in diagnostic labeling, so that one individual may easily be given a host of labels by different diagnosticians. For example, the designations *schizophrenia, manic-depressive* or *bipolar illness, borderline personality,* and even *neurosis* may all be given to a person who is mildly schizophrenic and has a tendency toward mood swings. Ironically, the observers giving these apparently contradictory diagnoses may agree on the particulars of evidence, although they do not on the nominalistic category. More often, however, they will not have observed the patient very carefully, let alone engaged the patient in careful interviewing or testing.

One advantage, therefore, of specifying the degree of disorder is that some of the arbitrariness of nominalism may be avoided or at least exposed. Resistances against the specification of degree have been great, however. Some resistances are made clear by a review of diagnostic practice historically and within the context of the entire mental health enterprise, as indicated in Chapters 1 and 2. Other resistances may be reactions to the greater assessment challenge, especially as most clinicians are unaware of, let alone practiced in, rigorous assessment. Of course, there are also the limitations of the currently available methodology, but common current practice lags far behind the frontiers of assessment research and methodology.

Paranoid-Nonparanoid

Most patients labeled schizophrenic in clinical practice have at some time shown evidence of paranoid ideation, at least ideas of reference, often to the point of delusional intensity. Paranoid persons interpret events in the environment as referring to the self more often and with greater intensity than an objective observer would consider warranted. When this tendency to attach highly personalized meanings to impersonal events is pervasive, it is customary clinical practice to label the person *paranoid.* The diagnostic questions that remain pertain to the severity of the tendency and the extent to which the mistaken interpretations are logical, given a core assumption. When the tendency is severe and there is pervasive illogicality, the clinician is likely to label the individual *paranoid schizophrenic.* But where there is little illogic in relation to an individual's core belief or premise, the label should be *paranoid* without the designation *schizophrenic* or, in the words of the DSM-III-R, a paranoid disorder rather than a schizophrenic disorder of the paranoid type. These paranoid disorders include paranoia, a relatively rare condition remarkably free of the pervasive illogicality of paranoid schizophrenic disorder. In paranoia, the individual reasons quite logically but from an incorrect premise that represents a false conviction; the person therefore has a particularly well-systematized delusion.

As noted in the DSM-III (p. 195), the boundaries between severe paranoid disorder and paranoid schizophrenic disorder and paranoid personality are unclear. This lack of clarity is due, certainly, to the arbitrariness of nominalism as well as the difficulty of specifying the degree and pervasiveness of illogicality in these disorders. If we accept that the pervasiveness of illogicality should be considered a matter of degree and so attempt to estimate the degree, we overcome the arbitrary difficulty imposed by rigid categories that have no justification in terms of the reality of the phenomena. But we must still attempt to ferret out evidence from paranoid individuals, whose very paranoid guardedness makes it difficult to assess them.

Acute-Chronic

If we keep in mind the matter of degree, the acute-chronic dimension should be seen as a handy but crude grasp of the phenomenon of change, or the lack of it, in the course of a schizophrenic disorder. The DSM-III and the DSM-III-R have ruled rather arbitrarily that a schizophrenic condition lasting less than six months should be called a schizophreniform disorder rather than a schizophrenic disorder. Although this distinction may seem to simplify diagnosis, and although it gives some acknowledgment to the temporal dimension, it has great limitations because people who become schizophrenic actually present as varied courses as it is possible to observe in mental disorders. Often, the individual labeled schizophreniform will become schizophrenic, in the sense of an apparently lasting disorder, only to revert to relative normality at a future date. Thus, while the distinction has some descriptive value perhaps, the predictive powers of the terms *schizophreniform disorder* and *schizophrenic disorder* are weak. We are less presumptive and more accurately descriptive when we recognize the real complexity of the acute-chronic dimension because individuals may move back and forth along this dimension with any degree of irregularity. We should proceed to the more important task of trying to capture some sense of the individual's pattern by means of accurately describing the pattern up to the present and integrating knowledge of other phenomena, including stressors, personal psychodynamics, and planned therapeutic interventions, in order to forecast further developments.

The DSM-III-R Axis V—the "highest level of adaptive functioning past year"—is a way of providing a comparison base against which the degree of chronicity or regression may be rated. The diagnostician is asked to rate the patient's highest level of functioning on a seven-point scale from "grossly impaired" to "superior." Again, the DSM-III and the DSM-III-R are improvements on the DSM-II in this respect, but a more detailed pattern of adaptation level should be explicated.

Psychosocial Stressors

The DSM-III-R Axis IV "provides a scale, the Severity of Psychosocial stressors Scale . . . for coding the overall severity of a psychosocial stressor or multiple psychosocial stressors that have occurred in the year preceding the current evaluation" (p. 18) and that may have contributed to the development, recurrence, or exacerbation of an already-existing mental disorder. Posttraumatic stress disorder is an exception to the requirement that the stressors must have occurred during the year before the evaluation. Although the concept of psychosocial stressors is a very useful consideration in assessment, the positing of one year as the crucial premorbid stressor period is somewhat arbitrary. Making posttraumatic stress disorder an exception to the rule is also useful but also somewhat arbitrary because many, if not all, persons with severe disorders have a history, remote or recent, of being severely stressed in ways that surely help to determine their disorder. A comprehensive assessment system should focus just as much on seemingly remote stressors, especially childhood stressors, which affect persons when they are the most vulnerable. Furthermore, recent stressors should be gauged in terms of their possibly critical symbolic significance in the light of "remote" stressors. In essence, assessment should address the complexity of the determinants, taking into account known stressors, symbolic precipitators, previous higher levels of adaptive functioning (before the breakdown), and the psychodynamics involved.

Psychodynamics and the Content of Thought

Traditionally, psychodynamics has been regarded as the concern of psychoanalysis and its offshoots. Splits among professional "schools" of psychiatry and clinical psychology have tended to promote reductionism within each school or orientation. Sometimes psychoanalytic observers have tried to explain too much in terms of unconscious motivation and theories of dynamic conflict. At least as grievously, many nonpsychoanalysts have practiced a dry descriptive psychiatry that is linked to prediction and treatment only by superficial considerations, most often mere attempts to banish readily observable secondary or positive symptoms. Notably, the DSM-III and the DSM-III-R omit psychodynamic considerations except by implication. They do not attempt to outline particular psychodynamic configurations or their special importance in making "diagnosis" meaningful. In turn, many clinicians of the psychoanalytic and psychodynamic persuasions, or even clinicians of other persuasions who would emphasize the importance of interpersonal relationships, balk at assessment procedures that would formalize evaluation in the structural sense, for fear, it would seem, that the person who is a "patient" would be too objectified into someone set apart from real humans, who, after all, are interpersonal psychodynamic creatures.

Many otherwise inexplicable breakdowns can be understood, and even predicted, by knowledge of what constitutes an individual's major preexisting weaknesses in personal development and personal unresolved conflicts. Such knowledge can be used to predict otherwise seemingly discrepant reactions to what are apparently minor events but that have special significance to the individual. Though some events may be distressing to everyone, other events may be particularly distressing to one person and trivial to another. Therefore, one must know the individual's psychodynamic history and its current states of resolution in order to know to what degree certain current or future events may "cause" a breakdown of adaptive ability. It is quite possible, otherwise, to perform an excellent assessment covering all of the other dimensions that need assessment, only to find that one can account for only a small fraction of the schizophrenic phenomenon. Learning the individual's history and ascertaining current weaknesses of adaptive response in certain psychodynamic content areas are absolutely essential to adequate assessment.

As Eugen Bleuler (1911/1950) emphasized, the structure of the person's thinking critically distinguishes schizophrenic disorders from related disorders. But the content of thinking is also of great importance because it reveals the person's psychodynamics, especially when examined in relation to the structure. That is, examination of the content of what the person thinks when the person's thinking is unwittingly illogical and impaired can reveal what is so distressing.

Personal Strengths, Needs, and Desires

A person has a personality, including certain strengths and particular needs and desires. Learning these facts about the person may help one to predict outcome, especially when this knowledge is taken into account in recommendations of treatment approaches and the kinds of living situations and social supports that will be helpful. In other words, schizophrenic persons, like all others, are characterized by idiosyncracies that are vitally important for us to know if we are to be able to predict their behavior and to help them. It would be unnecessary to make this statement if schizophrenic persons were not often treated as if they were a homogeneous group rather than individuals.

Nomothetic and Idiographic Assessment

Assessment of schizophrenic persons solely by means of the "hard science" or nomothetic science approach inevitably falls short of its own goal of accurate prediction because the subject is a human personality with a unique life history, replete with distinctive life experiences having idiosyncratic meanings to that person. Merely generalizing from "schizophrenics" fails to capture the richness and complexity of the critical affective, cognitive, and social influences on a person's mental functioning abilities and proclivities. As the physician William Osler advised, "Care more for the individual patient than the special features of the disease" (quoted in Auden & Kronenberger, 1981, p. 215). Osler thought, wisely, that it might be more important to know who has the disease than to know the disease.

Psychologist Jaan Valsiner (1986) and his colleagues have argued persuasively that nomothetic science, though it may present itself quantitatively (often considered a *sine qua non* of science), cannot capture the individual. Close examination of individuals labeled *schizophrenic* shows so many idiosyncratic and critical differences among them that even valid generalizations from the label to the person are extremely misleading unless they are balanced by a knowledge of the individual.

Even "intelligence," that object of relentless nomothetic study, cannot be adequately revealed by an "IQ" score, partly because that score may vary substantially on reexamination and there may be variable levels of achievement within a single examination (Matarazzo, 1990). Thus, even IQ scores and their components represent changing, idiosyncratic variations that distinguish the person both intra- and inter-individually. But such a measurement, *if* properly interpreted within the historical and circumstantial contexts of the person's life, may predict short-term functioning ability.

Overall, nomothetic classification and prediction efforts are greatly facilitated by an opportunity to experiment, but, with good reason, we are limited ethically and otherwise from using human beings to develop schizophrenic disorders experimentally. Both the limitations on opportunities to experiment and the seemingly limitless idiosyncratically determined variations of the higher mental processes in humans point to the importance of going beyond the nomothetic into the idiographic and of integrating these two basic approaches.

Traditionally, there has been a conflict between psychologies emphasizing individual differences and those emphasizing general processes, a conflict that has been sharpest among personality psychologists. Whereas nomothetic psychologists studying personality have tended to rely on personality inventories, idiographers have relied on case studies and biographies. A crucial challenge to resolving this conflict and making optimal use of the two approaches in terms of a meaningful gestalt of theory, methods, and findings is answering the "question of how an individual's uniqueness may be incorporated into a general understanding of how to define him or her" (Silverstein, 1988, p. 425). Silverstein proposed an answer:

> The key concept used is that of the developmental functional history (DFH) of the individual, the career of material functioning throughout an individual's existence that, among other general laws it follows, must be unique. The DFH is also developmentally cumulative in its effect. Earlier events have more far reaching consequences on its organization than later ones. (p. 425)

A good example of the integration of nomothetic and idiographic approaches is the assessment of intellectual functioning ability versus intellectual capacity in schizophrenic disorders. As discussed earlier in this chapter, the higher forms of mental functioning are the first to be affected in schizophrenic disorders, and there are continua of functioning abilities that, when adequately developed originally but failing later, show a generally predictable pattern of developmental regression.

But a given individual's particular pattern of regression into a schizophrenic condition is a function also of that individual's past and present experiences and their mental representations. Not only is the content of an individual's thinking disorder determined largely by that individual's unique experiences, but the regressive pattern itself is determined in part by the gestalt of personal experience. For example, there may be a certain readiness to form a delusion, which is often associated with a rather severe thought disorder, without there being much generalized thought disorder.

Thus, the general tendency to regress under extreme stress, which applies to everyone, is conditioned by the individual's personal developmental history. Idiosyncratic irregularities in the regressive structural pattern and sequence, as well as in the content of any schizophrenic process, will distinguish any individual from others who have become schizophrenic. In essence, a general nomothetic principle accounts for the commonalities in the regressive sequence of schizophrenic cognitive deficit, but an idiographic approach is needed to account for the characteristics of regression in an individual.

Individuals who are becoming schizophrenic or more schizophrenic tend to "lose IQ points." Thus, in a case illustration in the next chapter, Sylvia Frumkin, who was very superior to the average person in "intelligence" during her middle adolescence, achieved only an average or slightly above-average IQ score several years later. But the "deterioration" of intellectual ability, or what used to be called the *dementia* of dementia praecox, is limited largely to the period of the person's schizophrenic disorder. Vaslav Nijinsky, another case illustration in the next chapter, functioned more intelligently or adaptively in terms of the learning he had acquired before his schizophrenic breakdown than he did in terms of current events in his life (unless one were to say that it was no longer intelligent for him to play an active part in the life around him). In general, the more recent the schizophrenic breakdown, the better the preservation of intellectual ability.

Many schizophrenic persons give evidence that their intellectual *capacity* has not lessened even though their current intellectual *ability* may have lessened greatly. This lessening of functioning ability may be strikingly correlated, especially in acute cases, with certain distressing topics, events, and personal relationships, all of which vary greatly among individuals.

Positive and Negative Symptoms

Having noted how important it is to assess the degree of disorder and the roles of psychosocial stressors and psychodynamic influences, as well as the dimensions of paranoid-nonparanoid and acute-chronic and the recency of the breakdown, we may integrate these and other considerations into a framework for understanding the assessment of symptoms. It is symptoms, after all, that constitute the information classically relied on to make a diagnosis of mental disorder. Clearly, symptoms are not all-or-none phenomena, nor are they independent of time or circumstance, nor are they absent in "normals." As Arieti (1974) noted, Eugen Bleuler emphasized in his classic 1911 monograph, "the individual symptom in itself is less important than its intensity and extensiveness, and above all its relation to the psychological setting" (Bleuler, 1950, p. 295).

Bleuler also emphatically distinguished fundamental (primary) from accessory (secondary) symptoms. Such exclusive attention has been paid to the secondary, or positive, symptoms, such as delusions and hallucinations, that such authors as Andreasen (1981, 1982) and Kay, Fiszbein, and Opler (1987) have emphasized and clarified the difference by designating "positive" versus "negative" symptoms. Kay *et al.* listed as positive symptoms: delusions, conceptual disorganization, hallucinatory behavior, excitement, grandiosity, suspiciousness, and hostility. Their negative symptoms are blunted affect, emotional withdrawal, poor rapport, passive-apathetic social withdrawal, difficulty in abstract thinking, lack of spontaneity and flow of conversation, and stereotyped thinking (p. 266).

A "primary" difficulty, or "negative" symptom, is found in what Bleuler called "disorder of the process of association." Many authors call this a thought disorder or, much more precisely, a disorder of the ability to think, as inferred from studying the thoughts produced in certain tasks requiring an active thinking process. Bleuler regarded this inability as primary or fundamental and regarded as secondary, or accessory, such symptoms as delusions, hallucinations, and catatonic posturing. He implied that the primary inability led to or somehow caused the secondary symptoms. One may question the notion of a causal sequence, but it has long been observed that careful assessment is likely to disclose thinking disorder before secondary symptoms have occurred in a developing schizophrenic disorder. Because thinking disorder is the most sensitive indicator of schizophrenic breakdown, it is both the most distinctive and earliest characteristic of schizophrenic disorders.

One should remember, however, that the mere appearance of some evidence of thinking disorder does not a schizophrenic disorder make. As Quinlan, Harrow, Tucker, and Carlson (1972) showed, one can readily find some thinking disorder in nonschizophrenic persons, a finding that is in accord both with Eugen Bleuler's view of a continuum and with the inexactitude of psychiatric diagnosis. There is no suitable substitute for clearly stating the intensity and extensity of signs and symptoms as well as noting what they are.

Distinguishing primary from secondary symptoms is similar to distinguishing negative from positive symptoms. A person showing a mild inability to think logically (primary symptom) need not be delusional (secondary symptom). For example, the person may show "looseness of associations" without the appearance of delusions. If, however, there is a strong need to believe in a false construction of reality, a product of what Eugen Bleuler called "autism," then the inability to think rationally plays a facilitating role complementary to this wishful or autistic tendency. A paranoid delusion, for example, may be based on strong autistic tendencies complemented by relatively little inability to think rationally. But without a strong autistic need—for example, an overarching desire to be given attention as an extraordinary person—such an individual is not likely to form a delusional belief. The individual who shows only an extensive inability to think logically is schizophrenic but not paranoid. On the other hand, a paranoid delusion may be formed in the absence of widespread thinking disorder, in which case the individual is paranoid but not paranoid schizophrenic.

One can readily see, then, how relying on evidence of an accessory symptom may not only make an assessor late in discovering the process of breakdown but also lead to a wrong diagnostic conclusion, particularly because the accessory symptoms may be common to other than schizophrenic disorders. Whereas extensive inability to think logically, where this inability is not due to central nervous system damage, is unlikely to characterize other, nonschizophrenic disorders, delusions and hallucinations can and do occur in many other conditions of a so-called functional nature, as well as in cases of brain damage.

Emphasizing the importance of a fundamental inability to think rationally and to resist wishful thinking has immediate relevance to treatment. Clearly, unless the schizophrenic person's ability to think improves, a reduction in the accessory symptoms has little merit and may even be quite harmful, and neither therapist nor patient may be motivated to work on the fundamental inability if there is such "symptomatic improvement." Accordingly, from the standpoints of both early detection of schizophrenic disorder and meaningful criteria for evaluating treatment needs and outcomes, the assessment of thinking inability is essential. Thinking ability is probably the most sensitive sign of the overall ability to behave adaptively, to gear one's behavior to the naturally ever-changing requirements for living outside a highly constricted and artificial environment. Improving thinking ability favors the person's "making it" in real life instead of vegetating in a hospital or halfway house. Assessment aimed at predicting the success of treatment in these meaningful terms needs to focus on ability and not merely on whether secondary symptoms have been quelled.

Neuroleptic drug treatment often results in worsening the patient's condition, not only neurologically but by facilitating the pursuit of extraneous and distracting goals in ways that may deepen the patient's despair and further erode any remainder of hopefulness in the patient and those who genuinely care about the patient. For example, even Munetz and Schulz (1986), who strongly believe that "schizophrenia is a serious brain disease" (p. 170) and claim that "neuroleptics are very helpful when used properly" (p. 171), noted frequent kinds of drug treatment errors in terms of treating positive versus negative symptoms:

> While these negative symptoms are generally not improved by neuroleptic drugs, it is not uncommon for psychiatrists to increase neuroleptic dose in the hope of alleviating these symptoms. Similarly, psychiatrists frequently increase drug dosage in patients with persistent positive symptoms (i.e., hallucinations and delusions) in the hope of achieving increased antipsychotic effects. While a trial of high dose neuroleptic treatment may be reasonable for patients with persistent psychotic or negative symptoms, high doses should not be maintained over time in the absence of a clearly increased benefit. (p. 171)

The neuroleptic drugs also tend to confuse the symptom picture, making the distinction between positive and negative symptoms quite difficult. As stated in the DSM-III-R, the presence of affective disturbances is already "often difficult to detect except when they are in an extreme form. Furthermore, antipsychotic drugs have effects that may appear similar to the affective flattening seen in Schizophrenia" (p. 189).

Inferring Thinking Disorder

Remarkably, thinking disorder, which Eugen Bleuler considered the most fundamental disturbance in schizophrenic disorders, does not have a very clear definition in the latest edition of the *Diagnostic and Statistical Manual* of the American Psychiatric Association, the DSM-III-R (1987):

> *Form of thought.* A disturbance in the form of thought is often present. This has been referred to as "formal thought disorder," and is different from a disorder in the content of thought. The most common example of this is loosening of associations, in which ideas shift from one subject to another, completely unrelated or only obliquely subject [*sic*], without the speaker's displaying any awareness that the topics are unconnected. Statements that lack a meaningful relationship may be juxtaposed, or the person may shift idiosyncratically from one frame of reference to another. When loosening of associations is severe, the person may become incoherent, that is, his or her speech may become incomprehensible. (p. 188)

Given the lack of a clear conceptual definition and operational means for assessing the kinds, degrees, and motivational dynamics of thought disorder, it is not difficult to understand why there is such excessive diagnostic reliance on simply observing secondary symptoms like hallucinations. And because secondary symptoms have little distinctive merit in differential diagnosis, it is not difficult to understand why there is not generally higher diagnostic reliability in labeling schizophrenic versus related disorders such as manic-depressive and central nervous system disorders.

Thinking is a function that must be inferred, rather than merely observed, as it is quite private; we cannot simply read a person's mind. We all know that someone can say one thing and be thinking something else entirely, and paranoid persons are especially adept at guardedness and deception. Thus, what may be the single most important task in assessing schizophrenic disorders is also the most difficult. Rather than dodge this crucial issue, let us understand it and arrive at measurement concepts, strategies, and methods.

Concepts of Schizophrenic Thinking

The first concepts of the nature of schizophrenic thinking grew out of the clinical observation of cases of dementia praecox, in which the dementia, or loss of intellectual acuity, was most impressive. Great declines in intellectual ability were observed in individuals formerly regarded as having normal or even superior intellectual ability, who began thinking and behaving like demented persons. However,

> Intellectual capacity, in the formal sense, is not reduced; many persons with schizophrenia have accomplished formidable intellectual tasks. The name "dementia praecox," once given to this illness, was a misnomer. The more disturbed the patient's thinking, however, the more he will be hampered in intellectual activity. (Lewis, 1967, p. 1466)

A crucial distinction is made here between formal intellectual capacity and intellectual activity. What is meant by *capacity* is what the individual is capable of doing, in contrast to what he or she is doing. There are ways of estimating capacity versus current intellectual efficiency, and they will be noted later in this chapter. The important point to be made now is that a discrepancy exists between a schizophrenic individual's capacity and her or his current intellectual activity or demonstrated intellectual ability. Schizophrenic individuals do not have a true dementia, unlike those persons classified as being mentally retarded or mentally deficient, or as suffering from central nervous system damage, unless, like some minority of schizophrenic individuals, they also happen to have central nervous system damage or are mentally retarded.

The distinction between intellectual capacity and current intellectual ability or efficiency is critical to an understanding of the differences between schizophrenic and brain-damaged and mentally deficient persons. The latter two groups are characterized by impaired capacity rather than just impaired ability. Furthermore, as Eugen Bleuler originally noted (E. Bleuler, 1911/1950), the characteristic illogicality and bizarreness in the thinking processes of schizophrenic persons distinguishes them from brain-damaged patients. Carl Jung's word association experiments (Jung, 1903/1936) had already given evidence of a dynamic or motivationally determined significance in schizophrenic thought processes, which helped to explain their bizarre nature. Thus, a meaningful start was made toward conceptualizing the relatively distinct nature of schizophrenic thinking.

Various terms have been used to describe the illogicality characteristic of schizophrenic thinking, including *paleologic thinking* (Arieti, 1976), *predicate thinking* (Von Domarus, 1944), *autistic thinking,* and *dereistic thinking* (Bleuler, 1912/1951). Each of these terms for schizophrenic thinking has features that are associated with a particular viewpoint, and these viewpoints must be understood if we are to arrive at a clear perspective on the use of these terms.

Each term used to label schizophrenic thinking arises from a particular conceptual system, which must be understood if we are to evaluate the significance, usefulness, and limitations of the term. The term *autistic thinking,* for example, was used by Bleuler to describe his observations of schizophrenic thinking in relation to similar phenomena in mythology, superstition, daydreams, poetry, and nocturnal dreams. Bleuler was most impressed by the "wish-fulfilling" aspects of each of these psychological expressions. The term *autistic,* then, refers to a particular motivational characteristic and function of schizophrenic thinking without giving much attention to the structure of that thinking per se. Bleuler later replaced the term *autistic thinking* with *dereistic thinking,* which indicates a kind of thinking that disregards reality.

Paleologic is a term pertaining to a private (i.e., consensually unvalidated) use of symbols that likens schizophrenic thinking to the most primitive forms of thought, in a manner intended to have ontogenetic significance. *Predicate thinking* refers to an aspect of paleologic thinking, that is, the equating of objects merely on the basis of their predicates or functions. Because each of these terms refers to a different aspect of schizophrenic thinking, it would be a mistake to regard any one of them as a comprehensive description.

Another concern that arises with the use of certain labels for schizophrenic thinking is the need to be alert to the limitations that should be placed on the use of that specific label during observation or testing. Any specific method of observation or assessment yields data that must be understood in terms of that method and the data themselves, as well as in terms of the particular conceptual system. Thus, to say, for example, that "schizophrenics are incapable of abstract thought" may be true in terms of the assessment results obtained with a particular test device, but it may not be true generally. Likewise, to say that schizophrenic thinking is equivalent to "regressed" thinking, or the thinking of childhood, may be true only of one aspect of the thinking measured by a certain test or observational method.

Not recognizing the limitations in the generalizability of a given theorist's conceptual framework or assessment method means that apparent but meaningless contradictions in theory will emerge, will be taken seriously, and will serve to confuse the issues. An adequate explanation requires a theory that integrates factual knowledge of the phenomena in such a way as to enable prediction and subsequent alteration of the phenomena.

Passive versus Active Investigatory Methods

The difficulties of conceptualization discussed thus far originate in the failure to investigate the phenomena actively and to recognize the limitations of particular conceptual or assessment systems. Quite often, investigations of schizophrenic thinking are severely limited by an exclusive reliance on passive investigatory methods that involve observation but not active testing of the subject, for example, just observing psychiatric ward behavior.

A passive method is defined here as one that merely records the products of thinking as reflected in the voluntary or spontaneous behavior of the subject. The subject is not required to demonstrate various abilities or inabilities by having to perform but is merely observed in a situation where the phenomenon of schizophrenic thinking *may* be manifested. This kind of methodological limitation is analogous to a neurologist's merely observing a patient's spontaneous movement and trying to conclude that the patient does or does not have particular kinds of damage to or disorders of the nervous system. The competent neurologist has the patient actively perform certain tasks designed to reveal particular inabilities.

Most formal assessment methods, as well as methods of naturalistic observation, do not provide or guarantee active testing of the subject. A weakness of the Rorschach technique, for example, which is discussed in Chapter 7, is an excessive reliance on the spontaneous productivity of the subject. Or a test may simply not address itself to the task at hand. For example, the Bender-Gestalt test and the Minnesota Multiphasic Personality Inventory (MMPI) do not in themselves yield much evidence of schizophrenic thinking.

Most of the literature on schizophrenic thinking relates to modes of inquiry that are either passive or not directly relevant. Typically the investigator interviews, observes, or give standard psychological "tests" to a group of "schizophrenics." Generally, these methods are not focused on assessing abilities specifically relevant to this disorder. The interviews, observations, or test results are analyzed and compared with data from "normal" or "neurotic" groups of subjects. Then, conclusions are drawn about the nature of schizophrenic thinking. The limitations of such a procedure make it impossible to interpret the data meaningfully. These limitations include inadequate subject selection, the use of poorly suited assessment methods, and interpretations of data that fail to take into account the first two limitations; the result is misleading conclusions. To be adequate, an assessment method must operationalize a clear and meaningful conceptualization of schizophrenic thinking.

Schizophrenic Thinking as an Inability

Whatever the particular manifestations of schizophrenic thinking, these products of thinking should not be equated with the thinking process itself. Schizophrenic thinking has to be inferred, and thus, it must be elicited and expressed in such a way as to make accurate inference possible. The first task in this endeavor is to construct a clear conceptual definition of schizophrenic thinking. I define schizophrenic thinking generally as a relatively marked inability to think logically and wittingly in comparison to one's intellectual capacity.

The illogical nature of schizophrenic thinking is itself an expression of inability. To put the matter in the language of psychoanalytic theory, it is an ego deficit in reasoning or secondary-process thinking. In linguistic terms, it is a deficit or inability to construct syntactically correct sentences and to use words in a semantically correct manner. In cognitive terms, it is an inability to engage consistently in logical thinking processes.

To conceive of schizophrenic thinking as an inability—that is, a deficit in ability—is to provide a particular orientation to assessment. Some psychological tests, such as the Wechsler intelligence tests, are addressed primarily to the assessment of ability. Other "tests," such as the Rorschach technique, are concerned largely with the assessment of proclivity, that is, an individual's tendencies, preferences, or inclinations. One cannot depend with any certainty on the subject's proclivity to demonstrate openly, without active testing, his or her inability to think rationally. One is so handicapped by the proclivity approach as to make exclusive reliance on this approach a sure road to clinical and theoretical chaos. The specific hazards of the proclivity methods are discussed in Chapters 5, 6, and 7. Ideally, there would be a way of defining schizophrenic thinking operationally, as an inability, which would stipulate the exact requirements for an assessment method, and such a method would be constructed accordingly.

A Conceptual Definition of Schizophrenic Thinking

The conceptual definition that I have developed is an integrated composite of the features attributed by a great many authors to schizophrenic thinking, most notably Arieti (1974, 1976), Eugen Bleuler (1950, 1951), Cameron & Cameron (1951), Cameron (1963), Fenichel (1945), and Rapaport (Rapaport, Gill, & Schafer, 1946). This definition represents a core of consensus among these authors and conforms to the most prevalent usages of the term *schizophrenic thinking.* At the same time, it is more directed to the issue of assessment than some of the definitions on which it is built.

An instance of thinking is defined here as schizophrenic if it is all of the following:

1. *Illogical.* This characteristic is manifest in the semantic and syntactical aspects of an individual's language usage, in the relationships existing among the ideas expressed, or in the relationships between those ideas and the logical requirements of a given task or problem situation.
2. *Impaired.* This characteristic refers to the marked discrepancy between an individual's capacity to think and the level of adequacy of his or her thinking in a given instance.

3. *Unwitting.* The individual lacks awareness, deliberate intention, or control in relation to a given instance of thinking.

Common to all three points in this definition is the consideration of degree. Thinking that is mildly illogical, mildly impaired, or mildly unwitting may not be considered "schizophrenic." Specification of the degree of the characteristics *within* the range of schizophrenic thinking is also essential, because some instances of schizophrenic thinking are mild; others, moderate; and others, severe. Thus, the proposed definition does not assume that a dichotomous distribution of instances of thinking into "schizophrenic" or "nonschizophrenic" is adequate. Neither is it assumed that there is necessarily much consistency in the adequacy of an individual's thinking. For example, the "schizophrenic" kind of thinking may occur occasionally in persons who are considered, in an overall evaluation of their personality functioning, nonschizophrenic or even "normal." Also, many persons diagnosed "schizophrenic" may often think in nonschizophrenic ways.

The term *grossly illogical* refers to the individual's failure to provide logical connections in thinking, and this failure may take either or both of two forms, negative and positive. The negative type may be expressed, at the extreme, in an inability to respond at all. Or less extremely, the individual may be unable to respond in a timely manner.

Toward the positive error end of the continuum, on the other hand, the individual may make halting attempts that flaunt logical requirements, for example in the form of "loose associations," which proceed in the manner of "free associations" and are not appropriate to the situation. Such looseness may, if severe, be expressed by clang associations and "word salad." Actually expressing markedly illogical associations manifests positive thought disorder that, at the extreme, may be expressed in stubbornly held but erroneous convictions of delusional intensity. This type of failure is distinguished by the individual's verbalizing purportedly logical but grossly illogical arguments from which certain conclusions are drawn. It is exemplified by delusional trains of reasoning in which the individual sets forth premises and makes inferences from them in a markedly illogical manner.

The two types of error, negative and positive, may be considered errors of omission and commission, respectively. An individual may engage primarily in one or the other type or, more often than not, may combine them. In the succinct formula suggested by Donald Stilson (personal communication, 1972): "Schizophrenic thinking equals looseness plus slowness" looseness mostly represents positive thought disorder, and slowness mostly represents negative thought disorder.

The inability to be logical, whether covert or manifest, must be inferred. Clearly, it is easier to make such inferences when the thinking disorder is, at least primarily, positively expressed, but it is certainly no less important to measure thinking disorder of the negative type.

Relatively impaired means that, relative to the individual's own capacity for reasoning, the individual is functioning on a defective level. For example, an individual whose Full Scale IQ on the Wechsler Adult Intelligence Scale (WAIS) was

130 three months ago or three years ago and whose IQ is 100 today is "impaired" today. Likewise, if an individual gives correct answers to the last three Similarities subtest questions on the WAIS but fails a number of earlier items, it may be inferred, on a probability basis, that the individual's functioning on these earlier items is impaired. Impairment may be reflected in not giving answers, in giving answers very slowly, and/or in giving wrong answers.

Relatively unwitting means that the individual's thinking is not sufficiently within his or her awareness or control. Whereas the schizophrenic individual's thought products may appear humorous to others, the individual, unaware of their inherent nonsense or illogic, finds no humor in them. Lacking a realistic perspective, such an individual lacks control, that is, the ability to produce other, more reality-oriented conclusions and to behave accordingly. By contrast, a more witting person may behave in ways that are grossly illogical and that represent levels of functioning considerably below his or her capacity but that are under conscious control. For example, deliberately humorous behavior, such as in playacting, may involve behaving ostensibly in a grossly illogical and impaired manner. As another example, malingerers have more control and perspective than is evident in their behavior. In fact, the ability to feign inability is itself an indication of wittingness.

From the standpoint of test construction, there must be ways to measure illogicality in terms of both negative and positive behavior, with controls for intelligence and wittingness. There must also be controls on certain conditions of the individual and the environment that would make it difficult, if not impossible, to determine whether a given instance of thinking is "schizophrenic": the individual to be tested should be free of the influences of narcotic and toxic substances, severe basic biological need deprivation, sensory deprivation, extreme time pressure, and especially, anxiety-inducing testing circumstances. These conditions may make behavior schizophreniclike in an individual who is not schizophrenic. Age is also an important assessment consideration. The definition of schizophrenic thinking offered here is directly applicable only to persons aged 16 or over who are not afflicted with a form of senility such as Alzheimer's disease or advanced cerebral arteriosclerosis.

General Considerations

Because schizophrenic thinking is not a directly observable variable, it is quite unlike the readily observed behavioral signs often associated with schizophrenic disorders, such as catatonic posturing, peculiar gesturing, and bizarre self-mutilative behavior. Even inappropriate-affect expression is more directly observable than schizophrenic thinking. Thinking processes have to be inferred from various behaviors, chiefly verbal ones, that are not themselves the variables being assessed. A peculiarly constructed sentence, for example, may or may not be a manifestation of schizophrenic thinking.

Making inferences about what verbal behaviors are schizophrenic is especially difficult under certain circumstances. Lack of formal education, an unfamiliar cultural background, or any lack of knowledge of the language used by the interviewer may lead to an impression of schizophrenic thinking when, in fact, it is not present. Likewise, borderline mentally retarded individuals are difficult to assess in terms of language usage.

A more formidable difficulty is that one cannot rely on the patient to express with any appreciable spontaneity the particular cognitive inability that is the prime, and sometimes the only, evidence of this disorder. Paranoid schizophrenic patients, especially, are often able to conceal their disorder quite effectively. Many severely withdrawn individuals and patients institutionalized for long periods may also refrain from manifesting thought disorder in any *spontaneous* way.

The following is an illustration of these possibilities from my experience:

> A male patient was being interviewed by a psychiatrist at a teaching hospital before an audience of students. The psychiatrist, who was skilled and knew the patient, conducted what seemed to be a sophisticated interview that left the impression that the patient was normal, at least in terms of schizophrenic symptomatology. Following the interview, most of the students left the room, but the psychiatrist, the patient, and two of the students remained. The psychiatrist then leaned toward the patient and asked softly, "John, now tell me what happened this morning in the breakfast line." The patient replied excitedly that the kitchen staff were still up to their "old tricks" and had poisoned him again, causing his insides to continue rotting.

This particular psychiatrist was aware of the shortcomings of a regular interview technique with this patient; however, even a skilled interviewer or clinical observer who is quite knowledgeable about a patient may remain unaware that the patient has a thought disorder. Sometimes, one wonders whether the patient is consciously aware of the concealment, for example:

> A female patient recently discharged from a state psychiatric hospital was referred to a clinic in her community for follow-up treatment. Her therapist was amazed at the apparent improvement in her condition. He had worked with her for several months previously at the clinic, attempting to prevent further gross psychotic episodes, but she had resumed behaving bizarrely and had been placed in the state hospital. After her discharge, he concluded on the basis of interviews with her and discussion with her employer that she was no longer psychotic. In an effort to further assure himself, he administered the Whitaker Index of Schizophrenic Thinking (WIST) to her, and she obtained a very high index value, which suggested that she was severely schizophrenic. Using her incorrect answers to the test to phrase interview questions, he learned that the patient was having and had been having, through her period of "normality," flagrant paranoid persecutory and grandiose delusions, on the basis of which she was about to execute a specific plan for killing her employer.
>
> This patient appeared quite straightforward in the testing situation that served to elicit and make manifest her delusions, but she was seemingly unaware herself of the relevance of her (delusional) thinking until then.

Borderline schizophrenic individuals present yet another special problem because their assessment requires considerably more methodological precision than is available with interview or observation methods. Such precision is afforded only by a method that controls or otherwise takes into account the effects of variability in intelligence, education, cultural background, and the possible lack of a spontaneous manifestation of symptoms or signs of the disorder.

Assessing the Assessment Methods

The adequacy of any specific method for assessing schizophrenic disorders depends, first, on the inherent qualities of the method itself and, second, on how it has been validated. We have seen that the method itself should be designed to address the important dimensions of schizophrenic disorders. Such a method has the potential to reveal both general and specific characteristics of schizophrenic individuals in ways that potentially distinguish these schizophrenic individuals from nonschizophrenic individuals and that distinguish the schizophrenic individuals among themselves. Examination of the method itself will show its promise: Does it have the potential built into it to address degree of disorder and the paranoid-nonparanoid and acute-chronic dimensions? Does it address psychodynamics and the content of thought? Can it be used to infer thinking disorder, both positive and negative? And can it reflect changes over time? Few methods are designed with these measurement criteria in mind. Most methods are more global in design, constructed to show something about personality differences but not necessarily to distinguish schizophrenic individuals.

Ultimately, both those methods designed specifically to assess schizophrenic disorders and those methods less deliberately structured for this purpose must pass certain tests of their own adequacy. The tests must be tested.

Rigorous studies are needed to test the tests, whether the tests are interview methods, projective techniques, highly standardized psychological tests, or biological methods. The necessary steps in this process are selecting subjects, developing examination strategies, collating and analyzing results, and systematically drawing conclusions about various aspects of the test's validity and then supporting or refuting these conclusions by means of replication and cross-validating. Typically, many studies are needed to validate a test adequately, so that users may have reasonable confidence in its efficacy.

Selecting Subjects in Studies of Schizophrenia

The adequacy of any procedure for selecting subjects in a scientific study can be judged by three criteria: reliability, representativeness, and replicability. If any or all of these criteria are not satisfied, the results of the study are difficult to interpret. When the literature on a given topic fails to meet these criteria, we can expect that literature as a whole to be misleading, confusing, and limited in value. It will be misleading or confusing if we do not recognize investigators' failure to meet these selection criteria; if we do recognize this failure, we will not have confidence in the results of the study.

In order to judge the adequacy of the procedure for selecting subjects in studies of schizophrenia, Shearn and Whitaker (1969) surveyed the literature on data studies from late 1963 to April 1968. The stated procedure for subject selection was examined in every fifth article appearing in 12 major journals during this period. Forty-one such articles were distributed among the following: *Journal of Abnormal Psychology, Journal of Consulting Psychology, Psychiatry, American Journal of Psychiatry, American Sociological Review, British Journal of Psychiatry, Mental Hygiene, Psychiatric Quarterly, Medical World, Acta Psychiatrica Scandinavica, Archives of General Psychiatry, and Journal of Abnormal and Social Psychology.* Each of the 41 articles was scrutinized for the presence or absence of indications of the reliability, representativeness, and replicability of its selection procedure.

For the purposes of this review, indications of reliability in an article meant one or more statements describing an estimate of the reliability of the selection procedure used, gained from either work in that study or work done elsewhere. For example, the article might indicate that two or more raters had been used in selecting subjects, or that a rating device had been used on which studies of reliability had been done elsewhere.

Indications of representativeness meant one or more statements about the population from which the sample was drawn, so that one might reasonably generalize the results of the study to this population. For example, representativeness was considered present if there had been a random, stratified, or consecutive admission sampling procedure, or even if the authors suggested that the sample was representative of the population.

Replicability meant that the study was described in sufficient detail with respect to the subject selection procedure to permit investigators at other institutions to select a comparable sample on the basis of statements in the article. If, on the other hand, on the basis of the statements in the article it would be possible to duplicate or replicate the study only in the original institution, replicability was not considered possible.

Of the 41 articles, 9 gave evidence of reliability; only 1 gave some indication of the representativeness of the procedure; and 2 gave evidence of replicability. Of the 41 studies, 10 met one of the three criteria, 1 met two of the criteria, and the remaining 30 failed to meet any of the criteria. Thus, unless these articles represented a biased sampling of the literature, which is highly unlikely, the research literature on schizophrenic disorders from that period of over four years failed generally to provide valuable scientific data judged even by minimal standards for subject selection.

Of the 41 articles, 33, or 80%, indicated the use of psychiatric diagnosis alone as a basis for selecting subjects, 6 indicated the use of psychiatric diagnosis together with scaling or rating devices, and 2 indicated the use of scaling devices only.

Fitzgibbons and Shearn (1972) reported a factor-analytic study of concepts of schizophrenia among 183 mental health professionals. They interpreted their findings of extreme variability "as casting doubt on the remaining usefulness of the term 'schizophrenia' " (p. 288).

About five years after the Shearn and Whitaker survey, Cash (1973) reported his survey of 166 studies covering the interim period. He examined these studies for their adequacy in selecting subjects, classifying them, establishing controls, using measurement procedures, and discussing therapeutic implications. He concluded, "In general, the survey data indicated that during this recent five-year period little progress has been made in overcoming various deficiencies in these areas" (p. 278).

Because the vast majority of studies rely exclusively on psychiatric diagnosis as a means of selecting subjects, we should consider the adequacy of such a procedure. It is indeed tempting to assume that schizophrenia is a well-defined illness that can be readily diagnosed, and that subjects with this diagnosis represent a homogeneous group for study. As anyone who has worked in a mental hospital for a number of years can attest, an amazing variety of patients are given the label of schizophrenia at one time or another during their hospitalization. The problem of diagnostic variability and unreliability was reflected in the second edition of the *Diagnostic and Statistical Manual* of the American Psychiatric Association (1968), which lists under the category "schizophrenia" a group of 11 disorders, some of which, behaviorally, have very little in common with the others.

The many studies of the reliability of psychiatric diagnosis up through the era of the DSM-II (for example, Beck, Ward, Mendelson, Mock, & Ebaugh, 1962; Foulds, 1955; Sandifer, Pettus, & Quade, 1964; Schmidt & Fonda, 1956) usually produced discouragingly low estimates of the reliability of psychiatric diagnosis. Reliabilities tended to be especially poor if any attempt was made to go beyond the crudest of discriminations, such as a rough grouping into organic, psychotic, and characterological disorders. Furthermore, as Spitzer, Cohen, Fleiss, and Endicott (1967) noted, it is difficult to compare such studies because of the diversity of the statistical methods used in analyzing the data.

As will be discussed in Chapters 5 and 6, both the inherent limitations of traditional interview methods and the lack of sophistication about, or actual use of, structured interview methods, even in recent years, has meant little, if any, improvement in subject selection procedures using interview approaches. One is forced, therefore, to conclude that a study of schizophrenia in which the subjects are selected by psychiatric diagnosis alone cannot be very meaningful unless, at least, there are supporting data to show that a reliable, representative, and replicable procedure was used to select subjects for the study.

Studies in which subjects are well described, including their specific signs and symptoms, are valuable on that basis. The more accurate and detailed the descriptions, the more useful they are. Similarly, the method of procedure, such as the process by which the subjects were tested, ought to be clearly described so that a reader can judge the testing atmosphere, the instructional set given to the subjects, and the nature of the procedures themselves. It may even be important to describe the testers or interviewers themselves. Some personal characteristics of the tester or interviewer may be a crucial determinant of the results.

The analysis of results has often been limited to brief indications of whether there were significant differences between two or more groups of subjects. It is easy but not particularly meaningful to show a statistically significant difference, whereas the power of that difference to discriminate is especially important, as are other distinctions that go beyond simple nomothetic classification. The analysis of results should include reference to as many dimensions of schizophrenic disorders as the test instrument can possibly measure. These further results are important in themselves, of course, and also in terms of evaluating the discriminatory efficiency even of simple nomothetic classification.

The analytical tools, including statistical methods, should be tailored to the particular conditions of the study and should be described in some detail with a view to enabling a comparison of the study with others. Base rates should be calculated to show the practical as well as the theoretical importance of various discriminations. For example, if the expectancy rate for the diagnosis of schizophrenic disorder at a particular institution is about 50%, an instrument that is discriminating with 70% accuracy is practically useful. Where the expectancy rate is low, however (say, 10%)—the instrument will have to discriminate successfully at more than a 90% rate to be practically useful in and of itself, because one could simply predict in terms of such a low base rate that "no one will be schizophrenic" and be right 90% of the time. When base rates are low, a test may be practically useful only if it can serve initial screening purposes. For example, a test might be used as merely one in a battery of screening devices to gather results useful in pattern analysis.

Summary

The assessment of schizophrenic disorders must be made with precision and careful qualification if it is to have much predictive power. Several dimensions of schizophrenic disorders need to be addressed: the degree of disorder; the paranoid-nonparanoid dimension; the acute-chronic dimension; psychodynamics and the content of thought; and positive and negative signs and symptoms. Both nomothetic and idiographic assessment approaches should be used. Signs and symptoms should be rated for the degree of their severity as well as their positive and negative aspects, especially because negative symptoms or inabilities are often minimized or ignored in ordinary psychiatric diagnosis. The most important inability, the thinking disorder, has been poorly defined generally, and particularly in terms of negative thought disorder; it is especially difficult to assess a subject without special methods enabling one to infer thinking processes. Concepts of schizophrenic thinking were reviewed, and schizophrenic thinking was defined as illogical, impaired, and unwitting. Testing and interview methods should themselves be assessed in terms of their potential to address the basic dimensions of disorder and their proven ability to do so as shown by a variety of formal studies.

The vast majority of subject selection procedures in formal studies of schizophrenic disorders have not shown adequate reliability, representativeness, or replicability, at least before the advent of the DSM-III. Thus, it has been extremely difficult to determine the reliability and validity of either psychiatric diagnosis or the many assessment devices that have used psychiatric diagnoses as criteria, except that psychiatric diagnoses, at least through the era of DSM-II use, have generally low reliabilities.

4

The Narrative as Assessment
Biographies and Case Histories

The importance of detailed, early understanding of an individual who becomes schizophrenic is made clearest by studying individual persons in their interpersonal and social contexts over time. What appears cut-and-dried when we merely view the person in a cross-section of time or from a distant position takes on a wholly different appearance when we add the rich detail of close familiarity over the person's lifetime. Although closeness may result in a loss of objectivity—the kind of problem we refer to when saying one can't see the forest for the trees—an exclusively distant viewpoint results in segregation from and lack of identification with schizophrenic persons (Deikman, 1971). But in the study of "schizophrenia" there has been much more merely cross-sectional study and distancing of "the mentally ill" than overidentification with schizophrenic persons and overinvolvement in their lives.

The distancing orientation, when used exclusively, results in such abstracting and compartmentalizing of the schizophrenic person that all sense of the person is lost. As in visual perception, one is most likely to achieve a realistic perspective by seeing a phenomenon from both close and far positions, as well as from various angles. The combination of vantage points, including closeness to and distance from the individual person, offers a realistic perspective, whereas either of these two vantage points by itself is inadequate and prejudicial. The narrative accounts in this chapter, chosen to illustrate narratives as assessment of individuals in terms of their psychosocial and interpersonal lives, also show the oversights caused by merely distancing.

This chapter presents two biographically described "cases of schizophrenia" that illustrate two different eras of 20th century assessment and treatment, including the prejudices peculiar to these eras. The famous ballet dancer Vaslav Nijinsky, born in 1890, began to be considered schizophrenic at the age of 29. He was seen by many famous psychiatrists of that era, and his life has been superbly chronicled. "Sylvia Frumkin," who came to clinical attention in her teens, is also famous because her life as "a schizophrenic" has also been superbly chronicled; her case is illustrative of the "modern treatment era." Clinical narratives of other cases are also presented.

Vaslav Nijinsky

Vaslav Nijinsky (1890–1950), one of the most outstanding dancers who ever lived, has been the subject of many excellent accounts, most notably by his wife, Romola (1972); his sister, Bronislawa (1981); the art critic and biographer Richard Buckle (1975); and his fellow dancer Anatole Bourman (1936). There is also *The Diary of Vaslav Nijinsky*, which was sold in unexpurgated form at the Sotheby Parke Bernet galleries in London in 1980, and which is available to the public in attenuated form (R. Nijinsky, 1936/1968). Altogether, we have easily one of the most thoroughly documented accounts of schizophrenic breakdown and the life context ever made available. We have not merely the period of his schizophrenic disorder on record but the whole detailed panorama of his life from birth to death.

Because Nijinsky was a creative genius and he became schizophrenic, as defined by his psychiatrist Eugen Bleuler, who originated the term "schizophrenia" and was the world's greatest authority on the subject, these eloquent accounts are especially interesting in terms of the widely held belief that creativity is close to madness. They portray brilliant ability descending into stark inability with merely occasional sparks of the previous ability and spirit. In the summary to follow, there is only a sketch of some of the most salient events, but even a brief account of these events illustrates how vital it is to know the individual's history.

Nijinsky was the second of three children born to two accomplished dancers. He is said to have inherited his great capacity to leap and to control his body from his parents. This bequeathed talent was trained, especially by his father, virtually from infancy. Vaslav made his first public appearance as a dancer when he was 3. His father had been trained in the Warsaw School of Ballet and, as a Pole trained in Poland, would never be accepted into the Russian Imperial Theater. But Vaslav, though the son of Polish parents, was born in Kiev (in the Ukraine) and was accepted into the Russian Imperial School, directly on the path to the world's foremost theater of the ballet, the Russian Imperial Theater. A series of tragedies enveloped the family during Vaslav's childhood. His older brother failed to gain acceptance into the School on his first try, and his development was completely halted by a fall, which produced shock and a concussion. He never advanced any further mentally, was eventually placed in a mental institution, and died there in a fire many years later.

As recounted by both Anatole Bourman and Romola Nijinsky, Vaslav himself suffered a severe head injury as a boy when a jealous classmate played a trick on him, and was unconscious for five days. Vaslav's father began to have a love affair with another woman and left the family, at first providing support and visiting them but finally, through many complications, becoming lost to the family. The Nijinskys suffered considerably from prejudice against Poles, who were easily identified by their accents.

At 17, after many years of not seeing his father and having been trained intensively by other men (including his great teacher and supporter, Nicholas Legat), Vaslav had a reunion with his father, who wished to see him. Romola Nijinsky (1972) re-created the event:

> So slowly, Vaslav approached his father, whose loss may well have caused the tragedy of his life. It was a great moment for both of them when they finally met. Vaslav, at this time, was physically almost the image of his father, and Thomas Nijinsky saw himself completely in the dark, lithe youth, who had fulfilled his own most cherished hopes. Perhaps as an artist he felt an unconscious pang of jealousy, but at the same time he was exuberantly proud of his famous son.[1] His conscience was burdened with his neglect and injustice, as he faced the boy who had become the provider and protector of his family. But Vaslav had no word, no gesture of reproach. He smiled his irresistible, charming smile, expressed his respect for his father, and his gratitude for the talents he had transmitted to him. For Vaslav knew then that the amazing power of being able to jump so high, to float in the air, and to descend more slowly than to rise, he inherited from his father. The few days they spent together in Kazan were very happy. They became great friends as Vaslav told his father all about himself, the work at the Mariinsky, his ideas, and his life. They danced for each other. Thomas was literally speechless when he realized that Vaslav's dancing revealed what was the hopeless dream of most dancers, the quality of genius. As a parting gift Thomas gave his son a pair of cuff-links. Vaslav always wore and treasured highly these inexpensive gold buttons set with some semi-precious stones from the Urals—his father's only present to him. Thomas promised to come the following winter to St. Petersburg to see him dance at the Mariinsky, but fate decided otherwise, and they never saw each other again. (pp. 45–46)

A series of further tragedies was in store. Nicholas Legat committed suicide, and a young prince, who had befriended Vaslav and his family in their great need, broke off contact completely on the orders of Sergey Diaghilev, the impresario who took over Vaslav's life after his first spectacular rise to fame. His mother, always a psychological support for him, was also a great responsibility, as was his younger sister, who followed him in the Imperial School and Theater.

Vaslav Nijinsky battled with the jealousy of others and succeeded despite Diaghilev's orders, which removed him forever from the protection of the Imperial Theater. A few years later, Diaghilev rejected him entirely and banned him from his own dance troupe. The occasion was Nijinsky's marriage to Romola, which Diaghilev condemned, as he denigrated women as sexually unattractive and demanded sexual obeisance from Vaslav. Left to struggle without professional support, forced to move from one country to another during World War I, and then having the responsibility of a daughter as well as of his career as a dancer, he suffered increasingly from what he alluded to as a death of his spirit.

Nijinsky was 29 and living in Switzerland when the signs of his breakdown became unmistakable. The close accounts of his wife actually show a gradual succession of inner disturbances that he could not resolve and that, in retrospect, led clearly to his more complete loss of self-possession. He was cruelly led to believe again in Diaghilev and two of his male associates, who evidently did all they could to prevent him from becoming independently successful. His greatest personal need, the need for a reliable and truly helpful father figure, came close to satisfaction many times, only to be dashed. Diaghilev had even taught him despair by insisting that Vaslav's love of women must result in his loss of the love and any acceptance whatever of this possessive father figure.

[1]This was the year of his triumphant debut at the Imperial.

Nijinsky had never learned to grieve. Instead, he met each tragedy as a matter of fate, keeping to himself the hurt, anger, and sadness. News of his brother's death, his father's death, Legat's suicide, the prince's leaving him, and even the final betrayal by Diaghilev resulted mostly, on the surface at least, only in stony silence. Further, he had never learned to deal with the practical business of life, never having had even to book a room for himself and always relying on others to make arrangements for him. His lack of practical experience was compensated for well into his 20s by managers, who took care of virtually all of his business. When losses came, his personal sense of loss seemed beyond words, more like death than grieving, and he had no practical means of getting help.

As Nijinsky became more bizarre in his behavior and help was needed to oversee him, a male psychiatric nurse was hired by his wife. He improved, but the nurse stayed only 10 days, apparently convinced that Nijinsky did not need him because he seemed well. The nurse announced to Romola:

> "Madame, I am a psychiatric nurse, and have been so for thirty-five years. I know more than the greatest professors, and I have had greater experience. I nurse the patients, I live with them, while the Herr Professors only drop in for a few moments and go away. You are wasting your money in keeping a nurse. Mr. Nijinsky is the sanest person in the whole of St. Moritz Dorf." He departed, and Vaslav, who was now quite a friend, took him down to the station and saw him off. (R. Nijinsky, 1972, p. 422)

Thus, Vaslav lost yet another father figure.

Vaslav's wife, Romola, became convinced that he was altogether recovered, as all the alarming symptoms had disappeared. Vaslav had fooled everyone, including her. In fact, Vaslav planned a return to dancing and offered a private recital in which he would compose a dance in front of the audience. Two hundred people, including his physician, a Dr. Bernhard, first were exposed to Vaslav just staring at them intimidatingly for half an hour. Finally, he danced what he said was the World War (I). His artistry won the audience despite their initial terror, and it seemed that his claim was true, that he had merely been brilliantly portraying a madman during the previous months, and that he was not insane.

Meanwhile, Vaslav had been suggesting to his wife that she find someone who would understand him, that he wanted a son, and that he was feeling that he himself might be turning into God or at least a representation of God. His diary was dominated by Diaghilev and God, Diaghilev with a big *D* and God with a small *g*.

Romola searched for someone who would understand him, and she found for him Professor Eugen Bleuler, the world's leading authority on what Bleuler called "schizophrenia." But she first saw Bleuler alone, as Vaslav did not yet want to accompany her. She and Dr. Bleuler talked for two hours about the possibility of her having a child and whether her husband was insane. Dr. Bleuler told her "we do not become insane; we are born it. I mean, the disposition is there. Genius, insanity, they are so near; normality and abnormality, there is almost no border between the two states" (R. Nijinsky, 1972, p. 427). Professor Bleuler said he would be interested in meeting her husband. He noted that Vaslav's symptoms, as described by Romola, might be worrisome in any other man but that, as Vaslav was an artist and a Russian, his symptoms did not in themselves prove any mental disturbances. Vaslav felt reassured by his wife's report, including her saying that Professor Bleuler was a nice man, and he reassured himself by noting that, except for typhoid fever, he had never been seriously ill.

One must remember that, in this era (not to mention the present era), there was considerable confusion between physical and "mental" illness. The latter tended to be equated with physical disease, so whether it was Vaslav's brother's "mental illness" or Nietzsche's "mental illness" (which was advanced syphilitic infection of the brain), they were all considered insanity, as was "schizophrenia." Furthermore, insofar as causes were known, they were physical, such as brain damage from a fall in the case of Vaslav's brother and brain disease from syphilis in the case of Nietzsche. The question would then be whether Vaslav had an inherent, endogenous disease process that was essentially independent of interpersonal influence, not whether there might be interpersonal psychological causation, which would imply the possibility of corrective emotional experience. The lack of reliable males in his life, the treachery of Diaghilev, having to migrate from country to alien country, and the loss of his professional life, which had been virtually his only lifelong security, would not count much in the assessment of Vaslav Nijinsky. With the help of his wife, the only person he then trusted very much, Vaslav Nijinsky was about to see a "nice" father figure.

Romola and Vaslav drove to the state asylum with its iron-barred windows. Bleuler interviewed Vaslav while his wife waited. After only 10 minutes the professor ushered Vaslav out of his study smilingly. Romola recounts that Bleuler then said to her:

> "All right. Splendid. Won't you step in for a second? I forgot to give you the promised prescription yesterday." I smiled at Vaslav as I passed him, following the Professor; what prescription I could not remember. As he closed the door of his study behind him, he said firmly, "Now, my dear, be very brave. You have to take your child away; you have to get a divorce. Unfortunately, I am helpless. Your husband is incurably insane." (R. Nijinsky, 1972, p. 428)

Romola soon stopped listening, feeling she had to get out of the study quickly. Dashing through the door to the waiting room, she saw Vaslav:

> He stood near the table looking absent-mindedly at the illustrated papers, pale, strangely sad, in his Russian fur coat with his Cossak cap. I stopped and looked; it seemed as though his face was growing longer under my gaze, and he slowly said, "*Femmka,* you are bringing me my death-warrant." (R. Nijinsky, 1972, p. 364)

Romola's parents, on hearing that day that Vaslav had been pronounced insane, tried unsuccessfully to persuade their daughter to divorce her husband. Romola's mother then diverted her by taking her on a walk, while the police and fire brigade, called by her parents, arrived at the door of Vaslav's room, where he was in bed awaiting breakfast. They seized him immediately and even tried to carry him out in his pajamas. Vaslav maintained his composure, but like Franz Kafka's protagonist in *The Trial* (1925/1946), he got no answers when he asked what he had done to warrant such treatment. Nor would the authorities say what they wanted of him or tell him the whereabouts of his wife. Later, finding Vaslav's room deserted, Romola enlisted Bleuler to help her find him. They found him among 30 other patients in the state asylum, where he had just had his first catatonic attack, owing to the shock of his treatment at the hands of so many "sane" authorities. It became clear to Romola that this treatment had caused an acute breakdown, whereas Vaslav might have remained integrated at his higher level of self-possession. The "I" of Nijinsky had been drastically reduced immediately by the world's best available medical diagnosis and treatment. The genius of artistic sensitivity had been diminished by means of a 10-minute assessment interview with Bleuler and his in-laws' alarmist reaction to his diagnosed "dangerous insanity."

After six months' care in the Sanatorium Bellevue Kreuzlingen, Vaslav developed hallucinations, and Romola took him home. She called in the greatest specialists in Europe and the United States and "They all agreed it was a case of Schizophrenia" (R. Nijinsky, 1972, p. 432). The famous psychiatrists Eugen Bleuler, Wagner Jauregg, Emil Kraepelin, Sandor Ferenczy, Sigmund Freud, and Carl Jung advised her to give him the best physical care, quiet surroundings, and the care of a psychiatrist, and to "Let him dream his dreams" (p. 432).

Several years later, Diaghilev went to see him, and he offered Vaslav the opportunity to dance again for his company, but Vaslav shook his head. Turning away, Diaghilev burst out crying: "It is my fault, what shall I do?" (R. Nijinsky, 1972, p. 433).

Nijinsky was actually more fortunate in his exposure to psychiatry than most of his contemporaries, who did not receive even good physical care and most of whom were treated less kindly because they were considered less important personages. Nijinsky did receive kindness at the Sanatorium Bellevue Kreuzlingen, though apparently not at some other institutions. Furthermore, being a man of great integrity, Eugen Bleuler apologized for his mistakes, both immediately after Nijinsky's initial devastating treatment and years later, when, despite all of the uniformly dire and authoritative predictions of incurability, Nijinsky had recovered so much of himself with his wife's help that a major artistic comeback was planned. Bleuler then apologized to Romola about his advice to divorce Nijinsky and graciously acknowledged that she had been right about not giving up. Unfortunately, Nijinsky had developed a kidney ailment, of which he died at the age of 60.

Few people at that time would have believed that they might understand Nijinsky and even be able to help him by capitalizing on his great assets of personality and character—for he was a physically gifted, extremely disciplined, and highly creative, intelligent, ethical, and kind man—and by helping to supply those stable and reliable relationships, especially with men, that he desperately needed. But even Bleuler, Freud, and Jung did not understand the psychological development of functional psychoses. All of these great clinicians and theorists believed that "schizophrenia" was somehow a world apart from "normal persons," though it was Freud's genius that had related the normal and the abnormal so closely in his psychoanalytic theorizing. Freud lacked any close familiarity with schizophrenic persons. And none of the other authorities, though they were all familiar with schizophrenic patients in hospitals, could imagine, with the possible exception of Jung, that schizophrenia was not a physical disease, though there was no scientific evidence whatever for that medical bias. Accordingly, they thought that only a physical form of treatment, as yet undiscovered, would offer any hope.

Romola Nijinsky (1972) was caught between the dogma of medical authority and her own more intuitive understanding. She observed:

> In his insanity, as in his health, he is the same, kindly human. He never attacks, only defends himself. His illness is one before which medical science is at a loss. It is a Schizophrenia—a disease probably due to the malfunctioning of the glands; one of which the origin is little known and the cure not at all; one which leaves the organism intact, and is known as a functional disease. Unfortunately it is not caused by a germ, such as paralysis as the result of syphilis, and therefore is incurable. (p. 432)

The great human need to reduce the terrifying specter of bizarre language and behavior to the realm of the occult, or at least to the physical domain, is tremendous. As in the age of witchcraft, there is ample evidence that people around the witch or "patient" were in some fundamental sense as much out of touch with reality as the person being assessed and treated. Now we can say definitely that those who persecuted witches at Salem, Massachusetts, were paranoid. The fact that they agreed among themselves, however, may prevent us from calling them "psychotic," as psychotic persons are, by definition, idiosyncratic and do not agree among themselves. Likewise, there were ways in which those around Nijinsky, including the professionals, were "delusional," if that means grossly out of touch with reality.

It should be obvious that one can neither assess a person adequately in 10 minutes nor predict an inevitable deteriorating course and base the assessment on disease concepts when there is not a shred of evidence of a disease. No one had ever—nor has anyone yet—satisfactorily defined the etiology, course, effective treatment, or prognosis of "schizophrenia" in terms of physical disease. But in the case of Nijinsky and, indeed, today's patients, the certainty that "schizophrenia" is a disease, a distinct entity with an inevitable deteriorating course, subject to modification only by somatic intrusion, has held sway. Sometimes—probably most of the time—the patients also wish to believe that they have a physical disease, especially if only physical disease is presumed to be treatable, or even respectable.

Sylvia Frumkin

Sylvia Frumkin said, "I'm not a nut, I have something wrong with my brain" (Sheehan, 1983, p. 25). The lack of really meaningful assessment and the quickness with which drugs are administered surely can be explained largely by the eagerness of psychiatrists to quell disturbing behavior, as well as by the eagerness of patients and their families to avoid the stigma of being a "nut." But the continuance of physical treatment practices in the face of physical and psychological damage and therapeutic failure must mean collusion with society at large as well as with patients and their families. In Sylvia Frumkin's words, she was not a "nut," that is, someone to be stigmatized; she was merely the victim of a brain disease or defect. In excluding herself from a psychological explanation, to which society attaches great stigma, she herself acknowledged and internalized the stigma. It seems significant of her own poor self-acceptance that she said, reading about Creedmoor State Hospital, her frequent residence, " 'Philosophy of Treatment. . . . The individual with a problem is best served in his own environment.' I'm against polluting the environment, always have been" (Sheehan, 1983, p. 26).

Susan Sheehan's book *Is There No Place on Earth for Me?* (1983) illuminates the myriad problems inherent in modern psychiatric diagnosis and treatment, documented in the experience of the fictitiously named but real person Sylvia Frumkin. It is a book certainly worth reading in its entirety, the discussion here covers mainly assessment issues.

The diagnostic process in Sylvia Frumkin's case appears to illustrate many typical pitfalls. Based on her symptoms, she would have been classified as "schizophrenic, schizo-affective type," a diagnosis defined in the second edition of the American Psychiatric Association's *Diagnostic and Statistical Manual* (DSM-II; 1967) but merely mentioned in the third edition (DSM-III; 1980), without diagnostic criteria. It is a diagnosis, however, that acknowledges the lack of a dichotomy between so-called affective disorders and schizophrenic disorders.

Within seven hours, Frumkin was seen by three psychiatrists, each of whom gave her a different diagnosis based on an interview of one hour or less. The disagreement clearly demonstrates that such psychiatric diagnoses are nearly always based on the presentation of overt "symptoms," and that even psychiatrists at the same institution may have quite different diagnostic "styles." The unavailability of the patient's history of "mental illness," from age 15, and the fact that, like many psychiatrists in state institutions, one of the psychiatrists was foreign-born and had mastered neither the English language nor the American culture increased the possibility of unwitting assessment errors. The maze of technical language used further mystified her assessment and treatment. Sheehan remarked, "In psychiatry, simple words are never used where complicated ones will do" (p. 28).

As is typical in most state institutions, and even many private facilities, the physical conditions and interpersonal atmosphere in which the assessment and the treatment took place on this and innumerable other occasions were debilitating in themselves. A starkness of environment was guaranteed by poor funding, chronic theft, and inattention to any amenities of civilized living. For example, if Sylvia wished to dry herself after a bath or shower, she could do so only with a sheet, because towels were not available. Pictures and plants could not be maintained, and of course, no pets were allowed, nor was commerce with the outside world easy. This was not the place to learn the social skills vital to functioning in real life.

As is also common in psychiatric hospitals, lack of adequate numbers of reliable, genuinely able staff and the poor staff morale, often resulting in poor work attendance and "going through the motions" while just on the job, made therapeutic success less likely. Fatalistic attitudes are easily learned and confirmed in psychiatric hospitals.

For example, the common declaration that patients who are determined to kill themselves will kill themselves teaches fatalism to staff and patients alike. Similarly, the assumption that "schizophrenia" is an incurable disease guarantees poor treatment, if not further, iatrogenic illness. This atmosphere of therapeutic nihilism promotes the easy reductionism of "medical science." Thus, the assessment and treatment of Sylvia focused on the positive symptoms to be reduced; that is, Sylvia was to be made more passive rather than to learn to take charge of her own life.

Because about two thirds of the chronic patients never received any outside visitors, though they never stopped feeling the absence of visitors, and because the vast majority of the patients were heavily drugged, there was little incentive for them to do anything but stay in bed. Even eating tended to be distasteful, as people do not feel very alive in such a physically and emotionally draining atmosphere.

All of these conditions are fairly typical of most psychiatric hospitals; thus, we can expect major iatrogenic practices that will cloud both assessment and "treatment." The message to patients is to lie low; most gravitate to bed or become further stupefied by sitting in front of the community TV set.

Frumkin's life in the hospital was very eventful because she refused to lie low. Instead of eating and soon leaving the table, or not eating at all, she ate a lot. Instead of retiring to bed as early and often as possible, she stayed up and sought attention. Instead of giving up entirely on any kind of interpersonal sex life, she occasionally made sexual advances, saying that she had not had sex in five years and felt the desire to fulfill a normal need. One might say, if so much expert opinion were not against it, that she was a woman of spirit. She was failing to give up on her life. Various disgusting behaviors, such as eating sloppily and making hostile remarks, were largely in keeping with the blockage of normal avenues of social expression. Frumkin became the most "troublesome" patient on her ward, one who could not be subdued by seemingly endlessly varied attempts to find the "right medication" for her.

Like the majority of patients admitted to Creedmoor, Sylvia was a "readmit," one of the legions of "revolving-door" patients who may not stay long but who are unable to function adequately in the "real world." The challenge of enabling the patient to live in the real world as a self-supporting and self-possessed member of the community has had few takers. It is still commonly assumed that "schizophrenia" is an inevitably deteriorating condition that can be treated only symptomatically in terms of the "positive"—that is, outwardly disturbing—symptoms, such as bizarre and abusive language. "Treatment" seldom addresses the "negative" symptoms or inabilities of the patient. Thus, patients typically fall far short in their ability to function as whole persons. Still worse, the "negative symptoms" may worsen as a function of this skewed treatment approach. For example, as Carpenter *et al.* (1977) noted:

> It is often assumed that noxious side effects of neuroleptic treatment of schizophrenia are limited to unpleasant autonomic alterations, extrapyramidal effects, rare allergies, and infrequent tardive dyskinesias. Recent evidence . . . has more carefully documented the relationship between drug treatment and the inducement of reinforcement of defect or negative symptoms (e.g., anhedonia, social isolation, post-psychotic depression, and amo-

> tivational syndromes). Nevertheless, relatively scant attention has been paid to this problem or to possible later effects of long-term drug use on affect modulation, communication, perception, or other central nervous system functions. In addition, little notice has been given to the so-called secondary side effects, such as the impact on a child's development should his mother be on long-term heavy medication. This results in a situation not entirely dissimilar to that of past enthusiasm for lobotomies, when attention was focused on the positive attributes of the procedure to such a degree that the short- and long-term hazards were overlooked. (p. 15)

The amotivational syndrome produced by the neuroleptic drugs is often looked on as an improvement, in terms of patients' "manageability," as well as a desirable goal generally; but as the stress researcher and theorist Hans Selye (1974) wrote, "Deprivation of motivation is the greatest mental tragedy because it destroys all guidelines" (p. 79).

Sylvia Frumkin was subjected to a seemingly endless variety of drug regimens by a wide assortment of psychiatrists at several treatment centers. Such marked discontinuity and inconsistency of treatment are inherently stressful. Sylvia was only one of many patients whose drug regimens were not what they appeared to be on paper. Patients and staff may fail to make sure that prescribed dosages are actually ingested by the patient, though the patient's chart may indicate that medications have been taken.

At Creedmoor, many patients were reported, according to their charts, to have taken their medication on February 29 and 30, 1979 (Sheehan, 1983, p. 101). The potencies of many of the drug prescriptions, when taken, were often seemingly enough to reduce even the most agitated person to inactivity, but the person may have responded otherwise. For example, Sylvia actually "took all the medicine prescribed for her—1800 milligrams of Thorazine. . . . That night she and another patient stayed up pestering the other women in the dormitory and keeping them awake until morning" (Sheehan, 1983, p. 103). She was later given 90 milligrams of Haldol, the equivalent of 4,500 milligrams of Thorazine, before she calmed down. Giving her the Haldol was a way to get around the restriction on Thorazine dosages mandated by New York State authorities for Creedmoor, as the Thorazine limit was only 1,600 milligrams per day, but the limit on Haldol was 100 milligrams, more than three times the equivalent of her maximum Thorazine dosage. The reader should keep in mind that there are "main-effect" and "antipsychotic-effect" equivalents for the various neuroleptics, but that the various drugs have different side effects. Furthermore, a dosage of only 100 milligrams of Thorazine may easily produce extreme drowsiness and lethargy in a person who is not agitated and is not accustomed to the drug. Thus, Sylvia, like many other patients, was being given extreme dosages. Her calming down, after being given high-dosage Haldol, was seen as a great improvement.

Meanwhile, there was little attention to her history and the possible meanings for her of her psychotic status. As she relinquished her delusions that she would marry a famous personality, she remarked:

> "You know, it was fun believing some of those things I believed, and in a way I hate to give up those fantasies. There's a charm to being sick. I like to be in the twilight zone of the real

> world. Absolutely real is getting up every day and going to work. I once thought, when I was about to finish medical-secretarial school, before I had a breakdown on the last day of school, that I'd graduate and get a job. I was looking forward to earning my own money, to having a credit card, to being a grown woman in my own right." (Sheehan, 1983, p. 112)

Here Sylvia expressed both her attraction to being psychotic and her grief over giving up on becoming "a grown woman in my own right" and lapsing into psychosis. The question is: What was being done to help her face and master the threat of greater autonomy, which was also attractive to her? Who was recognizing her conflict and helping her with it? Her escapist tendencies were being rewarded by her "sick" status and the reduction of her positive symptoms, in favor of an amotivational syndrome. Might we not expect, then, a higher and higher level of conflict and inner disturbance, produced in large measure by her "treatment"? What, then, would become of her "own right" as she put it?

Logically, the patient must escalate the battle or resign herself to a colorless life. The tendency to fear freedom and the wish to make others responsible for oneself, even at the cost of tyranny, is a universal human tendency. Erich Fromm's book *Escape from Freedom* (1941/1965) illuminates the myriad faces of this fear and its destructive consequences when it is not mastered. Similarly, psychiatrist Arthur Deikman's book *The Wrong Way Home: Uncovering the Patterns of Cult Behavior in American Society* (1990) shows the insidious attractiveness of relinquishing personal responsibility for one's own life. Like many adolescents approaching the expected development of responsible adult functioning, Sylvia had panicked. The signs of her difficulty were apparent long before her first hospitalization, but no help was obtained for her. But not all adolescents approaching adulthood become schizophrenic, even if they are disturbed and help is not obtained. Certain life histories and circumstances make the approach to adult autonomy and self-possession more difficult for some than for others.

In Sylvia's case, though relatively little description of her psychological history is given, there were important clues showing that autonomous functioning was discouraged. For example, her own money was taken by her parents, who put it into an account that she could not touch, and it was not spent on her. When she was given an apparent opportunity at least to choose an opening-of-an-account gift from the bank, she made a great effort to assert herself by making a lengthy list of her preferences. One at a time, each item on her list was turned down by her parents until, after long bickering, she was allowed to select a high-intensity lamp, which was then actually kept at the parents' home. Eventually, Sylvia simply gave the lamp to her mother to keep permanently.

Meanwhile, one somatic approach after another was suggested, the father suggesting megavitamin therapy again even though it had failed previously. Significantly, her first choice of a gift had been a calculator, with which she could tally her calories and do her budget, both representative of her efforts at self-control. But after being refused that and all of her other choices, she had become exasperated and had confronted her mother over not being allowed to choose. Surely, this kind of material deserved attention from her therapists, but their focus remained on drugging her. It was seen, however, that it would not be good for Sylvia to go home from the hospital.

When Sylvia was reported to have "improved," she had lost some of her engaging qualities, such as her whimsy and her way with words. And though she was no longer delusional and had stopped hitting people, she was verbally vicious, abrupt, overtalkative, and hypercritical. In addition, what had passed for simply peculiar mannerisms, such as tongue rolling, lip smacking, and lip biting, turned out to be tardive dyskinesia, finally recognized after one and one-half months of these characteristic symptoms. She had been "stabilized on medication" but was able only to go once again to a sheltered workshop, where she typed but made little or no improvement in her functioning abilities. It was thought that, as she was "schizophrenic," her "inevitable deterioration" could only be slowed, not reversed. At age 30, she could hope only for a "secure retreat." Thereafter, the drug regimen had to be reduced in potency because of her tardive dyskinesia, and she began again, after a month, to have delusions and hallucinations. Meanwhile, she was insisting on getting her own apartment.

The historical perspective, even on her life from late adolescence to the age of 30, was not known to most of her seemingly innumerable psychiatrists, who came and went even as she came and went from one facility to another. No professional was held responsible for her continued care, though her most effective therapist, a clinical psychologist named Francine Baden, tried to continue psychotherapy with her but was cut out of Sylvia's life by a psychiatric resident. This fragmentation of assessment and treatment served, in effect, to fragment the patient. A psychiatrist who at least knew that the patient had never before made peculiar motions of the lips and tongue might have immediately recognized that her greatly increased drug dosages were responsible and might have made it possible to arrest or at least slow the tardive dyskinesia that was her real—iatrogenic—disease. And her alleged "improvement" would not have been impressive to anyone following her course even for a few months, as even the temporary reduction of her positive or secondary symptoms was effected at the expense of permanent brain damage.

If any of her psychiatrists had had even a sketch of her childhood and adolescent history, they might have seen the many early steps in the slow development of the crisis that had precipitated her first psychotic breakdown. Susan Sheehan's biographical account provides rich insights, especially into family dynamics. Most significantly, Sylvia grew up as the "second-best" child, always playing a poor second to her older sister, who herself could never be good enough. Sylvia tended to view her situation as hopeless even as a child but never gave up trying to be the center of attention by whatever means. Real accomplishment was not successful, even though, like her sister, she was a gifted child and did accomplish a great deal intellectually. Evidently, her attention getting, which expressed needs for recognition and acceptance, annoyed and disturbed others. Lacking legitimate and workable means to gain recognition, she "chose" psychotic ones.

Psychiatrists, and perhaps by now most mental health professionals, assume that one cannot do anything with such severely disturbed persons as Sylvia except to give them drugs. They are considered "untreatable," especially if they have passed their early 20s. Accordingly, the outwardly disturbing symptoms are simply to be reduced so as to give the patient at least "symptomatic relief." But it is possible that the symptom, properly understood as a disguised representation of a need in conflict with fear, may become the starting place for genuine improvement.

Recognition of the patient's personal and social human needs is essential in every assessment if truly good results are to be obtained and mere reduction of the person's life possibilities is to be avoided. In the case of Sylvia, it was known that she had very superior intelligence and that, as a child, she had demonstrated poetic ability, which was reflected in her "way with words" when she was acutely psychotic. During her senior year of high school, Sylvia was accepted into the Hunter College honors program for outstanding students. Her story is replete with many other examples of opportunities to assess and understand her needs and take serious stock of her assets as well, so that she could be helped to fulfill her needs creatively. Instead, the needs and assets themselves were attacked, as it were, by the "treatment."

There was a notable exception to the medical nature of her treatment when Sylvia had Francine Baden as a psychotherapist. As Sheehan (1983) noted:

> Francine Baden was the only therapist with whom she would ever try to work out her problems. "With Francine, something just clicked. . . . She helped me in the short run with everything from the way I looked to the way I thought about myself. . . . But perhaps she hurt me in the long run, by making me rebel against my parents. Maybe she opened Pandora's box." (p. 219)

There are few psychotherapists able and willing to help people like Frumkin, and the therapist must stay with the patient long enough to help her work through the emancipation from her parents and to master her ambivalence about growing up. Seventeen years after not seeing her one really helpful therapist, Sylvia needed real help more than ever. She had told Francine Baden once, " 'Getting well is growing up. I'm not sure I want to grow up. I'm going to stay Wonder Woman forever' " (Sheehan, 1983, p. 333).

In this case, it is difficult to imagine what else could have been done to the patient physically, except to lobotomize her. Just listing the various drug regimens prescribed for her takes up ten typed pages, as a student demonstrated to me. She was also given many series of electric shock treatments and insulin coma treatments, placed in straitjackets and seclusion rooms, and given megavitamins in five series, though none showed positive results. Even if one were to endorse purely physical modes of treatment, the lack of an ongoing assessment of her condition is glaring. The psychiatrists made responsible for her case rarely had any awareness even of her more immediate history of physical treatments. By any recommended standards of drug administration, her treatment was incompetent, and if one looks at the larger picture, there was gross neglect of her family and psychodynamic history, except for brief, rather fragmented episodes of psychotherapy. The emphasis was almost always on the immediate reduction of the positive symptoms of her disorder. After 17 years of fragmented treatment, she seemed considerably worse than when she had begun treatment, as an acutely upset adolescent.

This case, and innumerable others like it, reflects a great irony. Illogicality and hopelessness are classic characteristics of schizophrenic conditions. Illogicality and hopelessness also frequently characterize the treatment of schizophrenic conditions. In the case of Sylvia, "no treatment she received over a period of thirteen years bore any logical relationship to a previous treatment" (Sheehan, 1983, p. 282). But a psychiatric expert on psychopharmacology, commenting on her drug treatment and attributing its failure to her not being given enough drugs by, seemingly, her most successful psychiatrist, criticized the latter: "He was taught in medical school that schizophrenia is incurable, and he should not have forgotten that" (Sheehan, 1983, p. 284). Surely, "schizophrenia" will never be "curable" when there is such illogicality and hopelessness among mental health professionals, who, because of their own irrational fatalism, aid and abet the illogicality and hopelessness of their patients.

The Shrinking of Psychotemporal Space

Silvano Arieti (1974) elucidated the cognitive, emotional, and social regression in schizophrenic disorders in terms of psychotemporal space. The more severe the regression, the greater the reduction in psychotemporal space. That is, the world of the schizophrenic person shrinks. The full dimension of time—past, present, and future—tends to be reduced simply to the present. The more schizophrenic the person, the more he or she loses temporal perspective. The benefits of past experience become less available, and planning ahead with a view to consequences becomes impaired. Similarly, the space or breadth of the person's concerns, interests, and awareness, even in the present, is reduced. This is why, cognitively, the person appears demented and why, emotionally, the range of affect expression lessens. Because of the lack of awareness of psychotemporal space, the person's thought sequences, emotional expressiveness, and gauging of actions take place in an inadequate context of awareness. Perhaps the favorite words used to describe schizophrenic persons are *inappropriate* and *bizarre.* They do not have as adequate an awareness of psychotemporal space as more optimally functioning persons.

Psychodynamic theory suggests that schizophrenic persons have been excessively frightened, indeed panicked, by their awareness and so retreat from it. They tend to be both fixated at earlier stages of awareness and impelled to regress; the result is a variety and inconsistency of levels of functioning that give a bizarre appearance. At the other extreme from psychodynamic explanations, some attribute the shrinking of psychotemporal space, literally, to the shrinking of brain tissue. The shrinking of a person's psychotemporal space, whether due to drugs or apathy or both, may actually shrink brain tissue by means of insult and/or disuse. In any case, there is a reduction in the ability to be aware of and to exert control over both internal psychological processes and external events. The so-called mental deterioration is different from that observed in various forms of definable brain damage, however. The shrinking of psychotemporal space in schizophrenic disorders is an irregular phenomenon (especially in the early or acute stages) that is strongly affected by interpersonal events.

Assessment of every important question about the status of a schizophrenic person should relate to whether and to what degree the person conceives of various kinds and degrees of psychotemporal space. Phrased in psychoanalytic terms (à la Bettelheim, 1984), the basic question is whether the person's "I" is adequate to the demands and personal ambitions of the person's life. We have seen that Nijinsky and Frumkin were both far more ambitious than their personal awareness and control abilities warranted, but that they were curiously unambitious as well. Both became a combination of grandiosity and resignation in the face of their decompensations from previously higher levels of functional ability. Their sense of self was inadequate, and both ordinary and creative abilities were diminished.

The neuroleptic or so-called antipsychotic drugs limit the psychotemporal challenge to the individual because they reduce the stimulation that, normally, one has to organize and to act on. They are particularly effective with many acute or first-break schizophrenic persons in the sense of reducing sensibility. What cannot be worried about becomes less worrisome, at least temporarily, though there are paradoxical reactions to neuroleptics, too, evidenced in persons who insist on stretching their limits of awareness rather than having them reduced. For example, there are athletically inclined men who become more agitated as they lose sensitivity, including sexual potency. And Sylvia Frumkin had some paradoxical reactions to would-be tranquilizing drugs. There may have to be an attitude of acceptance of the drugs and their reductive power if they are to be "effective." But this effectiveness itself is at least primarily limited to a reduction of the positive symptoms, those outwardly manifest disturbing symptoms like bizarre and disruptive behavior and delusions and hallucinations and perhaps some positive forms of thought disorder. The negative symptoms—inabilities that are not always so manifest, such as social inadequacy, inability to experience pleasure, immaturity of concept formation, and irrational fears that have never been resolved—tend to persist and even to create by their persistence a greater imbalance than before. Thus, it is common, in the short run, to observe "improvement" in terms of more "sober" behavior but to observe, if one bothers to keep observing, that the patient never really gets better in the long run as a result of such "treatment." For all of Sylvia's innumerable "improvements," she did not learn much in terms of building a more adequate "I," though she learned a great deal about being a passive object to whom things were done.

As must be obvious by now, I believe that the assessment of schizophrenia and related disorders has been dominated by the physical reductionist approach, which does to already-shrinking patients things that shrink them further. One may rationalize this approach by saying that the patients need help with their defenses against awareness, and perhaps that is so in the short run. The reductionist approach is most represented today by so-called biological psychiatry, which seems to find "chemical imbalances" to be the cause of every mental condition, inability, or discomfort. Scientifically, of course, correlation—no matter how strong—does not necessarily mean causation. Even when it is thought, although often quite wrongly, that there is a chemical imbalance, there is no reason, logically speaking, to conclude that "it" is the cause and that chemical intervention is the cure of the "disease." But the behaviorist approach, too, can be, and very often is, used reductively when the person is treated as a mere collection of positive symptoms, or even as one or more inabilities that are conceived of as independent entities. Psychoanalytic approaches can be used reductively also. To say seriously, and unwittingly, that someone becomes schizophrenic just because she or he had a "schizophrenogenic mother" has misleading connotations because, at best, it oversimplifies. As applied to treatment, all forms of reductionism tend to limit further the already severely limited psychotemporal space of the schizophrenic person.

The proper task of assessment is to assess what is most relevant, that is, to be especially careful to examine the psychosocial as well as the possible biochemical and hereditary determinants of schizophrenic disorders. The notion, still unproven, that schizophrenic disorders have important hereditary and biochemical determinants has often served to shrink the awareness of investigators as well as patients. We must not be "shrinks," even if that is what we are asked to be.

The assessment of treatment effectiveness should be based on measuring the increase or decrease in the person's awareness and ability. Accordingly, such criteria of improvement as "dischargeability" and the patient's becoming less disturbing to others will be recognized as interesting and of some practical importance but as sorely misleading in and of themselves. Real improvement is not mindless docility, exemplified by patients' vegetating in a "community care facility" for the rest of their lives. Professionals and "laypersons" alike should be careful not to mimic the schizophrenic psychotemporal space shrinkage themselves by failing to develop a whole picture of the person. Treating a person without bothering to learn about the broad range of that person's life history as well as the current social and physical influences on her or him is simply irresponsible, no matter how "efficient" and "economical" it may appear in the short run.

The treatment of Sylvia Frumkin, and very probably of the great majority of persons labeled schizophrenic, is replete with "professional" interventions ungrounded in any understanding of the patient. It is as if it is safe and even necessary to do something to the patient right away. What results is most often a long series of medically based "treatments." By absolving psychiatrists and other mental health practitioners of constructing or even reading case histories, by not making them think about what they are doing in relation to a real person, the opportunity for truly adequate assessment and treatment is lost. "Treatment" then proceeds to shrink the patient's psychotemporal space even further, rather than to help enlarge it.

Among the many resistances to careful assessment is the old saw "We're going to end up doing the same thing to the patients anyway, so why assess them?" I have heard both "well-trained" psychiatrists and clinical psychologists make this and highly similar remarks. When one medical-school-faculty clinical psychologist was questioned about this attitude, he revealed a host of prejudices, all in the direction of fatalistic resignation, thus setting a tone of hopelessness for both the patients and the clinical psychology interns under his supervision.

Even case conferences, which are designed ostensibly to present for understanding a broad range of information and opinion about a patient, may readily collapse into grossly unscientific orgies of prejudice. I have sat in case conferences where the psychiatrist leading them has thrown out would-be serious oral and written assessment reports before hearing or seeing them. For example, a psychiatrist who ranked high in a teaching hospital declared that he could already tell—guess, actually—what the results of a psychological test evaluation were and he knew they were "wrong," so he was discounting them in advance. It so happened that he "knew" the patient's "disease" without even seeing the patient or hearing about him. He also knew the patient's prognosis, which was "extremely poor," though the patient was only 19 and obviously highly motivated and eager to work on his problems. Furthermore, the psychiatrist declared in advance that the patient's case was a case of "schizophrenia, a chemical imbalance disease," that treatment by chemical means was already clearly warranted, and that good results could not be expected. However, the patient appeared, during a conference interview, to be quite well motivated and demonstrated some insight into his condition. Several "naive" undergraduate college students attending the conference were better able to understand the patient and did not write off his potential. They left the conference with their eyes opened to the real world of practice, after having been exposed only to the generally much higher level of assessment and treatment described in the literature.

Though many professionals and institutions teach and practice at very high levels of understanding, the economic incentives are such as to make quick physical interventions the "treatment of choice." The fees for doing something physical and technical to patients, no matter how simpleminded, are far greater per hour than talking with patients or reading or hearing about them. This approach also seems more "efficient." When one has already decided on the "treatment," why, indeed, bother to do a real assessment? As Starr (1982, p. 386) noted, doctors earn more for time they spend in a hospital and more when they perform a technical procedure on a patient. Outpatient services and talking to a patient are "losers" financially. Thus, psychiatrists have incentives to perform technical procedures, that is, somatic interventions like drug prescriptions, preferably within hospitals.

Another resistance to assessment is predicated on the notion that assessment and treatment are entirely different activities. Actually, the relationship of assessment and treatment is quite intimate. Having to do something about the patient does not preclude careful assessment; rather, it should demand careful assessment. Even patients who present as emergencies should be assessed even as they are being treated. Nor does the treatment have to be doing something to the patient. Highly effective treatment, in both the short and the long run, is most feasible when one bothers to understand what it is that the patient needs. If one is given the latitude to consider various approaches and to be creative, many superficially insuperable problems can be resolved quickly when the patient's help is enlisted. The following are two examples of emergency admissions to a psychiatric hospital that, ordinarily, would have been "treated" immediately with drugs or other physical interventions such as seclusion and forced feeding.

Joe was a 19-year-old admitted to a psychiatric ward through a hospital emergency room. When he appeared on the ward, he was highly agitated and threatening. He paced rapidly up and down the ward all night long, threatening to beat up everyone he saw. He made punching motions, kept flexing his biceps, and acted "like a man possessed." No reassurance or plea to stop his terrifying behavior was effective. Though he continued this behavior throughout the night, he was not drugged or secluded and was told that he would not be as long as he didn't actually hit anyone. The next day, his ranting and delusional claims, including "I'm Superman," came to the attention of a psychiatrist, who asked me to interview the patient behind a one-way screen so that about 20 psychiatric residents could observe a display of schizophrenic thinking. Actually, the psychiatrist was more sophisticated than he let on to the residents; he suspected that the "diagnostic interview" might be therapeutic also.

That day a fearful but ranting and threatening Joe was led to the quite small interview room and was told that, while being interviewed, he would be watched by psychiatric residents behind a one-way screen. Staff were careful to keep Joe fully informed about whatever they were doing with or about him, as instructed by the author and the ward psychiatrist.

The interviewer entered the room slowly and was very "laid back," though friendly and observant. He was positioned between Joe and the only door. Joe had a wide-eyed look and flexed his muscles even as he sat in his chair. The interviewer asked what he liked to do in his spare time. A bit surprised at the question, Joe answered that he liked to fix up old cars. For 20 minutes, he taught the interviewer about his hobby, as the interviewer, a true mechanical idiot, listened appreciatively until Joe spontaneously switched the topic by asking whether the interviewer would like to know what had caused his coming to the hospital. He then lucidly described how he had come home at 5 P.M. the previous day and had been confronted angrily by his father, who was "always getting on my case." Joe "blew up" and got into an actual fistfight with his father that ended with police forcibly taking Joe to the hospital. The interviewer then remarked on Joe's flexing his muscles and saying he was "Superman," and observed sympathetically that he must have needed to feel very powerful. Joe grinned at the idea, leaned forward, and said, "I like you"; and the interviewer said, "I like you, too."

The interviewer then said, "I like to feel strong, too," and suggested that both Joe and he have fun by flexing their biceps and pretending that they were "Supermen." The interviewer satirized himself a little as he did so, and Joe grinned in satisfaction. The interviewer then suggested that anytime he wanted to play the game during group therapy sessions, Joe could start just by flexing his biceps and grinning. The interview ended on this friendly note. The psychiatric residents, however, said that they were quite disappointed by not hearing or seeing any manifestations of schizophrenic thought disorder whatever during the entire 50-minute interview.

Throughout his 1½-month stay in the hospital, Joe occasionally flexed his muscles and grinned in group therapy while looking at his former interviewer who was now his group therapist. The assessor-therapist would grin back, flex his own biceps, and acknowledge to everyone that Joe and he liked to play this game occasionally as they both liked to feel strong. Joe was never a "management problem" on the ward after his "diagnostic interview," and there was plenty of time for further assessment and treatment.

Had this young man been treated conventionally, with seclusion and/or forced drug administration, there would have been a deepening of his already great fears of and resentment toward authority and, most important, further damage to his already low self-esteem and sense of self-control. Instead, the interviewer, a male authority figure, provided an experience that corrected his experience with his father by being empathic and accepting, and by taking a real interest in Joe, reciprocating his saying he liked me, and introducing a shared awareness of his need for power and his fear of destruction. This humane kind of interview helped immediately to correct what had been a deadly serious and blatantly destructive relationship with his father, which had carried over into the hospital situation. Joe gained a measure of self-awareness and self-control through a therapeutic alliance, which took less than an hour to establish. Lest such an example of immediately effective assessment-treatment seem atypical, I should state that similar results were obtained regularly with other "management emergencies," as these patients, too, were desperately needy and thus highly motivated.

The assessment should disclose important needs so as to facilitate engaging the enormous underlying motivation of the patient to fulfill them. This approach may seem "unfairly easy," in cases when the patient performs the work with almost fanatic diligence, once he or she sees what can be understood and how immensely gratifying it is to be understood. Acutely disturbed first-time admissions are often easiest to fathom insofar as "emergency management" is concerned, but long-term disorders may be managed quite effectively, too, if the patient's great resources of mind can be enlisted.

Louise was a tall 28-year-old black woman who was conspicuously thin. Her weight had gradually dropped below 90 pounds. She was recognized as anorexic, but previous psychiatric contacts had not stopped her determined control of her own weight. I was asked to conduct an interview with her as part of a ward conference. The patient appeared sullen in front of her white interviewer and the predominantly white ward staff. After the preliminary formalities, including introducing myself and the staff, I began to talk with some feeling about the hospital budget, which I said was in dire straits, and I complained that the hospital food was abominable. I said that I was mostly concerned about these two problems and, along with the staff, needed practical solutions. Observing her thinness and complimenting her on it, I said that I hoped that she would continue to avoid food intake, as the hospital budget was in trouble and the food was bad anyway. I said I wanted to enlist her help in this way. The patient looked around at the staff wonderingly and asked, "Is this man crazy?" The staff members said they were not quite sure about my mental condition and that she would have to determine it for herself.

Alternately frowning and breaking into a grin, the patient appeared both perplexed and amused. I gradually allowed that I perhaps had some weird ideas. It was enough for Louise to feel that she might be sharing in some funny conspiracy. The staff and I felt that she had become more witting. My last words were admonishing: I said that I was counting on her to solve important administrative problems. Following this morning "diagnostic conference" and the lunch period, the staff reported that Louise had been utterly rebellious against my authority. She had eaten large helpings of the regular courses and had consumed three desserts. Thereafter, Louise and I occasionally exchanged knowing looks. She had no further eating disorder during her hospital stay. Regular psychotherapy later, following a full-scale assessment, proved adequate to her need to gain further control of her own life, as a follow-up three years later showed. She remained slender, at about 100 pounds, but was not emaciated.

These cases illustrate that an immediate and practically effective assessment-therapy can be done if patients' self-control needs are taken seriously as a desire to be in control of themselves. Wittingness, a combination of awareness and control on the part of the patient, was cultivated by being friendly and humorous in order to impart a relieving kind of insight and to legitimize the patients' motivation to be in control. Their own intense motivation could then be used in their own behalf, nurtured and abetted by a willing coconspirator. This approach results not in humoring patients (i.e., appealing to their temptation to stop aspiring to lead their own lives and merely to acquiesce to "being treated"), but in helping them, sometimes with the aid of humor to develop wittingness, to develop their own resources, and to develop a larger psychotemporal space.

Good assessment often leads quite quickly to a path of mutual collaboration by the therapist's finding out what the patient needs, portraying the patient's own potential power, and helping to ascertain what legitimate means of satisfaction may be found. Obviously, quick assessment is no substitute for thorough assessment, but it can help the patient immediately and may lead to the expectation that further assessment will also be helpful.

Biography and the Whole-Person Perspective

The study of schizophrenic and related disorders has suffered greatly from the distractions and coercions of pseudoscience. What seems obviously relevant and important in the larger picture created by a biography spanning the years of a person's life and the breadth of his or her relationships to persons and places may never even be noticed in the narrow, rigidly set focus of the empiricist-experimenter. The latter approach by itself may lead only to vast stores of useless and/or misleading "data."

There are so many doubtful but enduring presuppositions in the assessment and treatment of persons called schizophrenic that we must ourselves try to envision the problem in a larger psychotemporal space. Then, we will allow more space for psychological as well as physical "genetics," for early psychological as well as physical developmental influences, for sociocultural influences, and crucially, what we have done to the person ourselves in the form of "treatment."

Looking for the pattern, the developmental gestalt of a person's life, may be the most important method of study now. This pattern cannot emerge simply as numbers, which give our work the superficial appearance of a hard science. What is critically necessary, if not sufficient, are the soft sciences, including aspects of biology, a great deal of psychology, and all of the social sciences; they are more basic than the hard sciences because they do and must precede "hard science." Science should serve, not dominate, humanity. Even *more* basic, then, are those very broad areas of study called the humanities. Without sensitivity to the broad issues of human well-being, we might all be "mad" in the pursuit of aims at once too narrow and too blind. We must avoid a blind veneration of the hard sciences lest the blind lead the blind. In this sense, the good biographer, able to observe in a humane, empathic way, and also able to develop great psychotemporal perspective, is essential to our not "outschizophrenicking" the patients.

In essence, it is safe to pursue a scientific understanding of schizophrenic persons only when we do it in the context of their humanity. Otherwise, the person is reduced to some fraction, which misrepresents the reality of the person and allows the mad-scientist reductionist to run rampant. Having noted the context of assessment, which cannot be reduced to the hard sciences, we can be specific in stating the guiding principles for criteria that any nomothetic hard-science approach must meet.

The nomothetic approach aims to generalize among people classed as schizophrenic and to distinguish this class of people from people classed otherwise. It suggests that predictions can be made from this combination of grouping into classes and distinguishing among classes. Further, it may attempt to form and distinguish among subclasses of people called schizophrenic. In the statistical language of analysis of variance, it aims to test hypotheses about between-group and within-group differences. If powerful statistical differences cannot be discovered, the validity of the classification itself tends to be disproved, as it lacks predictive and/or control value. Essentially, the nomothetic approach attempts generalizations about classes and differences within and between classes that will have predictive and control value and will thus achieve real usefulness.

The usual failure to specify who the "schizophrenics" are in ostensibly scientific studies of "schizophrenia" clearly shows a need for people who will productively apply the nomothetic approach to learn from the idiographic. What scientists would not carefully specify who their subjects are if they knew much about them and therefore grasped something of their individual differences? Ignorance of individual differences has defeated the nomothetic science requirements for subject selection. By not clearly defining whom we are studying, we produce meaningless data but take them seriously, a practice similar to the nonsensical drawing of conclusions characteristic of schizophrenic thinking. Much of the nomothetic research literature on "schizophrenia" is nonsensical, although the authors and the readers may not know it. Because the selective criteria for the subjects have not been adequately defined, we cannot tell who or what is being written about in the "scientific literature."

Real science, which postulates logical relationships among and from its premises, is often limited more by the falseness of its premises than by the illogicality of its construction of postulates based on the premises. Scientific constructions, in this sense, are not themselves "schizophrenic," a condition of pervasive illogicality, but they may approach "paranoia," a condition of logical intactness in which one argues rightly from wrong premises.

Pseudoscience may suffer simultaneously from inadequately comprehensive premises, false, premises, and internal inconsistency, as Sheehan (1983) documented so well in the grossly presumptuous and illogical treatment of Sylvia Frumkin.

Pseudoscience pretends success but leads to failure and promotes hopelessness. Real science has little room for hopelessness. What seems utterly beyond possibility may be accomplished by real science, caring, and human ingenuity. Real science keeps on performing, at a continually accelerating rate, "miracles" of cure and prevention. Whereas even in the early 1970s there was no cure for Hodgkin's disease, today medical science has made Hodgkin's not only "treatable" but often curable because the previously "inevitable" progression of the disease can be stopped indefinitely. Epidemiology has proved itself as a clearly successful answer to infectious disease. So-called legionnaire's disease seemed utterly mysterious, and yet its deadly beginnings were discovered, and further contagion was stopped at its source. But solutions to schizophrenic disorders cannot be found by a mere mimicking of the technology of biomedical discovery.

From the psychodynamic standpoint, illogic and hopelessness are intertwined, as one furthers the other in a vicious cycle. If one assumes that "schizophrenics" are hopeless cases, it makes no apparent sense to try to understand them. And if one pursues an illogical course of thinking, "schizophrenics" may appear to be hopeless cases and one may perpetrate harmful treatments on them.

Actual observation of schizophrenic persons suggests that hopelessness and despair breed illogic in them, the implication being that the schizophrenic mistakenly perceives logic or rationality as leading to a recognition of inevitable disaster. On that premise, irrationality has a short-term defensive function, whereas long-term staving off of disaster seems impossible. As a young schizophrenic man said in a moment of great lucidity about his premise, "The unfolding of the truth is the inevitable scare!" Though it may be scary for both schizophrenic and nonschizophrenic persons, it is the proper business of all the sciences to contribute to the unfolding of the truth, and it is the particular proper business of the mental health professions to help develop tolerance for the truth.

Summary

Whereas both objectivity and empathy are needed to understand people, and neither by itself can provide a realistic perspective, the study and treatment of schizophrenic disorders has suffered greatly from a too exclusively distancing orientation and too little empathy. This chapter presented and discussed two famous cases of "schizophrenia." Vaslav Nijinsky and "Sylvia Frumkin" represent the old and modern treatment eras, respectively. Both illustrate extreme neglect of assessment and the imposition of generally harmful treatment practices, though Nijinsky fared better because he was not as aggressively treated. Predictions of a hopeless course in Nijinsky's case by several famous psychiatrists—including Eugen Bleuler, who coined the term *schizophrenia*—were shown to be invalid. Sylvia Frumkin was subjected to a relentless barrage of illogically related pseudoscientific modern somatic treatments, which resulted in an iatrogenically produced deteriorating course in keeping with the prejudice "Once a schizophrenic, always a schizophrenic."

Generally, treatment in the latter part of the 20th century is no more based on sound assessment than it was in the early 20th century. The credos of illogic and hopelessness, so salient in schizophrenic persons and their treaters alike, have a powerfully synergistic effect, producing results that confirm the dire predictions of the pseudoscientific "treatment experts."

In order to illustrate both the falsity of certain myths and the artificial dichotomy between assessment and treatment, illustrations were given of how patients who presented as acute schizophrenic and anorexic "management emergencies" could be "assessed-treated" effectively without reductionist methods or coercion. Instead of further reducing the "psychotemporal space" of the schizophrenic person, the proper business of the mental health professional is to cultivate tolerance of the spectrum of past-present-future and personal-social wittingness, enabling greater self-possession rather than humoring patients' human tendency to escape from their own freedom.

Because we need to empathize as well as to objectify in order to be realistic and effective, the idiographic approach must accompany nomothetic science so that it does not become pseudoscience. Ironically, a too-exclusive focus on nomothetic science and the aim of generalizability produces a reductionism that loses sight of the person and mimics and abets the shrinking of psychotemporal space that already afflicts schizophrenic persons. More attention to biographical and case-history accounts is needed to develop a balanced understanding that will make treatment humane and effective instead of iatrogenic. The cultivation of and tolerance of real knowledge, as distinct from the prejudices of pseudoscience and the cultural stigmatization of psychological disorder, need considerable encouragement in mental health professionals and patients alike. Assessment of schizophrenic and related disorders is often neglected altogether or is characterized by hurry and prejudice, thus paving the way for treatments that borrow inappropriately from the physical sciences.

5

Clinical Case History, Observation, and Interview

The earliest and still most often used methods for assessing persons who may be regarded as having schizophrenia or, indeed, any disorder of the mind, are history taking, clinical observation, and the psychiatric interview, including a mental status examination. These methods are essentially part of medical tradition. Each method grew out of clinical medicine—descending primarily from neurology, in the case of psychiatry, with its emphasis on diseases of the nervous system. Whereas clinical observation and the interview are methods used in all of clinical medicine, mental status exams have been inherited specifically from neurology.

Psychiatry failed, in a sense, to uphold the medical tradition because it produced little reliable evidence of physical pathology or even of a physical predisposition to "functional" disorders of the mind, whereas neurology can point to definite diseases of the nervous system. The so-called functional disorders, like the "schizophrenias," are less related to medical science per se, but they became part of the medical domain because medical doctors had undertaken their treatment. Accordingly, psychiatry has been regarded as a step-child rather than a solidly respected medical discipline firmly grounded in the natural sciences. Medicine itself is supposed to be an application of the natural sciences and is subject to experimental as well as clinical validation. Logical positivism, the philosophy of science devoted to direct, sensory, physical evidence of the existence and nature of any *thing,* is an ideal far more in keeping with actual physical diseases of the mind, like syphilitic infection of the brain, than with mental aberrations, whose existence cannot be proved by the natural science methods of physical diagnosis.

The fact that psychiatrists have been medically trained but work in a field outside the medical mainstream has exerted pressure on them to achieve "legitimacy" by trying to use mainstream medical theory and methodology in psychiatry. Assessment and treatment in psychiatry that uses the clearest and best established sources of medical knowledge have done much to illuminate actual diseases of the nervous system, but little to show the nature of the "functional psychoses" like "schizophrenia." The medical methods have acted beneficially to distinguish neurological from functional disorders, by dint of exclusionary criteria, as neurological disease is demonstrated by physical evidence and functional psychosis is not.

In the absence of any other major source of light on mental disorders, there was and is a desperate insistence on moving schizophrenia and other mental disorders into the respectable sphere of clinical and experimental medicine. Thus, besides the benefit of differential diagnosis conferred by physical diagnosis, there is also the folly reminiscent of the drunk man searching for his watch under a street lamp: Asked if he had lost his watch under the light, the drunk answered, "No, but the light is better here." As a result, relevance in the study of schizophrenia and related disorders has been severely compromised by the medical insistence on discovering, or often presupposing, a physical pathology.

General Considerations

History taking, interviewing, and clinical observation have in common great latitude both in discovery and in error. They all leave a great deal up to the ingenuity, sophistication, attentiveness, and ambition of the investigator. They also depend greatly on the cooperativeness of the patient and any other informants. Hence, one may find any degree of richness of information, ranging from virtually nothing that is definitive to a highly definitive picture of the individual.

Both the investigator's skill in gaining information with these methods and her or his skill in interpretation depend on personal and professional attributes that inspire a sense of trust and cooperativeness. The old and still-practiced notion that the psychotic person is so "out of it," so "completely crazy," that it is all right to relate to the person no more sensitively than to an inanimate object is obviously disproved in the eyes of all but its practitioners. Yet there are still "fully qualified" mental health professionals who talk in front of patients as if they were not there, apparently never sensing the harmful effects of their own behavior.

Schizophrenic persons, on the whole, are supersensitive, not insensitive. Thus, the personality and manner of the assessor or therapist are enormously important, a situation at the opposite extreme from that of many clinical medicine investigators, such as the physicians and technicians who do X-ray examinations. The subjective nature of the clinical-case-history, observation, and interview methods is paramount, although these methods are often used as if they are purely objective and therefore equally effective across examiners.

The notion that an interviewer's personality and personal manner, a "personal touch," are or should be irrelevant has no basis in reality. As Chrzanowski (1984) noted in speaking for psychiatrists, "The psychiatrist, as the basic instrument for arriving at a diagnosis, needs to include the particular make-up of his own personality as a significant medium that enters the field of his observation" (p. 457). "Doctor factors" are critically important:

> Physicians are also a product of their culture and past experience and bring predetermined feelings and behavior patterns to encounters with patients. A number of factors can affect

> the doctor-patient relationship adversely. Culturally determined prejudice is one, either outright prejudice against individuals as representative of a particular group or, more likely, subtle prejudice of which doctors are unaware. (Leon, Bowden, & Faber, 1985, p. 449)

The notion that the interviewer's personality is irrelevant is based on the assumption that the patient is, indeed, simply some sort of insensitive object that is merely a disease entity. Thus, if the patient has no personality, there is nothing to resonate with the personality of the interviewer, and of course, there would be no need for a collaborative exchange if the patient is merely a "which" and not a "who." Psychiatrist Ian Stevenson (1974) noted:

> Formerly a question-and-answer type of interview satisfied the requirements of psychiatric interviewing, as it did and still does satisfy those of medical history-taking with regard to exclusively physical illnesses. But the modern psychiatric interview, although it includes questions, puts much more emphasis on a free-flowing exchange between the psychiatrist and the patient. (p. 1138)

The Patient's History

Traditionally, the patient's history has been obtained by a psychiatric social worker or a psychiatrist, the social worker meeting with the patient's relatives to obtain their accounts and the psychiatrist emphasizing the recent history of the patient's presentation of symptoms and other difficulties in living. These viewpoints may be compared in the traditional case conference, which may also feature an on-the-spot interview of the patient by the psychiatrist. Of course, in common practice outside hospital or formal clinic settings, whatever emerges of the patient's history is obtained by the treating mental health professional, usually a psychiatrist. Often, in ordinary practice, little or no history is obtained, the patient being merely one of a vast number of psychotic or otherwise disturbed individuals. At one state psychiatric hospital that I visited several times in 1955, patients were generally represented only by a brief admission note, after which, typically, there was nothing but routine nursing and medical attention, the latter consisting almost exclusively of brief physical examinations twice a year. Teaching hospitals and clinics, however, generally practice extensive history taking.

Assuming that accounts can be obtained from both the patient and significant others, including family members, the patient's history and the ways it is expressed by the various contributors may reveal much of what needs to be known in order to predict the patient's future course and to be of help.

Because all accounts are biased and do not reveal just strictly factual truth, comparisons of accounts and modifications and additions over a series of sessions can be of considerable value in ascertaining those areas of the patient's life that are most likely to need further attention, because of either contradictions or omissions. Such contradictions and omissions often correspond to key areas of difficulty in the patient's life and therefore give direction to further inquiry and treatment. The fact that no case history or even any autobiography or biography is ever entirely complete or without contradiction need not make us despair. Often, if one considers the sources of the accounts in relation to the contradictions, one gets a meaningful impression of important relationships in the patient's life.

The history taker should attempt to construct a chronology of significant events that includes the family background as well as the patient's life. The circumstances of gestation and birth, whether the child was wanted by the parents and others in the family, and the parents' life circumstances, emotionally and physically, around and before the time of birth—all should be described. A family tree is valuable; it should be as complete as possible, with at least brief accounts of other family members' emotional or physical disorders. The specific circumstances may tell their own story.

In her autobiographical novel, *The Words to Say It* (1983), Marie Cardinal told of her discovery that because of the imminent divorce from Marie's father, her mother attempted repeatedly to abort her. Not succeeding in her abortion attempts and never having been able to grieve the loss of a previous child, her mother related to Marie as a nonentity, on the one hand, and as someone who had to be extraordinary, on the other hand. The message received intuitively by the child and reflected in her psychotic breakdown later was that straightforward success was not possible and that developing abortion symptoms herself was useful as a kind of retroactive birth control. Having experienced this ambivalent message, the patient did not simply kill herself physically but had an enormous fear of dying and almost did die psychologically through her psychosis, though psychotherapy later led her to a full development of her life.

The history taker ought to wonder why the patient became psychotic at a certain point and, conversely, why there was not an earlier breakdown. One ought to ask questions about traumatic and other possibly debilitating events and about those kinds of nurturance and support that can prevent breakdown. A commonsense question is often asked: Why can some people have a traumatic childhood and not break down and others with seemingly less trauma break down? The answer, in part, as is well known from studies of wartime situations of trauma, is that consensual validation and support characterize the lives of many people who have been exposed to severe trauma but have developed normally. Others may have led seemingly "easy" lives without clear traumas but have lacked nurture and support and may not have been wanted.

Similarly, one wishes to know the patient's history in terms of his or her personal strengths as well as weaknesses. Addressing the patient's personal areas of strength readily results in a working alliance effective in treatment as well as history taking, as was illustrated in the case of "Joe" in Chapter 4. Questions about what the patient likes and/or does best, couched as positive interest rather than negative challenges, can "bring out" the patient and give perspective to the whole history. Often, the symptoms of disturbance also contain hints of the patient's strengths and genuine interests. Many severely schizophrenic patients in my experience as a psychotherapist and a psychotherapy supervisor have presented delusions or other frankly aberrant behavior that, on close examination, have reflected a great genuine interest, but the patient was trained, as it were, not to pursue it and also not to create an appropriate social expression of that interest. For example:

> A 47-year-old veteran had been hospitalized with a diagnosis of paranoid schizophrenia for most of the past 20 years. One of his symptoms was a delusion that he could sense and receive electronic messages, in the absence of any electronic equipment. He also had cancer, and he had threatened homicide, particularly toward women, including his wife. As part of a special program in which I supervised psychotherapy with especially difficult patients, he was seen in therapy by a woman psychiatric resident who ascertained that his "hobby" was electronics but that his interest in electronics had been viewed as morbid. Psychotherapy proceeded well, and after a year, the patient was able to develop his former hobby into a profitable business and to live peacefully with his wife.

Symptom presentation and history often have a relationship in which the symptom represents, although in a disguised and inappropriate form, a genuine and potentially constructively expressed need or desire. When the need or desire represented in the symptom can be located in the person's history, one gains crucially valuable predictive and therapeutic information.

The fundamental purpose of all history taking is to find and to start putting together the pieces of the patient's life that can tell the story both of how the person's life development was fostered and of how it was disturbed, so that prediction and treatment can be made effective. One of the apparent dilemmas in predicting the course of someone who is schizophrenic is that the historical antecedents, by themselves, do not predict much of the variance in outcome. As is evident throughout this book, however, I believe that the answer to this apparent dilemma is not to disregard the history, but to take it seriously in addressing how to help the individual to legitimize the unfulfilled needs and desires that are implicit in the history, including the recent history of breakdown in acute cases. Gearing treatment to historical understanding will probably prove to be a powerful predictor.

> Anne was a 38-year-old never-married women who lived alternately with her mother and in psychiatric hospitals. She had never held a job of any consequence since leaving high school. She was diagnosed at a medical-school psychiatric teaching-hospital as schizophrenic, hebephrenic type, severe, and was regarded by her psychiatrist and other staff as having the worst prognosis of any patient in the hospital.
>
> Fortunately, this grim outlook also resulted in permission to work with her because no one else wanted to. In order to demonstrate the feasibility of even a novice psychotherapist's achieving good results, a clinical psychology intern with only brief experience as a therapist and virtually no experience with severely disturbed patients was assigned as her therapist. In her first session with the intern, Anne behaved typically. Either she was mute and stared off into a ceiling corner or she ran around his chair giggling and holding her skirt up. Both behaviors made the therapist acutely uncomfortable, but when asked which behavior was more acceptable, he chose the latter. Therapist and supervisor then discussed the meaning of this symptomatic behavior in terms of its attention-getting quality and its stark contrast to the silent staring off into space. The therapist was advised to "join her psychologically" by looking at her

and smiling at her "playfulness." She then began to pay more attention to him and was able in the next session to sit down and talk with him. She did so rather exuberantly, and he kept appreciating her "enthusiasm" until she saw that he was thoroughly attentive and quite reliable in continuing to see her whether she used extreme attention-getting methods or not.

As she made progress, including by getting perspective on her morbidly dependent relationship with her mother, and it was recognized that she had long wanted more attention from men, especially as she had lost her father at an early age, plans were made to have her share an apartment with another young woman after her discharge from the hospital. She obtained a job as a saleswoman in a clothing store and did reasonably well but was poorly paid and unhappy in selling primarily to women. A few months later, she was in therapy with me because the intern had finished his year of internship. Her confidence had increased, and I asked her what would be her very favorite kind of job. She chose to be a "go-go girl," landing such a job despite being 38 years old by then, and she became the most popular go-go dancer in a large city that employed many dozens at that time. She had, with help, entirely "legitimized" her need for male attention. She did nothing illicit, though the go-go atmosphere might have lent itself to prostitution. Eventually she met a man she decided to marry. Follow-up after two years in psychotherapy showed a continued ability to function at a high level of occupational and personal adequacy without further psychotherapy. No drugs were used during this psychotherapy; she had been on drugs at the very beginning, but they were discontinued shortly after her psychotherapy began.

The most common problem in history taking is that it may be restricted to the disclosure of one or more present secondary symptoms, and this initial, grossly limited "history" then forms a rigid basis for all subsequent treatment and management. We have seen how this practice has occurred at a wide variety of public and private hospitals as discussed by Rosenhan (1973). One can counter one's skepticism about reports of such practices by interviewing ordinary practitioners. For example, in 1985, I interviewed a psychiatrist practicing in a rural area who was reported to be more careful and "conservative" in his prescription of neuroleptic or "antipsychotic" drugs than the vast majority of his colleagues:

Dr. A stated that he saw 1,200 patients per year, including all those discharged from a local state hospital for the mentally ill and retarded. His contacts with them rarely exceeded a half hour per session, and the frequency of the sessions seldom exceeded a few times per year. He started or continued all (hastily diagnosed) "schizophrenic" patients on neuroleptics ("antipsychotic" drugs), the diagnosis having been based on the secondary symptoms of delusions and/or hallucinations. He found that patients over age 40 readily complied but that young patients often resisted taking the drugs; if they failed to do so and were hospitalized or rehospitalized, he refused to continue as their psychiatrist, whereupon they fell under the care of a psychiatrist who was less "conservative," in other words, "more aggressive" in forcing drugs. The psychiatrist whom I interviewed stated that he was willing to "trade the tongue movements" of tardive dyskinesia for keeping patients stable and out of the hospital. If they did remain stable, he ordinarily saw them just twice per year. He made no mention of the patients' ability to function other than in a community shelter or a nursing home. During his typically twice-yearly half-hour sessions, he discussed with them only (positive) symptoms and treatment by

> drugs. If a patient showed further secondary symptoms and was "unstable" he or she was given an additional appointment, and the drug dosage was increased on that occasion.
>
> This psychiatrist had seen many breast problems induced by the neuroleptics but had not recognized that the patients were becoming brain-damaged, though they had developed tardive dyskinesia as expressed in their peculiar tongue movements. He said that he had no time himself to do psychotherapy and that he seldom knew of anyone else who did psychotherapy with schizophrenia and related disorders. He summed up his approach as attending only to the patients' "stability" and whether they had a "process illness" and therefore "lifetime phenothiazines."

We can see from this example that a narrow, severely reductionist approach admits of little time or need for taking a history of a patient's life influences and personality development or even of those interpersonal and physical events in life that may have important influences on the person's "stability." Similarly, little attention is paid to the patient's course of life either before or after hospitalization, especially as there is nothing to relate it to except drugs and the seeming entity called "process schizophrenia." The fact that young people question these narrow practices has little effect because alternative approaches are not available except for those that would be even more immediately reductive, such as greater amounts of drugs or perhaps electroshock or lobotomy.

It used to be common, and perhaps still is, to construct elaborate case histories and descriptions but not to use them meaningfully. I had occasion in the 1950s to read over 100 case histories of patients hospitalized at a major private psychiatric institution. One history in particular stands out as an instance of the elaborate histories that were never used in treatment and that were used only for legal and insurance purposes:

> A woman's history began as a detailed recapitulation of her life, including her breakdown at age 25, which had evidently been precipitated by a young man's breaking off with her. She had apparently grown up feeling that marriage was the only justifiable life course for a woman already in her mid-20s. She had had no role models of women who had "succeeded" in life without being married and having children. The history clearly indicated that she was shamed and humiliated by her rejected, still-single status. She expressed her despair in her early years in the hospital by attempting suicide periodically. The history told of how nurses and aides had sometimes erred in their surveillance duties but had saved her from attempting to drown herself in a pond. The years rolled on and nurses', attendants', and doctors' notes were properly entered, but without evidence of any attention to her clear need to be shown and encouraged toward a constructive role in life that might be to her own liking. The patient's chronic condition began to mark her as what might today be called a case of *process schizophrenia,* as she became more and more withdrawn and insisted that she was the mother of a baby, clearly a delusion of the restitutional or compensatory kind that might alert some more astute clinicians to the nature of her plight. The history ended with the patient in her 70s, thoroughly institutionalized and relating only to her delusions.

In this case, as in vast numbers of others, one suspects that prediction of outcome was never a problem. Virtually 100% of the outcome was predictable, that is, dictated by the absence of any treatment that would have related constructively to this patient's desires. The patient had gradually—one might say, insidiously—made a "successful adjustment" to the hospital, which she perceived correctly as the inexorable keeper of her hopeless condition, and not a facilitator of her legitimizing her own desires for a role in life that would accord her satisfaction and self-esteem.

As in any case of mental disorder, attention to the person's history usually clarifies the meaning of her or his presenting symptoms. Psychodynamically understood, the symptoms are compromise formations representing both desire and defense, but neither wholly. One may be able to infer from the history what the desires were and what happened to them. Schizophrenic persons have often become so alienated from their own desires that they no longer perceive them as their own desires. A good history may answer such questions as "What persons and/or events served to cause the alienation?" and the consequent question "Are there persons and/or events currently that tend to preserve, decrease, or increase the alienation?" Just how quickly knowledge of the history and the presenting symptoms can lead to direct therapeutic intervention is illustrated by the following example:

> Sixteen-year-old Tom had been placed in a psychiatric hospital immediately after he was observed on a street corner attempting to cut off his exposed penis with a knife. Fortunately, he was immediately observed in this act, and the police intervened so that no physical harm occurred. During his hospital stay, Tom was one of my patients in adolescent group psychotherapy, where he began to relate well to his fellow teenagers. He told them he had been taught that sex was bad and so he had decided to cut off the offending member, as it caused him to want to masturbate. The group said explicitly that his desire to enjoy sex was entirely normal and that he should keep his penis because it was quite attractive and useful. Tom was clearly gratified and relieved by their heartfelt advice, which I wholeheartedly endorsed.
>
> Following his discharge from the hospital, however, Tom failed to attend the next group therapy session, and the other group members speculated that he might have been kept from doing so; his history included the fact that he had been kept in an attic for a couple of months by his parents. Taking the matter into their own hands, the other patients decided to go to Tom's home, with my permission, where they called him out and brought him to the session. He confirmed the speculation that his parents had told him not to attend any further sessions, and he expressed his gratitude to his fellow teenagers for so warmly and directly soliciting his continuing with them in the group. The forces that had been responsible for his alienation from other people and, inevitably, from himself were successfully opposed.

The Drug History

The patient's *entire* drug history is an important and often difficult part of the history to assess. In recent decades especially, the use of potentially psychosis-inducing drugs has been so widespread that one has to ask routinely that all patients provide an account of their use of illicit as well as prescribed drugs. Although no drug reactions totally accurately mimic the signs and symptoms of schizophrenic breakdown, some come close in certain respects. Most obviously, lysergic acid (LSD) and the amphetamine ("speed") psychoses have often been mistaken for schizophrenic disorders. But the fact that the visual hallucinations of LSD are unaccompanied by auditory hallucinations is a characteristic distinguishing sign. Amphetamines may produce such extreme heightened alertness as to resemble the hyperalertness of paranoid schizophrenic disorder, but the motor agitation, including the rapid neck-turning movements of the "speed freak," often clearly marks an amphetamine-induced psychosis.

Close examination of the history of the patient's drug use often shows a link between intense experiences of loneliness and alienation and the decision to use drugs. The difficulty of differential diagnosis is greatest when the patient is already strongly inclined to schizophrenic breakdown and then uses drugs that seem to precipitate a psychotic episode that lasts not only throughout the period of drug storage in the body but also beyond the time of reasonable recovery from drug intoxication:

> A young man in psychotherapy called to report that he was having very frightening experiences of unreality since eating some brownies at a party. He knew, after he ate them, that they had been spiked with strong hashish, but he feared that he would remain "psychotic" after the drug effects had worn off. Though he had a tendency to engage in illusory thinking bordering on delusions, the therapist estimated that the patient would not be psychotic 24 hours later and told him so, adding that it might be tempting to remain psychotic but that they would go ahead and have their outpatient session as usual. The next day, the patient had virtually resumed his regular degree of reality contact and developed further insight into how he saw the drug experience as offering him an escape but had resisted letting it be one. He also resolved to stay away from further exposure to drugs.

More serious effects of using LSD or even marijuana result when the individual is already denying reality in major ways and using drugs extensively, even though there have been no delusions or hallucinations:

> An 18-year-old college student had suffered the loss of her older sister in an auto accident the year before and, like her mother, could not tolerate full awareness of her sister's death; she had wish-fulfilling fantasies of seeing her alive, together with nightmares about her death. At a party, she was challenged to smoke some strong pot, which quickly made her feel as if she were in an inescapable nightmare and as if she herself might die. During psychotherapy sessions, she was able to view the experience with some detachment and understanding, but she suffered recurrences of the "waking nightmare" for several months, though there was no further drug use.

The most severe apparent consequences occur in relation to frequent heavy drug abuse and marked escapist tendencies. Such cases present an admixture of extreme drug abuse and a motivation to escape reality as complementary strivings. For example, Mark Vonnegut's *Eden Express* (1975) describes his long-term heavy use of drugs, including LSD, together with personal issues that were more denied than addressed until he became frankly schizophrenic. He then remained schizophrenic long after he had stopped using the illicit drugs. One often sees the greatest use of drugs in those who can least afford to use them, rather as if they are searching for a way "to go crazy." Both drugs and psychosis offer escape.

Alcohol is quite probably the most popular long-term drug among schizophrenic persons, with the possible exception of cigarettes. As alcohol has an immediate fear-reducing effect on the brain, although it is sometimes countered by a fear of losing control, both persons who are predisposed to schizophrenia and those who have already been diagnosed have strong alcohol proclivities. A study of alcohol and other substance abuse (Barbee, Clark, Crapanzano, Heintz, *et al.,* 1989) among 53 schizophrenic patients seen at an emergency psychiatric service showed that 25 met the criteria for a lifetime diagnosis of alcohol abuse–related disorder, and all 53 of the patients reported taking various illicit drugs daily for at least two weeks during some period in their lives. Drake, Osher, and Wallach (1989) reported a study of 115 schizophrenic adults discharged from a state hospital who were participating in an aftercare program; 45% of them used alcohol, 22% heavily. The authors noted that even mild alcohol use may be a problem for schizophrenic patients; it was associated with many negative patterns, including increased symptomatology, psychosocial problems, and rehospitalization.

It is unlikely that drugs themselves can either exactly mimic or produce schizophrenic disorders, though some use patterns may result in such a depletion of the capacity for cognitive and emotional control that the level of impairment resembles that of a severely regressed schizophrenic person. Even then, the schizophrenic person is likely to show more inconsistency of functioning ability than someone who is incapacitated by neurological and other physical damage. But continued use of drugs, including alcohol, may weaken already insufficient coping skills. Karon and VandenBos (1981, pp. 296–310) give a further excellent discussion of the psychological motivation and effects of alcohol as well as illicit drugs in schizophrenic disorders.

As is emphasized in several other sections of this book, the patient's history of prescribed drug use is also vital to assessment and treatment. Patients become different neurologically and psychologically through the effects of especially the more powerful psychiatric drugs. For example, acute symptomatic signs, particularly of the secondary sort, may subside although social recovery is delayed. Most patients who have previously been diagnosed as schizophrenic have been prescribed "antipsychotic" drugs. The virtual universality of such drug regimens should cause the assessor to pay careful attention to their particular effects on a given individual.

The Changing Life History

The life history is always changing. Because life histories are subject to bias, omission, and contradiction, it is wise to regard all histories as tentative and in need of corrections and additions. The process of long-term psychotherapy is especially likely to reveal the inadequacy of early versions of the history. Frequently, the most important facts of the history are not revealed before considerable therapy because the patient is initially unable to recall, much less present accurately, much of what is most important. One should be highly skeptical, therefore, of claims that "there is nothing in the history to suggest a psychological cause of schizophrenic disorder," especially as the vast majority of schizophrenic patients have never been in serious psychotherapy, let alone psychotherapy that is thorough enough to adequately reveal the history. Often patients are too afraid to tell themselves, much less others, what has happened to them or what they have done. We are used to taking these insufficiencies into account when working with "neurotic" persons, but we may fail to recognize that psychotic persons are even more apt to provide insufficient histories. In essence, the history-taking method may result in anything from a quite helpful beginning sketch of the patient's life to a virtually blank piece of paper.

Clinical Observation

The usefulness of clinical observation depends on the setting, the skill of the observers, the amount of observation time available, and the patient's openness. Psychiatric and other hospitals are generally regarded as settings where there are great observational advantages. One hears, for example, that the patient has been kept for hospital observation so that a clearer clinical picture can be developed. Some settings provide a variety of situations that allow the sampling of the patient's behavior. A psychiatric hospital conference usually includes reports from a variety of mental health professionals, each of whom has observed the patient from a particular vantage point or in terms of certain activities.

Sometimes, the observations are largely naturalistic, as the patient is free to sit, read, talk, watch television, and so on. However, the patient seldom feels free and knows that he or she is being observed. Thus, there is no purely "spontaneous" behavior akin to what the animal naturalist might observe from an undetectable vantage point. But a mild kind of testing, as it were, may occur when the patient is asked to perform, for example, in occupational therapy, by working at some handicraft.

Assessment and the Milieu

Each patient setting places limits, implicit and explicit, and provides, wittingly or not, various "role models" in the form of staff and other patients. All of these influences tend to shape the patient's behavior into a pattern of adjustment. It used to be common, and perhaps still is, to judge the patient's progress in terms of "how well the patient has adjusted to the ward or hospital," quite as if "good adjustment to the institution" will translate into good adaptation to life's ever-changing demands outside the institution. Although patients institutionalized for a long time certainly become "institutionalized," they usually do so at the expense of becoming able to adapt to the requirements of reality in the outside world. "Progress," as measured by various "ward adjustment scales," often means the dilapidation of the spontaneity and creativity needed to live a useful life outside the hospital. Such patients are tamed, as it were, but not helped.

Most psychiatric hospitals have paid only lip service to "milieu therapy," the structuring of psychological environments so that they are therapeutic influences. Typically, the patients sit around, idly staring at television to pass the time, and staff spend little active time with them, bestowing a sort of "benign neglect" that fosters passivity and disillusionment. Rosenhan's findings (1973) in this respect can be generalized to most institutions because the staff seldom attend much to the patients as would-be striving and contributing members to either the ward society or society at large. A number of excellent psychiatric hospitals, however, are distinguished by their thoughtful use of the great gains that may be made by taking seriously the patient's need for helpful caring and interest rather than the detachment and neglect that masquerade as useful clinical attitudes.

Taken seriously, milieu therapy (e.g., Cumming & Cumming, 1970; Schlesinger & Holzman, 1970; Woodbury, 1964) offers immense opportunities for assessment as well as treatment. By doing something interactional with patients in ways geared to trying to help them both in general and in tailor-made ways, much is learned about what treatment is or will be helpful. Deikman and Whitaker (1979) provided an example of a thoroughgoing milieu treatment ward. The patients themselves became essential "treatment personnel" as they shared the responsibilities for one another and learned about themselves through their efforts to help one another. In its responsible give-and-take, life on the ward became much more like real life. As a result, the staff could observe the patients and assess how they were progressing in terms of the challenges they would have to face in real life if they were to become productive citizens. Likewise, the staff shared with the patients their ideas about how each of them could be helped and solicited the patients' ideas on how they and the staff could be most helpful. Instead of producing anarchy, which some hospital staff predicted, this approach made the management of the ward easier, as management became secondary to the milieu treatment. Patients make good observers and advisers, especially when they are given a stake in the possibility of real progress.

Observers must take into account the kinds and degrees of the patients' "institutional savvy." Patients who know their way around psychiatric hospitals or who have been indoctrinated in the ways of the military or other highly structured settings may be psychotic to a marked degree, but their psychosis may not be clinically observable. An example was given in Chapter 3 of a woman, long observed in a state psychiatric hospital, who appeared to have recovered completely from paranoid schizophrenic disorder but who was revealed by psychological testing to be severely psychotic and quite dangerous.

Because active testing is not an inherent part of clinical observation, there is a crucial weakness in clinical observation that may make it difficult, if not impossible, to make valid inferences from the data. Passivity, institutional savvy, and guardedness are three patient characteristics that may critically limit the available observational data. Yet, a great deal of diagnosis is done rather simply, according to even casual clinical observation; in these cases, there is considerable if not exclusive reliance on the patient's presentation of secondary symptoms. Furthermore, when the clinical observation is done outside a close observational setting such as a hospital, direct observation under controlled conditions is not feasible.

The Psychiatric Interview and Mental Status Examination

Among all of the techniques for assessing persons who may be schizophrenic, none depends more on skill than the interview. At one extreme, an interviewer may both draw out the individual and begin a psychotherapeutic process; at the other extreme, an interviewer may not only fail to obtain useful information but may reduce the chances of successful psychotherapy or even of further assessment. The amount of time taken for the interview and the setting and atmosphere of the interview are also vital. Brief interviews, such as Eugen Bleuler's with his famous patient Nijinsky, may provide such an insufficient sample of the patient's life and status as to be grossly misleading. Similarly, some settings and atmospheres can produce greater unwillingness in the patient to participate in any assessment or therapy:

> It was the custom in a large public mental hospital to hold clinical conferences in a large room; the staff were lined up in chairs on either side, except for the presiding psychiatrist-interviewer, who sat behind a large table at the front of the room. The patient would be brought into the room and would then walk between the assembled staff to sit in a chair facing the psychiatrist across a table. Thus, the patient, seated in the middle of this horseshoe arrangement, in a chair without arms, unable to look comfortably at anyone but the presider, was an utterly vulnerable figure. This rather intimidating atmosphere was not relieved by any particular kindness on the part of the presider, who would proceed to ask questions in a cold and impersonal way.

Although common practice includes many insensitive interview techniques, there is a long and rich tradition of more sensitive and productive interview approaches, exemplified in Sullivan (1954), Gill, Newman, and Redlich (1954), Menninger, Mayman, and Pruyser (1962), Ewalt and Farnsworth (1963), Stevenson (1974), Stevenson and Sheppe (1974), and Ginsberg (1985). But the art of psychiatric interviewing may be declining: "Before an accurate assessment can be made, a productive doctor–patient relationship must be established. It is becoming more difficult to do so as technological advances lead physicians away from the human factors in their patients" (Leon *et al.,* 1985, p. 449).

In addition to knowing what to look and listen for and having good interviewing skills generally, the interviewer of someone who may be schizophrenic requires considerable flexibility and creativity. The interviewer may need to change orientation quickly and sensitively in accord with the patient's responsiveness. For example, the interviewer may need to be quite active if that approach may encourage the individual or, at the other extreme, to be very quiet and willing to wait if the individual is easily intimidated by gregariousness. The most important requirement for a productive interview is developing trust and confidence in the interviewer; reliability and continuity of the interviewer's interest and acceptance are essential to sustaining this trust and confidence. Many patients have long ago learned not to place faith in someone who may readily leave them.

The interviewer's flexibility may also have to include a willingness to adjust the interview's duration to the individual's tolerance. Many individuals cannot tolerate a regular 50-minute interview; they may withstand only shorter periods of dialogue or may even be able to respond only when they surmise that the interviewer does not have much time for them:

> A 20-year-old hospitalized schizophrenic man was extremely withdrawn. Attempts had been made to interest him in psychotherapy, but he had remained adamant about not talking to anyone. Instead, he formed plans to escape from the hospital, such as by lowering himself with knotted sheets from a second-story window. The prospective new therapist's supervisor suggested that he approach the patient with an apology for his, the therapist's, unavailability. The therapist told the patient that he had been assigned to be the patient's psychotherapist but that he did not have the time and hoped the patient would understand and forgive him. The therapist added, however, that he could, if the patient really wanted it, offer one 20-minute session per week. The patient accepted and soon after asked for longer and more frequent sessions, which were "allowed" gradually. The patient improved, was discharged, and continued in outpatient psychotherapy.

In this case, as in many others, there was great conflict between the patient's need for help and his fear of human closeness, which the psychotherapist had to take into account. When an interviewer backs off but advises the patient of his or her continued availability—although it is limited—the patient, feeling more need than fear, may surmise that the interviewer will not engulf the patient, as he or she had feared. The patient is reassured to know, on the one hand, that there is some definite availability and, on the other hand, that he or she will be protected from too intense a contact.

Particularly creative approaches may be needed to draw out chronic "burned-out" patients, who present a monotonous facade of withdrawal and apparent lack of interest in everyone around them. Such patients usually feel quite expendable, and it may be a revelation to them that they are needed. Arieti (1974) cited the marked improvements in back ward patients who were asked by an overworked nurse to help in her daily chores. The improvements were clearly caused by this unpremeditated but highly effective form of occupational therapy. Likewise, "hopelessly withdrawn" patients have been known to respond with helpful and even heroic acts in times of emergency, such as fires that threatened everyone's life. The feeling of being needed, which is tantamount to feeling worthwhile and having increased self-esteem, often has very positive effects on patients' openness and willingness to cooperate:

> While working on a research project at a long-term state hospital, I had difficulty obtaining the cooperation of a sufficient number of chronic schizophrenic patients. But a particular research assistant was quite reluctant to concede that any patient was

> untestable. An especially great challenge came one day in the form of a middle-aged chronic schizophrenic man who was reputed to take no appreciable interest in the events around him and did not speak to, much less let himself be interviewed or tested by, anyone. He was observed in solitary and apparently oblivious masturbation on a back ward when approached by the research assistant, who in a calm and friendly way greeted him and told him that she really needed his help. The patient responded by stopping masturbating, zipping up his fly, and taking the test.

Sometimes, it is best to address the patient's interest as straightforwardly as possible, even though it may mean helping to "act out" a delusion:

> A 12-year-old boy had become paranoid schizophrenic. The boy's distrust and suspicion extended to a refusal to talk about himself. His only admitted interest was in proving that his mother had a special radio device in her car though which she could hear everything he said, including whatever he might say in the therapist's office. Instead of asking questions, the therapist wondered with the boy where the wires were. The result was a thorough, mutually conducted search of the therapist's office area, both inside and out, until the boy concluded that the therapist and his office were indeed an exception to his mother's surveillance. Thereafter, he talked freely about himself, as well as his parents.

Many adult schizophrenic or otherwise psychotic individuals are best "interviewed" in ways and in settings ordinarily associated most with how we would work with children, yet our approach must not be condescending. Going for a walk with a patient, playing Ping-Pong, or performing routine work with the patient often opens the conversational door and also becomes informative in its own right.

Although it is commonly thought that great numbers of schizophrenic patients will simply not talk, the actually thoroughly unwilling patient is rare. Referring to the context of psychotherapy, Karon and VandenBos (1981) observed that

> most psychotic patients clearly do not come in with the expectation that the therapist will be of any help. It is the therapist's job to create the therapeutic alliance by every possible means. Strangely enough, it is often not that much work. The advice . . . that most schizophrenic patients will talk freely if asked what seems to be the trouble, and if they are actually listened to when they do talk, may seem oversimplified. Yet we have seen patients listed on the ward charts as "totally uncommunicative," only to have the patient speak meaningfully when asked, "What seems to be the trouble?" Indeed, when we were invited as consultants to interview the "most difficult and uncommunicative" patient, to teach residents and graduate students to deal with recalcitrance, we have been embarrassed by having the patients talk openly. (p. 156)

Different kinds of patients respond quite differently along the continuum of revelation and symptomatology, according to the interviewer's approach. Our attitudes toward the patient, including our acceptance of his or her peculiarities, largely determine what kinds of information will be elicited and whether core conflicts can be ascertained. The patient is unlikely to respond with a revealing outpouring of information to an unsympathetic listener intent only on discovering symptoms to eradicate. Patients are often in terror of being engulfed and taken over by others, afraid that they will lose their personalities and their very persons. For the sake of both assessment and truly effective treatment, as well as humaneness, the patient must be regarded with respect.

As illustrated earlier in this chapter, the symptoms often express combinations of fears and needs. The needs have not been met in ways that are acceptable to the patient or others. Discovering what these needs are and how the patient may be helped to legitimize them is a hallmark of the kind of assessment that can lead to effective treatment. The patient and the interviewer should share a common purpose, which is to determine the patient's needs and fears and ways to cultivate legitimate pathways to need satisfaction. Assessment should serve to expand our knowledge of the patient's life, personality, and conflicts rather than to limit our knowledge to a bare description of some symptoms that then become the targets of reductive "treatment."

The schizophrenic individual contains the seedlings of his or her own growth toward a more fulfilling life. These seedlings will be found and cultivated by the astute and sympathetic interviewer. One astute interviewer observed:

> In the degree in which I have been privileged to know the intimate secrets of hearts, I ever more realize how great a part is played in the lives of men and women by some little concealed germ of abnormality. For the most part they are occupied in the task of stifling and crushing those germs, treating them like weeds in their gardens. There is another and better way, even though more difficult and more perilous. Instead of trying to suppress the weeds that can never be killed, they may be cultivated into useful or beautiful flowers. For it is impossible to conceive of any impulse in a human heart which cannot be transformed into Truth or into Beauty or into Love. (Havelock Ellis, Impressions and Comments, as quoted in Seldes, 1985, p. 124)

Interviews with family members may be particularly revealing of how the patient's needs and fears came into conflict and how strivings were converted into symptoms even in the presence of a "normal family environment." Karon and VandenBos (1981) illuminated this situation, which may easily present a blank wall to less astute observers. The contrast between interviewing a patient alone and with the family can make the difference between the patient's presenting as a weed or a flower. For example, Karon and VandenBos described the case of a catatonic boy brought by his parents for evaluation. While with his parents, the boy said nothing, but alone he talked freely. The parents had kept referring to him in the third person, quite as if he were not there and as if they did not want him to be there.

Because schizophrenic individuals are an enormously heterogeneous group of people and because idiosyncratic pathways to schizophrenic disorder can be expected, there is every reason to pursue these diverse pathways rather than to settle in advance on one or a few formulas that, when they do not fit the case, steer the interviewer away from open inquiry. Not every schizophrenic person fits a particular family constellation. Some interviewers are inclined, however, to conclude that the family had no role in the patient's becoming and remaining schizophrenic if Formula X or Formula Y cannot be fitted to the "facts." The facts themselves are, of course, provisional; many patients hold back information because of shame or distrust. Although certain formulas are useful in guiding inquiry, they are simply tools and not proofs. Clear, individually tailored formulas often emerge if the interviewer dares to keep an open mind:

> I was consulted by the parents of a five-member family, each of whom had experienced schizophrenic and/or schizoid phenomena. The parents' greatest immediate concern was their 17-year-old daughter, who was hospitalized in a catatonic stupor, but a 16-year-old son was also becoming schizophrenic as expressed in peculiar thoughts and the appearance of a delusion. A much younger daughter was quite withdrawn. The parents were devoutly religious and had been referred by their minister. A general formula made some sense of this family's problems but did not explain the differences among the family members.
>
> In general, the parents preached their own version of "goodness," indicating and their children that they "could never be too good," and that, in fact, they were never "good enough." The parents' sincerity was such that they included themselves in this family credo and provided a model, both male and female, of self-rejection. Their older daughter could not imagine that she had done anything bad but had forestalled the possibility of wickedness by becoming totally immobile. The son, however, had experienced such strong but uncomfortable and therefore alien sexual urges that he was beginning to believe that they came from another person. The youngest daughter, meanwhile, had begun practicing the withdrawal that her older sister had already taken to the extreme. The family, together and singly, were interviewed, and each was then seen individually in psychotherapy by different therapists, as well as together. As a result, each began to understand his or her own particular version of the compulsion to be impossibly good so as to make up for the parents' deep sense of inadequacy.

The Mental Status Examination

Psychiatric interview methods include the mental status examination, which had its origins in the diagnosis of severe psychiatric disorder but has taken on both broader categories of disorder and more subtle manifestations. It retains a sense of testing rather than just observing or gathering historical information, and in this way, it is more directed to assessing the patient's abilities and inabilities in at least a semistandard manner. Its full breath and complexity have been well explicated by Leon *et al.* (1985) and by Stevenson and Sheppe (1974). The latter suggested that the psychiatrist begin with questions about milder disorders and proceed only later to testing for more severe disorientation. When memory and other intellectual abilities are assessed, the inquiry proceeds from easier to more difficult questions. More rigorous versions of this kind of testing are done by clinical psychologists with the aid of standardized instruments such as the Wechsler Adult Intelligence Scale—Revised (WAIS-R) and other formally standardized and validated psychological tests. The modern version of the psychiatric examination may cover a broad range of the patient's cognitive and emotional functioning, and it may take an hour or more. But in general practice, it is less detailed, exacting, and time-consuming than a full-scale psychological evaluation using a battery of tests.

Although Stevenson and Sheppe (1974), as well as many other psychiatrists, suggested avoiding an outright formal testing approach because the patient might see it as a nontherapeutic approach, many psychiatrists ask some fairly standard questions in order to examine specific functions. Counting backwards by 7's from 100; telling the time of day, month, and year; and asking the patient half an hour later to remember five objects that he or she has been shown—these are obviously test items meant to reveal the patient's abilities. Often, patients are asked to explain the meaning of proverbs as a test of their abstracting ability; the specific probers used are chosen from the WAIS-R. Psychiatrists who know that the precision and standardization of psychological testing are important in terms of administration, scoring, and interpretation may do a brief mental status examination as an introduction to the patient and a prelude to formal psychological test evaluation.

Cultural differences, lack of formal education, and lack of formal standardization of the mental status items may readily combine to render the examination results and interpretation misleading. Testing for the understanding of proverbs illustrates these hazards. Although it may be presumed that proverbs are within the realm of nearly everyone's educational exposure, many people, in fact, have never heard that "The proof of the pudding is in the eating." The patient's unfamiliarity may result in a misconception that seems like schizophrenic thinking disorder when cultural and educational differences are really at issue. One must comprehend and control for many variables affecting the quality of response. Though fear of contaminating a therapeutic orientation with a testing orientation may make the examiner hesitant to resort to rigorously structured formal testing, one cannot expect tests that have had poor or no standardization to yield readily interpretable results.

Failing to understand that schizophrenic thinking cannot be accurately assessed by casual and unstandardized methods, many psychiatrists, and probably many clinical psychologists, rely for diagnosis on observing merely secondary, generally positive, symptoms, such as blatant delusions and hallucinations. Agreement rates among such examiners tend to be low, and even when there is agreement, it is superficial.

In essence, the mental status examination, as used to ascertain schizophrenic disorder, its degree, and various other differentiating characteristics, has considerable historical importance, but as a method of assessment, it lacks the essential qualities of good testing methods: sufficient standardization of administration, scoring, and interpretation and proven reliability and validity.

Summary

The earliest and still most often used methods of assessing schizophrenic and related disorders are history taking, clinical observation, the interview, and the mental status examination. The efficacy of all of these methods depends largely on the skill and the personality of the assessor. Genuine interest in the individual and a flexible, creative approach are needed to gain information that can lead to helpful treatment.

Several examples of flexible approaches to interviewing were given. Neglect of the patient's history and insensitive interviewing tend to limit the available information to secondary symptoms and encourage therapists to gear treatment simply to reducing the secondary symptoms. Several examples were given of the value of historical information and how particular kinds of patients may be interviewed.

The mental status examination is a kind of semistandardized method of testing that is related to formal psychological testing but lacks actual standardization of administration, scoring, and interpretation. Lacking an awareness of the need for and the uses of more comprehensive and rigorous means of assessment, especially to test for schizophrenic thinking, many diagnosticians are both inaccurate and superficial in their approach.

6

Structured Interviews and Diagnostic Systems

Basic Considerations

During the late 1970s, while the third edition of the *Diagnostic and Statistical Manual* (DSM-III; American Psychiatric Association, 1980) was being developed, the definition of schizophrenia in the United States narrowed, and the concept of schizophrenia as a unitary disease diminished (Haier, 1980). Two considerations contributed greatly to these changes.

First, it had become clear, at least to researchers, that the American definition of schizophrenia, which was far broader than most European definitions, did not readily lend itself to reliable classification because it allowed a very broad spectrum of patients to be diagnosed as schizophrenic. Second, the so-called affective illnesses of mania and manic-depressive disorder, including patients with schizoaffective diagnoses, seemed responsive to lithium carbonate (e.g., Hirshowitz, Casper, Garver, & Chang, 1980), and the new antidepressant drugs became available to treat the depressive aspect of affective disorders. The responders to these drugs might include "schizoaffective" patients who were diagnosed as schizophrenic according to DSM-II criteria (American Psychiatric Association, 1967), a group essentially excluded from the diagnosis of schizophrenic disorder in the new DSM-III in 1980. Thus, in the DSM-III, "schizophrenic disorder" became a more specific and narrowly defined diagnosis that would lend itself much more to reliability of diagnosis than the broad DSM-II description of schizophrenia.

Many researchers had begun to recognize the vagueness and the consequent unreliability of the DSM-II diagnoses; they attempted, in terms of both the DSM-III and more than a dozen other newly developed diagnostic systems for schizophrenic disorders, to increase the reliability and therefore the possible validity of this diagnostic category. If other factors are held constant, narrowness of definition favors the possibility of achieving higher reliability, though perhaps at the cost of ruling out important phenomena. Sophisticated researchers also knew that, to achieve reliability, they would need not only a clearer conceptual definition of schizophrenic disorders but also quite specific operational definitional criteria. Interviewers would have to know exactly what information was needed, what questions to ask, and how to rate the information. Accordingly, interviews had to be more "structured" in terms of specificity and rigor. In the process of developing "structured interviews" as part of diagnostic systems, interview technique was moved from a position of considerable latitude toward the greater rigor and the stricter methodology of psychological testing. For example, DSM-III system interviews might use the Diagnostic Interview Schedule (Helzer & Robins, 1988), developed to elicit in rateable form the information directly pertinent to the DSM-III criteria.

As we shall see in this chapter, it is extremely difficult to promote the effective use of interview systems, including the most prominent system, which is the DSM-III; it is difficult to get interviewers to learn the diagnostic criteria, let alone to learn and to use structured interview methods. The same considerations apply to the DSM-III-R, which is essentially the same as the DSM-III in terms of the diagnosis of schizophrenic disorders. Therefore, in this chapter, when I use the term *DSM-III,* I mean also to cover the DSM-III-R (American Psychiatric Association, 1987).

The Importance of Reliability

The *reliability* of an assessment method tells us the degree to which we know what is being assessed. The *validity* of the method tells us the degree to which the method actually measures what it purports to measure. The *usefulness* of the method is the degree to which it produces measures that enable us to predict and/or control given phenomena. Reliability is a necessary but not a sufficient condition for achieving validity. That is, reliability by itself guarantees neither validity nor usefulness, but it is an absolutely necessary foundation for validity. Thus, although there can be no validity without reliability, a diagnostic method may be both completely reliable and completely invalid.

To develop highly reliable methods for the assessment of schizophrenic disorders, there must be agreed-upon operational definitions of schizophrenic disorders. That is, there must be such clarity of definition that we know precisely what is meant by *schizophrenic disorders* according to quite specific instructions for deducing the phenomena. We prove reliability by showing repeated ability to achieve agreement over time and among assessors. Thus, the reliability of a method is demonstrated both by an individual assessor's consistency within herself or himself and by consistency among assessors.

Difficulties in Achieving Reliability

Despite many studies of the diagnostic reliability of the methods available for assessing schizophrenia and related disorders and many attempts to improve reliability, unreliability is still the rule. Saugestad and Odengaard (1983) emphasized that there has been a persistent discrepancy in international diagnostic practice since 1970. Among Norway, Denmark, France, England, Poland, Australia, and the United States, the range of frequency of diagnosis of schizophrenia for first hospital admissions was from 5% to almost 50% with the United States continuing to diagnose about 50% of first admissions as schizophrenic. Similarly, manic-depressive disorder was diagnosed from 4% to over 25% of the time among these countries. Obviously, both the terms *schizophrenic disorder* and *manic-depressive disorder* have highly divergent meanings in these various countries, with much less overlap in meaning than one might expect. Thus, whether one receives a diagnosis of schizophrenia may depend more on what country one lives in than on being "schizophrenic."

As discussed in Chapter 5, it is quite difficult to achieve diagnostic reliability even within the same diagnostic interview system. High reliabilities are obtained only when interviewers are trained and quite practiced in a method that has highly specific operational criteria for schizophrenia and related disorders and when adequate diagnostic data are available, the latter depending, as we have seen, on the skill of interviewers and the patients' "cooperativeness." Thus, in addition to whatever properties a given system may have for making high reliability possible, there is the issue of what percentage of possibly schizophrenic patients will produce enough relevant data to be included in any sample for a study. For this reason, as well as many others, all samples of "schizophrenia" are biased, so that their representativeness of the overall population of schizophrenic and other individuals with "major mental disorders" is limited. Given these problems of sampling adequacy, together with the limitations inherent in any system, one can easily imagine why cross-cultural diagnosis is extremely unreliable and why even a single diagnostic system tends to be inadequately reliable unless its users are skilled and can elicit the necessary data to be rated according to highly specific criteria.

Some problems of "reliability" stem from false assumptions about the nature of "schizophrenia." Even if "schizophrenia" is an entity, we do not really know what "schizophrenia" is. Often, problems of "reliability of diagnosis" stem from the assumption that there is a particular—and presumably only one—way to define schizophrenia. Actually, different systems—say, a system used in Norway and a system used in the United States—are different both in type and in the degree of their *inclusiveness* for the category schizophrenia. Neither of these differences need present a problem in reliability if we are aware of the nature of the differences and if they can be specified. But we must know, for example, what the term *schizophrenia* means in the United States and must be aware that it means a broadly inclusive category, especially before the introduction of the DSM-III in 1980. Even the less inclusive DSM-III and DSM-III-R definitions, compared to DSM-II, may be quite different from the Norwegian definition in terms of the degree of disturbance as well as the types of signs and symptoms required as criteria for "schizophrenia." If there is a clear definition of schizophrenic disorders, differences in inclusiveness among diagnostic systems throughout the world do not necessarily mean problems in reliability of the type that limit validity. But we must be aware of these definitional differences and we must know the definitions both conceptually and how they are operationally defined.

The Systems

The following systems for diagnosing schizophrenic disorders are among the most prominent:

1. E. Bleuler's restricted system of three of the four "A's" (1920)
2. M. Bleuler's system (M. Bleuler, 1971)
3. DSM-III (Spitzer & Fleiss, 1974)
4. Feighner, Robins, Guze, Woodruff, Winokur, and Munoz' system (1972)
5. Flexible System (Carpenter, Strauss, & Bartko, 1973)
6. Four A's (E. Bleuler, 1920)
7. E. Kraepelin's system (1919/1971)
8. G. Langfeldt's system (1971)
9. New Haven Schizophrenic Index (Astrachan, Harrow, Adler *et al.*, 1972)
10. Newmark, Raft, Toomey, Hunter, and Hazzaglia's system (1975)
11. Research Diagnostic Criteria (Feighner, Robins, Guze, Woodruff, Winokur, & Munoz, 1972)
12. Schneider's first-rank symptoms (Schneider, 1959)
13. United Kingdom (Edwards, 1973)
14. United States (Edwards, 1973)
15. WHO-IPSS (Carpenter *et al.*, 1973)
16. Yusin, Nihira, and Mortashed's system (1974)

Several of these systems, particularly the older systems, have not been integrally associated with structured interview methods but have been found adaptable. Some of the newer systems have been developed in association with structured interview methods, for example the Structured Diagnostic Interview in the case of the DSM-III and DSM-III-R.

Practical Implications

Achieving reliable classifications of schizophrenic disorders means that we know and can communicate what we are talking about. To achieve reliability among systems, we must have not only conceptual definitions but clear and testable operational definitions for each and every diagnostic system in order to make it reliable in itself. For example, though a Norwegian psychiatrist might not agree with the definition, that psychiatrist would at least know what an American psychiatrist was talking about when the American psychiatrist said that the "schizophrenics" in a research or clinical sample were classified according to the DSM-III. Therefore, whatever generalizations the American psychiatrist made from a given sample would refer to a defined group rather than simply to "schizophrenics," undefined.

Though the importance of reliability of definition is well known in science, it has taken several decades to bring it into prominence in psychiatric and psychological research, much less in clinical work. As discussed in Chapter 5, journals of psychiatry, psychology, and inevitably social work, sociology, and other disciplines, which used psychiatric diagnostic classifications, have published many hundreds of clinical and research articles that purported to deal with "schizophrenics," whom the authors did not define well enough to convey meaningful information. Making clear what it is that you are talking about is a *sine qua non* not only of science but of any form of meaningful communication. The argument has often been advanced, however, that the authors of an article were surely talking about "schizophrenics" because the symptoms were so severe. The questions remained: What symptoms? How severe?

> Prominent scientific researchers presenting papers at a major national conference gave a quite lengthy report on a major study of their treatment program for "schizophrenics," but they said nothing about subject selection. A member of the audience asked what they meant by "schizophrenics" in their sample of patients. One of the presenters, annoyed at the question, dismissed it by replying emphatically, "Oh, they were schizophrenics all right!"

Diagnostic Unreliability and Iatrogenic Treatment

Johan Landmark, a Norwegian psychiatrist who has also done work in Canada and other countries, has shown, in collaboration with his colleagues, the strengths and limitations of various diagnostic systems. "A Manual for the Assessment of Schizophrenia" (Landmark, 1982), developed as part of a larger research project and published as a supplement to *Acta Psychiatrica Scandinavica,* details and evaluates 13 of the major systems in terms of their diagnostic characteristics. The manual provides definitions of the symptoms encompassed by all of the systems, clear-cut rules of application and inquiry, and a structured interview format. Furthermore, Landmark and his group did the careful study and practice needed to produce high interrater reliability before using any of these systems with a large sample population of chronic patients.

The manual was used to show how 13 diagnostic systems had been applied to some 300 chronic and presumably severe "chronic schizophrenics," all of whom had been diagnosed as schizophrenic by the staff psychiatrists in the hospital and were on periodic fluphenazines (a long-acting phenothiazine) (Cernovsky, Landmark, & Leslie, 1985; Helmes, Landmark, & Kazarian, 1983; Landmark, Cernovsky, Merskey, & Leslie, 1986; Leslie, Landmark, & Whitaker, 1984). A detailed study of 100 of these patients showed that 42% were not classifiable as schizophrenic according to any of three systems: Bleuler's, Schneider's, or Langfeldt's. For all practical purposes, even if one assumes that the phenothiazines are the only efficacious way to treat "schizophrenics," apparently 42 of these 100 patients were being given massive long-term doses of a drug having a variety of harmful effects, often including a crippling and incurable disease, when they may not have had any chance of benefitting in terms of their "schizophrenia" because they were not schizophrenic. Many, perhaps most, of these misdiagnosed, phenothiazine-treated patients could be expected to develop tardive dyskinesia, an irreversible brain disease. In effect, such patients, in the course of being treated for a "disease" they did not have, may have been given real diseases.

Of the 100 intensively studied patients, 6 were found not to be schizophrenic but to have brain syndromes, a condition that contraindicates the use of phenothiazines. There is no sense, however, in being indignant about practices at the particular institution where this research was done, as this institution permitted and facilitated a genuinely scientific inquiry into its practices with the intention of reforming not only its own practices but practices everywhere. Nor do we have evidence that practices at this institution fell below average practice at other similar facilities. Practitioners at many other institutions, and in private practice as well, have made and continue to make these and greater treatment mistakes without recognizing or correcting them.

Let us approach the matter of reliable classification, assuming that the phenothiazines are the treatment of choice for "schizophrenia." A sincere advocate of this approach surely would not want to contaminate improvement indices by including patients who had no schizophrenic disorder to begin with. Such contamination of a subject pool would dilute what might be a valid demonstration of efficacious results for truly schizophrenic patients. So let us also assume that there is a genuine interest in careful and accurate diagnosis, at least in the sense of establishing highly definable and therefore potentially reliable diagnoses. If so, the psychiatrist should hold off prescribing phenothiazines, and very probably any other drug treatment as well, until the patient can be carefully diagnosed. Landmark (1982) noted the especially pernicious effect of instituting long-term phenothiazine treatment after a first psychotic episode:

> If the psychiatrist starts a long-term treatment the first time a patient "breaks down" he will never be able to verify whether or not such a treatment is necessary because he cannot know the difference between the natural course of the disease and the effect of the major tranquilizer. (p. 17)

What the Systems Have in Common

Every structured-interview system for obtaining, organizing, and interpreting data diagnostically represents an attempt at specificity that is clear and precise enough to enable a variety of investigators to reach highly similar conclusions about the same patients, with respect both to the general diagnosis and to the signs and symptoms on which it is based. In order to achieve these goals, the systems must be tested.

The issue of the reliability of diagnostic systems is twofold: how well investigators agree in the results of their use of any given system and how well the systems themselves agree. In the first instance, it is essential that investigators actively learn to use a given system until they can demonstrate agreement among themselves, for otherwise the system has no value; the achievement of interinvestigator reliability is an absolute prerequisite. In the second instance, however, there is no inherent need for high reliability. That is, partly because no system has yet clearly proved itself the most valid, it is not necessary that systems agree with one another as long as the differences are clearly stated and recognizable. Ultimately, validity takes supremacy over reliability, though the reliability is needed to achieve validity. In this sense, intrasystem reliability is more important than intersystem reliability, but any system must eventually demonstrate validity as well as reliability.

Validity is established when a system corresponds with independent, external criteria for schizophrenic disorders. A system might prove itself valid by this criterion but have a low or even nonexistent rate of agreement with other systems. For example, the majority or even all of the systems now extant may fail to measure the essence of the schizophrenic disorders, by taking into account only relatively superficial manifestations often shared with other disorders. For the skeptics, it should be noted that both Kraepelin (1919/1971) and Bleuler (1911/1950) emphasized a central disturbance in the relation of thinking and feeling, which is not readily measured or deduced from patients' outward behavior. Therefore, in addition to evaluating the reliability of diagnostic systems, one should evaluate whether they measure what it is important to measure—perhaps most importantly, thinking disturbance.

One way of considering whether a method of assessment is measuring what it is supposed to measure is referred to as its *construct validity:* "The construct-related validity of a test is the extent to which the test may be said to measure a theoretical construct or trait. . . . It derives from established interrelationships among behavioral measures" (Anastasi, 1988, p. 153). It is this aggregate or combination of measures in close interrelationship that provides a kind of evidence that the instrument will measure what it is intended to measure. It may be argued that, ultimately, construct validation is not necessary because it is predictive validity (and control of the phenomena) that is the essential test of validity. But construct validity enhances the chances of predictive validity; therefore, it may be a good index of the promise and potential usefulness of an instrument for a variety of prediction and control aims. In respect to schizophrenic disorders, construct validity may be shown by the close relationship of an instrument, such as a diagnostic system or test, to various behavioral manifestations of presumably schizophrenic persons. Of course, the question of what schizophrenic behavior is must be answered to provide the necessary validity criteria. Finally, even high validity in these terms does not necessarily mean that the instrument is useful unless it can be demonstrated that it will aid in the prediction and/or control of schizophrenic phenomena.

In any event, close examination of the current major diagnostic systems has generally produced only meager evidence of their reliability, predictive validity, construct validity, specificity, and comprehensiveness. Fenton, Mosher, and Matthews (1981) reviewed six of the major systems for diagnosing schizophrenia:

Schneider's first-rank symptoms; the New Haven Schizophrenia Index; the Flexible System; the Feighner *et al.* (1972) system; the Research Diagnostic Criteria; and the DSM-III. Fenton *et al.* found that none of these systems had established construct validity, and they concluded that choosing any one of the systems over another could not be data based, i.e., supported by evidence of construct validity. In regard to the DSM-III particularly, the authors found no evidence that its criteria for schizophrenic disorder were either less arbitrary or better, in identifying a group of "true" schizophrenics, than those of any of the other systems or the DSM-II. These authors advised that elevating any one diagnostic system, including the DSM-III, to an official status is premature and that users of the DSM-III should be both open-minded and cautious.

Some of the phenomena considered most important by the original conceptualizers of what are now called the schizophrenic disorders tend to be neglected or minimized in current diagnostic systems. Eugen Bleuler (1911/1950) emphasized the greater importance in "schizophrenia" of primary over secondary symptoms. Emil Kraepelin (1919/1971) epitomized the descriptive psychiatry approach in his listing of the symptoms of "dementia praecox" and is not usually noted for psychodynamic formulations. But Kraepelin wrote of the weakening and then loss of the volitional force that binds together volition, emotion, and intellect in a coherent whole. This loss would make prediction difficult because meaningful self-directedness and clearly purposive behavior are relinquished and our ordinary rules of behavior prediction may not apply. In fact, "schizophrenic" persons have been shown to be less predictable in verbal communication than other patient groups or "normals" (Ragin & Oltmanns, 1983). Perhaps the loss of meaningfulness or purpose—a severe form of existential despair, a kind of giving up and dying emotionally without physical death—will turn out to be the central phenomenon of the schizophrenic disorders, and it may even turn out to be measurable.

What the Systems Tend to Neglect

Traditionally, and perhaps inevitably, all diagnostic approaches to schizophrenic disorders have emphasized some criteria and neglected others. Most, and until recently nearly all, interview approaches have emphasized "positive," rather than "negative," signs or symptoms, that is, clearly outward florid expressions of disorder rather than deficits or inabilities. As an analogy, it was as if a neurologist were satisfied merely to observe a patient's spontaneous behavior. If the patient complains of pain, for example, or shows an unsteady gait, the neurologist has a positive sign or symptom of disturbance. But if the same patient is passive and the neurologist does not actively test the patient to see if there is a deficit or inability, the quite possibly invalid conclusion would be that nothing is wrong with the patient. Paranoid persons are especially likely to conceal signs of their disorder, and because "Patients suffering from the paranoid type constitute the majority of cases diagnosed schizophrenic" (Arieti, 1974, p. 34), reliance on only positive symptomatology results in many false-negative diagnostic decisions:

As an undergraduate student in the 1950s, I witnessed a demonstration of the false-negative diagnostic phenomenon and one way to correct for such "errors of omission" in the interview process. A psychiatrist sat with a patient who, spontaneously, depicted his daily activities as quite mundane. The patient appeared perfectly normal until the psychiatrist said, "Tell me, John, what was your day really like?" The patient then spoke emotionally about how he had been the target of various poisoning attempts throughout the day, beginning with breakfast. This astute psychiatrist had taken into account the patient's defensive covering up, which is part of a paranoid disorder.

The false-negative diagnostic error is also often made when a nonparanoid patient is passive. Silent, withdrawn, inactive people may pass for nonschizophrenic because they are not bringing attention to themselves. This situation is like believing that children are all right if they are quiet and not causing a disturbance. It is useful in this context to make a distinction between disturbing and disturbed behavior, which is analogous to manageable versus unmanageable behavior. Although we prefer that people not disturb us, the fact that they do not disturb us is no indication that they are not disturbed. In this light, it is clear that much of what is called treatment is the reduction of disturbing behavior, that is the reduction of the disturbance experienced by people other than the patient. Likewise, patients who are disturbed but not disturbing may be neglected because they are not disturbing anyone but themselves. In both kinds of cases, the "treatment" consists only of targeting the patient's positive symptoms, such as outwardly expressed threats, delusional ideation, explosive behavior, or verbal abusiveness, while neglecting to help resolve *the patient's disturbance.* This situation is reminiscent of the old joke about the man who tells his physician, "Doc, it hurts when I lift my arm," to which the doctor replies, "Don't lift your arm." Silent symptoms and making symptoms silent sometimes seem to be the criteria for successful "treatment."

The neurologist Hughlings Jackson clarified the crucial importance of distinguishing positive from negative symptoms and regarded the negative symptoms as basic. As Carpenter, Heinricks, and Alphs (1985) summarized:

> Hughlings Jackson . . . viewed negative symptoms as direct manifestations of tissue injury or necrosis, and positive symptoms as secondary disinhibitory phenomena. He also characterized positive symptoms as distortions and exaggerations of normal function, and negative symptoms as loss of normal function or capacity. It is in this latter, more descriptive sense that current workers are defining negative symptoms. (p. 440)

The implications of omitting active forms of inquiry and testing that will elicit negative as well as positive signs and symptoms are made clear by the masses of nonfunctioning "manageable" people outside mental hospitals who live vegetative existences. Such "deinstitutionalized" people seldom show any form of improvement in functioning ability or enjoyment of life but may show fewer disturbing symptoms, though their lack of the ability to care for themselves and their nonproductivity generally mean a debilitation of society as well as of themselves. In essence, an exclusive emphasis on reducing the positive symptoms of schizophrenic disorders leads to what we might call the zombie syndrome, a condition of stupefaction rather than the development of normal functioning ability.

It should not be assumed that there is a strong correlation between positive and negative symptoms in the schizophrenic disorders and that getting rid of the positive symptoms will mean getting rid of the negative symptoms as well. Nor should it be assumed that the negative symptoms are not important. A study of positive and negative symptoms in 61 unmedicated schizophrenic male inpatients (Guelfi, Faustman, & Csernansky, 1989) showed no correlations between positive and negative symptoms either in the entire group or in subgroups defined by duration of disorder or diagnostic subtype. Medicating schizophrenic persons tends to skew treatment toward the reduction of positive symptoms, leaving the person's deficits essentially intact. These deficits, or negative symptoms, then mitigate against social recovery and functioning ability in real life.

Interviewing is not well suited to "getting at" negative symptoms. Interview methods do not readily lend themselves to rigorous forms of testing that can both elicit and make measurable the negative as well as the positive signs. A recognition of the extreme limitations of ordinary interview methods has led to the development of various forms of "structured interviews," which are meant to increase both the reliability and the validity of diagnosis.

Interview structuring makes explicit the areas of inquiry and how the information obtained is to be ordered and rated. Nevertheless, structured interviews are limited because they cannot be rigorously tested. Thus, although structured interview methods possibly represent advances in the adequacy of assessment because they standardize the areas of inquiry and the analysis of the data and thus promote reliability, they may not provide the kinds of data that are most revealing, particularly of negative symptoms. Nowhere is this limitation clearer than in the discernment of the essential diagnostic variable "thought disorder"; thought disorder means an inability to think rationally, as well as a proclivity to produce verbalizations that explicitly show thought disorganization. For example, a patient may readily express delusions (a form of positive thought disorder) or may be unable to respond coherently (a form of negative thought disorder). That is, the patient may not be having delusions but may be unable to absorb and interpret new information normally, even though the patient is not mentally retarded, brain-damaged, or under the influence of drugs. In the case of the more subtle forms of thought disorder, it is especially difficult to elicit enough data in an interview. Yet thought disorder, as has been claimed ever since Eugen Bleuler's pioneering work on schizophrenic disorders (1950), may be the single most important criterion for schizophrenic disorders because of its power to predict ability to function adaptively.

Prediction and its close cousin control are the ultimate aims of science; all other aims are, at best, contributory. Sensitive and accurate elucidation of thought disorder may be a powerful predictor even when an investigation is limited to "positive thought disorder" (Marengo & Harrow, 1987), but when active testing for "negative thought disorder" is included, the prediction of an inability to function is likely to be far more accurate.

Even "positive thought disorder" that is spontaneously expressed may be better elicited and measured by psychological testing than by interview because interviewing methods lack the evocative and rigorous characteristics of testing.

Much of the confusion about what to look for as evidence of a schizophrenic disorder is rooted in a lack of clarity about whether one should assess deviance or morbidity. As has been discussed in Chapter 2, an emphasis on deviance easily lends itself to political pressures and the inclusion of "deviants" who are not really morbid in the sense of having an impairment of ability. Deviance criteria tend to include positive symptoms more than negative symptoms and to include outwardly disturbing symptoms more than measures of the person's inability. Deviance criteria are more likely to be used when assessment is one-sided (emphasizing positive symptoms) and when it is limited to passive investigation, that is, to relying on the patient's volunteering material.

Characteristics of the Specific Systems

The work of Andreasen (1979a,b, 1982) and Andreasen and Olsen (1982) on the conceptualization of data from clinical observation and interview illuminates some traditionally neglected information and shows the extreme importance of so-called negative as well as positive symptoms, but without going so far as to turn interviewing into testing. Their work progresses toward even greater comprehensiveness and rigor than most of the structured-interview systems in widespread use. In a later section of this chapter, the DSM-III-R is examined in the light of these and other authors' awareness of what is neglected by most systems. Understanding this neglect may help us to understand why the simple diagnosis of "schizophrenia" is neither simple nor very useful.

"Positive schizophrenia" is characterized by prominent delusions, hallucinations, positive formal thought disorder, and persistently bizarre behavior; negative schizophrenia is characterized by affective flattening, alogia, avolition, anhedonia, and attentional impairment (Andreasen & Olsen, 1982, p. 789). Essentially, negative signs are the absence of affect expression, logical thought and behavior, the expression of volition, the lack of evidence that pleasure is experienced, and a lack of attentiveness. These absences tend to be more ominous signs than the florid, positive signs of a schizophrenic disorder. It is as if, in the active or florid state, the individual is still struggling with his or her problems, whereas the more negatively schizophrenic person seems to have given up. Negative symptoms tend to be primary, and positive symptoms tend to be secondary: "Clinical observation suggests that patients whose symptoms are initially negative tend to remain negative when followed longitudinally, whereas in many patients with initial positive symptoms, negative symptoms eventually develop" (Andreasen & Olsen, 1982, p. 793).

Landmark and his associates (e.g., Cernovsky *et al.*, 1985; Landmark *et al.*, 1986) have shown intercorrelations among the diagnostic systems as well as correlations of the specific systems with many social variables. Their large sample was of

Canadian patients diagnosed schizophrenic according to at least one of the systems. These researchers have produced many remarkable findings, which they have interpreted in sophisticated ways. The diagnostic systems show considerable differences in what they designate as evidence of a schizophrenic disorder; their intercorrelations are not strikingly high, though the systems were carefully and rigorously applied only after high rates of interassessor reliability were established.

The correlations among the systems ranged from .08 to .72 (Schneider compared to E. Bleuler's Four A's and M. Bleuler compared to Edwards, respectively). Because the square of a coefficient of correlation equals the variance accounted for by the correlation, not much of a core concept of schizophrenic disorders is represented by the intercorrelations among the systems. Even the .72 correlation accounts for only 52% of the variance (as .72 times .72 equals .52). Most of the intercorrelations fell into the range of .40 to .60, so most of the variances accounted for were between 16% and 36%.

The researchers in the Landmark studies pointed out that some diagnostic systems fare rather well, however, when one rates them on their combination of interrater reliability, inclusion of the broad range of schizophrenic signs and symptoms, and concordance with other systems. In this view, Langfeldt's system and the DSM-III are favored. One must, of course, bear in mind that a system may be high in these attributes without being valid, or at least without being useful for prediction and control. Accordingly, these and other researchers have been intent on discovering the relationships between the diagnostic systems and many other variables that reflect social, economic, and other forms of functioning in life.

The diagnostic systems that had the highest concordance with the whole (diagnostic agreement with the other systems) are characterized by an emphasis on hallucinations, thought disturbance, and delusions. These systems are limited primarily to what the researchers call "hard-core" items. These systems are high in both interrater reliability for a given system and intersystem reliability. In essence, users of these systems can be more sure that they and others will agree on what they are talking about. Whether what they are talking about will prove valuable is another question. Finally, in the quite careful and extensive Landmark studies, "the results clearly showed that, to make a reliable diagnosis of schizophrenia, the assessment must be done longitudinally and not solely on the basis of cross-sectional symptomatology" (Leslie *et al.*, 1984, p. 639).

Another study of reliabilities and agreement between diagnostic interview systems (Endicott, Nee, Fleiss, Cohen, Williams, & Simon, 1982) compared the diagnostic rates for schizophrenia among systems of essentially equal interrater reliabilities: the New Haven Schizophrenia Index; the Carpenter *et al.* WHO-IPSS (4-, 5-, 6-, and 7-item) system (1973); the DSM-III; the Research Diagnostic Criteria (RDC; full and chronic); the Feighner *et al.* 1972 system; and the 1975 criteria of Taylor and Abrams (1977). These systems varied as much as sevenfold in their rates of diagnosing schizophrenia. For example, given an undiagnosed pool of subjects, to be diagnosed by these systems only, the New Haven Schizophrenic Index diagnosed schizophrenia in 44 of 168 newly admitted psychiatric hospital patients, and the Taylor and

Abrams (1977) system diagnosed schizophrenia in only 6 of the 168 patients. Rates of the diagnosis of schizophrenia of the other systems were in somewhat greater agreement, but the authors' conclusion appears warranted: "The disparity illustrates the degree of difficulty associated with the diagnosis of schizophrenia, and in the concept of schizophrenia" (Endicott *et al.*, 1982, p. 888).

In addition to the problems of achieving high enough levels of interrater and intersystem reliability to make diagnostic interview systems adequate for clinical and research purposes, the problems of inadequacy—and therefore, the lack of validity—in the data obtained in a single interview are great. In regard to the cross-sectional (as distinct from longitudinal) nature of the data, Strauss and Carpenter (1981) noted that "it is now clear that the diagnosis of schizophrenia based on cross-sectional symptomatology—no matter how stringent—fails to predict outcome in the individual patient" (p. 60). And the structured psychiatric interview itself has severe limitations even within the limits of cross-sectional evaluation. Brockington and Meltzer (1982) argued that "the structured psychiatric interview, which has become the foundation of much modern clinical research, is not a sufficient method of documenting an episode of psychiatric illness" (p. 485). These authors proposed that there be more than one interview and that the interview data be supplemented by a high standard of recorded observations, by all staff in contact with the patient, throughout the period of hospitalization. Their proposal takes into account that patients change over time and often do not themselves give a clear or comprehensive account of their "episode of illness." One may conclude that structured psychiatric interviews are far from adequate by themselves.

The studies just cited represent more careful and rigorous approaches to assessment than the typically hasty and imprecise approach that characterizes much, if not most, diagnostic practice. Yet, one can see that it is extremely difficult to reach a consensus in terms of intersystem reliability, much less a demonstrably valid diagnosis, even when the question is merely whether or not an individual is schizophrenic. We must remember that what appears to be a dilemma for the scientist who wants to establish a nomothetic category called *schizophrenia* may not be a great dilemma for the idiographic clinician, who may be of great help in making assessment statements that have important predictive and therapeutic value for the individuals assessed. In other words, the accurate and sensitive assessment of individual differences may be essential if we are to get beyond the apparent severe limitations of the concept of a relatively homogeneous disease entity; the mere lumping of people together in a single disease called schizophrenia has little empirical support after all, in terms of prediction or control of the phenomena. In fact, there is little agreement among systems even about the phenomena and their specification.

The DSM-III criteria for schizophrenic disorder, as Andreasen and Olsen (1982) noted, "may give an excessive prominence to positive symptoms, considering that negative symptoms may be more important as prognostic indicators" (p. 794). Furthermore, because DSM-III eliminates cases of less than six months' duration from the diagnosis of schizophrenic disorder, on the one hand, and tends to eliminate chronic cases characterized mostly by negative symptomatology, the two ends of the chronological spectrum of the disorder are apt to be missing. In this light, it is not surprising that the diagnosis has little or no validity in its prediction of the course or outcome of the disorder. It is rather like trying to predict the route of a car when one's data are restricted to the middle of the journey. Paying more attention to where the car (or the case) started, where it went next, where it will end up, and how fast it will get there would greatly increase one's predictive power. And because prediction and control are the goals of science, a truly longitudinal study of the phenomena of schizophrenic disorders is essential to the validity of any diagnostic system.

In trying to explain the seeming arbitrariness of the DSM-III, one wonders if attention to the prevailing mode of treatment of the schizophrenic disorders and the prevailing mode of treatment of the manic-depressive disorders have not overridden the basic tenets of diagnosis. That is, if one is already "sold" on phenothiazine treatment and lithium treatment, the tendency is to apply the label *schizophrenic* to those whose (positive) symptoms are reduced by phenothiazines, and to call *manic-depressive* those whose mania (also a positive symptom) is reduced by lithium. Thus, to a great extent, the diagnoses are determined by the availability and popularity (with prescribers) of certain treatment substances.

This approach to diagnosis makes diagnosis secondary to somatic treatment response, when both *treatment* and *response* are narrowly defined. The DSM-III-R (1987) specifically encourages making a diagnosis of schizophrenic disorder "that has validity in terms of differential response to somatic therapy" (p. 187). This approach fails to ground diagnosis in criteria that are truly independent of either diagnosis or treatment. This approach also postulates, or even claims outright, specific etiologies, implying that manic-depressive disorder is a lithium deficiency and that schizophrenic disorder is a phenothiazine deficiency; the latter etiology is based on the theory that schizophrenic persons suffer from excessive dopamine reception in the brain and that phenothiazines help patients by reducing dopamine reception. Dopamine reception may be reduced, but neither the need for its reduction nor the supposed benefits have been proved, whereas the harmful effects are becoming well documented (to be discussed further in Chapter 10).

For the assessment of the schizophrenic disorders, we need more than a definition based solely on the effects of the so-called antipsychotic drugs. As Carpenter *et al.* (1985) noted:

> It is the longstanding practice of reporting treatment effects in terms of either ill-defined global measures or narrowly defined positive symptoms that has left the field poorly informed concerning the long-term effect of anti-psychotic drugs on core aspects of schizophrenia. (p. 440)

The Use of the DSM-III in Common Practice

Clearly there are major problems and limitations in the use of structured interviews and the diagnostic systems on which they are based, even when they are assiduously studied and practiced. For purposes of research, their use must be carefully structured and practiced if it is to achieve sufficient reliability to serve any purpose at all. But what about common diagnostic practice? Do clinicians profess to use these systems, and if they do, do they know the diagnostic criteria well enough to apply them?

The DSM-III (and its close cousin the DSM-III-R) has become the most widely publicized and, presumably, the most widely used diagnostic system, particularly in the United States, where it originated. Shortly after the introduction of the DSM-III in 1980, Lipkowitz and Idupuganti (1983) surveyed U.S. psychiatrists to find out their diagnostic orientation to schizophrenia; they discovered that the DSM-III criteria were not being used to any great extent. On repeating their survey in 1982, Lipkowitz and Idupuganti (1985) found that, although psychiatrists had had a couple of years to learn and use the system, the DSM-III still had no major influence on their approach to diagnosing schizophrenia.

During a five-month period in 1983 and 1984, Jampala, Sierles, and Taylor (1988) surveyed a random sample of 1,000 U.S. psychiatrists and all of the graduating psychiatric residents regarding their use of signs and symptoms to diagnose major depression, mania, and schizophrenia. These surveyors achieved remarkably high response rates for this type of study (56.2% of the psychiatrists). Their results suggest very strongly that, more than three years after the introduction of the DSM-III, even fourth-postgraduate-year graduating psychiatric residents, whose entire psychiatric training occurred after 1980, had little applicable knowledge of the system. Psychiatric residents graduating in 1984 were not significantly more conversant with the DSM-III than were the already qualified practicing psychiatrists. The respondents to this survey generally lacked diagnostic knowledge in respect to all three disorders: major depression, mania, and schizophrenia. In regard to schizophrenia, the authors noted:

> For the diagnosis of schizophrenia, DSM-III requires that six criteria be satisfied: (A) presence of symptoms of active psychosis, (B) deterioration in function, (C) duration of illness more than six months, (D) absence of major affective disorder, (E) age of onset before 45, and (F) absence of organic mental disorder. . . . No psychiatrist correctly listed at least five of the six criteria necessary, and about one fourth of the psychiatrists did not report using any of the criteria acceptable by DSM-III standards. . . . The subsamples of respondents favorable to DSM-III were not meaningfully different from their parent samples. (pp. 42–43)

In addition to now knowing the DSM-III system, the respondents were generally unaware of their ignorance. Of the residents who claimed that at least 75% of their patients receiving DSM-III diagnoses satisfied all the necessary criteria, none listed all the DSM-III criteria necessary to diagnose mania, major depression, or schizophrenia. One would expect that these respondents, who also reported being trained in the use of the DSM-III and reported using it extensively, at least knew, and were therefore able to report, the DSM-III criteria for the diagnosis of these major disorders. In fact, these respondents were no different from their peers in their requirements for the diagnosis of these three syndromes (Jampala *et al.*, pp. 44–45).

In conclusion, common psychiatric diagnostic practice continues to be grossly deficient in two major respects apart from the question of the adequacy of the available diagnostic methods themselves. The majority of practicing psychiatrists in the United States apparently profess to know, and apparently think they correctly practice, their official American Psychiatric Association DSM-III diagnostic system. But they do not know the system and are not really applying it despite their belief that they are. One would suppose that there are psychiatrists who know and practice the system correctly, but they evidently constitute a minority.

In the light of evidence of the unreliability and the lack of awareness of their diagnostic reliability in common psychiatric practice, pronouncements like the following by Paul Fink, President-Elect of the American Psychiatric Association, in the *American Medical News* of February 12, 1988, are interesting: [Psychologists and other nonpsychiatrists] "don't have the training to make the initial evaluation and diagnosis [and] are not trained to understand the nuances of the mind. . . . Doctors should refer to doctors" (as cited in Mindell, 1988, p. 17). This claim contains four doubtful premises: (1) that psychiatrists as a group are well trained in evaluation and diagnosis; (2) that they use this training effectively; (3) that they are aware of their use or nonuse of their training; and (4) that nonpsychiatrist mental health professionals are less well trained and effective. The first three assumptions are clearly disputable in light of the available evidence. The fourth assumption is certainly open to conjecture, but barring a legal monopoly, the weaknesses of psychiatric training and its application invite competition in the free market.

The DSM-IV in Progress

Work on the DSM-IV is in progress at the time of this writing:

> The DSM-IV work group evaluating schizophrenia and related psychotic disorders has been trying to achieve the optimal balance between three somewhat conflicting goals. The first is to refine the reliability and validity of the diagnostic categories. The second is to make DSM-IV as compatible as possible with the tenth edition of the *International Classification of Diseases* (ICD-10), both of which are scheduled for publication in 1993. The third and perhaps the most important goal is to achieve those two goals in a manner that maintains as much continuity as possible with existing diagnostic criteria, to minimize the reclassification of patients. (Andreason & Flaum, 1990, p. 954)

Hopefully, as chair of the work group and as someone who has emphasized the importance of negative symptoms, Andreason will be able to change the system enough to develop more validity by bringing this emphasis into the DSM-IV:

> A literature review supported the validity of negative symptoms as a central construct of schizophrenia. Negative symptoms were deemphasized in DSM-III and DSM-III-R because they were considered potentially unreliable, but they will be given more prominence in ICD-10. (Andreason & Flaum, 1990, p. 954)

Supporting this intent is the fact that the base rate (frequency of occurrence) of negative symptoms was found by those authors to be extremely high in samples of schizophrenic patients, whereas the base rate of Schneiderian first-rank symptoms, which were given considerable prominence in the DSM-III-R and the ICD-9, were relatively low.

A further major change is needed in the diagnosis of schizoaffective disorder: "How to conceptualize and describe the boundary between schizophrenia and mood disorders has been a matter of controversy for many years. Schizoaffective disorder is the much traveled border-zone between these two conditions" (Andreason & Flaum, 1990, p. 955). As of this writing, it is too early to tell whether the drug-treatment-era opposition to allowing schizoaffective disorder full legitimacy will be overcome.

Summary

During the 1970s, certain considerations, including the diagnostic unreliability of the DSM-II system, the discrepancies among diagnostic systems internationally, and the increasing emphasis on drug treatment, combined to warrant the development of the DSM-III and structured-interview systems. Compared to the DSM-II, both the DSM-III and the DSM-III-R define schizophrenic disorders more narrowly, in keeping with most European definitions, and as being much more dependent on the response to somatic treatment. But studies of the major systems, including the new DSMs, have not shown high reliability, predictive validity, specificity, or comprehensiveness. Both the interviewing and the diagnostic systems have especially neglected negative symptoms, as do the somatic treatments. Hopefully, the DSM-IV, which is scheduled for publication in 1993, will place much more emphasis on negative symptoms, as well as give better definition and legitimacy to schizoaffective disorders, and will thereby prove more valid than its predecessors.

Several problems have combined to produce less than efficacious assessment results from interview techniques. These problems are the inadequate definitions of disorder; the basically unstandardized nature of interviewing techniques, despite attempts at structure; perhaps the cross-sectional nature of the interview method itself; and the absence in actual, ordinary practice of a knowledge of the definitional criteria. Any one of these problems might be crucial; en masse they are certainly crucial. Not even a single episode of "psychiatric illness" is adequately documented by interview methods, although some interviewers are quite skilled. Comparing the results of even skillful interviewers has not contributed adequate nomothetic knowledge.

7

Psychological Tests

Basic Considerations

The Nature of Test Validity

Establishing the validity of a psychological test is a complex task, especially when the available validity criteria are themselves questionable. As Meehl (1977) stated, "Construct validity must be investigated whenever no criterion or universe of content is accepted as entirely adequate to define the quality to be measured" (p. 5). Because the psychiatric diagnosis of schizophrenic disorders is seriously flawed in and of itself, it is not fully acceptable by itself for developing test validity, though it may have an important guiding function, particularly in the early development of a test or technique.

Construct validity may embrace content relevance and coverage and criterion-related concurrent and predictive measures. It is not limited to a single measure or criterion: "On the contrary, construct-related validity is a comprehensive concept which includes the other types" (Anastasi, 1988, p. 163). Accordingly, "Even when a test is constructed on the basis of a specific criterion, it may ultimately be judged to have greater construct validity than the criterion" (Meehl, 1977, p. 11). Sometimes, this possibility is overlooked when a test is evaluated, especially when great weight has been attached to measuring it against a particular criterion that carries considerable, though perhaps misguided, authority, as has often been the case with psychiatric diagnosis.

In this light, some test measures may be more meaningful in the prediction and amelioration of severe mental disorders than the psychiatric diagnostic label. For example, test evidence of thought disorder may turn out to be a better predictor of the ability to live adaptively outside a hospital than the person's diagnosis. Therefore, a single-minded devotion to making a test measure correlate with a psychiatric diagnosis not only has a severely limited benefit in itself but may distract attention from more meaningful efforts at test validation. Thus, in accord with the argument advanced by Messick (1980), the validity of a test (its interpretive meaningfulness) should be stated in terms of its construct validity rather than simply in terms of a given criterion.

Kinds of Psychological Tests

The psychological measurement instruments most useful for assessing schizophrenic disorders fall into two general categories; projective techniques and standardized tests. The differences between these categories have lessened in recent years, but they are still significant.

Tests in the sense of highly standardized instruments include the Wechsler Adult Intelligence Scale (WAIS) and the Minnesota Multiphasic Personality Inventory (MMPI). Such tests have, on the whole, more rigidly set methods of administration, scoring, and interpretation than projective techniques. The interpretation of results follows definite guidelines based on the results obtained in large standardization samples of subjects whose answers have been correlated with other behavioral variables. By contrast, projective techniques are not so rigidly formalized. The Rorschach, the Holtzman Inkblot Technique (HIT), and the Thematic Apperception Test (TAT) do provide standard stimulus materials and, in some systems at least, even considerable standardization of administration and scoring, but projective technique instructions present the subject with an ambiguous task and considerable latitude in both the degree and the variety of responses, which may make the interpretation of the responses more difficult.

To conceptualize the spectrum of the clinical assessment methods used to delineate people psychologically, envision various degrees of latitude of instructional cues and allowable responses. At one extreme, the examiner may ask for a certain and specific "correct answer" (e.g., "How much is 4 times 6?" "What is your age?" or "Define the word *table*"). At the other extreme, the examiner may point to a cloud or an inkblot and ask, "What might that be?" This rather vague and ambiguous cue does not limit the subject to a concrete or literal response ("A cloud" or "An inkblot"); it encourages the subject to take into account the objective properties of the perceptual stimulus, on the one hand, and also to use his or her imagination and mental associations with real objects. In essence, projective techniques, in contrast to strictly focusing psychological "tests," encourage individually expressive answers that will manifest the broad dimensions of human personality.

In order to capture the spirit of these two types of psychological assessment, one might consider two kinds of detectives. Let us have Columbo, the television detective played by Peter Falk, represent the projective techniques. He was not content with merely asking straightforward questions. He might seem to be unconcerned about gathering more evidence, but on his way out the door, he would turn around and say casually, "By the way, I was just wondering, do you suppose that something else was going on that night?" Columbo's subject would be encouraged to respond speculatively to this vague question. In contrast, Joe Friday, the television detective played by Jack Webb on "Dragnet," was famous for his strict focus on objective information.

His informant would be giving her impressions and reflections, and he would say, "Just the facts, ma'am!"

On the Rorschach or Holtzman, depending on the individual subject, the same inkblot may be a bat, a bear, a butterfly, or the Empire State Building; none of these answers is "correct" or "incorrect." As the examiner says in giving instructions, "There are no right or wrong answers." The variety of answers among individuals is an expression of individual differences across the very broad spectrum of styles of thinking and emotional expression, as well as perceiving. In short, projectives such as the Rorschach inkblot technique are designed to encourage the full expression of personality rather than just certain narrowly delimited abilities or aptitudes. But certain kinds of responses, particularly uncommon answers that are difficult to justify on the basis of the perceptual characteristics of the stimulus, may be classified as "deviant" or "pathognomonic" of some disorder, especially schizophrenic disorder and especially if the subject is shown to be unaware that his or her responses are not justifiable on the basis of the inkblot's objective perceptual characteristics.

To use projective techniques to assess an individual is to encourage a full expression of individual personality and then to categorize the responses in accord with a particular system of interpretation. Each of the systems takes into account the kinds of responses that other people give as well as how the individual shows an awareness of and justifies the bases for his or her responses. The scoring and interpretation of responses include ratings on many personality dimensions. Responses suggestive of schizophrenic disorder, such as responses implying thought disorder and other failures of "reality testing," are inferred from certain response criteria if the individual is a cooperative subject who is fairly freely expressive.

Encouraging a full expression of the subject's personality, and therefore the full panoply of individual differences among persons, is simultaneously the advantage and the disadvantage of projective techniques. Although many "rich" response data may be evoked, the data are difficult to interpret because of their very richness. The initial promise of projective techniques was that they would be the "X-ray of the psyche" (Gilbert, 1969, p. 9) and another "royal road to the unconscious" like Sigmund Freud's interpretation of dreams. But their interpretation has proved difficult in several respects. Varying methods of administration and scoring, and variable numbers and detail of responses, mean considerable difficulty from a psychometric or test-measurement point of view. In short, too many variables are left uncontrolled for projective techniques to qualify as "tests" in the strictly traditional sense.

To put the matter somewhat facetiously, it is as if the subject—after being asked "What might this be?"—confronts the examiner with data so difficult to interpret that the examiner is being asked the same question: "What might this be?" Just as the subject is told that there are no correct answers, so the examiner finds it extremely difficult to come up with correct interpretations. It is as if both the subject and the examiner have all too much freedom to express their personalities in terms of the subject's interpretations of the stimuli on the one hand, and the examiner's interpretations of the responses on the other hand. How much is the interpretive report an expression of the examiner's personality rather than the subject's personality?

Vicissitudes in the Development of Projective Techniques

The wide-open use of projective techniques, beginning with the inception of the Rorschach in the 1920s, became more and more restricted by the 1960s. The enthusiasm and widespread use that peaked in the 1940s and 1950s subsided dramatically, and there was a tendency to abandon projectives altogether because they were too "unscientific." But during the 1980s and early 1990s, the projective techniques—the Rorschach, in particular—have been holding their own and tending to gain in use in some quarters, as they have been made more psychometrically sophisticated, that is, more like tests in terms of standardization.

Defenders of projective techniques assert, with some justification, that although the techniques often, if not uniformly, reveal much useful information about the individual, this information has not been used to the best advantage. They say that simple attempts to correlate projective technique data with certain behaviors have failed for lack of theoretical sophistication (Blatt, 1975; Karon, 1978). Greater sophistication in conceptualizing the data would result in greater predictive validity. There is evidence to support this point of view. For example, Kenneth Purcell (1965) demonstrated as early as 1957 that he could predict antisocial behavior using the Thematic Apperception Test. The TAT presents ambiguous pictures to the subject, who is asked to tell a story for each picture. Instead of merely noting aggressive content in TAT stories by itself, Purcell also took into account response content expressing inhibitory themes. The same aggressive story content that means behavioral aggression in one case may be associated with inhibitory controls in another. No actual behavioral aggression is indicated in the latter case even though just as much internal aggressive drive is evidenced. Purcell concluded that, to achieve "behavioral prediction from projective material, the same attention must be given to repressive, inhibitory forces manifested in the data as is given to the impulse or drive system" (p. 559).

If projective techniques are as revealing of the human psyche or personality as X-rays are revealing of human bodies, it must be added that the interpreter of projective technique responses also seems to need as much training and specialized expertise as the X-ray specialist. Many projective-technique interpreters have relied as much on their own experiences with the technique—their own personal sets of "internalized norms," the results of hundreds or perhaps even thousands of sets of response data and what they corresponded to, all stored somewhere in the memory bank of the interpreter—as they rely on published research data. As Howes (1981) put it, "many clinicians consider projective tests as more valuable than might be suggested by the equivocal reliability and validity studies, probably because many clinicians accord their personal clinical experience with these tests greater weight than the experimental evidence" (p. 347).

In addition to needing clinical experience and sophisticated psychological theory that takes into account psychological coping methods (as in the theories of psychoanalytic ego psychology, for example), the projective technique interpreter needs awareness of the often severe limitations of psychiatric diagnosis and classification. Attempts to match interpretations of the results of projective technique data with psychiatric diagnosis, including "schizophrenia," have generally been disappointing. However, as we have seen, neither the reliability nor the validity of psychiatric diagnosis is impressive, so that we should not expect high correlations, even if projective techniques yield valid depictions of human personality. In this sense, approaches like Purcell's (1965) to predicting actual behavior have been far more compelling scientifically than attempts to match projective data with psychiatric diagnosis. The blind acceptance of psychiatric diagnoses as criteria for evaluating the validity and usefulness of projective and other psychological assessment instruments has been as misleading as it is pervasive.

In this chapter, two of the projective techniques most often used to assess people for schizophrenic disorders—the Rorschach and Holtzman inkblot techniques—are discussed. A special effort is made to resist having the labels of ordinary psychiatric diagnosis distract from basic concerns about their validity by judging the validity of a technique or test solely and uncritically in terms of its correlations with one or another method of psychiatric diagnosis.

Rorschach Inkblot Technique

Origins

Hermann Rorschach, the son of a teacher of drawing, became a psychiatrist at a time when Sigmund Freud and psychoanalysis were trying to develop an all-encompassing understanding of human personality. During this period, extending from just after the turn of the century through Rorschach's untimely death in 1922, psychoanalytically oriented theorists saw the expression of deeply meaningful human drives and defenses in everything people did. Dreams were considered by Freud to be the "royal road" to the unconscious. Similarly, art and people's responses to art were seen as especially meaningful expressions of unconscious and preconscious drives, conflicts, and defenses. Art reflected the personally meaningful imposition of a person's wishes, fears, conflicts, and defenses in relation to the stage props, as it were, of the objective world. It was what the person did with these props, when given the latitude to be creative, that distinguished that person from others while also showing the "type" of person she or he was.

Rorschach, the first inventor of a systematic projective technique, made his props for the imagination by mounting symmetrical inkblot formations on cards, 10 in all, some achromatic (black and white and shades in between), and some chromatic. Subjects were instructed to engage in a self-chosen degree of apperception, a combination of perceiving, in the objective sense of recognizing objects, and of interpretation. This mixing of the perceptual and the interpretive modes provided a response set somewhere between daydreaming and the perceptual recognition of real objects in the real world. Rorschach thus devised a kind of waking-dream process in which the props were constant over subjects and the subject's set or orientation was to some degree apperceptive, a mix of subjectivity and objectivity. By standardizing the stimuli for all subjects for this waking-dream task he gave it one of the essential attributes of a test.

Standardization versus Apperception

Further standardization of the Rorschach into a test has proved enormously difficult. The test requisites for standardization of scoring and interpretation were not agreed on except within certain "schools" of practitioners. Perhaps it was the nature of the method itself that defied efforts to make it fully "scientific" in the sense of being standardized. After all, the method starts with an art form, in this case symmetrically formed inkblots, which, by definition, have no exact resemblance to anything existing objectively in the real world. Therefore, as even the instructions to the "test" say, "There are no right or wrong answers." The only objectively correct answer is "It's only an inkblot," as a modern leader in Rorschach technique noted (Exner, 1980). Exner wittingly noted the objective truth in a subject's protest at being required to distort objective reality when the subject says, "But it's only an inkblot."

Because all Rorschach examiners require the subject to distort objective reality with such instructions as "What might this be?" or "What does this look like?," they usually preface this demand for apperception with a sober acknowledgment: "I am going to show you a series of cards; each card has an inkblot on it." In any case, "When the subject is forced to convert the ambiguity of the blot into something else, that is to violate reality, an intriguing complex of psychological activity is stimulated" (Exner, 1980, p. 566). Actually, it is not the inkblot that is ambiguous; it is the examiner's instruction that is ambiguous because it asks, in effect, that the subject "violate" objective reality by mixing a strictly objective perceptual orientation with a subjective impression.

Some examiners further acknowledge the objective reality of the inkblots by telling the subject how the Rorschach cards were made (e.g., "Ink was dropped onto a piece of paper; then the paper was folded in half". By this time, the subject is expected to have grasped the fact that cooperation means making more of this objective reality than (literally) meets the eye, though Rorschach himself (1921/1951) insisted that the task was not imaginative. However, even the most common responses require some imagination. For example, a common response to Card I is "a bat," though all that this response means is that the form of this inkblot and its black coloring may remind many people of the visual characteristics of a bat with outstretched wings. Thus, the Rorschach is largely a technique used to gauge a person's wittingness and awareness in combining perception, in the strict sense of recognizing the actual identity of the stimulus, with subjective associations, so as to admix one's recognition orientation and subjective impressions in the assigned task of apperception.

The Rorschach's apperceptive nature and the subject's great latitude for responding subjectively lend themselves to great variation in numbers and kinds of responses, as well as in orientations to the task in terms of style. These characteristics may make the Rorschach an ideal technique for assessing how the subject characteristically goes about integrating his or her personal needs and conflicts with the demands of external, objective reality; these characteristics also make it difficult to standardize the technique.

The Rorschach as a Reality-Testing Process

Rorschach himself regarded his technique as revealing an important aspect of personality: the degree to which the subject takes a perceptual-identification (recognition-of-objects) orientation or an interpretive orientation. To assess the subject's "reality-testing" ability, following the phase of initial administration, the examiner tries to clarify, during the inquiry phase of testing, how witting the subject is when given time for reflection about his or her responses. At one extreme, is the subject convinced that the task is merely to recognize and identify the Rorschach "pictures"? If so, the subject has failed to recognize that he or she has actually interpreted the stimulus, because the Rorschach card really just shows an inkblot. At the other extreme, is the subject not even bothering or able to engage in an objectively perceptual mode, but responding without consideration of any perceptual likeness between the response and the visual characteristics of the inkblot?

The first extreme is exemplified by the subject who claims, with great confidence, that Card I is a picture of a bat or even that what the examiner presents as an inkblot is actually a bat. For example, a subject whom I tested declared that one of the Rorschach cards actually had a mountain on it; the subject could not be convinced that he was wrong—that the card just had a two-dimensional inkblot on it—until he turned the card sideways and saw, to his great surprise, that the card was indeed flat. Such an inability to "take distance" from one's own ideas and responses, and thereby to recognize the difference between one's fantasies and reality, is called *loss of distance.* Loss of distance is also illustrated in the old joke about projective testing: "Doctor, why are you showing me these dirty pictures?"

The second type of extreme is called *increase of distance.* The subject seems to go off into a world of fantasy and fails to match the form of the inkblot with the form of the object indicated in his or her response. An extreme example is "Empire State Building" as a response to the whole of Card I, which doesn't look at all like the Empire State Building. In these cases, the stimulus seems to make little difference in what the subject says. The responses cannot be "justified" by the stimulus characteristics of the inkblot. Poor form responses have traditionally been regarded as possible signs of schizophrenic disorders, especially when they occur often in the total response record.

Both a marked decrease and a marked increase of distance are regarded as failures in reality-testing ability, especially when the subject displays no awareness of the unrealistic nature of the response; either while initially giving a response or later when asked to reflect on the response during the inquiry phase of testing. The rationale underlying the distance–closeness concept of reality testing is the premise that effective reality testing brings together external representations of reality and the individual's internal reality of wishes, fears, and conflicts in such a way as to show awareness and control of the respective influences of these two aspects of reality. In this sense, reality testing is neither merely a perceptual identification task nor merely an expression of internal reality; it requires being aware of and judging the roles played in one's interpretations by both external, "objective" reality, on the one hand, and one's internal, "subjective" reality, on the other.

The Rorschach assessment of reality testing requires at least the following four steps: obtaining the initial responses; inquiring about the initial responses (the inquiry phase); scoring the subject's responses, taking into account both the initial and inquiry responses; and determining from the total response record and scores the extent and the nature of the individual's reality-testing ability. If the examiner fails to do a careful and thorough inquiry, it may be quite difficult or even impossible to assess the subject's reality-testing ability; yet this is a common examiner error. Trying to determine the significance of Rorschach responses without obtaining the subject's thoughts on or associations with the responses is like trying to determine the meaning of a dream without obtaining the dreamer's own associations to the dream.

Returning now to the standardization problem, one can grasp the strengths and weaknesses of the "test" and how it can, but may not, provide a valid measure of the individual's reality-testing ability. It does not directly test the individual's sense of objective reality, as no objects are presented, save cards with inkblots on them, and the examiner has already deprived the subject of the response "It's an inkblot." The individual does have an alternative, however. He or she can say nothing, in which case the examiner has nothing to score or interpret. Nonresponsiveness is a major source of difficulty in standardization and in establishing reliability and validity. A test is not a test if it evokes no responses, unless of course one can prove that nonresponses can be given a reliable and valid interpretation. But nonresponses are exceedingly difficult to interpret within the assumptions of the technique. Using his own methods of administration, scoring, and interpretation, and referring to a very large data base, Exner (1987) stated, "The data indicate that 3 of every four records of less than 14 answers are probably not valid" (p. 6).

Similarly, subjects who declare that they see merely inkblots are not providing revealing responses. The person who does not agree to mix objective with subjective reality, in accord with the directions, is not playing by the rules of the game. Assessing the Rorschach nonresponder is like assessing a person's ability to play basketball when he or she refuses to participate except perhaps to acknowledge the presence of a basketball.

While nonresponsiveness and even low responsiveness are critical and common problems, especially with possibly schizophrenic subjects, their close relative—variable responsiveness—is also a major psychometric dilemma, because it limits the standardization of scoring and interpretation. For example, in summarizing Rorschach scores, how should one weigh the relative importance of the percentage of certain types of responses versus their absolute number?

Nonresponsiveness, low responsiveness, and variable responsiveness, as well as the great latitude given to the subject not to respond or to respond in any way he or she chooses, are all indicative of the psychometric dilemma of the Rorschach technique. The freedom from objective-reality limitations accorded to the subject, and actually required of the subject, means a waiving of some of the constraints that serve to make a technique a test. Like dreams, Rorschach responses tend to be richly expressive of human personality, but both dreams and Rorschach responses are difficult to harness in the scientific test mode. The interpretation of the Rorschach, one suspects, must involve the talents and skills of the artist as well as the scientist, just as Rorschach himself was both an artist and a scientist.

Perhaps it has been the acceptance of the flexibility provided by the artistic viewpoint that has delayed attempts at Rorschach standardization even in terms of scoring. Though scoring may be operationally defined within a given system, Rorschach research has lacked the rigor usually associated with science. For example, contributors to Rorschach research literature in the *Journal of Personality Assessment* did not have to meet the usual scientific requirement of demonstrated scoring reliability until Weiner (1991), as editor, required it.

Regard for the Rorschach

Early expectations that the Rorschach would be an X ray of the mind, readily interpretable by a trained technician and readily validated against behavioral criteria, have been difficult to realize. There has been a kind of radical splitting of professionals into camps, rather like the camps of those who adhere to psychoanalytic tenets and those who vehemently reject them, or of those who promulgate the concept of "schizophrenia" and those who totally refute the existence of any such "disease" or even any such disorder.

Critical reviews of the Rorschach research literature over the past several decades have done little to strengthen belief in the Rorschach technique from a scientific standpoint. Two considerations, however, have kept the Rorschach in serious contention as a sophisticated leader in the assessment of schizophrenic disorders. First, by its very nature, the technique is a method for assessing reality-testing ability, particularly the ability to think logically and rationally in the face of challenges to demonstrate awareness and control of both aspects of reality: inner and outer. Thus, it is a measure of the person's ability to relate his or her own emotionally directed fantasy life to the objective world. The instructions challenge the person to venture beyond the obvious ("It's only an inkblot") into a fanciful series of responses, and then to justify these responses during the inquiry phase of assessment. The examiner inquires "What makes the inkblot look like" the object that the person has named. In citing the form of the inkblot and/or the color and/or the shading and other visual characteristics of the inkblot, the person shows the degree of his or her ability to match the response with the objective characteristics of the visual stimuli, and to make a judgment about the match. Perhaps the person says, "It just reminded me somehow of . . . " and realizes there is no objective justification. Or there may be little or no awareness that the response does not fit, which indicates that the individual's reality-testing ability, and therefore the individual's ability to behave adaptively in the world, may be impaired.

The second consideration that keeps the Rorschach alive in clinical assessment is the great advance in the empirical study of how responses and the scores attached to them correspond to certain kinds of diagnostic signs and symptoms and also entire diagnostic categories, most notably the schizophrenic disorders.

Theoretical constructions that linked the Rorschach with reality-testing ability outstripped empirical validation at first. David Rapaport constructed an enormously erudite and creative synthesis of psychoanalytic theory, as it is related to reality testing in general and the "psychopathology" of thinking in particular. This synthesis is elaborated especially in Volume 2 of *Diagnostic Psychological Testing* (Rapaport *et al.*, 1946), and in *The Organization and Pathology of Thought* (Rapaport, 1951b). The extensive footnotes alone in the second book reflect profound theoretical insights. Rapaport focused especially on the function of thinking in reality testing, recognizing that thinking, the most complex and difficult of mental functions is therefore also the function most sensitive to, and most readily disrupted in mental disorders generally and the schizophrenic disorders particularly.

Rapaport *et al.* (1946) asserted that "the effects of maladjustment on the intellection can be discovered earlier in concept formation than in any other aspect of thought process" (p. 148). Thus, emphasis was placed on the active aspect of thinking, rather than on perception, memory, or simply the products of past learning; that is, the process of concept formation was considered the most important. This process has to be inferred rather than observed directly, as we cannot see into a person's mind or brain and actually observe the process itself. Insofar as the Rorschach technique can elicit a sample of the subject's ability to form concepts, it provides evidence from which the concept formation process can be inferred.

Provided that the subject does produce responses to the Rorschach and these responses are interpretable in terms of the processes of concept formation, what is there about the Rorschach exactly that will enable an assessment of reality-testing ability? Part of the answer to this question has already been given: The task provides a measure of the subject's ability to achieve perspective by being aware of and in control of her or his distance from a stimulus that is presented externally (i.e., the inkblot). Achieving this task requires awareness on the part of the subject of the external world, his or her internal reality, and the roles that both play in his or her conceptualization process and its outcome. In other words, the subject must take into account contributions both from the inkblot and from internal sources in order to respond appropriately, neither merely in the mode of objective perceptual identification ("It is a bat!") nor merely in the mode of blocking out the objective reality of the stimulus ("Empire State Building"). Then, during the inquiry, the subject must justify the response by referring to the visual attributes of the inkblot or must recognize the degree to which the response cannot be justified. In essence, what is being tested is the subject's awareness of both inner and outer reality, his or her integration of the two, and his or her ability to be free of domination by either one alone.

Robert Martin (1968) interpreted Rapaport's further consideration of reality-testing ability (Rapaport, 1951a, 1958) in terms of the "stimulus barrier" that the person uses to avoid a kind of enslavement to either internal or external reality and to achieve relative autonomy from both:

> Rapaport considered the ego as able to achieve some measure of autonomy from both external and internal stimulation. Such autonomy was always relative since the ego was never completely insulated from either source of stimulation. Paradoxically, the autonomy that is achieved depends on the ego's ties to the two major sources of stimulation. Its autonomy from drive forces derives from the apparatuses that are responsive to the external environment and its autonomy from the environment comes from the ego's responsiveness to drive forces. (p. 486)

Although the ability of creative geniuses to develop something new and different has often been likened to the bizarre productions of some schizophrenic people, creative geniuses are able, unlike schizophrenic persons in the throes of psychosis, to excel in reality testing. Intense, accurate awareness of both external reality and internal reality and the relationship between the two is the basis of creations that ingeniously relate the two. Commenting on this kind of genius, John Malcolm Brinnin (1982) wrote about the young Truman Capote's first novel:

> With no preface to cue me in, I grasped only that a character named Joel was being put through a small series of misadventures meant to test his courage and sense of reality. The story didn't matter. What did was the quality of a prose that mixed hard observations with extravagance, without ever losing a grip on either. (p. 4)

In contrast, the schizophrenic process is characterized by a failure to grasp reality or, more accurately, to be sufficiently aware of, and independent enough of, both external and internal reality to integrate them. As Martin (1968) noted, inattention to either internal or external reality lessens one's ability to place the attended to "reality" in perspective. According to this theory, in order to have good reality testing, one must be able to grasp *both* external and internal reality as a prerequisite to being able to relate the two to each other, to be independent of either alone, and to achieve perspective by means of stationing oneself psychologically at vantage points between the two and perceiving each from a certain distance. As I conceive of reality testing ability, it is the ability to be aware of both external reality and internal reality and the differences between the two by going back and forth between them, *contrasting* one with the other and thereby gaining a perspective on and an understanding of each. This process requires active thinking.

Pathognomonic and Deviant Verbalization

Theoretical considerations and clinical observations of the language usage associated with schizophrenic disorders suggest certain kinds of failure in the thinking processes of schizophrenic persons. Eugen Bleuler (1911/1950), who coined the term *schizophrenia,* noted the characteristic illogicality and bizarreness in the thinking processes of schizophrenic persons, which he believed distinguished them from brain-damaged persons. Bleuler called this characteristic "dereistic thinking" to indicate a disregard of reality. Further clinical observation led to attempts to label the various kinds of language usage that reflected such "thinking." These kinds of language usage became, collectively, signs of "thought disorder," a primary indicator of schizophrenic disorder according to Bleuler and a long succession of psychiatrists who predominated until the 1950s. By this time, Rapaport and many other Rorschach theorists had devised ways of scoring Rorschach responses for signs of thought disorder. The Rorschach became an important part of diagnostic assessment at the most advanced psychiatric centers. For example, the prominent American psychiatrist Robert Knight (1952), who headed the Austin Riggs Center in Massachusetts, stated:

> In the early stages of such a [psychotic] process clinical observation may not be sufficient to detect the presence of the thought disorder, and reliance must be placed on competent diagnostic psychological testing and interpretation. The patient's responses to projective tests . . . do permit the early detection of the thought disorder. (pp. 12–13)

This statement reflects both the theory that Rapaport elaborated and the operationalization of this theory into a system of scoring Rorschach verbalizations as "pathological" or "deviant" (Holt, 1968). It had already been common practice to score Rorschach responses four ways, for location, determinants, content, and popularity versus originality. Beginning with the publication of *Diagnostic Psychological Testing* (Rapaport *et al.*, 1946) a fifth category, labeled deviant verbalizations, was added, together with the theoretical rationale of the distance concept. Holt (1968) attempted to specify loss or increase of distance in terms of each kind of deviant verbalization, explaining as follows:

> We may profitably conceive of the reality of the testing situation in terms of the distance maintained by the subject between himself and the inkblot. If the subject's responses show too little regard for the inkblot (absurd form responses), or if his responses carry too much associative elaboration of a response which itself is good, then we have an indication of increase of distance from the card. On the other hand, if the subject's response shows that he is conceptually and/or affectively taking the inkblot as an immutable reality, with its own real affective and logical propensities not admitting of critical control, we have an indication of loss of distance from the card. (p. 429)

By restricting themselves to scoring only the most strikingly deviant verbalizations, Rapaport *et al.* (1946) hoped to establish their theoretical rationale and permit further development of this scoring category and its theoretical basis. They noted that, "As a consequence, the bulk of the verbalizations extracted reflect schizophrenic pathology of thinking . . . this basis permits inferences from clear-cut to masked schizophrenic thinking when the course of the thought process is more obscure or entirely hidden" (Holt, 1968, p. 426). Although this system of scoring deviant verbalizations has continued to be valued in both the Rorschach and the Holtzman inkblot techniques, there are two serious, related problems in addition to the psychometric difficulties associated with the variable numbers of responses to the Rorschach cards. Holt (1968) commented in one of his editorial footnotes that, in general, even the more extreme pathological verbalizations are not as specific to schizophrenia as the Rapaport *et al.* (1946) text implies. He added:

> In particular, I have found it difficult to work with the notions of loss and increase of distance from the card. In practice the distinction between too little and too great distance proves too slippery for reliable use. Concepts such as failure of reality testing, or slippage in set, will probably eventually replace disturbances of distance. (p. 425)

The second problem is that insufficient attention was paid to the adequacy of the subject's control in coping with his or her "primary processes," i.e., the initial, raw form of impulses or desires. As described earlier in this chapter, Purcell (1965) had shown the crucial importance of registering evidence of the individual's inhibitory or regulatory forces when attempting to gauge the potential for deviant behavior from Thematic Apperception Technique (TAT) responses. In essence, assessment must take into account the subject's awareness and control of impulses, as well as the impulses themselves. It is not merely an individual's proclivity to perceive, imagine, and think in primary-process ways that determines whether the individual is "schizophrenic"; in fact, strictly speaking, an individual may have extremely "deviant" proclivities but may be so able to direct them as to be a creative genius, rather than a schizophrenic. But Martin's observation (1968) still tends to hold today, namely, that

> more than most other psychological processes attended to by the clinician, concept formation tends to be handled in a "sign-oriented" manner. The clinician is apt to consider a certain concept an example of "sick" or "pathological" thinking without explicating the processes involved. (p. 485)

In practice, most clinicians are not skilled in taking into account those inhibitory and controlling processes that are crucial in determining the schizophrenic disorders or in predicting whether "pathological" fantasies will be "acted out," that is, expressed inappropriately. This lack of skill helps to explain, perhaps, a considerable measure of the unreliability and invalidity of both the diagnosis of the schizophrenic disorders and the prediction of the potential for violent behavior. The problems associated with this lack of skill are compounded when the simple "cookbook" or "sign" approach is followed, for example, merely correlating Rorschach response types with "schizophrenia" as diagnosed by psychiatric interviews.

Because of the lack of a clear-cut rationale for deciding what categories of verbalizations are really "pathological," perhaps because psychiatric diagnosis has been regarded as definitive, even the best efforts to improve the discriminatory ability of the fifth category (deviant verbalizations) have relied mainly on the sign approach, statistically sophisticated though as it may be (e.g., Exner, 1982). Insofar as psychiatric diagnosis is unreliable and invalid, this approach is quite weak. As previously discussed, several kinds of considerations cast great doubt on the merits of the DSM-III-R system when used to diagnose schizophrenic disorder. At the very least, one would expect that basing a method for scoring, including weighting scores, solely on DSM-III-R diagnoses would quickly become severely limited. What Strauss and Carpenter (1981) called the "bootstrap affair" of psychiatric diagnosis of schizophrenic disorders means that trying to improve one system of diagnosis by correlating it with another (weak) system can result only in poor success. Given a weak criterion, even a perfectly valid system of scoring for deviant verbalization may go beyond correlations at a chance level, but not a powerful level, of discrimination of "schizophrenic" from nonschizophrenic persons. Neither the clinical nor the research utility of these results are impressive if one recognizes these inherent limitations. Furthermore, a non–DSM-III-R assessment method, such as the Rorschach, may be superior in validity, although comparing it to DSM-III-R diagnoses would not reveal its superiority.

Attempts have been made to evaluate disordered thinking on the Rorschach in terms of definitions of categories independent of the DSM-II, the DSM-III, and other psychiatric diagnostic systems (e.g., Quinlan *et al.*, 1972; Weiner, 1966). But given this "explication approach," which rates the integrity of the person's thinking as the independent variable, it is not surprising that disordered thinking is not unique to psychiatrically defined "schizophrenia," as Harrow and Quinlan (1977) reported. Similarly, other, non-Rorschach measures of "schizophrenic thought disorder" correlate positively with such psychiatric diagnostic systems as the DSM-III and the Research Diagnostic Criteria (Feighner *et al.*, 1972), but by no means perfectly, and "thought disorder" appears in other diagnostic categories besides schizophrenic disorder (see, e.g., Harrow, Silverstein, & Marengo, 1983; Marengo & Harrow, 1987).

As neither *schizophrenia* nor *thought disorder* has been defined with great rigor or reliability—especially in the systems of psychiatric diagnosis—we should expect (1) that there would be no more than a modest correlation between "schizophrenia" and "thought disorder" and (2) that "thought disorder" would be found in related conditions such as "mania." The latter finding would not be surprising because all conditions related to mania have been removed from the category of schizophrenic disorders in the DSM-III and other "narrower" diagnostic systems, on which it is based, like the Research Diagnostic Criteria.

Altogether, we might expect a less-than-perfect correspondence between thought disorder and "schizophrenia" in the DSM-III or the DSM-III-R than in the DSM-II because (1) many of the DSM-II criteria for "schizophrenia" were moved, in the DSM-III-R, to "manic-depressive illness"; (2) some acute forms of schizophrenic disorder were eliminated, in the DSM-III, by the six-month-duration criterion; and (3) the DSM-III virtually eliminated the category schizophrenia, schizoaffective type. Furthermore, certain kinds of inability to think rationally are not clearly evoked by projective techniques, particularly when the subject does not respond.

Many individuals who are "schizophrenic" according to their case histories do not respond enough to be diagnosed schizophrenic by the Rorschach. As Mason, Cohen, and Exner (1985), for example, stated, "Some schizophrenics who have been institutionalized learn to conceal their pathology and will give very barren records . . . so that the indicators of thought disorder . . . will not be present" (p. 302).

In essence, one should be very surprised indeed if any measure of thought disorder inferred from projective technique responses correlated almost perfectly with any clinical diagnosis of "schizophrenia," including one based on the DSM-III-R.

The Efficacy of the Deviant Verbalization Category

Among the hundreds of studies attempting to correlate Rorschach indices with the clinical diagnosis of schizophrenia, the only scoring category that has proved a notably successful discriminator is *deviant verbalization.* For example, as Saccuzzo, Braff, Sprock, and Sudik (1984) reported in their study of the Rorschach, the Minnesota Multiphasic Personality Inventory (MMPI), and the Visual Backward Masking technique, "of all traditional test variables examined, only one discriminated among the [diagnostic] groups, and this was the number of deviant verbalizations (DV)" (p. 1292).

Since the early 1960s, the best-known work on deviant verbalization scoring on the Rorschach has been associated with the systems of Exner (1974, 1982) and Weiner (1966). Their work represents both a well-explicited understanding of thought processes and many empirical studies of how deviant verbalization scores match up with clinical diagnoses, including those based on the DSM-III. Not all independent studies have confirmed the usefulness of the verbalization "signs" they have used for diagnosis, however, particularly when signs other than deviant verbalizations were used to discriminate schizophrenic from nonschizophrenic hospitalized patients, for example, as reported by Schwartz and Ewert (1969) and Lambley (1973). But recent and ongoing work by the Exner group promises useful refinements that will make sense both theoretically and empirically. From a theoretical perspective, this group has developed a much-needed differentiation of degrees of thought disorder as reflected in two levels of "special scores" among the four types: DV (deviant verbalization); INCOM (incongruous combination); DR (deviant response); and FABCOM (fabulized combination). All four of these score categories apply to answers in which illogical, fluid, peculiar, or circumstantial thinking is present. A Level 1 value is assigned to mild or modest instances of such thinking, and a Level 2 value is assigned to moderate or severe instances (Exner, 1987).

The following definition and illustration of a deviant response is quoted here to provide a sense of this new development:

> DR is used to indicate the presence of a marked strangeness or peculiarity in an answer. It may manifest itself in either of two ways. The first is a phrase that is very inappropriate or completely irrelevant to the response such as, "That looks like a butterfly, *but I hope it's not one on display somewhere.*" DR phrases are quite uncommon and usually will be of a Level 2 variety. The more common type of DR involves circumstantiality in which there is a fluid-like rambling such as, "That sounds like a dancer on the stage, she's so beautiful

> there, *trying so hard to convey the meaning of her dance to everyone so that they will get caught up in it too, but sometimes as much as you try you just can't get others involved.*" DR's usually jump out because of their strangeness. If you find yourself debating about whether a DR is present, it probably isn't. (Exner, 1988, p. 71; italics in the original)

From an empirical perspective, there are now data to support the reliability of scoring and the validity of Exner's system. The reliability coefficients of Level 1 and Level 2 differentiation of the four special scores range from .82 to .93. Validity is supported by the finding

> that the presence of at least two Level 2 scores correlates very highly with structured interview estimates of serious thinking problems and with the differentiation of diagnostic categories (mild versus severe) [and] that the presence of two or more Level 2 scores in the *discharge* protocols of inpatients is a very good predictor of relapse. (Exner, 1988, p. 7)

Furthermore, the use of Level 2 scores increases the true-positive rate for identifying schizophrenia by about 6% to 10% and decreases the false-positive rate among nonschizophrenics by about 55%. This new system supports the view that distinguishing the degree of thinking disorder is empirically useful, especially if it leads to greater predictive accuracy, for example, in terms of relapse.

Predictive accuracy is also critical in distinguishing certain related kinds of disorders from schizophrenic disorders. So-called borderline and schizotypal personality disorders show some important differences from the schizophrenic disorders, which the Exner (1986) system helps to elucidate. In a study comparing 84 subjects with borderline personality disorders, 76 subjects with schizotypal personality disorders, and 80 first-admission schizophrenics, the borderline subjects appeared markedly different from the other two groups. In particular, the borderline subjects had fewer of the special scores, including indices of cognitive slippage, or of disordered thought. The differences among groups are considerable when the scores are weighted for magnitude; the borderlines have the lowest scores, and the schizotypals fall between the borderlines and the schizophrenics. Thus, validation of a sort is provided for these diagnostic categories themselves through using the Rorschach scores as the independent variable, rather than assuming the validity of the diagnostic categories and using the Rorschach as a dependent variable. Practically, these results suggest that individuals in the diagnostic category of borderline personality disorder, who often behave in ways that strike the observer as psychotic, have significantly better reality-testing ability then those with schizophrenic or even schizotypical personality disorders. Yet, because normal subjects do even better, there is evidence to suggest a continuum of reality-testing ability rather than of strictly discrete categories.

A Summary Evaluation of the Rorschach

Many of the criticisms leveled at the Rorschach have been countered rather well, especially as the Exner system has developed. From the perspective of test standardization, there are substantial improvements in administration, scoring, and empirically derived modes of interpretation. The technique can now make meaningful distinctions among important diagnostic categories and can suggest whether and how these categories are themselves meaningful in terms of underlying cognitive and psychodynamic processes as well as in terms of some behavioral correlates. Major flaws persist in cases of variable and low responsiveness and nonresponsiveness, notably in the testing of persons with schizophrenic and related disorders and particularly with chronic and/or paranoid persons, who constitute a great segment of the schizophrenic population. Although there are special methods recommended for dealing with such subjects (e.g., different test instructions asking for more responses), the Rorschach sometimes falls short of being a test in the active sense of eliciting interpretable responses.

Holtzman Inkblot Technique

Psychometric Structure

Wayne Holtzman and his associates have attempted to develop a technique that would retain the advantages of the Rorschach but that would be better psychometrically. Their fundamental test (Holtzman, Thorpe, Swartz, & Herron, 1961) presents both a carefully conceived theoretical rationale and considerable supportive data. Most notably, the Holtzman group developed a detailed weighted scoring system for assessing schizophrenic thinking; the system is based on Rapaport's nominalistic categories of deviant verbalizations, and it is closely related to independent assessments of the schizophrenic disorders. Those by-now-familiar demons of low and variable responsiveness, which made the Rorschach so vulnerable to criticism from a psychometric standpoint, had seemingly been harnessed.

Subjects were shown 45 inkblot cards to respond to but were limited to one response per card. The stimuli themselves extended the parameters of the Rorschach inkblots. Whereas all of the Rorschach inkblots are bisymmetrical, Holtzman inkblots may be asymmetrical, and their much greater number provides much greater stimulus variety. Holtzman (1988) summarized his vision of the psychometric advantages:

> It was clear to me right from the start that a new inkblot technique of the kind I visualized would have several distinct advantages over the standard Rorschach. First, the number of responses per individual could be held to a relatively constant value. Second, because each response would be given to an independent stimulus, the resulting protocol would be much more amenable to psychometric treatment. Third, a fresh start in the production of stimulus materials could result in a richer variety of stimuli capable of eliciting far more information than the original 10 Rorschach plates. Fourth, two parallel forms of the inkblots to use in test-retest studies of personality change could be constructed easily from item-analysis data in the experimental phases of development. And fifth, adequate estimates of reliability based on internal consistency and parallel test-retest correlations could be obtained independently for each major variable. (p. 581)

Thirty years of research have shown that the Holtzman technique does live up to much of its psychometric promise. The Rorschach problems of inadequate and variable responsiveness have been partially overcome by the provision of more cards to respond to, on the one hand, and the restriction of subjects to one response per card, on the other hand. But the problem of what to make of card rejections, which are more frequent in the schizophrenic population, has not been wholly solved.

Pathognomic Verbalization

All 22 Holtzman scoring variables may be entered into formulas that discriminate the schizophrenic disorders. But the heart of Holtzman discriminatory efficiency for this diagnostic category is what Holtzman called "pathognomic" verbalization:

> Pathognomic [sic] verbalization has been shown to be the best single indicator of psychopathology. The bizarre perception and autistic logic underlying high scores on this variable are characteristic either of schizophrenia or extreme artistic license in responding to inkblots. Normal individuals tend to give fabulations with notable affectivity, mildly fabulized combinations of otherwise acceptable percepts or even give occasional queer responses that are often described in a playful manner. Schizophrenics, on the other hand, manifest a loss of distance between themselves and the inkblots, often giving severely fabulized combinations, contaminations, queer responses, or special kinds of autistic logic that show faulty, fantastic reasoning as a justification for the response. (Holtzman, 1988, p. 583)

Pathognomic verbalization (V) scores denote the degree of autistic, bizarre thinking inferred from responses; a five-point scale is used, on which 0 denotes no pathology. The nine categories of V and the ranges of their scoring weights are Fabulation, 1; Fabulized Combination, 2, 3, 4; Queer Response, 1, 2, 3; Incoherence, 4; Autistic Logic, 1, 2, 3, 4; Contamination, 2, 3, 4; Self-Reference, 2, 3, 4; Deterioration Color, 2, 3, 4; and Absurd Response, 3. From the outset Holtzman and his associates presented clear conceptual and operational definitions of these response categories. For example, part of the conceptual definition of Contamination is that "two superimposed concepts are reported as one percept because of an inability to separate disparate associations" (Holtzman *et al.*, 1961, p. 62). This definition is elaborated, and the elaboration is followed with numerous examples.

As Holtzman (1978) stated, "The best single variable for revealing pathology in thought processes is Pathognomic Verbalization, the one variable on the HIT that requires some clinical experience and can be scored only for the individual method of the HIT, not the group" (p. 251). This requirement immediately raises the issue of scorer reliability.

An early study of reliability was supportive but turned up the familiar problem of inadequate responsiveness. Whitaker (1965) compared the Rorschach and the Holtzman in terms of V to determine their degree of agreement and the extent of the Holtzman's potential psychometric advantages in assessing schizophrenic disorders. Holtzman's scale for scoring was applied by two scorers to both the Rorschach and the Holtzman testing of 45 psychiatric inpatients. Each scorer was already experienced with the Rapaport nominal scoring system, on which the Holtzman ordinal scoring system is based. The study aimed specifically to measure scorer reliability, card rejection rates, and the degree of correlation between Rorschach and Holtzman pathognomic verbalization.

Blind, independent scoring of 19 randomly chosen Holtzman protocols yielded a reliability coefficient of .81, suggesting that psychologists previously unfamiliar with the Holtzman but experienced with the Rapaport system can score the Holtzman reliably for "pathognomic" verbalization. Similarly, the two blind scorers achieved an interscorer reliability of .76 on the Rorschach protocols of the same subjects. Card rejection rates were 17% for the Rorschach and 44% for the Holtzman, though the examiner encouraged the subjects to use their imagination if they initially rejected a card. Thus, under somewhat special response-encouraging conditions, on the average about 8 out of 10 Rorschach cards elicited responses, and 25 out of 45 Holtzman cards elicited responses. As the rejection rates of schizophrenic patients tend to be higher than those of other patients, the problem of low and variable responsiveness was appreciable. The correlation between Scorer A's Rorschach scores and Scorer B's Holtzman scores for pathognomic verbalization for the 19 patients was .76, and Scorer A's scoring of all 45 Rorschach and Holtzman protocols yielded a correlation of .94, suggesting that the Rorschach and the Holtzman were measuring essentially the same variable; but it was clear that scorers need to be well practiced to achieve sufficient interscorer reliability to provide the potential for high validity.

Variations of the Holtzman Inkblot Technique have been developed, partly to reduce the otherwise lengthy testing process that may be feasible for research purposes but is too laborious and time-consuming for routine clinical use. A major limitation of the more efficient group methods of administration and/or scoring is that pathognomic verbalization is not included.

Users of the new, individually administered experimental version of the Holtzman, the HIT 25, ask subjects to give two responses per inkblot to each of the 25 stimulus cards. Although rejection rates of schizophrenic subjects are greater than those of normal subjects, the difference may be less on the HIT 25 than on the standard Holtzman. A study of 30 schizophrenic subjects (reported by Holtzman, 1988) showed that 7 of the subjects gave the maximum total of 50 scorable responses. But the HIT 25 provides less differentiation between schizophrenic and normal subjects than the standard Holtzman, in terms of both pathognomic verbalization and what he calls "integration" scores. Using formulas to analyze all of the data by postdiction (restrospective prediction), the HIT 25 discriminated 30 schizophrenic subjects from 30 normal college students in all but 2 of the 60 cases. Although discriminating hospitalized schizophrenic subjects from normal subjects is much easier than discriminating schizophrenic from other severely disordered patients, the results do suggest that further development of the HIT 25 may be worthwhile.

Studies of the regular Holtzman have shown that it does effectively discriminate schizophrenic from other clinical groups as well as from normals. For example, Mosely (1963) found the best linear combinations of 16 Holtzman variables, based on the Holtzman standardization studies, and then cross-validated them on independent samples of normal, depressive, and schizophrenic subjects. V was added to his model for use with doubtful cases and the result was a formula classification that was 88% correct. In the most difficult discrimination task, that between schizophrenics and depressives, 78% of the subjects were correctly classified.

The Rorschach and Holtzman in Perspective

The Holtzman technique represents an advance beyond the Rorschach in terms of its psychometric properties. In has an especially well-developed system for the precise scoring of variables relevant to schizophrenic disorders, particularly with the use of pathognomonic verbalization (V) scores. This advance, however, involves greater labor for the administrator and the scorer as well as for the subject. As I can attest from having administered and scored Holtzmans and Rorschachs to the same 45 patients, though the Rorschach can be very arduous and time-consuming, the Holtzman is more so. The Holtzman's even more arduous nature and the Rorschach's greater tenure, together with major Rorschach research developments, have combined to keep the Rorschach ahead of the Holtzman in regular clinical use.

Both the Rorschach and the Holtzman have become much more sophisticated in the hands of their modern developers and users, partly because of the use of computer technology which makes possible ever more ingenious constructions of empirically based formulas. The Holtzman probably has more potential for sophisticated research use, and perhaps also for empirical validation, whereas the Rorschach will probably continue to appeal more to the clinician. Both continue to require quite considerable training, experience, and skill on the part of users, and both manifest their artistic origins, as they demand artful as well as scientific application and judgment. Although the Holtzman has moved projective methodology further into the realm of empirical science, "As with any projective technique . . . the clinical utility of the HIT depends to a great extent on the skill and experience of the clinician using it" (Holtzman & Swartz, 1983, p. 247).

Neither technique wholly achieves the properties of a test by the most rigorous definition. But administration and scoring are now much more standardized and reliable across a large spectrum of users. The Exner group has achieved considerable success in standardizing the administration and scoring of the Rorschach technique and in developing more sophisticated kinds of scoring and empirically based interpretation. The Holtzman group had already designed and developed a rather sophisticated system by the time their 1961 text and testing materials were published. And the Holtzman does lend itself to more far-reaching kinds of empirical validation because of the way it is constructed. But neither technique comes very close to overcoming nonresponsiveness. Card rejections are still a significant problem, even when special encouraging instructions are used. The question remains: What is being missed and what does it mean when a subject does not respond?

There are certain ways to interpret a lack of responses on the Rorschach or the Holtzman, but they fall short of yielding certainty of interpretation. Nonresponsiveness *may* mean an inability to respond and thus a kind of deficit, but what kinds and degrees of deficits are involved? And can we be sure that we are finding evidence of a deficit in the sense of a lack of ability, or does nonresponding mean, at least sometimes, a proclivity rather than a deficit? One can retort that the proclivity not to respond and the inability to respond are the same thing, but such an argument is like saying that a patient is mute because the patient is unable to talk, or that a patient "has flat affect" because the patient is not expressing affect. Both Exner and Holtzman have been quite explicitly aware of this dilemma but have not resolved it by any means. The dilemma of how to avoid low projective-technique responses is especially great in the assessment of schizophrenic disorders. Furthermore, even when there is an appreciable number of responses overall, variations in responsiveness both within and among protocols pose particularly significant problems for both intraindividual and interindividual comparisons in the schizophrenic disorders as well as between schizophrenic and other disorders.

The traditional diagnostic oversight, recently recognized as a crucial problem in the planning and evaluation of treatment, is failing to take into account and to distinguish the difference between positive and negative signs and symptoms. As discussed in other sections of this book, it has traditionally been assumed that "symptomatic cure"—that is, the skewed treatment results that show curtailment of positive symptoms but little or no progress in the patient's development—is satisfactory and all that can be expected. But skewed treatment results may mean not only no real improvement but harmful neglect and even inhibition of the patient's developmental needs. A similar oversight is possible in the use of the Rorschach and the Holtzman, although many, if not most, of its users may be well aware of the limits of their interpretive ability. Relatively nonresponsive or variably responsive subjects may be concealing much more than they are revealing. Paranoid and long-institutionalized persons have learned to conceal both their inabilities *and* their abilities; their proclivity to conceal may be readily and chronically activated by distrust. The more paranoid and/or chronic the person, the more likely it is that not only interview and ordinary observation information but also projective technique data will not be sufficiently revealing. This dilemma cannot be satisfactorily resolved simply by correlating projective technique data with interview and observation data, because all of these assessment methods may fail to elicit certain kinds of evidence. And thus, comparing DSM-III diagnoses, for example, with the results of Rorschach or Holtzman or any other assessment technique has a considerable inherent limitation because the so-called validation criteria themselves are seriously flawed.

The Whitaker Index of Schizophrenic Thinking

The Whitaker Index of Schizophrenic Thinking (WIST) is a relatively new test that first appeared in print during the early 1970s (Whitaker, 1973) and was then further developed, so that a more comprehensive practical and theoretical guide to

WIST use was provided by the end of that decade (Whitaker, 1980). Some 50 publications about the WIST have appeared up to the time of this writing.

Structure and Aims

The WIST is an attempt to improve on the projective techniques as a measure of "schizophrenic thinking," or, more precisely, the severe inability of intellectually capable persons to think logically in even the dull-normal range of intellectual ability. In contrast to the Rorschach and the Holtzman, the WIST is structured quite deliberately to elicit and reveal this inability rather than to serve as a technique for ascertaining a broad spectrum of personality proclivities by calling for relatively spontaneous expression. The structure of the WIST provides a definite and standardized method of actively testing for thinking inability. The problems of nonresponsiveness and variable responsiveness, which are intrinsic in the projective techniques, are extremely rare in the use of the WIST, which is also a more objective, more narrowly focused, and much briefer instrument. It is predicated on a particular conceptual definition of schizophrenic thinking, which is built into the text.

An instance of thinking is defined as schizophrenic if it is *all of the following:*

1. *Illogical.* This characteristic may be manifest in the syntactical or semantic aspects of an individual's language usage, in the relationships existing among the ideas expressed, or in the relationships between those ideas and the logical requirements of a given task or problem.
2. *Impaired.* This characteristic refers to a marked discrepancy between an individual's capacity to think and the level of adequacy of his or her thinking demonstrated in other instances.
3. *Unwitting.* The individual demonstrates a lack of awareness, deliberate intention, or control in a given instance of thinking.

The WIST is a multiple-choice test with two forms, A and B, each containing 25 regular test items. Form A and Form B are identical in structure but different in content. The subject is presented with one of the forms and is told, "Please read the directions on the front of this test and go ahead with it when you are ready. When you are finished with the test, I will go over your answers with you." The examiner does not set a time limit but does time the subject to see how many minutes she or he will take to complete all 25 items. The subject does an example item before the series of regular items in each subtest and is given the correct answer before proceeding with the regular test items.

The 25 items in each form are distributed among three subtests: 9 Similarities items present a stimulus word; 9 Word Pairs items present two stimulus words; and 7 New Inventions items present a sentence. As will be explained later, all Form A items present inherently anxiety-provoking verbal content, except for the example items preceding each subtest. Form B items present neutral emotional content. Each of the five alternative answers for each item receives a weighted score according to an ordinal scale, as described in a later section. The following is an item illustrative of the Form A Similarities subtest (except that the answers are not listed randomly) together with the score assigned to each answer according to its type:

Kill	Score	Type of answer
Bapple	4	Nonsense association
Mill	3	Clang association
Bloody me	2	Reference idea
Stab	1	Loose association
Cause to die	0	Correct answer

During the inquiry, which the examiner begins when the subject has completed all of the items, the subject is told of any incorrect answers and is given an opportunity to correct them. The examiner points with a pencil to the first wrong answer and says, for example, "This is not the correct answer for number 1. What is the correct answer?" Further incorrect answers are handled in the same manner until the subject has managed to arrive at all of the correct answers. To score the test, the examiner assigns *each* wrong answer a weighted score in accordance with the "type of answer" system illustrated above. The sum of *all* of the weighted wrong answers is the score, to which is added the time, which is the number of minutes required to complete the initial answers. The score plus the time equals the Index of the degree of schizophrenic thinking overall.

Subject Qualifications

The WIST was designed for use with persons who have at least low-average intellectual capacity, have the equivalent of an eighth-grade education, are 18 years of age or older, and are not brain-damaged or under the influence of nonprescribed drugs. These criteria are meant to make certain that inability shown on the test cannot be attributed simply to deficits due to mental retardation, inadequate education, physical brain impairment, or certain drugs, including alcohol. As intended, thinking inability, as shown on the WIST, is not attributable to lack of intelligence or education; the low negative correlations of WIST indexes with intelligence and with education have not adversely affected the WIST's discrimination of schizophrenic thinking.

Though the WIST was not designed for the purpose, WIST studies with brain-damaged persons have suggested some capacity to distinguish brain-damaged from schizophrenic subjects, as will be discussed in the next chapter by Antonio Puente.

Inevitably, virtually all of the schizophrenic persons tested with the WIST have been on neuroleptic drug regimens of various kinds. But none of three WIST studies (Pishkin, Lovallo, Lenk, & Bourne, 1977; Simpson, Bourne, Justesen, & Rhodes, 1979; Whitaker, 1973) examining the relationship between WIST indices and dosage levels of various phenothiazines have suggested that these "antipsychotic" drugs have any effect overall on the degree of schizophrenic thinking. These results are in accord with Chapman's study (1975) showing that, as a group, schizophrenic patients neither improved nor worsened when proverb testing was used as a method of assessing thinking disorder. Yet neither the general issue of whether or in what ways these drugs influence thinking disorder nor the specific question of their possible effects on WIST performance has been wholly resolved, especially as the WIST studies are only correlational.

Validity

The WIST was constructed to measure a certain kind of thinking deficit that is considered basically characteristic of schizophrenic disorders. WIST validation began with an overall theoretical rationale for test construction, together with empirically derived ways of developing and selecting test items and the formulation of hypotheses to be tried both in developing and standardizing the test. This process, including the theoretical rationale, subject selection methods, and the sequence of correlating WIST data with empirical criteria at various stages of development, is described in detail in the WIST manual (Whitaker, 1980).

One of the hypotheses was that the WIST would correlate relatively highly with a particular empirical criterion of validity, which in this case was diagnoses of schizophrenic disorders based on especially carefully assessed interview and observation evidence.

Briefly, the rationale for the WIST is based in part on a theory of levels of cognition. The alternative answers for each test item comprise a hierarchy of these levels. Whereas the answers are randomly arranged in the actual items, the answers below, to item 1 in the Form A Similarities section, are arranged, for the sake of illustration, in their hierarchical order, showing their respective levels in terms of score, association type, semantic adequacy, and the degree of cognitive ability shown by the choice of each answer:

Kill	Score	Associative	Semantic	Cognitive
Cause to die	0	Correct	Designation	Thinking
Stab	1	Loose	Connotation	Perception
Bloody me	2	Reference	Connotation	Perception
Mill	3	Clang	Rhyme	Sensation
Bapple	4	Nonsense	Irrelevant	Blocking

In essence, as one goes down the scale of values, the closeness of fit between stimulus and response decreases to the point of virtually complete inadequacy and irrelevance. Correspondingly, there is a downward shift in the cognitive level of the responses, from the most complex and advanced to the simplest and most undeveloped.

Though both score 1 and score 2 are on the level of connotation and perception, score 1 answers show stronger connotations and broader perceptions. In the present example, *stab* is a less limited connotation and a less limited perceptual referent of *kill* than the exclusively personal *bloody me*.

The validity of this hierarchical or ordinal scale for scoring was substantiated empirically by finding that the various levels of wrong answers corresponded generally to blindly and independently diagnosed and severity-rated schizophrenic disorders. Other early validation studies compared WIST results to pathognomonic verbalization scores obtained by schizophrenic and nonschizophrenic hospitalized patients on the Rorschach, the Holtzman and Wechsler Adult Intelligence Scale (WAIS). The results of these studies and the WIST testing of presumably normal subjects all supported further development. Normal subjects found the test quite easy to complete correctly and quickly, and they tended to laugh at the wrong answers, reflecting their wittingness. Schizophrenic subjects, on the whole, took much longer to complete the test, gave wrong answers, and did not find wrong answers absurd enough to be amusing.

A study of 164 hospitalized psychiatric patients and 61 normal subjects (Whitaker, 1980) showed substantiation of all of several hypothesized outcomes. Schizophrenic subjects had significantly higher scores, times, and indices than nonschizophrenic hospitalized patients, who, in turn, performed significantly worse than the normal subjects. Also, as predicted, acute schizophrenic patients did worse on Form A than on Form B, and they generally showed improvement on the WIST over a two-week period, whereas the chronic schizophrenic patients did not.

As is well known from clinical observation, acutely schizophrenic persons are hyperalert to their surroundings, whereas chronically schizophrenic persons tend to be withdrawn and inattentive. Accordingly, it was hypothesized that acutely schizophrenic persons would be especially open to the higher stimulus values of the inherently anxiety-provoking items of Form A, whereas chronically schizophrenic persons, because of their high stimulus barriers to external stimulation, would be unaffected. It was predicted that the thinking inability of the acute subjects would be particularly exacerbated by Form A because of its anxiety-provoking content. The confirmatory WIST results added an important dimension to the WIST's construct validity in terms of others' research results with acute and chronic patients. For example, Gray (1975) showed correlates of autonomic nervous system functioning for chronic schizophrenic patients by means of a reaction-time paradigm explainable by a "loss of receptivity to task relevant cues . . . the price these patients pay to avoid painfully high arousal" (p. 195).

Several other empirical studies of the WIST have supported and extended the basic English-language standardization and validation study briefly described above (Whitaker, 1980). For example, recognizing that the considerable variation among psychiatric diagnostic systems makes test validation suspect when only one system is used, Leslie *et al.* (1984) used 13 different diagnostic interview systems and compared them with one another and the WIST in a study of 85 chronic Canadian outpatients. The WIST showed a mean agreement of 70% with the systems, as high as could be expected in view of the demonstrably limited reliability of diagnosis among the systems. A more refined analysis suggested that the WIST has quite high validity:

> When the 13 diagnostic systems and corresponding Indexes for the patient sample were examined individually, consistently higher Indexes across both WIST Forms were found for currently psychotic patients over the non "presently psychotic" schizophrenic patients. Moreover, when individual symptoms associated with schizophrenic thought disorder were examined in relation to patients' Indexes, consistently higher Indexes were found associated with the presence of the symptom. (Leslie *et al.*, 1984, p. 646)

In reference to the last point, without exception, WIST mean indexes, from both Form A and Form B yielded correct and substantial discriminations for every one of the following symptoms: thought withdrawal; disturbances of association; autism; disturbances of attention; auditory hallucinational passivity feeling; lack of insight; poor rapport; complex thought disorder; hallucinations present for more than six months; and delusions and hallucinations. That is, if an individual showed a particular symptom, there was a strong tendency, other symptoms being held constant, for that symptom to be linked to a higher WIST index on whatever form the individual was given. Because discrete observations of particular symptoms tend to be much more reliable and valid than general judgments, whether considered within or between diagnostic systems, or whether persons are schizophrenic, these results are especially important.

The WIST's construct validity was also broadened by studies using it as an independent classificatory device (Bourne, Justesen, Abraham, Beeker, Brauchi, Whitaker, & Yaroush, 1977; Pishkin *et al.*, 1977). These studies showed that the WIST validly distinguished degrees of schizophrenic thinking by predicting, within the range of schizophrenic disorders, the level of performance on conceptual learning tasks. Whereas the diagnosis of schizophrenia by itself has little predictive power, refinement of that diagnosis by use of the WIST shows promise for measuring the individual's degree of thinking inability, probably the most important variable in gauging the individual's ability to live productively outside a hospital.

Cross-cultural research, parallel to the validation and standardization studies in the United States and Canada, has suggested that the WIST is effective in discriminating schizophrenic subjects in other Western cultures. Spanish-translation versions of the WIST yielded highly supportive results in Puerto Rico (Acevedo, Gonzalez, Puente, & Whitaker, 1985) and Mexico (Bolado & Whitaker, 1990). A German translation was effective in a West German study (Yaroush, 1982).

The Minnesota Multiphasic Personality Inventory

Few psychological tests have been designed and interpreted with more attention to empirical correlates than the Minnesota Multiphasic Personality Inventory

(MMPI). Indeed, much of the claimed superiority of actuarial over clinical judgment has arisen in connection with the development and use of this test. Actuarial prediction is based on a statistical model that is relied on by insurance companies. The companies try to achieve a profit by finding out the actual occurrence rates of key events (e.g., deaths and accidents) and then calculating premiums that will, in aggregate, give them a profit even though they will lose money in individual cases. Such a prediction depends on adequate sampling of the relevant population so that the statistical calculations can be validly extrapolated to the entire population in question.

Meehl (1954) defined the clinical versus statistical prediction approaches in psychology, and L. R. Goldberg (1965), as reported below, demonstrated their specific applicability to discriminating neurotic from psychotic persons.

> Goldberg derived various decision rules through statistical analysis of scores on 11 MMPI scales and psychiatric patients' discharge diagnoses. The single most effective rule for distinguishing the two conditions was quite simple: add scores from three scales and then subtract scores from two other scales. If the sum falls below 45, the patient is diagnosed neurotic; if it equals or exceeds 45, the patient is diagnosed psychotic. This has become known as the "Goldberg Rule." (Dawes, Faust, & Meehl, 1989, p. 1669)

In this study of 861 cases, this actuarial judgment yielded 70% correct discriminations, whereas the clinical judges, who viewed the same MMPI material, achieved 62% accuracy. Although this and other studies suggest that actuarial judgment is usually more accurate than clinical judgment, questions remain about the usefulness of this discrimination task, given the reliability and validity problems of psychiatric diagnosis. Furthermore, the discrimination rates themselves have not been impressive. Essentially, the MMPI has not been highly effective in discriminating psychiatrically diagnosed clinical groups, such as patients with schizophrenic disorders, although it was originally intended to do so.

The later developers of the MMPI have not perceived clinical diagnosis in psychiatry to be as valuable as it was once thought to be, nor as valuable as diagnosis is perceived to be in clinical medicine today (Graham, 1987). What began in the late 1930s as an attempt to find test sentences that would collectively yield patterns of answers corresponding closely to diagnostic categories has evolved into an interpretive device that places the primary importance on behavioral description. The MMPI has not been a loser in this evolution; it is now the most widely used personality test in the United States.

The fact that its 566 test items make it an extraordinarily time-consuming task for the subject has not kept the MMPI from widespread use. Users have found in the MMPI many practical advantages, as it is a paper-and-pencil test that can be readily administered and scored by someone with only technical training, and interpretation can follow clear empirical guidelines. In fact, the MMPI is probably the most empirically based test device in the personality tester's repertoire. Vast amounts of empirical research, correlating its 10 clinical scales and 4 validity scales with myriad forms of behavior descriptions, have made it a statistical wonderland in which facts rather than theories predominate. The meanings of test answers are not assumed but are inferred by means of the considerable standardization data that have been used to substantiate interpretations. This dependence on gathering great stores of data has propelled increasing efforts to reach more and larger standardization groups, including black populations, as it is realized that previous normative standardization samples are not adequate to the task of making interpretations on this limited and biased data base.

MMPI raw scores are tabulated and transformed linearly into *t* scores that indicate the individual's scores' statistical positions on each of the scales. For example, a *t* score of 70 on Scale 8 (Schizophrenia) shows that the person's raw score on that scale falls at the 70th percentile of the normal, nonpatient, sample and indicates that the particular subject has scored higher than 70% of "normal" subjects.

Clinical Scales

The clinical scales have retained their original names, but a number has been assigned to each name. Significantly, the numbers are now referred to more than the names, which merely suggest clinical categories and are referred to parenthetically, as follows:

Scale 1 (Hypochondriasis)
Scale 2 (Depression)
Scale 3 (Hysteria)
Scale 4 (Psychopathic Deviate)
Scale 5 (Masculinity-Femininity)
Scale 6 (Paranoia)
Scale 7 (Psychasthenia)
Scale 8 (Schizophrenia)
Scale 9 (Social Introversion)

None of these scales offers a straightforward correspondence, in empirical results, with psychiatric diagnosis. Scale 8 (Schizophrenia) was designed to correlate highly with the psychiatric diagnosis of schizophrenic disorders but, especially when considered in isolation from other scales, it does not closely match diagnoses. John Graham (1990) provided this succinct description:

> Scale 8 was developed to identify patients as schizophrenic. This category included a heterogeneous group of disorders characterized by disturbance of thinking, mood, and behavior. Misinterpretations of reality, delusions, and hallucinations may be present. Ambivalent or constricted emotional responsiveness is common. Behavior may be withdrawn, aggressive, or bizarre.
>
> All 78 of the items in the original scale have been maintained in MMPI-2. Some of the items deal with such frankly psychotic symptoms as bizarre mentation, peculiarities of perception, delusions of persecution, and hallucinations. Other topics covered include social alienation, poor family relationships, sexual concerns, difficulties in impulse control and concentration, and fears, worries, and dissatisfactions. (p. 76)

Although one should not conclude that an individual is schizophrenic solely on the basis of a Scale 8 score, *t* scores from 75 to 90 are said to suggest the possibility of psychotic disorder. Some individuals using drugs—prescription or nonprescription, and especially amphetamines—may have Scale 8 elevations.

Scale 6 (Paranoia), which has 40 items, is also relevant to the clinical category of schizophrenic disorders, especially when considered in combination with Scale 8 (Schizophrenia). Scale 6 was designed to identify patients with paranoid symptoms, including ideas of reference, persecutory and grandiose ideas about themselves, suspiciousness, and what may be considered excessive sensitivity, rigid opinions, and rigid attitudes. Many subjects with *t* scores above 70, especially if Scale 6 is highest in the profile, may show frankly psychotic behavior, together with diagnoses of paranoid schizophrenia or paranoid state. But as reported by Graham (1987), some subjects with clearly paranoid symptoms may be able to produce average scores on the MMPI Paranoid scale, and it is possible to produce a *t* score of 70 without selecting any of the frankly psychotic items.

Schizophrenic Disorder Profiles

The relations among scale scores are more informative than isolated scale scores. Code types, whether of two or three digits (depending on what configurations best correspond empirically to diagnostic categories), tell which clinical scales are the highest in the profile, starting with the highest of the two or three scales. For example, a profile code of 138 tells us that the subject scored highest on Scale 1, the next highest on Scale 3, and the next highest on Scale 8. As noted previously, each scale has a number assigned to it, and the schizophrenia scale number is 8.

As Graham noted in his 1990 book on the MMPI-2, no data have been reported for correlates of the MMPI-2 code types, and so the present discussion pertains to the original MMPI. It may also pertain to the MMPI-2 because the currently available evidence indicates considerable continuity between these two versions of the test.

Schizophrenic subjects often fall into a couple of MMPI profiles, in which 8 is prominent but not necessarily the most prominent: 138 and 687/867. Subjects with the 138 profile code, indicating higher elevations for Hypochondriasis and Hysteria than for Schizophrenia, are usually diagnosed as having paranoid schizophrenia or paranoid personality disorder, and clear evidence of thought disorder may be observed. The 687/867 code, indicating greater elevations on the Paranoia and Schizophrenia scales, respectively, and both involving Psychasthenia, suggests very serious psychopathology and is sometimes referred to as the *psychotic valley.* The most common diagnosis associated with this profile is schizophrenic disorder, paranoid type. Graham (1987) commented as follows on the specific issue of thought disorder:

> When scale 7 is 10 or more T-score points greater than scale 8, the likelihood of thought disorder is not great. As scale 8 becomes higher than scale 7, the likelihood of a thought disorder increases. When both scales 7 and 8 are elevated, persons may be rather confused, but a well-developed delusional system is not to be expected. (p. 115)

The Validity Scales

Self-report devices, which ask the subject to indicate his or her preferences, values, and personal experiences, cannot be assumed to give an accurate depiction of the individual. Various forms of false reporting, whether due to deliberate falsification or self-deceit, occur often. Furthermore, subjects cannot simply be assumed to have so much self-knowledge as to give a comprehensive picture of themselves. To assume that self-reporting is always accurate is like assuming that the author of an autobiography is always giving a complete and accurate picture.

There are four validity scales on the MMPI: the Cannot Say (?) Scale; the L Scale; the F Scale; and the K Scale. Scores on these special indexes of reporting accuracy provide the MMPI interpreter with data from which to infer whether and to what extent the other scales and their profile, formed in relation to one another, can be considered valid. In addition, like the clinical scales, and in the spirit of such an extremely empirical device as the MMPI, the validity scales have come into use as measures for inferring extratest behavior, in other words, as themselves revealing personality.

The Cannot Say score is the number of items omitted by the subject plus those items that the subject answered both true and false. The examiner may encourage subjects to answer all items, both as part of the pretest instructions and after testing if it is seen that the subject has omitted items. Protocols with more than 30 omissions are considered invalid.

The L Scale, designed originally to detect deliberate and unsophisticated attempts to present oneself in a favorable light, consists of 15 items. More intelligent, educated, sophisticated subjects tend to score low on the L Scale. College students typically produce L Scale raw scores of only 1 or 0.

The F Scale, designed originally to detect deviant and atypical ways of responding to test items, has 64 items, some of which are relevant to schizophrenic disorders, such as items pertaining to paranoid thinking. High F Scale scores tend to be associated with elevated clinical scales, especially Scale 6 (Paranoia) and Scale 8 (Schizophrenia), but a high score may also invalidate the test protocol. An examination of individual item answers may be needed to determine the basis for a raw score in the range of 10 to 15 (a *t* score of 65 to 79), specifically, whether it means serious psychopathology or restlessness, dissatisfaction, and moodiness. A very high raw score, equal to or greater than 26 (a *t* score of 100 or more) may mean random answering or "faking bad" or even answering all items as true. On the other hand, for hospitalized psychiatric patients, it may be associated with delusions of reference, hallucinations, withdrawal, and other behavior symptomatic of psychosis.

The K Scale, which has 30 items, was designed to be a more subtle index of denial of psychopathology or its converse, attempts by subjects to exaggerate psychopathology. It was meant to pick up signs to which the L Scale is insensitive. But the K Scale turned out to have much more complex associations than anticipated, including the fact that higher scores may mean that the subjects are better educated and of higher level socioeconomic status. And for purposes of determining psychological disturbance, the K Scale itself does not appear useful: "There is no definitive way to determine when elevated K scores indicate clinical defensiveness and when they indicate ego strength" (Graham, 1987, p. 25).

Conservative users of the MMPI may consider a profile invalid and uninterpretable if more than 30 items are omitted or if a *t* score of more than 70 occurs on one or more of the L, F, and K Scales. This conclusion would eliminate the test profiles of many schizophrenics or other psychotic subjects. Many users may decide to interpret such profiles rather than discard what they may consider valuable information, though it must be interpreted with caution. An examination of specific item answers and experience with the MMPI and particular subject populations may serve to lessen the risk of making invalid interpretations.

The MMPI-2 has three added validity indicators, which are merely noted here, as they have not yet been tested for usefulness in assessing schizophrenic disorders: the back-page infrequency (Fb) scale; the variable-response-inconsistency (VRIN) scale; and the true-response-inconsistency (TRIN) scale.

Valid Uses of the MMPI to Assess Schizophrenic Disorders

Sophisticated users of the MMPI are aware that the test does not provide a very close match with psychiatric diagnoses, though it was originally designed to do so. Use of the MMPI to discriminate clinically diagnosed schizophrenic persons is especially fraught with difficulties, particularly if Scale 8 (Schizophrenia) is viewed in isolation. This use does not make sense, given the considerable available empirical evidence, which, after all, is the chief virtue of MMPI development. The MMPI does yield discriminatory patterns or profiles that are more effective than Scale 8 by itself in discriminating schizophrenic disorders, but even these cannot be regarded as sufficiently correlated with the clinically defined category to be used as an independent method of defining "schizophrenia." Often, if not usually, the MMPI interpreter needs to know whether the subject has already been diagnosed as schizophrenic in order to be confident in making inferences about the subject's current or even past "extratest" condition.

As discussed earlier in this book, one may argue with some merit that the clinical psychiatric diagnosis of schizophrenic disorders is questionable for both conceptual and practical reasons. Conceptually, "schizophrenia" is a broad category that includes an evidently highly diverse population. Practically, there is—especially in regular practice—considerable diagnostic unreliability, with the result that the validity of the diagnosis is severely limited. Therefore, why should the MMPI match up with clinical diagnoses, except that it was originally designed to do so? It may be argued that the "failure" of the MMPI to produce close correspondences may even be serendipitous, as this failure has probably helped its developers and its regular users alike to search for more "telling" correspondences with actual highly definable behaviors and manifest attitudes, instead of a nebulous and perhaps arbitrary diagnostic category. In any case, the MMPI has gone the way of quite basic empiricism in terms of its chosen criteria, and it has become the most popular personality test.

Clearly, the most sensible and effective use of the MMPI in the assessment of persons clinically diagnosed as cases of schizophrenic disorder is the MMPI characterization of the individual "schizophrenic" person and a comparison of the individual with others who are given this diagnosis. These aims are indisputably important unless one takes the thoroughly uninformed doctrinaire position that "All schizophrenics are the same anyway." MMPI users can verify that "schizophrenic" persons may have a lot in common, but that they are quite significantly different from one another in important kinds of behaviors, attitudes, and ideas.

MMPI-2 and the Future

Because the MMPI-2 is the most empirically based and fact-dependent of personality tests, MMPI research must demonstrate that meaningful interpretations can be made by referring to its standardization samples. To the extent that MMPI items are found to contribute substantially to correlations with important behaviors and personality attributes, it makes sense to keep them, provided that valid generalizations can be made on the basis of the available standardization samples. These two factors—item adequacy and standardization adequacy—are inextricably linked. The success of current efforts to improve the MMPI by means of a new form, the MMPI-2, and new and broader standardization samples will be determined in the coming decade.

The MMPI-2 contains many different items but is about the same length (567 items) as the MMPI. In addition to having to demonstrate the adequacy of this new form itself, researchers need to relate MMPI-2 findings to the vast research findings on the MMPI. Pancoast and Archer (1989) depicted the complexity of these developments. They noted that the MMPI has been frequently criticized in terms of the adequacy of the adult MMPI forms, for which the standard reference is still the 724 persons who were used to develop both several of the clinical scales and the norms. Neither its size nor its national relevance has made the normative sample adequately representative. On the other hand, the MMPI in its present form has been very popular with users.

Psychologist Starke Hathaway and neuropsychiatrist J. Charnley McKinley (1989), the original developers of the MMPI, noted several important changes incorporated in the MMPI-2, which was released for general use in 1990. Instead of the original 724-member, rather ethnocentric nonpatient normal sample, the MMPI-2 has a normal reference group of 2,600 persons representing a broad geographic, socioeconomic, and ethnic sampling, though this sample is admittedly somewhat biased toward upper-socioeconomic populations, and both Hispanic and Asian-American subgroups are underrepresented. Sexist wording, outmoded idiomatic expressions, and the use of increasingly unfamiliar literary and recreational material have been omitted. One result of these changes is that patients' *t* scores, based on the new norms, are not as deviant as those based on the original norms; the new nonpatients had higher scores overall. Uniform *t* scores were designed for the MMPI-2 to result in essentially uniform ranges and distributions for all of the basic clinical scales used for coding patterns of scale scores.

The newness of the MMPI-2 leaves open to speculation questions about its overall efficacy and its particular contribution to the assessment of schizophrenic disorders. Perhaps more definitive code profiles for schizophrenic disorders will be discovered, or at least as important, the MMPI-2 will better identify certain constellations of behaviors associated with these disorders. But the MMPI-2, like the MMPI, does not test directly, by any means, for the deficits in thinking ability that have classically been deemed to be integral to all schizophrenic disorders. Although they may be the most empirical and experimental of the personality tests, the MMPI and the MMPI-2 are structured in such a way as to get at the thinking-disorder phenomenon only indirectly. Thinking disorder may be inferred as a fairly likely component of the clinical picture frequently associated with certain profiles, but the measures based on this self-report device are quite removed from the active testing of thinking ability.

Summary

The psychological test assessment of schizophrenic disorders began more than 80 years ago, almost as soon as Eugen Bleuler coined the term *schizophrenia.* The heterogeneity of what Bleuler brought together as a group of disorders has been partly responsible for both the usual inexactness in clinical diagnoses, which are made largely by means of observation and interview, and the frequent lack of correspondence with psychological test evidence.

At one extreme, it can be argued that the category *schizophrenia* is far too nebulous itself to permit of any definitive test. At the other extreme, it can be argued that clinical diagnosis is rightfully paramount and that failures to find definitive test measures are due to shortcomings in the tests. Both arguments contain some truth. Clinical diagnosis is not nearly reliable or valid enough to be the sole criterion for any test. On the other hand, there is enough evidence of important common denominators among these disorders to allow them to be grouped meaningfully, especially—following Bleuler's insistence—in terms of the thinking disorder, which takes both positive and negative forms. Most often, psychological tests, like many observational and interview approaches, have not sufficiently addressed the negative (deficit) kinds of symptoms.

Like every other author, I have a bias, in this case a preference for active testing of the subject, who is thereby required to demonstrate ability and not merely to express a proclivity. Failures to respond on the Rorschach, the Holtzman, and the MMPI continue to be major impediments to making valid inferences, whereas the WIST rarely shares this dilemma. But the three older and more established tests have merit in their construction and their considerable data bases. The Rorschach and the

Holtzman can be quite useful both in demonstrating the subject's overall personality functioning, usually including abilities, and in having a telling relevance to determining the kinds and degrees of thinking disorder, particularly as demonstrated in pathognomonic or deviant verbalizations. For the user primarily interested in assessing schizophrenic disorders, their major drawbacks are low and variable responsiveness, various associated psychometric problems, and the need for considerable interpreter sophistication, experience, and knowledge of the standardization data.

The MMPI and the new MMPI-2, though they are the tests that are most empirically based and rigorously linked to factual correspondences to subjects' extratest behavior, do not have the ingenious structure of the projective techniques. Although the Rorschach and the Holtzman do not directly elicit an expression of the subject's reality-testing style and orientation, they may reveal thinking disorder, as well as a great deal of information about the subject's personality and behavior.

The Whitaker Index of Schizophrenic Thinking has shown at least as high a correspondence to carefully made clinical diagnoses as any other test, as demonstrated by rigorous studies in the United States and Canada, supported by Spanish- and German-language cross-validation research. WIST research has been theoretically based on and empirically supportive of the assumption that "thought disorder," an inability to think rationally, is of core importance in the schizophrenic disorders. WIST validation has included matching WIST results with clinical diagnoses and specific symptoms, plus using the WIST as an independent classificatory device. It provides measures of both negative and positive components of schizophrenic disorders by revealing the types and degrees of subjects' thinking inability in both its negative and its positive test manifestations.

Compared to the other tests discussed in this chapter, the WIST does not offer anywhere near as broad a picture of personality functioning, but it is very much shorter and simpler to use, and it does promise considerable specificity in measuring what is probably the most critical component of schizophrenic disorders.

Together, the four tests discussed in this chapter can provide valuable inferences about both the interindividual and the intraindividual characteristics of persons who may be designated schizophrenic. In large part, these are complementary devices rather than substitutes for one another, though the Rorschach and the Holtzman have strong similarities, and in regular clinical use, a tester usually employs one or the other.

8

Assessment of Possible Neural Substrates

Antonio E. Puente

Introduction

For an understanding of schizophrenic disorders, biological as well as psychological variables and their assessments should be taken into account. Notably, psychiatry has become increasingly interested in biological explanations of schizophrenic disorders, a reductionistic approach reflected in contemporary definitions (Andreasen, 1987).

In this chapter, I review the disparate neurobiological literature in an attempt to show whether and to what extent schizophrenic disorders can be considered brain disorders. Neuroradiological, neurological, psychophysiological, and neuropsychological assessment strategies are reviewed as they pertain to helping to distinguish schizophrenic from other psychiatric and neurological disorders. Following a review of selected studies, the hypothesis that schizophrenic disorders may be associated with brain dysfunction is presented. Numerous methodological and theoretical issues, which prevent clearly substantiating this hypothesis, are also discussed.

Assessment Methods

The differentiation of schizophrenic from organic disorders has typically relied on nonpsychological techniques (e.g., neuroradiological techniques such as computerized tomography). As a consequence, although a theoretical framework yields a working psychological approach to distinguishing schizophrenic from closely related (both functional and organic) disorders, little in the way of acceptable empirical information is currently available. Nevertheless, clinical differences have been reported and are presented in this section.

Neuroradiological Methods

The advent of sophisticated neuroradiological techniques has provided numerous assessment devices for studying schizophrenic disorders. The most robust appears to be computerized tomography (CT scan), a neuroradiological technique that gives a relatively accurate anatomical representation of the brain through horizontal "pictures" (top to bottom) of white and gray matter. The measurement of ventricle size, especially the lateral dimension, has been emphasized in the use of technique. Reports of cerebral as well as cerebellar density and atrophy are also found in the literature. More recently, researchers have used such sophisticated technologies as cerebral blood flow, positron emission tomography (PET), and magnetic resonance imaging (MRI). Cerebral blood flow analyses allow a careful study of the effects of mental functions on alterations of blood flow throughout the brain. The advantage of the PET over the CT scan is that it allows a more precise neuroradiological measurement of ongoing brain activity (rather than anatomical structure) by measuring glucose uptake. The MRI, in contrast, allows refined analysis of anatomical (and not physiological) deviations of the brain, such as brain tumors. For the most part, diagnosis has focused on the structural differences between nonneurally impaired patients with schizophrenic and affective disorders (especially mania) and normal controls.

Neurological Methods

The behavioral neurological approach, as espoused by researchers such as Luria (1973), focuses on a psychiatric-neurological interface in the diagnosis of disorders. In distinguishing schizophrenic from related disorders, the behavioral neurologist focuses on the administration of relatively unstructured neurological tasks such as finger tapping in an effort to measure a possible inability to engage in fine eye–hand coordination. Such a functional inability cannot be detected by classical electroencephalography (EEG) analyses but may be detected by analyses of the so-called soft neurological signs. Soft signs are qualitatively assessed symptoms that suggest a lack of neurological integrity. Recent attempts to differentiate schizophrenic from manic and personality disorders and minimal brain syndromes, while focusing on analyses of soft signs, are of special interest.

Psychophysiological Methods

The measurement of central as well as peripheral nervous system activity by psychophysiological devices has yielded important information about schizophrenic symptomatology. Early work in this area focused on skin activity as measured by the galvanic skin response (GSR), but recent investigations have almost exclusively concentrated on central nervous system activity, such as cortical firings measured by

EEG. Classical qualitative and intuitive neurological analysis remains an accepted method of differential diagnostics in neurology. However, greater scientific acceptance has been given to a more quantitative analysis of the amplified electrical signals of the brain. Brain arousal has been effectively measured by such methods as averaged evoked potential (AEP) as well as more classical methods, such as EEG response to eye-opening exercises. Evoked potentials occur in response to very specific sensory stimuli (e.g., auditory clicks) and are averaged over numerous trials for a comprehensive "mean" response. Spectral or bandwidth analysis has been effectively used in the assessment of a wide range of EEG frequency (though not amplitude or voltage) activity. These methods analyze specific patterns of electrical activity by focusing on the speed and intensity of neuronal firing in the cerebral cortex. This robust quantitative analysis has allowed examinations of hemispheric asymmetries, an approach that yields valuable information about such issues as interhemispheric processing and hemispheric coherence (i.e, similar and simultaneous EEG patterns in both hemispheres of the brain). One of the most recent applications of the EEG to research on schizophrenic disorders has been brain-electrical-activity mapping (BEAM), which allows a comprehensive topographical analysis of activity by examining EEG activity at different cortical sites and developing a "geographical" map of brain activity (Duffy, 1985).

Neuropsychological Methods

The psychometric assessment of central nervous system dysfunction has only recently gained appreciable clinical as well as research importance. Although it is a potential contributor to the differential analysis and understanding of schizophrenic disorders, the literature on this topic is rather limited. Traditional tests, such as the Minnesota Multiphasic Personality Inventory (MMPI) and the Wechsler Adult Intelligence Scale (WAIS), stand as the psychometric devices most widely used to differentiate schizophrenic from related disorders. Numerous MMPI "neuropsychological" subscales, such as the Psychiatric-Organic (P-O) Scale, have been used for this purpose (Watson, 1984), as have the Halstead-Reitan Neuropsychological Battery and the more recent Luria-Nebraska Neuropsychological Battery (e.g., Puente, Heidelberg-Sanders, & Lund, 1982a).

Differentiation of Schizophrenic from Related Mental Disorders

As indicated previously, a wide variety of biopsychological tests have been used to distinguish schizophrenic from other psychiatric populations. The following is a review of attempts at such differentiation by the use of neuroradiological, neurological, psychophysiological, and neuropsychological indices. Special emphasis is placed on methodological considerations including selection of subjects and effects of medications on neuropsychological functioning.

Neuroradiological Indices

CT scan evidence suggests that significant differences are observed in the brain structures of "schizophrenic" and "control" subjects (e.g., those with affective disorders, especially mania). Wood and Short (1985) reported that, next to those with dementia, subjects with schizophrenic disorders had the highest incidence of abnormal CT findings. Nasrallah, McCalley-Whitters, and Jacoby (1972) reported that cerebral cortex atrophy or neural deterioration of the cortex was more frequently observed in schizophrenic than in other "functionally" psychotic psychiatric populations. Specifically, the cerebral density in the cortical areas immediately dorsal to the body of the corpus callosum was slightly larger in schizophrenic than in manic subjects.

CT scans have also been used to examine ventricular, especially lateral, size in schizophrenic subjects, the supposition being that changes in ventricle size would affect the integrity of the surrounding neural tissue and thus the related functions. Nasrallah *et al.* (1972) reported that schizophrenic subjects did not exhibit larger ventricles than manics, whereas Luchins, Lewine, and Meltzer (1984) reported that ventricle size did differentiate schizophrenic and manic groups. In an effort to determine whether ventricular enlargement predated neuroleptic treatment and the onset of hospitalization for psychoses, Luchins *et al.* tested 35 individuals with first-episode schizophreniform disorders and concluded that structural changes were evident not only in the chronic schizophrenic subjects but in the acute schizophreniform sample as well. However, all subjects were on neuroleptics, and neuronal inhibition or structural changes may already have occurred. In contrast, only 3 of the 23 affective subject controls exhibited similar symptoms. (Drug administration as it affects brain functioning will be addressed later.)

Luchins *et al.* (1984) found that depressed subjects with enlarged ventricle size were (most often) misdiagnosed as schizophrenic, but these findings do not appear to generalize to cerebral or neuronal atrophy. Yates, Jacoby, and Andreasen (1987) reported no difference among affective, schizophrenic, and control subjects on global cerebellar atrophy. Thus, these studies raise questions about the adequacy of initial diagnoses and of subject selection procedures. As in the case of Luchins *et al.* (1984), subjects' classification may be based on incorrect criteria. Further, it may be at best academic to divide subjects into categories (e.g., depressed vs. schizophrenic) by the use of the current inadequate diagnostic criteria (e.g., the revised third edition of the American Psychiatric Association's *Diagnostic and Statistical Manual,* or DSM-III-R, 1987), and then to attempt to determine whether an underlying neuroradiological problem exists.

Neurological Indices

Qualitative neurological analysis has revealed the existence of soft signs suggesting that neurological integrity (e.g., frontal lobe dysfunction) in schizophrenics has been compromised, especially when they are compared to subjects with alcoholic, depressive, manic, bipolar, and emotionally unstable character disorders (Cox & Ludwig, 1979). However, Nasrallah, Tippin, and McCalley-Whitters (1983) reported little difference between manics and schizophrenics, noting that similar performances were observed on 27 of 30 structured neurological tasks designed to test for soft, or difficult-to-detect, signs.

Psychophysiological Indices

Using sophisticated analyses of both amplitude and frequency, as well as EEG cerebral asymmetry indices, Shagass, Roemer, and Straumanis (1983) were able to differentiate schizophrenic from nonpsychotic (e.g., neurotic), depressive, and manic subjects. Another report, by Shagass, Roemer, Straumanis, and Josiassen (1984), showed that eye-opening exercises resulted in significantly higher activation levels in schizophrenic and manic than in depressive, neurotic, and normal subjects. Scott and Schwartz (1975) reported qualitative EEG changes in a single patient suffering from both depression and schizophrenic disorder. Their results indicated that the quantity and organization of 8- to 12-cycles-per-second activity with atypical spikes and waves distinguished the schizophrenic from the depressed state. These results were extended by Abrams and Taylor (1979), who reported more abnormal EEGs in schizophrenic subjects ($N = 27$) than in subjects with affective disorders ($N = 12$). These findings, which appeared to be unrelated to demographic or pharmaceutical variables, suggested abnormalities in temporal areas of the cerebral cortex. However, the subjects were on neuroleptics, and replication of this study with drug-naive subjects would be of crucial interest.

Analyses of hemispheric EEG activity have yielded promising information for differentiating schizophrenic from related, nonneural psychiatric disorders. An analysis of amplitude asymmetry, which is not frequently performed, revealed large right–left variances in schizophrenics but small to nonexistent variances in persons with personality disorder, graduate students, and mental-health-center staff (Rockford, Swartzburg, Chowdhrey, & Goldstein, 1976). Such differences have been postulated by some (Dymond, Coger, & Serafetinides, 1980) to be restricted to frontal-temporal areas, whereas others (Flor-Henry, Koles, & Tucker, 1982) have suggested less cortically defined differences. Flor-Henry *et al.* reported that left-hemispheric overactivation is seen in schizophrenic disorders, whereas right-hemispheric overactivation is observed in affective disorders. Gruzelier (1987) endorsed these findings by suggesting that different asymmetrical hemispheric patterns actually distinguish schizophrenic from clinical controls as well as from schizophrenic subtypes.

Neuropsychological Indices

There is a growing literature on the differentiation of schizophrenic from neuropsychologically intact clinical controls by the use of neuropsychological tests. The MMPI is the most frequently used, scientifically based personality test. Hence, it is not surprising that it has been used in the type of studies reviewed in this chapter. For example, Trifiletti (1982) used Russell's MMPI key method to successfully discriminate brain-damaged from schizophrenic subjects but was not able to classify the depressed subjects. In a more recent effort, Puente, Rodenbough, and Horton (1989) compared the relative efficacy of several MMPI subscales used to detect brain dysfunction in psychiatric groups. Although schizophrenic subjects could be differentiated, the authors raised numerous cautions about using a simplistic differentiation procedure, such as single-test analyses.

More comprehensive neuropsychological tests have yielded more promising results, suggesting evidence of an underlying organic problem. For example, Donnelly (1984) found that schizophrenic subjects performed significantly worse than affective disorder subjects on the Halstead-Reitan Neuropsychological Battery (HRNB). However, intellectual abilities were found to affect neuropsychological performance in both groups. Taylor, Redfield, and Abrams (1981) reported that "schizophrenics" did significantly worse than depressives on several psychometric tests, such as the WAIS. In a study using the HRNB and the WAIS, schizophrenic subjects performed significantly worse on both measures than nine psychiatric controls (Lawson, Waldman, & Weinberger, 1988).

Summary

Neuroradiological analyses indicate that "schizophrenic" subjects, both acute and chronic, *may* exhibit significant structural brain changes, most notably in ventricular size, compared to controls. Neurological assessment furthers clinical group differentiation by focusing on soft signs, and a variety of EEG measures appear sensitive for discrimination purposes.

Schizophrenic disorders appear to be differentiated from other major psychiatric disorders beyond chance levels, especially when more comprehensive neuropsychological tests are used to discriminate groups. Difficulties do arise when less comprehensive tests of brain function are used. Regardless of the measurement device, it is premature to suggest that there are specific patterns of brain dysfunction that distinguish schizophrenic from other psychiatric disorders. R. B. Cairns (1986) suggested that conclusions based on statistical probability alone (without consideration of ecological validity) have significant potential problems. Thus, the validity, meaningfulness, and importance of these findings remain to be established.

Differentiation of Schizophrenic from Cerebral Disorders

Standard psychological tests have been of little use in differentiating schizophrenic from brain-damage disorders. Traditional psychological tests have been used to measure the personality traits and the intellectual-cognitive functioning of schizophrenic subjects, as well as brain-damaged subjects and those with other psychiatric disorders. However, the differentiation of schizophrenic from brain-damage disorders is a more complex and tentative issue, and what has been published is preliminary. Several neuropsychological tests, administered individually or in conjunction, have served as a foundation for major assessment strategies used to distinguish schizophrenic from brain-damaged subjects. Neuropsychological tests compare favorably with the physiological approaches used in the differential diagnosis of schizophrenic and related nonneural disorders.

Neuroradiological, Neurological, and Psychophysiological Indices

The literature lacks neuroradiological, neurological, and psychophysiological analyses that differentiate schizophrenic and brain-damaged subjects.

Neuropsychological Indices

Use of the complete MMPI's 14 basic scales has not proved to be of clinical utility in differentiating schizophrenic disorders from brain damage. However, deviation on specific experimental scales of the MMPI has generally proved to be of some clinical usefulness. Watson (1984) reviewed the efficacy of the Schizophrenia-Organicity (Sc-O) and the Psychiatric-Organicity (P-O) special scales. He concluded that a two-thirds accuracy or hit-rate could be achieved with the Sc-O scale and the P-O scale. Specifically, schizophrenic subjects had considerably different scores from those with brain damage on these two scales. These findings are best exemplified by the work of Horton (e.g., Horton, 1982; Horton, Scott, & Golden, 1983). Puente *et al.* (1989) extended these efforts, using several special or organic MMPI scales with outpatients. Russell's MMPI key has also been effectively used to discriminate these two samples (Trifiletti, 1982). However, questions remain about potential gender differences. For example, Horton (1982) indicated that the P-O scale was not an effective discriminator for female samples, whereas Sillitti (1982) indicated the opposite. Such discrepancies may reflect subject selection problems.

The WAIS has been used by several investigators to differentiate schizophrenic from brain-damaged samples. Heaton, Vogt, Hoehn, Lewis, Crowley, and Stallings (1979) reported discriminating schizophrenic subjects from normal controls as well as from acute and chronic brain-damaged subjects. These results were supported by Chelune, Heaton, Lehman, and Robinson (1979). Better discrimination rates were obtained by Bigler, Tucker, and Piran (1979), who used a late adolescent and young adult population. Both the mean level of WAIS performance and more careful pattern analysis appeared to yield group discrimination. However, group differentiation may be largely due to specific factors evaluated by the WAIS (e.g., attention). Using paranoid schizophrenic and brain-damaged patients, Lewis, Nelson, and Eggertsen (1979) found that attention and speed measures were most useful in differentiating these two groups. Of these measures, the Digit Symbol may be most sensitive in differentiating schizophrenic from brain-damaged subjects (Wysocki & Sweet, 1985). The WAIS has also been used to discriminate schizophrenic subjects with brain damage from those without brain damage (Freeland & Puente, 1983). Nevertheless, the traditional "hold, don't hold" strategies suggested by Wechsler were not useful in discriminating these two samples. According to Wechsler, "hold" tests are immune to brain damage, whereas "don't hold" tests are more likely to be affected by brain impairment.

The Whitaker Index of Schizophrenic Thinking (WIST) has also proved useful in differentiating schizophrenic from cerebral disorders. The WIST, described in greater detail in Chapter 7, focuses on cognitive processes and uses a multiple-choice design. The first study on this topic (Albott & Gilbert, 1973) reported successful differentiation between non-brain-damaged schizophrenic patients and brain-damaged patients. In an extension of their efforts, Puente and Heidelberg-Sanders (1981) assessed the efficacy of the WIST in differentiating schizophrenic subjects with and without cerebral disorders. The results suggested that indexes (time plus score) and times on the Word Pairs subtest were significantly different in the two groups. Puente, Heidelberg-Sanders, and Lund (1982a) were able to replicate these findings on a smaller sample.

The 269-item Luria-South Dakota, now Luria-Nebraska, Neuropsychological Battery (LNNB), has been reported to be effective (at times 100%) in distinguishing schizophrenic from organic brain syndrome patients. In a series of studies by Golden and colleagues (Lewis, Golden, Purisch, & Hammeke, 1979); Purisch, Golden, & Hammeke, 1978, 1979), the LNNB was reported to discriminate the two groups of subjects based on pattern as well as overall scale analysis of the 269 items and 16 basic scales. Subsequent studies that controlled for chronicity and length of hospitalization helped to substantiate these findings. Moses, Cardellina, and Thompson (1983) reported that schizophrenic as well as schizoaffective patients were easily distinguished from brain-damaged patients with only a few LNNB variables. Using the LNNB, Puente, Heidelberg-Sanders, and Lund (1982b) reported successful differentiation of schizophrenic subjects with and without detected brain damage. These findings were successfully replicated the following year with a smaller sample of subjects (Puente *et al.,* 1982a).

The Halstead-Reitan Neuropsychological Battery has also been used to differentiate schizophrenic from brain-damaged subjects. The HRNB comprises a variety of individual tests (e.g., categories) that address a number of sensory, motor, and language and other cognitive functions. Heaton and colleagues (Chelune *et al.,* 1979; Heaton *et al.,* 1979) reported using both HRNB gross analysis and HRNB pattern analysis to discriminate schizophrenic subjects. For example, Chelune *et al.* reported better schizophrenic than brain-damaged subject performance, but deficit pattern analyses did not significantly differentiate these two groups.

Summary

Although no neuroradiological, neurological, or psychophysiological measures have statistically discriminated between schizophrenia and organic brain syndromes, psychological and neuropsychological tests have yielded a large body of data showing significant differences. Psychological tests such as the MMPI special scales, the WAIS, and the WIST and neuropsychological tests such as the LNNB and the HRNB have all proved of clinical utility in differentiating these two types of subjects.

The above review of the literature reveals some interesting trends. Before the development of sophisticated neuroradiological techniques (CT, MRI, and PET), as well as psychophysiological methods, the role of the psychological assessment of schizophrenic disorders was often differential diagnosis. But there has been a paradigm shift in both the role of the psychologist and the assessment of schizophrenic disorders, as well as in the theoretical approach to understanding schizophrenic disorders. Instead of focusing on differential-diagnostic issues, psychological testing has largely relinquished discriminating between organic and functional disorder to neurologically based assessment methods (e.g., CT). In contrast, recent efforts have been directed by both psychologists and neurologically oriented physicians interested in schizophrenic disorders to understanding the biological—namely, neurological—substrates. Unfortunately, this shift has largely ignored more rudimentary questions of subject selection and the definition of *schizophrenia.*

Schizophrenic Disorders as Brain Disorders

Neuroradiological Indices

A wide variety of neuroradiological techniques and measures, including CT, MRI, and cerebral blood flow, have been used to examine the possible central nervous system (CNS) substrates of schizophrenic disorders. Each method has been used to try to elucidate the relationship between the brain and schizophrenic symptomatology.

CT scans have been used for over 10 years. The numerous CT measures include, but are not limited to, the assessment of ventricular enlargement and structural pathology. In one of the earlier studies to address this issue, Weinberger, Torrey, Neophytides, and Wyatt (1979) reported that lateral ventricle enlargement appeared to be associated with chronic schizophrenia, but not to its pharmacological treatment. However, measurement problems have precluded a very precise estimate of the extent to which the ventricles are actually enlarged. For example, volumetric measures of the lateral ventricles differed significantly from digital plammetry and from mechanical plammetry analyses (Raz, Raz, Weinberger, Boronow, Pickar, Bigler, & Tukheimer, 1987). Nevertheless, the finding of lateral ventricle enlargement in "schizophrenics" is well accepted and is reported in a large number of studies. The question has now shifted to what the functional implication of such an enlargement is, as ventricle enlargement does not correlate well with a variety of symptoms (Farmer, Jackson, McGuffin, & Storey, 1987; Pfefferbaum, Zipursky, Lim, Zatz, Stahl, & Jernigan, 1988). However, Andreasen, Olsen, Dennert, and Smith (1982) reported that "large" ventricles appear to be associated with negative symptoms such as flat affect and avolition. In contrast, positive symptoms (e.g., delusions and hallucinations) were most frequently seen in patients with "small" ventricles.

CT technology has also allowed the analysis of specific structural pathology. Using discordant or nonidentical schizophrenic twins as subjects, Reveley, Reveley, and Baldy (1987) reported that the left hemisphere was relatively less dense than the right hemisphere. White matter density, asymmetry in white matter density, and global cortical atrophy were more prevalent in schizophrenic subjects than in headache controls (Smith, Baumgartner, Ravichandran, & Largen, 1987). Interestingly, none of the measures correlated well with neuroleptic treatment response to psychopathology scores on the Brief Psychiatric Rating Scale.

A family history of schizophrenic disorders (Turner, Toone, & Brett-Jones, 1986) was not associated with CT abnormalities, whereas a poor premorbid level of function was (Weinberger, Cannon-Spoor, Potkin, & Wyatt, 1980). Lateral ventricle enlargement at the onset of psychosis was reported by Iacono, Smith, Moreau, Beiser, Fleming, Lin, and Flak (1988). The question of whether these CT abnormalities progress over time has also been explored. Illowsky, Julian, Bigelow, and Weinberger (1988) completed a seven- to nine-year follow-up of schizophrenic subjects with known brain abnormalities. Although these patients had been continuously hospitalized and treated with neuroleptics, no significant changes in CT measures were noted. In a comprehensive review of the literature, Goetz and Kammen (1986) indicated that CT abnormalities in chronic subjects tend to change negatively over time and to exhibit a higher degree of neuropsychological impairment than in control subjects.

The relationship of drug treatment to CT abnormality has been explored. Losonczy, Song, Moh, Small, Davidson, Johns, and Davis (1986) examined 28 schizophrenic patients on and off neuroleptic medication (haloperidol). Neither the response to the medication nor the symptom type or severity was significantly correlated with the ventricle–brain ratio. These findings were replicated by Smith *et al.* (1987). Unfortunately, the question of past drug treatment and possible residual effects is not well understood or taken into account. For example, Breggin (1983) claimed that the neuroleptics' brain-damaging effects increase with age, and that past drug treatment effects may not show clearly until the patients are older.

Although CT technology may offer a window into the schizophrenic brain, Andreasen (1988) offered only cautious optimism about its "illuminating the underlying neural mechanism" of schizophrenia. Questions about the actual measurement allowed by CT and the functional relations of CT measures remain to be resolved, as numerous methodological and empirical questions persist.

The MRI is a more recent and sophisticated method used to examine general structural brain abnormalities. Using signal-density analyses, the MRI easily distinguishes gray from white matter. In general, the MRI appears to suggest that the frontal lobes are the most significantly impaired of brain structures in schizophrenic subjects (Andreasen, Nasrallah, Dunn, Olson, Grove, Ehrhardt, Coffman, & Crosett, 1986). This impairment may be due in part to the enlargement of the anterior portion of the lateral ventricles found by Kelsoe, Cadet, Pickar, and Weinberger (1988), who reported a 73% enlargement. Education, one of the crucial control variables, may also modulate cerebral size. For example, DeMyer, Gilmor, Hendrie, Augustyn, and Jackson (1988) reported that smaller right than left hemispheres were noted in schizophrenics, but this pattern was reversed when education was taken into account. In addition to the impairment in the lateral ventricle and the frontal lobe, corpus callosum thickness, especially in the anterior and middle portions (Nasrallah, Andreasen, Coffman, Olson, Dunn, Ehrhardt, and Chapman, 1986), and greater overall length (Mathew, Partain, Prakash, Kulkarni, Logan, & Wilson, 1985) have been found in "schizophrenics." Mathew *et al.* (1985) also reported a mean thickness increase as well as a lack of correlation between MRI findings and symptoms. Finally, it appears that the basal ganglia are affected in schizophrenic persons, but only in those with tardive dyskinesia, a neuroleptic-induced brain disorder (Bessen, Corrigan, Cherryman, & Smith, 1987).

Although the CT and MRI provide excellent representations of possible structural abnormalities, they fail to provide insights into specific physiological or metabolic deficiencies. Two very recent innovations in neuroradiology, PET and cerebral blood flow, now allow for this type of analysis.

Cerebral uptake of labeled fluorine-18 in the frontal lobes of schizophrenic subjects was initially measured by PET. Buchsbaum (1982) reported decreased glucose use in the frontal lobes compared to that in controls. More recent studies (e.g., Kishimoto, Kuwahara, Ohno, Takazu, Hama, Sato, Ishil, Nomura, Fujita, Miyanchi, Matsushita, Yokoi, & Iio, 1987) have identified subtypes of chronic schizophrenic disorder with PET. Their findings suggested that "Type A" experienced a 38% reduction in brain glucose utilization of the frontal lobe, and that "Type B" experienced 26% in the parietal lobe. Postmortem PET studies of chronic schizophrenic subjects have also revealed an increase in the number of specific dopamine receptors in the basal ganglia, which may be due to the neuroleptics. Wong, Wagner, Tune, Dannals, Pearlson, Links, Tamminga, Broussolle, Ravert, Wilson, Thomas-Young, Malat, Williams, Tuma, Snyder, Kuhar, and Gjedde (1986) suggested that this increase, especially in the carotid artery, is probably linked to schizophrenic disorder, and not to the neuroleptics themselves. However, metabolic rates in the basal ganglia increased with the administration of neuroleptics. Interestingly, drug-free schizophrenics exhibited lower metabolic rates in this region than nonschizophrenic controls (Buchsbaum, Wu, DeLisi, Holcomb, Hazlett, Cooper-Langston, & Kessler, 1987). Others have reported that hypofrontal metabolic patterns may occur with the administration of neuroleptics (Volkow, Brodie, Wolf, Angrist, Russell, & Cancro, 1986).

Related neuroradiological measures have been used to map the neural substrates of subjects with schizophrenic disorders. One of the more promising of these procedures is regional cerebral blood flow. For example, Weinberger, Berman and Zec (1986) suggested that a pathophysiological pattern was evident in the dorsolateral prefrontal cortexes of 20 inpatient schizophrenic subjects. Such patterns may be accentuated during specific cognitive tasks. Berman (1987) compared frontal lobe blood flow in 30 normals and 34 neuroleptic-free schizophrenics. Although the expected differences in frontal lobe function were observed, they were accentuated during performances of the Wisconsin Card Sorting Test, a visual abstraction task. In addition to frontal lobe deficits, the left temporal and right parietal lobes have been implicated in this type of schizophrenic patient (Mathew, Wilson, Tant, Robinson, & Prakash, 1988).

Neurological Indices

Standard neurological studies have also contributed to the understanding of schizophrenic disorders as brain disorders. Using a test of graphathesia and the face–hand test, Torrey (1980) examined 84 inpatient "schizophrenics" for neurological abnormalities. Approximately 8% of the subacute and acute inpatients showed abnormalities, and approximately 50% of the subchronic or chronic group were abnormal, although it is impossible to ascertain the role of neuroleptics in this study. In a recent review of the significance and meaning of neurological signs in "schizophrenia," Heinrichs and Buchanan (1988) concluded that "schizophrenics" exhibited more neurological signs than both nonpsychiatric and psychiatric controls, including subjects with affective disorders and nonpsychotic disorders.

Neuropathological Indices

Postmortem examinations are often the most conclusive criterion in any study of the CNS, and studies of CNS involvement in schizophrenic disorders are no exception. Recent studies address the complex neural substrates of these disorders, although there are problems in terms of specific measures and functional implications.

In a study that supports the CT findings reported earlier in this chapter, Pakkenberg (1987) found that Type II (chronic) schizophrenic subjects had larger ventricle volumes than Type I (acute), and that the total fixated (postmortem) brain of both types revealed significant ventricle volume reduction in both hemispheres and in all of the cerebral cortex. In addition, postmortem examinations have revealed altered hippocampal structures (Bridge, Kleinman, Karoum, & Wyatt, 1985). Seeman (1984) examined the dopamine hypothesis of schizophrenia by measuring dopamine receptors in a variety of schizophrenic subjects. Seeman concluded that high-density measures were most frequently noted in Type I, and that Type II tended to be associated with low-density measures.

Psychophysiological Indices

Although early studies used a variety of psychophysiological measures, more recent efforts have been directed to CNS function, especially with EEG-type measures. Another new technology, brain-electrical-activity mapping, has also contributed to an understanding of the electrical activity of the brain. BEAM offers the advantage of a noninvasive and sensitive approach to the topographic mapping of brain activity (Duffy, 1985) by "mapping" the electrical activity of the brain geographically with the use of EEG measures. Guenther and Breitling (1985), who applied this method of mapping brain activity to schizophrenic disorders, reported bifrontal delta and theta with low beta power values.

Both P300 latency and P300 amplitude, measured with evoked-potentional technology, appear to be affected in schizophrenic inpatients (Obiols, Bachs, & Masana, 1986). Such CNS pathophysiology is typically observed during task activity. Barrett, McCallum, and Pocock (1986) reported that the amplitudes of the P300 (both specific and late) were significantly reduced in schizophrenic subjects, compared with controls during an auditory target detection.

Neuropsychological Indices

Whereas early studies were often personality-based, recent efforts using neuropsychological measures have allowed a greater functional understanding of CNS abnormalities in schizophrenic disorders. Various standard and individualized neuropsychological measures have been used to determine the disorders associated with CNS impairment, as well as to classify subtypes of schizophrenic disorders. By far the most widely used of the tests is the Wechsler Adult Intelligence Scale followed by the Luria-Nebraska Neuropsychological Battery and portions of the Halstead-Reitan Neuropsychological Battery. Neuropsychological measures on these and related tests have been used to address cognitive, motor, and attentional dysfunctions.

Using a variety of neuropsychological instruments (e.g., the LNNB), researchers have been developing a concept of what behaviors appear to be impaired and, in turn, which ones are directly related to CNS dysfunctions. Cognitive dysfunction, including problems with visual abstraction and association, and with complex motor behaviors and attention, has been observed in schizophrenic subjects. Motor dysfunctions were studied by Bilder and Goldberg (1987), who used tests developed for the assessment of frontal-lobe-modulated function and elicited behaviors in chronic schizophrenic subjects that resembled frontal lobe motor damage. This and similar studies reveal cognitive defects that may be functional and/or organic. Goldberg,

Weinberger, Berman, and Pliskin (1987) used the Wisconsin Card Sorting Test to determine the abilities of inpatient schizophrenics to develop appropriate sorting strategies. Although the subjects could learn a related word list, most could not learn a strategy to sort the cards.

Going further, several researchers have used these preliminary findings to cluster or categorize groups of schizophrenic subjects. In the earliest study on this issue, Goldstein and Halperin (1977) administered the WAIS, the HRNB, and several related tests to 140 schizophrenic subjects. The subjects were classified according to one of the following: paranoid versus nonparanoid; neurologically intact versus abnormal; and long- versus short-term institutionalization. Although this classification into categories was achieved by means of neuropsychological test scores, the most significant classification of the subjects was between long- and short-term institutionalized subjects.

Using the criterion of brain damage versus CNS intactness to classify subjects into brain-impaired and nonimpaired categories, Puente *et al.* (1982b) were able to classify 90% of the subjects correctly simply by their *t*-scale scores on the LNNB. Paranoid and nonparanoid schizophrenic subjects differed similarly when their LNNB performance was impaired (Langell, Purisch, & Golden, 1987).

An alternative approach to studying schizophrenic disorders is to combine methods or measures rather than to use a single approach. Probably the best example of this effort has been the combination of CT and neuropsychological measures. Specifically, researchers have attempted to examine cerebral ventricular size in relation to neuropsychological impairment. Golden (1981) correlated plammeter-measured lateral ventricle size with *t* scores on the original 14 scales of the LNNB. A multiple correlation of .72 was noted. Kemali (1985) replicated and extended these findings, using more sophisticated cerebral ventricle measures, for example, ventricular brain ratio as well as both the LNNB and the WAIS. It would appear that there is a relationship between CT and other neuroradiological deficits in schizophrenic patients. This impression was supported by the early work of Golden, Purisch, and Hammeke (1980), who reported a positive relationship between LNNB scale scores and ventricular size in young schizophrenics.

Assessment of Assessment Techniques

Excluding the until-recently standardized Halstead-Reitan Neuropsychological Battery and the Luria-Nebraska Neuropsychological Battery, most of the psychometric devices used to established the neural substrates of higher-order behavior have been nonneuropsychological. Thus, comparisons of studies using nonneuropsychological or neurophysiological tools and the neuropsychological tests are weak at best. To aggravate matters, what does exist in the psychophysiological literature is plagued by a lack of standardization between laboratories and measures. An interface of psychometric and psychophysiological measures which use standardized techniques, should prove critical to understanding the existing disparate findings, as well as provide a heuristic impetus for future investigations. Until then, one can only make, at best, a weak interpretation of how schizophrenic disorders differ from related disorders with regard to the neural substrates of higher-order behavior.

Another critical methodological issue is the confounding of variables in the measurement of brain function. Including, but not limited to, chronicity, length of hospitalization, and the effects of somatic therapies, age, education, and intellectual ability. In this chapter, several studies were reviewed in which neuroleptic treatment was taken into account. However, by no means are the data clearly interpretable. In one of the most aggressive attacks on this situation, Breggin (1983) labeled neuroleptic therapy "brain-disabling therapy." He proposed the concept that the major tranquilizers produce "iatrogenic helplessness and denial" or, in essence, nonsurgical lobotomy. Reviewing numerous studies on the neurophysiological and neuropsychological effects of neuroleptic ingestion, Breggin proposed that these drugs impair first the reticular activating system and later the limbic system.

Regardless of whether one accepts Breggin's conclusions, there is no question that neuroleptics—which reduce dopaminergic activity—confound an understanding of the schizophrenic disorders from a neural perspective, at least in the great majority of studies. Long-term follow-up and cross-sectional drug versus nondrug studies are sorely needed to address this serious methodological (and clinical) issue. For example, Keck, Cohen, Baldessarini, and McElroy (1989) reported that, out of more than 1,300 research literature citations, only 5 studies were scientifically rigorous enough to address the efficacy and the time course of antipsychotic agents. Finally, another concern is whether statistical differentiation equals diagnostic or clinical significance. Ventricle size, for example, may not relate well to functional impairment. Thus, the possibility exists that even establishing measurable neural deficits may not lead yet to an understanding of the behavioral deficits in schizophrenic disorders.

Summary

Some "schizophrenics," relative to nonneurally impaired clinical subjects (e.g., those with affective disorders), exhibit decreased neural integrity as measured by various neural tests. That is, a portion of this population's disordered behavior may be linked to underlying disordered CNS activity (e.g., changes in ventricular size). Unfortunately, this conclusion must be tempered by numerous methodological concerns.

Though numerous types of clinical samples have been tested, including subjects with personality disorders, alcoholism, depression, and manic disorders, an uncontrolled variety of assessment methods have been applied to many of the populations investigated, especially manic subjects. Possibly as a function of these confounds, there is a lack of clear distinction—at least, according to several investigators—between the underlying neuropsychological substrates in mania and the schizophrenic disorders. During periods of active psychosis, clear neuropsychological differentiation becomes increasingly difficult, if not impossible. Other confounding variables involve subject selection; samples have usually been noncomparable, nonreplicable, and nonrepresentative, even when similar diagnostic systems have been used to select research participants. Selection tends to be biased toward more behaviorally disturbed patients or patients with a mixture of schizophrenic and neural impairment (e.g., Puente *et al.,* 1982a,b) or the inclusion of misdiagnosed "schizophrenics," who were actually brain-damaged (e.g., as reported by Landmark *et al.,* 1986). Other methodological considerations include the questionable reliability and validity of assessment devices and procedures. Further, more evidence needs to be obtained on the effects on brain function of neuroleptic drug use and other somatic therapies (i.e., electroconvulsive therapy, or ECT). Establishing their effects (or possibly using drug-naive subjects) would greatly enhance the understanding of the possible neural mechanisms underlying schizophrenic processes.

The question remains: How many of the observations and correlations are valid or, if valid, powerful enough to be revealing or clinically important? The implied neural defects may be due to many different variables, including (1) psychosomatic processes related to inadequate stimulation; (2) neuroleptic treatment, which reduces brain activity; (3) genetic defects; (4) factors developed during childhood; and (5) ongoing brain dysfunction of a viral or other somatic origin.

The available findings suggest that schizophrenic disorders are associated with neurological changes even when compared to organic brain syndromes. This evidence is stronger when Type I and Type II schizophrenic patients are compared, or when positive and negative symptoms are taken into account. Type I patients (see Crow, 1980), who exhibited delusions and hallucinations and tend to be acute, may have more of a metabolic disorder. In contrast, Type II patients, who are more chronic, exhibit more negative symptoms as well as more structural pathology.

A radical perspective suggests that schizophrenic disorders should no longer be viewed as functional psychoses (Tyrer & Mackay, 1986). If one does accept the findings of neurological deficits, questions remain regarding such issues as the etiology and the pattern of these deficits. Regarding etiology, for example, Weinberger (1987) implied that brain pathology remains silent until the nervous system matures; it is not until later that the pathology (e.g., of neurotransmitters) is exhibited in behavioral responses. Questions of the chronicity of the disorder and the etiology of the "injury" as discriminant factors remain to be answered.

Schizophrenic subjects do worse on neuropsychological tests than other psychiatric patients, but better than organics. As early as 1978, several researchers noted these differences (Goldstein, 1978; Malec, 1978), which may be due to limitation of the patient's attention and/or to left-hemisphere deficits. Specifically, the studies reviewed in this chapter indicate that some "schizophrenics" appear to exhibit deficits on CT, EEG, and a variety of psychological and neuropsychological tests, including the MMPI, the WAIS, and the HRNB. When compared to other psychiatric populations, schizophrenic subjects tend to exhibit behavioral deficits that may be attributable to an impairment of the ventricles, the hemispheres (especially the left), and the frontal lobes. "Schizophrenics" show what may be neurological deficits on the

MMPI, the WIST, the WAIS, the LNNB, and the HRNB, but these deficits are less appreciable than those shown by organic subjects. This tendency suggests that some schizophrenic disorders may have a central nervous system or brain disorder component. A variety of neuroradiological (i.e., CT MRI, and cerebral blood flow), neurophysiological (i.e., variations in EEG activity), and neuropsychological tests (e.g., the WAIS, the HRNB, and the LNNB) have revealed frontal lobe, hemispheric, and lateral ventricle disruptions that appear to be associated with such behavioral processes as attention, information processing, motor functioning, personality variables, and a variety of "executive functions." Such processes appear to be more disrupted during periods of task performance, exposure to novel situations or stimuli, and related unusual demands (e.g., stress) during standard cognitive activities.

However, it is critical to emphasize once more the numerous methodological limitations in the studies reviewed in this chapter. Thus, for the time being, the conclusions presented in this chapter should be considered preliminary. There is little question that behavioral and neurological deficits do exist in some "schizophrenics." Their relationship and significance remain open to question.

9

Conceptualization of Schizophrenic Disorders

The aims of this chapter are to capture the overall sense and nonsense of the concept of schizophrenic disorders and to prepare the groundwork for Chapter 10, on treatment and prevention, and Chapter 11, on legal considerations. Basic conceptual issues relevant to these topics are made particularly explicit with these aims in mind.

Myth, Construct, Disorder, or Disease

Careful study of people labeled *schizophrenic* suggests that a great many of them have quite serious, real impairments of a characteristic kind. Vaslav Nijinsky and Sylvia Frumkin, who were discussed in Chapter 4, were certainly severely impaired in cognitive and interpersonal functioning. Both had deteriorated from much higher previous levels of functioning. They were persons for whom the adjective *schizophrenic* makes sense in terms of a marked impairment of a functional rather than an "organic" kind. Neither, evidently, became schizophrenic because of central nervous system damage, though Sylvia did suffer brain damage later because of her drug treatment. But some persons who are labeled schizophrenic are actually just brain-damaged, and some are both brain-damaged and schizophrenic, as discussed in Chapter 8 by Antonio Puente. Still other persons who are neither brain-damaged nor schizophrenic are neverless labeled schizophrenic often merely on the basis of one or two possible symptoms. Such misdiagnosis is common, and in these cases "schizophrenia" is certainly a myth.

Thomas Szasz (1976) claimed correctly that "mental illness" generally and "schizophrenia" particularly are myths if one adheres to the classical definition of disease, propounded by Rudolph Virchow in 1858, in terms of cellular pathology:

> According to this view, "Disease of the body is a disease of cells. The cure of the body may be effected by curing the cells. The real question which the modern scientific physician puts to himself when called to treat a case is: What cells are out of order and what can be done for them?" This remains the basic concept and model of disease in Western countries and

in scientific discourse throughout the world. (Szasz, 1976, p. 9, including his quoting of *Funk & Wagnall's New Standard Encyclopedia,* 6th ed., on "Rudolph Virchow")

At the other extreme from this classic definition of disease, psychiatrist Samuel Guze gave the following extremely encompassing definition in his coauthored book *Psychiatric Diagnosis* (Goodwin & Guze, 1979):

> Any condition associated with discomfort pain, disability, death, or an increased liability to these states, regarded by physicians and the public as properly the responsibility of the medical profession, may be considered a disease. Whether a condition is regarded as a disease is a function of many factors: social, economic, biological, etc. As a society becomes better educated and more secular, disabilities often cease to be regarded as moral or theological problems and become medical ones. Many illnesses have passed through such a transition: epilepsy, mania, various psychoses. Similar shifts may currently be taking place for alcoholism and sociopathy. (p. 215)

At this extreme, we may someday be called diseased if we merely go to a grocery store and find ourselves uncomfortable with the prices, or even if we are simply liable to become uncomfortable, as long as physicians say so and the public acquiesces.

This extremely inclusive view of disease as anything that physicians say it is, provided their say-so elicits some public agreement, has been taking increasingly firm hold, as Paul Starr documented thoroughly in his book *The Social Transformation of American Medicine* (1982). More and more human conditions have come under the authority of the medical profession; particularly psychiatry, as the market for medical services has expanded and medical authority has consolidated. Although the classical disease criteria have not been satisfied for the "functional psychoses," including the schizophrenic disorders, the treatment of these conditions has become increasingly classical in terms of somatic interventions and underlying assumptions of, as yet unproven, cellular pathology. Thus, seemingly limitless numbers of human conditions are now considered diseases and are treated by physical means, and the public also generally accepts the notion that these "mental disorders" are really diseases and must be treated medically. In recent years, it has become commonplace to hear that such disorders are "caused by chemical imbalances."

Both the myth and the disease concept of the schizophrenic disorders may distract attention from the important phenomena. Szasz correctly refuted the basic assumption that "schizophrenia" is a medically well-established diagnosis of a disease, ostensibly a brain disease with a high genetic predisposition, which is helpfully treated by physical means such as drugs. Szasz was right in asserting that each of these premises lacks adequate evidence. But he did not address the phenomena of impairment characteristic of many people labeled schizophrenic. He was also right in pointing to the dangers of using deviance criteria for "mental illness." He was correct in condemning myriad forms of coercive treatment, especially when they cause iatrogenic harm.

Advocates of the disease concept may seem to provide a sense of certainty, but calling schizophrenia a *disease* is, at best, extremely premature. At present, we have no solid evidence suggesting a substrate of genetic or other biological bases for the kinds of cognitive and interpersonal breakdowns that are called schizophrenic. The "evidence" is nearly always correlational rather than experimental, and it does not necessarily imply causality. Thus, acting as though schizophrenic disorders are diseases in terms of classical cellular pathology is more a political than a scientific approach.

At the other extreme, if everything that is or may be uncomfortable is called a disease, we may have an interesting philosophical point of view but nothing practically useful. As Strauss and Carpenter (1981) wrote, "Theoretically, symptoms alone rarely constitute an adequate basis for defining a disease; the concept of disease implies an underlying pathological process with ramifications far beyond symptom description" (p. 34). It is one thing to claim a vast domain of authority but quite another to do something useful within that domain.

Labeling schizophrenic disorders diseases also appears presumptuous because of the still primitive nature of attempts to define schizophrenic disorders. The mere label *schizophrenia* has had little predictive or other explanatory significance. Though the term *schizophrenia* should be used to refer to quite seriously impaired mental conditions that ought to command serious attention, it is usually a poorly defined and rather weak concept, certainly not a well-defined disease. Arieti's 1974 observation still holds true: "It is a formidable task to define schizophrenia unless we accept an unsatisfactory definition that consists of a list of the most common characteristics of the disorder" (p. 3).

The term *disorders* might be satisfactory if even this term did not suggest more certainty about definition than is warranted. From a scientific standpoint, as Meehl (1972), Kendall (1975), and Neale and Oltmanns (1980) have proposed, it makes sense to treat schizophrenia as an open scientific construct, "an internal event whose existence is inferred on the basis of observable behaviors and the context in which they occur. . . .The construct cannot be directly observed, but it is tied to overt behavioral referents that can be observed." (Neale & Oltmanns, 1980, p. 19). At least, an "open scientific construct" indicates that "schizophrenia" should be linked in provable ways to observable phenomena. Ultimately, the question is whether any concept of "schizophrenia" is helpful toward the scientific goals of prediction and control and the humane goals of trying to prevent and treat "schizophrenia."

Schizophrenic disorders is a passable term, unless one vests it with more definiteness that has been established. Scientifically, *schizophrenic disorders* should be regarded as an open scientific construct that invites further understanding rather than premature certainty. Thus, the term *schizophrenic disorders* may be used to refer to impairments that are problems for schizophrenic persons and others. However, the term has been used nonsensically in the past, for example, to refer to persons who are not impaired (e.g. Russian political deviants who have "sluggish schizophrenia" or persons whose impairments are of different kinds and origins (or whose brain damage is mistaken for schizophrenic disorder). Persons may be hastily labeled schizophrenic without more than the briefest presentation of apparent symptoms, yet this label may stick as if it had some scientific value (Deikman & Whitaker, 1979; Rosenhan, 1973). One should be cautious in accepting the label even when evaluation is apparently thorough: "absolutism in the diagnosis of schizophrenia has such a shaky base as to cast doubt about the critical capacities of any unflinching proponent." (Strauss & Carpenter, 1981, p. 40).

Entity or Continuum

The presumption that schizophrenia is a clear-cut all-or-none entity is contradicted by the evidence. Eugen Bleuler (1950) noted degrees of schizophrenia along a continuum and emphasized that most schizophrenic persons were ambulatory and not so severely impaired as to be completely dysfunctional. If we view schizophrenic disorders as being a matter of degree as well as kind, and along a continuum of disorder representing the whole of humanity, the majority of schizophrenic persons are certainly far from "completely crazy." Furthermore, the kinds of cognitive and interpersonal impairments considered characteristic of schizophrenia can be observed among nonschizophrenic persons under severe stress, as in combat situations or in concentration camps (Karon & VandenBos, 1981). Thus, all of us can empathize with schizophrenic persons, if we are not afraid to do so.

Because schizophrenic phenomena are a matter of degree as well as kind, we can see the arbitrariness of various cutoff levels for declaring a person schizophrenic. Most European systems have had higher cutoff points than American systems, though this has been less true since the introduction of the third edition of the *Diagnostic and Statistical Manual* (DSM-III; American Psychiatric Association, 1980). Furthermore, it is arbitrary to insist on a rigid demarcation between schizophrenic and certain related disorders, particularly schizoaffective and other "affective disorders." How pervasive and how extreme must the schizophrenic kinds of impairment be to identify someone as schizophrenic? These questions of cutoff levels and demarcations from other disorders pose major dilemmas in the weighing of assessment evidence presented by courtroom psychiatrists and psychologists, especially as the issue of degree is seldom made explicit.

Although the task is difficult, to be genuinely useful, a diagnosis must specify how impaired the person is, to what degree the person has improved or worsened, and to what extent we may expect the person to be aware of and in control of his or her actions. Rarely, however, have clinical or research studies accomplished this task. Instead, we have vague statements of "improvement" or "exacerbation" without any definition of the person's previous degree and pervasiveness of disorder. None of the *Diagnostic and Statistical Manuals* of the American Psychiatric Association have been explicit about degree of impairment, much less provided a means of assessing it.

One may ask why we should attempt to specify degree when it is difficult even to specify whether a person is schizophrenic. As discussed in previous chapters, if assessors did have to specify degree, one might be able to distinguish substantive from superficial disagreements among assessors. For example, if a psychiatrist or psychologist using a relatively limited definition of schizophrenia and another "expert" using a more inclusive definition disagree about whether a subject is or is not schizophrenic, they may find that they disagree only on the degree and the pervasiveness of the signs and symptoms. If the definitions used by both are specific, they can easily pinpoint the areas of their disagreement.

As discussed in Chapter 3, differences in degree correspond, in part, to differences in kinds of symptoms, and even symptoms such as hallucinations, delusions, and thought disorder should be rated for degree. Taking into account both kinds and degrees enables a much more precise specification than is usual.

Deviance or Morbidity

Deviance from social norms is often used to represent morbidity, but although deviance and morbidity may overlap, they refer to different personal attributes. For example, a person may be described as having "above-normal intelligence." Does this mean that the person is abnormal, in other words, suffering from some form of intellectual morbidity? No, it means merely that the person has above-average intellectual ability, which is regarded as desirable. Somewhat similarly, persons who are politically deviant may be doing something that is quite the opposite of morbid, such as Germans who protested the Nazi regime. Deviance refers to difference from the average or the "norm," whereas *morbidity* refers to harmful influences or their consequences. When we equate deviance with morbidity, we fail to accept individual differences, including those that serve constructive purposes and work against morbidity.

These distinctions between deviance and morbidity have a crucial significance in how schizophrenic persons are diagnosed and treated. When people disturb others, they attract attention, whereas quiet persons who are very disturbed but not disturbing may be ignored. Most observers tend to focus more on deviance than on morbidity. They may also equate deviance with morbidity, especially in the ordinary diagnosis and treatment of "schizophrenic" persons. This tendency is found not only in Russian psychiatry's labeling of political dissidents as schizophrenics but also the hasty and lasting diagnoses of schizophrenic disorders in people who deliberately faked symptoms and were admitted into mental hospitals in Rosenhan's study (1973). Like the Russian dissidents, these "patients" were given phenothiazine treatment.

Labeling someone schizophrenic makes sense only if it can be shown that the person has suffered a considerable impairment of reality-testing ability and that his or her functioning ability is well below their capacity. That is, schizophrenic disorder refers validly only to impairment and disturbance of the individual, not to disturbance that the person is causing others. Again, disturbed persons may be disturbing, but that is not the essence of their disorder.

Consistent or Inconsistent

Inconsistency is a hallmark of schizophrenic disorders. Perhaps no other disorder is so much characterized by inconsistency along so many dimensions. Even viewed in a single short period of time, schizophrenic persons are more likely to be inconsistent than to present a uniform picture of functioning. Even patients at the severe end of the continuum of disturbance who may seem "crazy all the time," may be surprisingly normal when they are with certain people, when they are treated with great respect, when certain topics are mentioned, and when circumstances suggest that they can perform valuable services. Much of the variability in level of ability may be a function of the person's self-esteem. For example, Arieti (1974) reported how constructive and competent backward schizophrenic patients became when over-worked nurses called on them to help.

Viewed over long stretches of time, schizophrenic persons may be so inconsistent as to confound the most careful assessments of prognosis. Stated statistically, most of the outcome variance cannot be accounted for by predictive means. A seemingly "incurable schizophrenic" like Nijinsky, who was discussed in Chapter 4, may contradict even the most expert prognosticators of dire deterioration. Yet others diagnosed as having merely had a "psychotic episode" or as having just a "schizophreniform illness" may deteriorate into severe lifelong disability. Such cases of continued deterioration usually have a history of a more consistent, severely regressive level of functioning, although even the "obviously hopeless case" may prove surprising in certain circumstances.

Biological or Psychosocial Causation

The question of the causes of schizophrenic disorders has elicited countless answers, most of them now demonstrably wrong. This history of false explanations is fraught with great emotional intensity, even when ostensibly sober research scientists are involved. Many proposed causes and proposed cures have appeared later to involve denial and rejection. For example the practice of prefrontal lobotomy was allowed to continue while obviously reducing people to really hopeless prognoses and subhuman vegetative existences. Currently, proponents of neuroleptic drug treatment are producing many cases of tardive dyskinesia although the neurological signs and symptoms are blatant, and many experts continue to view "schizophrenia" as a disease with a course of inevitable deterioration, or at least as a lifelong illness, in contradiction to abundant contrary evidence. In all of these cases of incorrect but steadfastly held opinions about causation and treatment, correction has required humane concern from outside the "scientific" domain.

Given the immensity and the prolongation of errors in the biological "scientific explanations of schizophrenia," we should be quite skeptical of the "new discoveries" of the cause of schizophrenia that appear in newspapers, magazines, and scientific journals every year. Some authors tie the relentless pursuit of such explanations to the powerful commercial influence of the drug industry. Even establishing a somatic cause would not necessarily suggest drug treatment:

> Yet such thinking has dominated more than thirty years of research on the biochemistry of schizophrenia, generated endless research papers, made scientific and medical reputations, and brought incidental substantial profit to the big drug firms. The history of thinking among biochemists about schizophrenia over the period is inextricably intertwined with that of the pharmaceutical industry, for which psychotropic drugs have been one of the biggest money spinners. (Lewontin, Rose, & Kamin, 1984, p. 204)

As will be discussed in Chapters 10 and 11, the tendency to accept assessment and treatment as they are commonly practiced leads to many absurd "catch-22's," which can be resolved only by explicating the assumptions surrounding the assessment and treatment enterprises. For example, as will be discussed in Chapter 11, the landmark "right to treatment" and "right to refuse treatment" court cases and policies of recent decades have been based on the general unavailability of anything but somatic and coercive treatments. In essence, as long as the "givens" that support the current approaches to the diagnosis and treatment of the schizophrenic disorders are accepted, there will be no real reform. And the available "evidence" from formal assessment studies will continue to be replete with conclusions about biological causation, even though "somatic etiology is often assumed in the face of otherwise inexplicable psychopathology, even without supporting evidence" (Strauss & Carpenter, 1981, p. 79).

The possible role or even the existence of a genetic predisposition to schizophrenic disorder remains unclear for several reasons, including three that are especially complex. First, no currently known means of genetic transmission can account for the findings of apparent concordance of schizophrenia with genetic endowment. Second, the data are from correlational but not experimental studies, so that causal linkage is more difficult to establish. Because of the impossibility of controlling for the many possibly relevant variables, there is speculation about explanations other than genetic influence. For example, intrauterine life is clearly subject to many maternal influences, so even the separation of the child from the mother at birth does not mean that interpersonal influence of mother and child have been ruled out. The third complicating factor is the lack of a concrete definition of schizophrenia.

The genetic determination viewpoint may become more convincing as genetic science advances. Also, it may not be necessary to demonstrate a direct link between gene and behavior. All human beings have various genetically determined predispositions, not only to clearly evident physical characteristics such as eye and hair color, but also to a great array of behavioral tendencies that are not so clearly demonstrable. Whether a genetic predisposition to schizophrenic disorders exists, however, is yet to be demonstrated. In fact, "Despite numerous studies suggesting an association with genetic, toxic-metabolic, endocrine, viral-immunological, and other factors, the etiology of schizophrenia is not known" (Wyatt, Kirch, DeLisi, 1989, p. 717). Furthermore, "No laboratory tests as yet can diagnose schizophrenia" (Karno & Norquist, 1989, p. 699).

Though even recent genetic studies are badly flawed, it is significant that as the design of genetic studies has improved, estimates of the power of a genetic causation of schizophrenic disorders have become more modest. For example, studies of monozygotic (MZ) and dizygotic (DZ) twins have shown:

> For narrow concordance, the average has plunged from 56 to 26 percent for MZs; for DZs, the corresponding averages are 11 and 9 percent. . . . The data do make clear, however, that even in genetically identical MZs environmental factors must be of enormous importance. The concordance for MZs reported by modern researchers, even under the broadest criteria, does not remotely approach the preposterous 86 percent figure claimed by Kallman. (Lewontin *et al.,* 1984, p. 217)

"The notion that a functional excess of dopaminergic activity is related to the development of schizophrenia has been the most promising and widely accepted hypothesis of schizophrenia" (Wyatt *et al.*, 1989, p. 718). Basically, the theory behind this notion is that functional dopaminergic excess causes schizophrenia and that various neuroleptics or "antipsychotic" drugs block the dopamine receptors and reduce schizophrenic symptomatology. The dopamine theory has been the most prominent biochemical explanation of both the cause and the relief of schizophrenic symptomatology, but we lack hard evidence that schizophrenic persons have too much dopamine in their systems, and the result of neuroleptic treatment is skewing toward relief of the more secondary symptoms in acute schizophrenic reactions, and not any kind of cure. As discussed elsewhere in this book, it is doubtful whether neuroleptic drugs in the modern era have provided any long-term improvement over the previous era, when these drugs were not available. If there has been improvement, it may be due to lessening institutional influences which led to greater chronicity.

The role of psychosocial variables in the causation, course, and outcome of schizophrenia has received less attention than the role of hereditary and biochemical variables. Psychosocial variables do not fit easily into narrow medical models of causation or treatment. They do fit into the purview of the generally less prestigious professional and research fields of clinical and social psychology, cultural anthropology, sociology, and social work. These disciplines relate to and interact with schizophrenic persons almost entirely through the medical profession, which, naturally, emphasizes what it knows best. This hierarchical ordering of the variables according to how well they fit the medical model, as well as the striving of psychiatrists to legitimize themselves within the traditional confines of medicine, is a powerful political influence. The more ancillary professions tend to accept the premises handed to them rather than to embark on more independent inquiries. In the process, many mental health professionals other than psychiatrists develop the same blind spots, and as a result, the search for causes is strongly dedicated to physical variables. At the same time, many interpersonal variables, even those that are obvious to ordinary common sense, are denied. For examples, the real patients in the Rosenhan study (1973) all knew that the pseudopatients were not schizophrenic, but the professionals did not. And Romola Nijisky knew intuitively that her husband might recover if she did not give up on him, though the world's foremost experts agreed among themselves that his recovery was an impossibility.

The fact that most schizophrenic persons have only gradually, over long periods of time, developed their psychotic conditions make it seem quite implausible, at least superficially that psychosocial influences, including interpersonal relations, are causal in any major way. Seldom is anyone in ordinary life "driven crazy" by a single experience, so that only a detailed longitudinal study of a person's life makes the real psychosocial influences apparent. Such studies have generally been left to biographers, some social workers, and perhaps psychoanalysts and a few social scientists. None of these students of the human condition are accorded the prestige and the scientific acceptance of mainstream medicine. Their work, although it has a vital place in the psychology of individual differences, is dismissed as "anecdotal." However, any method of research and theorizing will be unproductive and even sorely misleading if the methods are not suited to the subject; such methods become a distraction from the truth. In the case of the schizophrenic disorders the proper subject of study is the individual and the effect on him or her of interpersonal, as well as physical influences over the life cycle.

The investigative methods and aims in the study of schizophrenia have proceeded in step with the treatment of schizophrenic persons toward the reduction of secondary symptoms, while primary impairments in cognitive ability, emotional responsiveness, and interpersonal skills have been neglected. As has been discussed previously and as Strauss and Carpenter (1981) note, we have a plethora of causal propositions, including the biological, which account for no more than a small measure of the development, course, and outcome of the schizophrenic disorders.

Deterioration or Recovery

Historically, dementia praecox, or, as it was later termed, schizophrenia, was assumed to be a disease of the classical cellular-pathology type, which had an onset beginning in early life and a course of inevitable and progressive deterioration. In short, it was assumed to be a disease like syphilitic infection of the brain. Nothing but the appeal of this assumption can explain the continued dogma that "schizophrenia is incurable" and that nothing better can be done for schizophrenic persons than what is commonly done today, for example, a lifetime regimen of neuroleptics. Naturally, this dire prophecy tends to be fulfilled. Yet there are excellent studies, including those cited in Chapter 2, which directly refute this stubborn assumption.

Given the relevant resources in adequate supply, including both enlightened professional and social influences, many patients who are so-called hopeless cases may indeed progress to levels of quite adequate, meaningful, and fulfilling personal and social functioning. Frequently, the pessimism of prognosticators is based on the assumption that only medical methods are helpful and that, admittedly, these have proven to be inadequate. Furthermore, as family therapists know so well, work with the families of schizophrenic persons is quite difficult for several reasons. To question family attitudes and behaviors is to open Pandora's box, a necessary move probably, but fraught with powerful resistances to upsetting what has been a family equilibrium of sorts. And there is the ever-present temptation, in the face of this difficulty and the short-term apparent ease and legitimacy of reducing disturbing symptoms and increasing the docility of the patient, to take a kind of short-cut by methods of drug administration or behavioral management techniques designed to curb disturbing behavior. For the moment, let us merely note that the more painstaking work of deconstructing morbid interpersonal patterns and nurturing the construction of a new foundation that is more powerfully secure and adaptive requires far more skill and practice than are usually available.

A Capsule Depiction of Schizophrenic Disorders

Reality Testing and Thought Disorder

By definition, schizophrenic disorders, like other psychoses, are characterized by a major impairment in reality-testing ability. What is most distinctive about the schizophrenic kind of impairment is the disturbance of thinking, or thought disorder. Although people who are not schizophrenic may show similar kinds of thinking disturbance, they generally do not do so to the same degree. Specification of the degree of disorder is an essential part of a definitive account. It is probable that people who have schizophrenic kinds of impairment are distributed along a very broad spectrum and that the vast majority are on the portion of the spectrum characterized by mild impairment and would not, even on careful assessment, be called schizophrenic. Regardless of the type of diagnostic system used, therefore, the term *schizophrenic* tends to be used to refer to the relatively extreme end of a continuum of disorder; diagnostic systems differ in their cutoff points along this continuum as well as in some of the types of signs and symptoms included in their definitions.

Both interindividually and intraindividually schizophrenic disorders are characterized by various degrees and mixtures of regressive phenomena. The simpler intellectual functions— first of all, sensation and then memory and perception—tend to be better preserved than the functioning ability to think, which, although itself tending to be variable in its efficiency and veridicality, is most impaired overall. Thus, the alleged preservation of intelligence is only relative, both in overall degree of general intelligence and among the various intellectual functions. Unlike brain-damaged persons, schizophrenic persons are much more impaired in intellectual functioning ability than in capacity.

This characteristic relativity of regression is consistent with the fact that, in all forms of regression, the more complex functions tend to be sacrificed first. It is also consistent with a retreat from anxiety that sacrificing thinking first often preserves or even enhances the lower forms of intellection, especially sensation. Sensory impressions become more vivid as they are given full reign in their individual and class separateness rather than being organized by the higher functions, as is typical of normal waking life. Thus, at a very regressed level of cognitive functioning, sensations are not superseded and organized by thinking or even memory and perception. Instead, they are accentuated in their own right, sometimes to the point of hallucinatory intensity. At the most extreme level of regression, even this primitive sensibility—the domination of the senses—may be omitted in a further retreat from anxiety, that sacrifices even sensory awareness as the person blocks out the most basic of all functions, simply registering sensations. These regressive phenomena are driven by such an extreme form of anxiety that the word *anxiety* itself seems inadequate to communicate its power.

Terror

Emotionally, schizophrenic breakdowns are promoted by anxiety, characteristically perhaps by levels of anxiety that are better designated as ineffable terror. The person cannot provide a rational account of the terror and, typically, does not trust that anyone can help him or her with it. In the absence of the ability to explain the terror rationally, the person may be incoherent or may become delusional, delusions serving to reduce the terror somewhat by at least providing an explanation. Acutely schizophrenic persons are motivated to search actively to find the cause of their terror, but often without searching out other people who might be of help, as there is little trust in others.

Experience in trying to help persons who are terrified and having schizophrenic breakdowns suggests that the anxiety itself, like many other emotions, may be denied, even immediately following an initial realization that one is afraid. The anxiety that, in the acute stage, was obvious at least to others, tends to become transformed into symptoms that both express the breakdown and function as attempts to deny and contain the anxiety. Ultimately, apathy and other negative symptoms replace overt anxiety and more positive symptoms.

Just as some emotions are felt but not expressed, some emotions may be expressed but not experienced. For example, everyone but the person having an acute schizophrenic breakdown may recognize that he or she is extremely anxious to the point of terror. But the person who is terrified may not admit to the terror even in the acute phase. Instead, the person may excitedly report "wonderful discoveries," may claim supernatural powers, or may do frenzied detective work to root out persecutors. Such behavior obviates acknowledgment or full awareness of the anxiety by acting it out and thereby denying it. Lacking trust in others and being unable to cope oneself lead to denial and avoidance. In contrast to the characteristic transformation of anxiety into delusions and other ways of "explaining away" the terror in schizophrenic disorders, a person who openly acknowledges anxiety can be helped more readily. For example, someone who says, "I feel terribly frightened, as if I'm going crazy!" has both acknowledged fear and asked for help.

If in the frenzied search for understanding of the causes, the person does not succeed in finding the real causes and in finding help to resolve the fear, she or he will fixate on false causes such as those provided by paranoid persecutory delusions and hallucinations that —in the case of "voices," for example—tell the person who or what is causing the terror. These are defensive mechanisms that serve to "bind the anxiety" instead of allowing it to pervade every facet of the person's concerns. Thus, a paranoid delusion may sufficiently encapsulate anxiety to permit the person to go about ordinary everyday functions quite as if nothing were wrong, except that now the "causes" are located in a seemingly malevolent environment. As illustrated in Chapter 1, such mechanisms store up considerable anxiety and, when touched on, may evoke extremely powerful, even explosive reactions.

The defensive mechanisms used to try to contain the anxiety are maladaptive insofar as they sacrifice reality testing and thus produce gaps in understanding both subjective experiences and the objective environment. The experience of not understanding becomes an anxiety generator itself, making the person feel still more vulnerable and helpless. But instead of turning to others for help, the person tends defensively to withdraw, retreating further from reality and possible opportunities to achieve realistic understanding.

Affect Expression

As certain defensive mechanisms are resorted to, without any real understanding occurring and therefore without any satisfactory resolution of the anxiety, the person retreats further from his or her emotions thereby further losing contact with inner reality. Having lost such awareness, the person may attempt to maintain irrational explanations even in the face of opposition from other persons, and to deny self-doubt. Because since especially threatening emotions are central to the actual causes of the terror, the person tends to retreat from these emotions particularly. Either "inappropriate" or "flattened" affect expression tends to replace normal emotional expression. At the extreme end of the path of retreat, the person appears "burned out," or devoid of emotional concern and responsiveness (Arieti, 1974).

The outward expression of emotion—or *affect expression*, as it is called —cannot simply be equated with either the person's actual emotional experience or the presence of emotional energy. The seemingly emotionless individual may be far more emotional, underneath a bland or even apathetic exterior, than people who are very emotionally expressive. Thus, affect must be distinguished from affect expression; highlighting this contrast helps the assessor to understand the person's motivation and dynamics. The often reported observation of "bland affect" in schizophrenic persons is usually based on the typically incorrect equation of affect and affect expression.

As discussed in Chapter 10, drug treatment with the neuroleptics appears to be most "effective" during the acute stage; it may reduce the severe anxiety or terror and alleviate the need to resort to radical defensive mechanisms that, as described above, are desperate attempts to bind the anxiety at the cost of false "explanations." For several reasons, however, these drugs have little or no effectiveness for chronic schizophrenic persons. Most importantly, they reduce the terror without the person's learning anything more than that the drugs can bring relief of a sort. The person still does not know the causes of the terror and may develop a dependency on the drug that dissolves any motivation to develop the personal understanding and competence to master the challenges that were overwhelming. Similarly, the patient's doctors and family may be satisfied that the "solution" has been found, a solution that may even take the form of "lifetime medication." Thus, the so-called antipsychotic drugs may have the antipsychotic effect of reducing the terror level of anxiety that is especially prominent in acute breakdowns, but there are various drawbacks that tend not to be obvious, at least in the short run. Chapter 10 further addresses the pros and cons of drug treatment.

Self-Esteem

Competence and a sense of being loved, including by oneself, are components of self-esteem. Competence includes the abilities to make one's way in the world without morbid dependencies—as opposed to normal (i.e., strengthening) interdependencies with other people. Stated somewhat differently, in schizophrenic impairment, there is a gross discrepancy between one's capacity and one's functioning ability to be organized and effective. Competence gives one a sense of confidence and options, in contrast to a sense of helpless dependency, in the face of life's challenges.

The competent person is more likely to take initiative and to figure out alternative ways of behaving when frustrated. But when the person has little ability to behave adaptively, stress is likely to produce destructive internal alterations. In other words, challenged by the ordinary stresses and frustrations of life, the schizophrenic person tends to undergo internal alterations instead of producing external changes in his or her environment. Repeated experiences of failure make the turning inward, the withdrawal from external reality, a cumulative response that further postpones the development of competence.

Feeling loved, or at least cared about, is a second crucial component of self-esteem that is especially lacking in schizophrenic persons, who usually find the acceptance of love and caring to be fraught with difficulties. Suspicion, distrust, and resentment over interference with a defensive system that guards against getting up "false hopes"—all work against the acceptance of love. Hostility may also be generated by not being loved or by not feeling loved in the past. Finally, the schizophrenic person may have intense fears that, as people get to know him or her, they will discover that he or she is worthless, empty, repulsive, and unlovable. This intense, but not always apparent need for and fear of being cared about often deter anyone who wants to help with the person's self-esteem by facilitating competence and a sense of being lovable. Although these needs and fears are certainly not exclusive to the schizophrenic disorders, they are usually present in an extreme form.

Alienation

Although the defensive mechanisms, self-esteem problems, and distrust of others characteristic of the schizophrenic disorders are often seen in other conditions, the idiosyncratic alienation of schizophrenic persons is sharply distinctive. Groups of bigoted people can band together and share their common "madness" and thus find in one another a reassuring consensual validation. The group members may share extreme irrationality, including stubborn delusions, but their bonding together keeps them from being alienated from everyone. In contrast, the eccentricity and strangeness developed in schizophrenic persons isolates them from others.

The terror of the schizophrenic person may be compounded by a sense of the isolation and alienation. A kind of vicious circle develops in which the sense of being without help from others is abetted by the person's withdrawal from help. People who may truly understand and want to help may be summarily rejected. Even people with caring attitudes may be perceived as people who want to take over, exploit, and destroy the person.

Typically, the schizophrenic person practices the attitude conveyed in the joke variously attributed to Harry Truman and Groucho Marx: "I wouldn't join any club that would have me!" This attitude expresses both the fear of belonging, which may mean being swallowed up and destroyed, and the hostile rejection of people who would be accepting. The alienating practices of the schizophrenic person may provoke hostile counter responses that produce further alienation, deepening the person's despair and abandonment of hope for desperately needed acceptance. This ambivalence toward the self and others sets up dilemmas that pervade every aspect of the treatment and management of schizophrenic persons, and it must be understood in terms of powerful self-rejection drives that are in conflict with the natural instincts to experience acceptance and pleasure.

The Rejection of Pleasure

The term *anhedonia* (Rado & Daniel, 1956) is used to denote an apparent inability or refusal to experience pleasure. The tendency toward anhedonia is not consistent, except perhaps in some extremely severe conditions, and is not found exclusively in schizophrenic persons, but it appears often in schizophrenic disorders as well as in some forms of depression. Anhedonia is not a true incapacity to experience pleasure, as schizophrenic "patients prove to be able to experience pleasure fully once they have overcome their psychological difficulties" (Arieti, 1974, p. 119). Rather, anhedonia is a highly motivated rejection which takes various forms, including apathy, refusal of nourishment, self-mutilation, and the rejection of people who are perceived as "corrupting influences" because they try to be nurturant and to facilitate the person's pleasure and well-being.

The so-called negative transference of schizophrenic persons derives not only from actual negatively nurturant experiences with people in the past but from the internalization of these experiences in the form of proscriptions against pleasure. Thus, kind and helpful people may be perceived as hostile and destructive not despite, but actually because of their positive nurturing qualities.

When pleasure is experienced, as tends to occur in all but the most guarded persons, the schizophrenic person may negate it later, for example, by spoiling it with thoughts about possibly negative aspects of the situation, or perhaps by creating a negative outcome, expressed in hostility toward the people who are seen as responsible for the corruption, thereby "teaching" them not to do it again. These people are then caught in a dilemma that cannot be resolved without a full understanding of the person's conflict and, specifically, the power of the person's terror that proscribes pleasure. Therefore, kindness, although surely a crucial ingredient in any attempt to be of benefit, is seldom sufficient.

Summary

This chapter first presented a discussion of the key issues in the conceptualization of schizophrenic disorders and then gave a capsule description of characteristics of the schizophrenic disorders. Whether "schizophrenia" is a myth, a construct, a disorder, or a disease depends first on the definition of disease. If *disease* is defined in classical cellular-pathology terms, the evidence that schizophrenia is a disease is certainly inadequate. If *disease* is defined as any condition of discomfort, the extreme broadness of the definition makes it meaningless. Even the term *disorder* may connote more knowledge than has been established. The term *construct* in the sense of an open scientific construct is unsatisfying, but it suggests the need to tie schizophrenic disorders more reliably and usefully to observable behaviors. Alleged cases of "schizophrenic disorders" should, at this stage of our knowledge, be well described and documented because the term is still used so loosely.

Assessment evidence strongly suggests that the schizophrenic disorders should be regarded as variables on a continuum rather than as entities. Although some symptoms appear to crystallize suddenly into clear psychotic presentations, even hallucinations and delusions are matters of degree, as are their forerunners, such as fixed ideas, that are later observed as delusions.

For social and political reasons, much assessment and treatment of the schizophrenic disorders has focused on deviance instead of actual morbidity; there has been much more concern about the person's disturbing than about her or his being disturbed. Deviance in itself does not mean morbidity but both ambiguity of definition and prejudicial attitudes have facilitated labeling persons schizophrenic when they are politically deviant or are considered undesirable for any reason. The term *schizophrenic disorder* makes sense when the condition is one of morbidity that may cause harm to the individual as well as possibly to others, but not when it only causes others discomfort or harm.

By and large, the schizophrenic disorders tend to be quite inconsistent, both intraindividually and interindividually. Schizophrenic persons as a group are extremely heterogeneous; what they have in common is considerable difficulty with thinking, affect expression, and interpersonal behavior. There is some tendency for individuals to become more consistent within themselves if they worsen over time and become chronically disabled.

Whether schizophrenic persons will deteriorate or recover is hard to predict, given our present methods of prediction, but several well-conducted long-term studies show that most schizophrenic persons improve over time, a great many to the point of leading productive lives.

The capsule depiction of the characteristics of the schizophrenic disorders covered thinking disorder and problems with reality testing, the experience of terror, problems with affect expression and self-esteem, alienation, and the rejection of pleasure known as *anhedonia*.

10

Treatment and Prevention

This chapter first addresses general considerations that are basic to any successful treatment approach and then discusses three major modes of treatment: psychotherapy; psychosocial approaches; and drug treatment. This ordering of the modes of treatment emphasizes the psychological and social approaches because they are the most currently underemphasized forms of treatment and are the most important to a favorable long-term outcome. This chapter concludes with a discussion of prevention.

General Considerations

Respect for the Individual

No principle is more important or more overlooked in the treatment of schizophrenic persons than respect for the individuality and uniqueness of the patients. As Strauss and Carpenter (1981) wrote:

> Heterogeneity of patients classified as schizophrenic is almost the hallmark of the disorder; yet, the modal schizophrenic patient is often processed through the health care system with surprisingly little attention paid to him or her as an individual and with unwarranted assumptions that the individual represents primarily one case in a homogeneous group phenomenon. To know that a patient fits in a diagnostic niche is not sufficient information on which to base clinical care decisions, and treatment and diagnosis of the schizophrenic patient will be severely compromised in any circumstance in which the patient's individuality is ignored. (p. 208)

Developing a relationship in which there can be at least a gradual increase in trust is the indispensable basis for any treatment. Patients who are simply "treated" without this foundation learn to be either actively rebellious or passively resistant, and it may be difficult to tell which is worse, though perhaps active rebelliousness is the better response in terms of long-term outcome because it implies that the patient has not given up.

There are several formidable obstacles in the way of respecting "schizophrenics" that need to be confronted immediately, repeatedly, and effectively. First, the severe stigma attached to being schizophrenic or having any kind of "mental illness" is perpetuated not only by laypeople but professionals, who have been known to refer to such persons as sickos, weirdos, crazies, and, for the genetically inclined, "piss-poor protoplasm." Stigmatizing conveys rejection, furthers alienation, and, by means of projection, results in fearful lack of identification with one's fellow human beings. It preserves ignorance and acts to distance rather than to facilitate getting to know schizophrenic persons. Anyone doubting that an enormous stigmatizing influence still exists in our culture only has to be reminded of the tremendous readiness, demonstrated in the 1988 campaign for the presidency, to jump on the (falsely) rumored possibility that a candidate may simply have seen a psychiatrist or been in psychological counseling. The fact that schizophrenic persons are treated professionally at all, much less have hospitalization records, is immensely stigmatizing in itself, even when professionals themselves are very respectful.

Second, schizophrenic persons are generally "hard to get through to." They are not easy to relate to, and, in most cases, they do not accept help easily. In fact, as has been discussed, they may actively reject would-be helpers, sometimes being the most hostile toward and the most rejecting of the people who would accept them. Yet it is essential to avoid merely "humoring" the negative orientation of the person, who, in a sense, "wants" to be persecuted because otherwise the much desired attention is not acceptable. Getting to know the patient individually is important in planning and administering any kind of treatment, psychosocial, psychotherapeutic, or somatic. In the latter case, knowing the patient is especially likely to be regarded as irrelevant. However:

> If drug therapy is to be carried out most effectively, timing of intervention is important. Drugs may be beneficial in some phases of illness without being required in all. In the initiation of pharmacotherapy, the social and psychological connotations of intervention must also be considered. A terrified paranoid patient suffers from anxiety, but some elements of the psychotic experiences may be gratifying or reassuring. We have seen, for example, patients who have woven such an elaborate paranoid frame of reference that they were enthralled with the intrigue of constant danger and surprise. To alleviate their apprehension immediately was to misunderstand the important self-perpetuating gratifications involved. With other patients, hallucinatory experiences were reported as uncomfortable, but removing the hallucinations was associated with a sense of loss and abandonment. (Strauss & Carpenter, 1981, pp. 148–149)

The patient's "negative transference" may readily evoke considerable counter-hostility in professionals and laypeople alike, whether we call this negative counter-reaction negative countertransference or simply the human tendency to strike back when someone is hostile and rejecting. Such negative countertransference, together with a stigmatizing orientation, may account for much of the abuse of hospitalized mental patients, the persistence of medical treatments such as lobotomy, and, more subtly, the typical inattentive "processing" of patients through the health care system.

Third, some schizophrenic persons are destructively aggressive and provoke reasonable concern about the safety of others or themselves. Often, such aggressiveness is motivated by fear, and the answer to the question of how to "manage" the person may be found in understanding the nature of the fear in that particular case.

Management techniques that merely pit aggression against aggression may cause the schizophrenic person to escalate his or her own fearful aggressive attempts as a "defense" against what are perceived to be threats from others. So it is important to get to know the individual in terms of what can be especially threatening and what can be especially security-inducing.

Though homicide is not as common as the media makes it seem, suicide, especially, is much more likely in schizophrenic persons than in the general population. At one extreme, the potential for such acts may be clear, especially on careful assessment; in other cases, prediction may be extremely difficult.

Fourth, patients may accuse treatment personnel of harmful or hostile acts, perhaps even out of a desire for attention, although of a negative kind, that cannot be expressed directly because the patient's self-esteem problems mask the desire itself for fear of rejection and because of the patient's tendency to convince herself or himself that positive attention is not needed. For example, Arieti (1974) pointed out:

> A situation from which the therapist must protect himself is the possible accusation of having sexual relations with the patient. Sexual intentions are often attributed to the therapist even by neurotic patients. However, with neurotics, this is not a serious problem. It is easy to discuss these feelings and interpret them. The situation is much more complicated with a psychotic, who in his tendency to concretize ideas, does not speak of intentions of the therapist, but of real acts. (p. 611)

Beyond the obvious need to abstain from actual sexual relations with a patient, the therapist should, where possible, interpret these feelings to the patient, recognizing the patient's desires for caring and closeness and their relationship to self-esteem.

These and other hazards pervade many modes of treatment and greatly influence treatment personnel to steer toward more impersonal modes and away from those emphasizing interpersonal approaches. Yet it is essential that therapists and other treatment staff not be unduly afraid of their patients and therefore unable to understand the expression of the important needs that are motivating harmful behavior. All human beings, including schizophrenic persons, feel more secure when it becomes obvious to them that they are respected, especially when that respect is based on a knowledge of themselves as individuals. Accomplishing a genuinely helpful therapeutic orientation is favored by knowledge not only of the patient but also of oneself.

Focus on the Basic Strengths and Deficits

Because no one is "completely crazy" and even severely schizophrenic persons are not merely schizophrenic but also relatively normal in some ways, the schizophrenic person has strengths that can serve as assets in any treatment. The person who is helped to use his or her strengths experiences thereby some awareness of competence and, if these strengths are appreciated by others, a sense of positive regard.

The common practices of leaving hospital patients to vegetate in front of television drivel and morbidity, to chain-smoke, or to lie in their beds most of the day are indefensible from any treatment standpoint. In fact, most mental hospitals are vegetative environments that promote institutionalization syndromes and chronicity. It is extremely tempting, from a "management" point of view, to allow and even to encourage patient passivity by rewarding inactivity and to punish, or at least frown on, patient activity. But instead of condemning patient initiatives as "inappropriate," staff should examine those initiatives to find what needs they express and how they can be used to help increase the person's understanding and competence. Dulling initiatives and discouraging emotional expression may make patients more manageable, but they foster withdrawal and chronicity as the patient becomes persuaded to give up. The principal focus should be on encouraging activities that make it possible to develop greater competence, confidence, and a sense of being appreciated.

Inabilities to think, to tolerate and express emotions, and to engage in constructive interpersonal relationships are the primary deficits in schizophrenic disorders. Simply reducing the positive symptomatic expressions of these inabilities—such as delusions, hallucinations, inappropriate affect expression, and bizarre behavior—serves mostly to put a different face on the person, rather like a mask. The product of these reductionistic means of quelling symptoms tends to look more like a zombie than a person. Such a skewed treatment approach borrows against the future for the sake of manageability and the quite superficial appearance of "improvement." The fact that this kind of treatment is by far the most prevalent approach and is regarded not only as acceptable but, in many quarters, as the most desirable and defensible approach does not help schizophrenic persons.

Focusing on the primary deficits themselves, rather than putting a mask on them, requires careful assessment together with a nurturing kind of treatment geared to the individual needs of the person. This approach addresses primarily the person's disturbance and secondarily the person's being disturbing. The fact that the person is disturbing is important, but the prevalent priorities for treatment should be reversed.

Practically speaking, reductionistic practices should be delayed as much as possible; management consideration must be given some weight, but with an attempt to treat in ways that result in constructive learning and not in passive resignation. Drug treatment, especially by coercion, and the use of isolation rooms should be minimized. Assessment should occur before, and not after, drug treatment whenever there is a reasonable chance of finding out from the person what is disturbing *to him or her and not merely to other people.*

The guiding principle in this recommended approach is based on child development, in recognition that there is virtually always a crucial component of failure of development, as well as regression, in schizophrenic disorders. Seldom is it enough to restore the patient to his or her previous level of functioning because at that level, the person was crucially vulnerable to breakdown.

Adults as well as children develop best when there is considerable encouragement and facilitation of relatively spontaneous interests and activities as well as adult guidance into beneficial activities and ways of thinking and relating. Otherwise there is only a rigidly programmed kind of competence that does not prepare the child or adolescent for the demands for the more autonomous and creatively flexible adaptation required of most adults. It is no mystery that the vast majority of schizophrenic breakdowns occur as the person is required to enter adulthood.

Implied in this developmental approach are the hope and expectation that certain kinds of development can still be achieved after the time when they normally occur, and that the developmental aim will be primary, whereas the stress-reducing aim will be secondary except when further breakdown would otherwise occur. As Strauss and Carpenter (1981) stated:

> A patient who decompensates under stress may require procedures which decrease stress when he is on the verge of decompensation, but during another phase of illness, if severe withdrawal and social isolation are prominent, the same stress-reducing procedures may cause a further deterioration in social functioning. (209)

Longitudinal Emphasis

The developmental approach also implies that treatment may be relatively long-term. Given the current emphasis on short-term treatment and the short-term savings that result in some cases, it may seem that longer-term treatment would greatly escalate costs. But the cost to schizophrenic persons, their families, and society is extremely high under the present system, which emphasizes brief hospitalizations and little, if any, outpatient treatment beyond a routine, superficial assessment of patient status and "progress" that ends simply with further drug prescriptions and thus further skewing of the treatment. Schizophrenic persons need mostly developmental help, not merely restorative help, unless it is decided that repeated breakdowns and long-term disability are acceptable, together with their extremely high cumulative costs.

Were it not for certain political considerations, such as elected officials campaigning for reelection on the basis of short-term accounts of their spending taxpayers' money during their two- or four-year terms, one could propose experiments in treatment that would examine and compare the outcomes of different kinds of treatment programs after 5, 10, or even 20 years. Many longer-term developmental programs might win cost-effectiveness battles easily. In addition, both mental health practitioners and patients would have the satisfaction of achieving more meaningful long-term goals than those of the "30-day wonder" hospital regimens based expediently on inpatient insurance provisions. Interest in long-term research, in more ambitious treatment of all sorts, and in psychotherapy with schizophrenic persons would be rejuvenated, and patients would have more reasonable bases for hope, the vital ingredient without which nothing ultimately satisfactory ever occurs.

Psychotherapy

The advent of the phenothiazines, or "antipsychotic" drugs, in the early 1950s reduced incentives to work with schizophrenic patients using primarily psychological means. The previously available drugs had seemingly little helpful influence except sometimes to ameliorate agitation. The supposed miracle of prefrontal lobotomy was finally being recognized for what it was: a way of permanently damaging patients rather than curing them. And even those who vaunted electroshock treatment could not point to major benefits for schizophrenic patients except that depressed schizoaffective patients might be temporarily relieved of depression, the cost being at least short-term memory loss and perhaps longer-lasting brain damage.

Meanwhile, psychoanalysis had become relatively well respected, and although it was thought originally that the standard psychoanalytic method of psychotherapy was not applicable, some therapists were adapting the principles of psychoanalysis to work with schizophrenic patients. These therapists recognized not only that there was little or no apparent positive transference to provide leverage against the patient's resistance, but that psychotherapy had to focus largely on the earliest developmental difficulties and would have to provide a basic restructuring of development in the person's early years. The psychoanalyst Harry Stack Sullivan (1962) emphasized that schizophrenia is a human process different from normal processes not as one genus is different from another, but only as a matter of degree, the schizophrenic person having had more disturbing early development experiences than most other people. So the work of the therapist could not be merely interpretive; it had also to be nurturantly reconstructive. Thus, effective psychotherapy with schizophrenic persons would be more extensive, involving, and ambitious than psychotherapy with less disturbed persons. Although this view makes sense, it is difficult to actualize because of the large amounts of time, effort, and financial support needed; the cultural stigma against the seriously "mentally ill," which causes them to be disenfranchised; and the considerable resistances of the patients themselves and, often, of their families.

Not surprisingly, relatively few therapists have actually worked to develop the understanding, skill, and perseverance to succeed with schizophrenic patients. Typically, those who start to work with schizophrenic persons eventually gravitate to patients who are less demanding and who, partly because they are functioning more adequately, can finance their treatment. In essence, there are tremendous incentives to veer away from extremely disturbed patients except to provide the much more lucrative forms of quick, ostensibly symptom-reducing somatic treatments which are more immediately appealing to all concerned. Psychotherapeutic approaches appear to be quite difficult, time-consuming, personally involving, and not at all guaranteed of success. However, highly detailed accounts of psychotherapy with quite severely schizophrenic persons leave little doubt that superb outcomes are possible.

Documented Accounts

Two of the most outstanding narrative accounts of successful psychotherapy with severely schizophrenic patients are the anonymous *Autobiography of a Schizophrenic Girl* (1970) and *I Never Promised You a Rose Garden* (Green, 1964). These accounts are particularly compelling for their elucidation of the richly complex interweaving of the patient's states of terror and how the therapists became able to reach these two patients through that terror, to provide the needed developmental experiences. The therapist in the former case, Margaret Sechehaye, developed a remarkable form of "symbolic realization" to make needed gratifications acceptable. The therapist in the latter case, Frieda Fromm-Reichmann, was able to get through to her patient by recognizing that a kind of emotional connectedness to herself and to the real world had to grow to replace the patient's addiction to a world of make-believe.

These therapeutic approaches surely involved intellectual work for all concerned, but severe thinking disorders, delusions, and retreats into make-believe worlds cannot be resolved by mere intellectual means. The therapists had to be emotionally involved personally. Hannah Green (1964) made this point by contrasting her regular therapist with a substitute therapist she had one summer:

> His work was clever and detailed and sometimes almost brilliant, and she had many times to agree with him, but the more profound he was the more profound was the silence that enveloped her. She could never get beyond the austerity of his manner or the icy logic of what he had proven, to tell him that his scalpels were intrusions into her mind just as long-ago doctors had intruded into her body, and that furthermore, his proofs were utterly and singularly irrelevant. At the end she marshaled all of her strength, and with as good a clarity as she could give him, she said, "Please, Doctor, my difference is not my sickness." It was a last cry and it went unheard. (p. 160).

These early, innovative, psychoanalytically oriented psychotherapists usually worked in the traditional framework of long-term psychiatric hospitalization, where not only the principal but sometimes the only effective forms of treatment were performed by a single professional, *the* therapist who was "the patient's doctor." Though the therapist might be extremely skilled, other hospital staff were generally not very skillful or involved. Furthermore, hospitalization itself has many drawbacks, including separation from what may be productive work environments, socializing influences, and important challenges to personality growth. Although some hospitals were quite good in many respects, the general effect was often harmful except for that small amount of time spent with the therapist. These conditions and the relative lack of knowledge about how to do psychotherapy with schizophrenic patients may explain partly why the early successes took many years of concentrated effort. In addition, there was and still is intense resistance to psychotherapeutic approaches to the treatment of schizophrenic patients.

Resistances Then and Now

The resistances of patients are never so great as when they are matched with resistances from the professionals who are supposed to be trying to help. It is easily and perhaps even "natural" to collude with patients by focusing on the superficial, the clever and expedient. Then, everyone is distracted from the critical concerns. When "manageability," "control," and "symptom reduction" are the only goals of treatment and no attention is given to the person's developmental needs, skewed treatment may produce worse results than if no treatment had occurred.

During a period of nearly one year, while changing a psychiatric ward from a primary emphasis on drugs to a primary emphasis on psychotherapy and psychosocial treatment, Deikman and Whitaker (1979) recorded both results with patients and results with staff. Despite dire predictions that suicides and elopements would abound without strict management in the form of drugs and seclusion practices, the patients did well. Although this "experimental" ward almost invariably kept even the most disturbed patients, instead of sending them to a long-term state hospital, no suicides or elopements occurred during the 11 months of the ward experiment. Another ward, which practiced the most "expert" application of drug therapy and was more fully staffed, had three suicides during the same period. The somewhat longer average stays on the experimental ward resulted in a lower rehospitalization rate despite the decision to keep and to treat even the most disturbed patients, whereas the other wards transferred their most difficult patients to a long-term state hospital. The experimental-ward patients tended to look after one another and to share in the treatment responsibilities in concert with the orientation developed in group psychotherapy (Whitaker & Deikman, 1980).

Meanwhile, the initially quite resistant experimental-ward staff developed considerable morale and cohesiveness. Many staff on other wards began to emulate the experimental ward, though not fully, as there was not full support from the supervisors who never gave up the "traditional" approach; some suggested that the "drug-free" ward was a case of "malpractice," as "schizophrenics always need phenothiazines." In other words, the positive results were not enough to overcome a steadfast resistance to change. The authors began to realize that, just as the experimental-ward staff had to examine their own resistances, including fears that there would be no "controls" if drugs and seclusion were not used, so older, more experienced supervisory staff would have to work through their own emotional resistances, which had become more rigidly set by their longer training and experience. Most remembered what they had been taught: "Schizophrenics are incurable."

Despite the current almost universal primary reliance on drugs, there are well-documented accounts of highly successful psychotherapeutic approaches. One of the most outstanding, in terms of both results and explication of approach, is the work of Karon and VandenBos, described in their book *Psychotherapy of Schizophrenia: The Treatment of Choice* (1981), which reports on the Michigan State Psychotherapy Project. They achieved quite successful long-term outcomes for severely schizophrenic patients by using relevantly trained psychotherapists, in contrast to other studies pitting drug treatment against "psychotherapy" but not using relevantly trained and experienced therapists. Karon and VandenBos did not rely on drug treatment, and they accomplished excellent results within relatively short periods of time, as compared to the early pioneers in this field such as Sullivan and Fromm-Reichmann.

Karon and VandenBos (1981) emphasized the importance of frequent, highly accessible psychotherapy and placed hospitalization and drug treatment in ancillary roles. They saw hospitalization as an extraordinary intervention that might be justified when it provided a secure place for persons who were actively suicidal, homicidal, or otherwise in jeopardy of their lives, but not as an ordinary requirement for successful treatment. Similarly, they preferred not to use drug treatment although they allowed their patients the option to use it:

> Acutely psychotic patients who require hospitalization will have progressed sufficiently without medication in 5-days-per-week therapy to be discharged within 2 weeks. Even the bulk of more chronic patients will take no longer than 8 weeks.
>
> We prefer not to use adjunctive medication. When medication is not used, any improvement that occurs is obviously the result of underlying changes. These changes result in enduring improvement. (p. 208)

Recognizing the appeal of drug treatment, Karon and VandenBos noted an alternative way of working: the therapist can begin with the patient on medication because it makes the patient more tolerable to the staff, the family, and the therapist, too. But the medication is reduced and discontinued as rapidly as the patient can tolerate the reduction, so that a greater focus on the psychotherapeutic work is facilitated. The efficacy of this approach is shown in a key result:

> Medication produces behavioral control, and an apparent change in the thought disorder by damping the disruptive affects of fear and anger. But medication slows down underlying personality changes resulting from psychotherapy, since part of the process of change in psychotherapy depends on emotional reactions and having to deal with them. . . . The improvement in the thought disorder with psychotherapy was slower (less) when the patients were also on medication. In the long run, this had consequences for rehospitalization. (p. 209)

The efficacy of the psychotherapeutic approach and the consequent lowered need of hospitalization and rehospitalization argue in favor of psychotherapy, as opposed to medication, for schizophrenic patients in terms of treatment costs, especially when the long-term costs are considered (Karon & VandenBos, 1975).

But there is a question of professional motivation. Why should professionals choose the more arduous route? Why should they choose a longer period of training, develop the skills and sensitivity necessary, and invest themselves emotionally in such work when it takes less training and skill and requires little emotional investment in patients to adhere to the more prestigious and more lucrative mainstream medical model of treatment? These practical realities generally deter professionals from pursuing the psychotherapeutic approach. Though it is personally meaningful and rewarding and makes sense in terms of both helping people in profound ways and one's own psychological growth, only a relatively small—and decreasing— number of psychotherapists now do such work.

Admittedly, the prospects for advancing the science and art of psychotherapy with schizophrenic persons, and especially chronic patients, are dim. Psychiatrist Alexander Gralnick (1986) predicted:

> There will be a negligible degree of dyadic psychotherapy in relation to the volume of chronic schizophrenics. Its effectiveness with these patients will be seen as inconsequential and newer drugs will be seen more and more as the solution for the chronic schizophrenic.

> Little headway will have been made in discovering the origins of schizophrenia, let alone in methods of arresting its insidious progress. We will be overwhelmed by the numbers of chronic and underproductive schizophrenics who will clog our streets and meager facilities. Their numbers will be limited by nature's attrition, the death rate (p. 422).

Only if socioeconomic circumstances and incentives in the United States change—for example, by legislators' taking a hard look at real long-term costs and beginning to support more effective long-term approaches—will there be genuine reform. For the present, as Schulz (1985) stated:

> If there are skilled therapists available to work over a long period of time in a setting that is coordinated to provide other treatment modes acting synergistically with schizophrenic patients who have a capacity to observe themselves, the situation deserves a chance to utilize the highest capabilities in self-understanding (p. 746).

Despite the many disincentives to develop psychotherapeutic approaches for schizophrenic patients in the United States, a sizeable group of dedicated professionals have persisted in showing the superiority of both individual and family therapy approaches over drug treatment. For example, Lidz and Fleck (1985) have made clear that the family approach makes good sense. As Lidz (1987) noted:

> . . . the disturbed or strange family environments in which virtually all schizophrenic patients have grown up form the only consistent lead concerning the etiology of schizophrenic disorders (p. 449).

Meanwhile, other countries have been less dependent culturally and therapeutically on drugs. For example, in Finland Alanen *et al.* (1986) found that most of their intensively treated patients improved, the more so if the patients did not receive neuroleptic medication or had only low doses. Furthermore, those patients who did receive medication did not relapse when it was discontinued, if they were receiving any psychotherapy. In fact, these authors observed that even tranquilizer doses about the equivalent of 300 mg. of chlorpromazine per day not only hamper improvement but may actually prevent any recovery.

Ultimately we must examine how irrational fears of working psychologically with schizophrenic persons combine with cultural and financial disincentives to discourage effective treatment (Karon & Whitaker, in press).

Psychosocial Approaches

The Rationale and Range of Psychosocial Treatment

As both the cause and the cure of schizophrenic disorders are probably largely based in the psychosocial environment, both primary prevention plans and treatment programs should include an improvement in environmental influences. Persons who have been through environmental and interpersonal experiences that seem stressful enough to "drive anyone crazy" need compensatory and corrective interpersonal experiences both during and after formal treatment. The now-predominant practice of merely treating mental patients with drugs, whether in hospitals or in clinics, and then dumping these still severely disturbed patients onto the streets armed only with their prescribed drugs is a sure design for therapeutic and societal failure. Schizophrenic persons, like the rest of humanity, cannot acquire social competence by taking drugs.

Liberman (1985) cited specific evidence for the crucial importance of psychosocial treatment:

> Studies carried out in England and the United States have found "expressed emotion"—criticism and emotional overinvolvement by family members of schizophrenic patients—to be the most powerful predictor of relapse in the 9 months following discharge. These findings point toward family therapy to reduce the level of family tension, social skills training to improve the patient's ability to cope with family problems, and psychosocial rehabilitation and group therapy to develop support from persons other than family in the patient's natural environment. (p. 724)

Psychosocial treatment takes myriad forms, including group, family, and milieu therapy, as well as planned-living situations that offer special kinds of learning and support that increase competence and confidence. There are no truly neutral situations; every social environment has positive and negative influences that help or set back the person. "Custodial" environments, which provide little personal attention to patients, may be designed to be neutral and nonharmful, but they impart a sense of impersonality and uncaring attitudes that only increase schizophrenic alienation. Interpersonal environments that convey a sense of caring and shared concerns, on the other hand, may do much to effect improvement.

As discussed early in this book, moral treatment was essentially a form of milieu therapy, and it produced quite good results before it gave way to an emphasis on somatic treatment and segregation into large, impersonal institutions. Fortunately, even in recent decades, after the neuroleptic drugs were introduced in the 1950s, some institutional programs of treatment provided carefully structured, effective therapeutic milieus, such as the Menninger Foundation in Kansas and the Fort Logan Mental Health Center in Colorado, to mention just two with which I have been familiar. These programs provided both generally positive environments and care tailored to the individual.

Resistances to Psychosocial Treatment

In all such psychosocial treatment programs, it is essential to focus on staff as well as patient resistances to taking responsibility for designing and actually carrying out social living arrangements that embody the treatment principles noted at the beginning of this chapter: respect for the individual; a focus on basic strengths and deficits; and a longitudinal emphasis on the person's development. I witnessed the fate of a highly effective program that first corrected a negative environment, only to be overcome by it later:

> A milieu therapy consultant was hired by a psychiatric hospital to help improve patient interest and involvement in treatment. The patients had been extremely reluctant

> to attend "patient–personnel" meetings, which were held three mornings a week. Those patients who did straggle into the meetings seldom said anything. The consultant restructured the format, beginning by announcing that only patients who were interested should attend and that the door would be closed five minutes after the announced starting times. The patients were also told that they would have to try actively to help solve problems on the ward during these meetings. Instead of exercising their right not to attend, virtually all of the heretofore apathetic patients came on time and were actively involved. These meetings aroused sufficient interest so that some patients on weekend passes even returned a bit early to catch the Monday morning meetings. Staff and patients agreed that morale had improved greatly, and that the patients were taking a more active interest in their own treatment.
>
> The consultant left after several weeks, and the meetings continued to be run effectively by two psychiatric residents whom he had trained. But after the residents moved on to another training rotation, the recommended format was dropped by the staff, even though most of them had liked it. After another month or two, the ward again experienced its old problems of low staff and patient morale. Evidently, the self-examination required of staff in these meetings produced enough anxiety to interrupt the momentum of the program and to let it return to the kind of self-protective apathy that represented a collusion between patients and staff.

Not only patients and staff resist change; the patient's significant others also resist forms of treatment requiring challenging personal or social interaction. Family therapists must deal with these resistances of family members and patients as well as their own resistances to facing instead of denying problems. When it is successful, psychosocial treatment is essentially of an active, dynamic give-and-take nature. The resistances most often take on a distancing character, embodied in such rationalizations as "We are here to treat the patients, not the staff," or "It is time we stop talking with patients and do something for them," which usually means doing something *to* them. Doing something to the patients instead of doing something with them is the antithesis of good psychosocial treatment.

The approaches of the "modern treatment era" have discouraged psychosocial forms of treatment, but some authors have persisted in advancing milieu therapy (e.g., Gunderson, Will, & Mosher, 1983), and the "psychosocial treatment of schizophrenia" in particular (Strauss, Böker, & Brenner, 1987). Zubin (1987) pointed out that

> The assumption that schizophrenia is necessarily a long-term disorder leading to deterioration or to severe reduction in quality of life may be a relic of a previous era which persists despite evidence to the contrary. The generally benign outcome of schizophrenia that has been demonstrated by three outstanding long-term European studies, i.e. the studies of Manfred Bleuler (1972), Luc Ciompi (1980), and Gerd Huber et al. (1980), has not yet been fully appreciated. (p. 30)

The extreme lag in the recognition of the evidence from these and other studies is probably due to the same kind of resistance embodied in the assumption that schizophrenia is a lifelong disease that cannot be cured. This attitude corresponds to therapeutic nihilism and it colludes with patients' own tendencies toward apathetic resignation and thus forestalls any improvement. Apathy, after all, is the most disabling condition for patients and therapists alike.

Resistances to psychosocial and psychotherapeutic treatment for schizophrenic patients have been considerably abetted by the availability of the "antipsychotic medications" beginning in the 1950s. Schulz (1985) noted:

> Except for the advent of psychotropic medications, the philosophy of treatment for schizophrenia at that time might have evolved into a broad-based, multimodal approach using psychosocial methods to bring about early rehabilitation and adaptation to community life. Instead, the obvious effectiveness of the new medications led to their narrow application to bring about behavioral change, with short-sighted goals of emptying hospitals to save money. Psychotherapy, if used at all, was viewed as effective merely in enhancing compliance with the taking of medications that were seen as the real therapeutic agents. Many of those patients were dumped into the community prematurely without further rehabilitative efforts. (p. 735).

Drug Treatment

The assumption of the "obvious effectiveness" of the new medications is as ubiquitous as their use even by most proponents of other approaches. These virtual universalities of belief and practice have already been noted and critiqued in various contexts in several places in this book. Now it is time to focus in a concentrated way on the nature of these drugs and their effects.

No evidence exists of the superiority of one antipsychotic drug over another (Simpson & May, 1985), except that a couple appear to be less effective and clozapine (Clozaril) is thought to offer some advantage in refractory patients (Kane, 1989). There are at least 10 commonly used generic types, such as chlorpromazine (Thorazine); fluphenazine (Prolixin and Permitil); haloperidol (Haldol); perphenazine (Trilafon); trifluoperazine (Stelazine); thioridazine (Mellaril); and thiothixene (Navane). These drugs have somewhat varying "main effects" and "side effects." The side effects tend to increase as the dosage is increased, but a slow increase may produce lesser side effects than a rapid increase. In the United States only fluphenazine (Prolixin Decanoate) is available as a long-acting injection.

The "neuroleptics," as they began to be called in the early 1950s, because they produced neurological disturbances of the extrapyramidal system (Simpson & May, 1985), were all of the class of drugs known generically as *phenothiazines* and were considered major tranquilizers. But the "antipsychotics," to use the term usually preferred now, also include the classes of drugs called *thioxanthenes* (e.g., Navane and Taractan), *dibenzoxazepines* (Loxitane), and *dihydroindolones* (Moban).

The "Obvious Effectiveness" of Antipsychotic Drugs

It *seems* clear that the neuroleptics can be effectively "antipsychotic" in at least limited ways for certain schizophrenic patients. Usually, acutely schizophrenic persons appear to show a decrease in positive symptoms such as agitation, anxiety, delusions, and hallucinations within a short time of administration. Negative symptoms, such as apathy and withdrawal, may also decrease, apparently, if they are present in association with positive symptoms that are preoccupying the patient. Furthermore, some evidence suggests that the chances of relapse may be lowered by maintaining patients on these drugs. But, as discussed below, such apparent efficacy is not so scientifically evident, even though, supposedly, "antipsychotic agents have been subjected to the most rigorous scientific investigation in the history of therapeutics." (Simpson & May, 1985, p. 716).

What is clearest scientifically is that the antipsychotics have a great many effects, some of which *may* be considered therapeutic, at least in reducing positive symptomatology, whereas others definitely cause a wide variety of types of physical harm as well as psychological problems. These unwanted "side effects" should be quite carefully monitored, and it may be necessary, especially if large doses are administered, to counter these effects pharmacologically or to reduce the dosage. Although even neuroleptic advocates proscribe their immediate use, the neuroleptics are used almost universally in the treatment of schizophrenic disorders as soon as there is even a provisional, often quite hasty, diagnosis. For example, Simpson and May (1985) stated:

> The first step in management is to make sure of the diagnosis. This is one of the reasons that the authors recommend withholding of formal treatment—in most cases antipsychotic agents—until such time as a good working diagnosis has been reached. . . . A quick decision to treat without a thorough diagnostic evaluation, however, may preclude firm diagnosis and complicate treatment; when basic principles are ignored a price often has to be paid. (p. 716)

This critically important advice is probably not followed in the majority of cases, at least in ordinary practice. Furthermore, as discussed earlier in this book, lack of clinical recognition of neuroleptic-induced movement disorders is common even when the disorder is severe and the signs are blatant (Weiden, Mann, Haas, Mattson, & Frances, 1987).

Patient manageability is often cited as a major benefit of drug treatment, both in terms of enabling patients to stay in the community and to be treated as outpatients, and in terms of easing the stress on hospital staffs and on other patients that is produced by acutely agitated patients. Further, patients whose terror can be reduced by the drugs experience themselves as more calm and more in control, although not by their own learned competence.

Recently, some community programs have been designed to counter and lessen some of the problems that characteristically occur when excessive reliance is placed on drug treatment. "Intensive case management" programs (Bush, Langford, Rosen & Gott, 1990) and "assertive community treatment programs " (Taube, Morlock, Burns & Santos, 1990) have shown promise for improving the functioning of chronically and severely disturbed mental patients in the community while decreasing the use of mental hospitals. The greater attention to and monitoring of the patients in these programs tend to ensure more reliable maintenance of medication schedules, which are otherwise typically followed only erratically by outpatients. But a reviewer of experimental studies of assertive community-treatment programs (Olfson, 1990) concluded that, although hospitalization is reduced, the findings of improvements in symptom control, social functioning, and occupational performance have not been replicated.

Qualifications and Complications

The apparent benefits of drug treatment are lessened, negated, or even outweighed in many cases by some obvious and some rather subtle influences inherent in the drugs themselves.

The most obvious problems in the use of the neuroleptics comprise the known side effects, which include

1. Central nervous system changes that can worsen schizophrenic symptoms, for example, by increasing agitation and catatoniclike behavior.
2. Extrapyramidal side effects, which are common and include acute dystonic reactions (muscular spasms), akathisia (inability to sit or stand still), and Parkinsonism, a condition that begins by affecting the muscles of the face and neck and that spreads to the shoulders, arms, and trunk and is indistinguishable from classical Parkinsonism.
3. Tardive dyskinesia, a generally irreversible brain disease in severe cases, which first shows itself in peculiar movements of the tongue and which has been reported in up to 50% of patients on long-term neuroleptics.
4. Autonomic side effects, including a kind of toxic psychosis marked by confusional states, as well as neuroleptic malignant syndrome, which is a very rare but potentially fatal condition most often affecting young males.
5. Electrocardiographic changes, often associated with thioridazine use.
6. Allergic effects, rashes and photosensitivity.
7. Ocular effects, including granular deposits in the eye and in the lens.
8. Endocrine and metabolic effects, including lessened sexual potency with erectile dysfunction and inability to reach orgasm.
9. Weight gain.
10. Effects on the newborn producing postnatal depression and dystonic symptoms.

All of these side effects are well substantiated and have been reported extensively in the literature (e.g., Kane, 1989; Simpson & May, 1985). But many more subtle, though no less serious, problems have received relatively little attention.

As noted earlier in this chapter, clozapine (Clozaril) is thought to offer some treatment advantage in refractory patients. This drug, though so expensive to administer that the State of Pennsylvania will not pay to monitor its use closely (Acker, 1991), is considered "a major breakthrough in the treatment of schizophrenia . . . effective with 60 percent of patients who fail to respond to other antipyschotics" (sic) (Acker, 1991, p. 1). But, as with other sensational somatic treatment "advances," sober scientific observation suggests that what may be limited clinical evidence of harm today, given that clozapine use is relatively new, may become a major story of iatrogenic harm tomorrow. Breggin (1990) observed that, although agents such as clozapine do not cause as many acute dyskinesias as other neuroleptics, clozapine "produces a typical neuroleptic suppression and reactive supersensitivity in A10 dopaminergic neurons that project fibers into the meso-limbic system and cerebral cortex" and "Because of their specificity for A10 neurons, these neuroleptics are probably an equal or greater threat in producing persistent cognitive deficits, dementia and atrophy." (p. 456).

As psychiatrist Peter Breggin (1983) claimed, with impressive documentation, the so-called antipsychotic effects of the major tranquilizers correspond neurologically to their damaging effects, including damage to the brain's frontal lobes and to the reticular activating system of the brain stem. These damaging effects appear to be responsible for the lobotomylike results in patients. Thus, the undesirable effects, traditionally called *side effects*, are also the main effects. Clearly, not only are the neuroleptics not curative, but they also achieve their ostensibly therapeutic effects by damaging the nervous system.

Among the many drug-induced forms of damage to patients, perhaps the most ironic is tardive psychosis. Once patients get used to the neuroleptics, they may suffer psychotic reactions on withdrawal from them, "as a result of rebound hyperactivity of the limbic system dopamine receptors, comparable to the rebound hyperactivity that plays a role in tardive dyskinesia." (Breggin, 1983, p. 141). Thus, patients may "require" lifelong neuroleptics and may therefore be vulnerable to psychosis all their lives *because* of the somatic treatment. Thus, patient failure to comply with drug treatment may be truly antipsychotic. But the very universality of neuroleptic drug use with presumably schizophrenic patients and the resulting neurologically compulsive dependency on the neuroleptic drugs probably give professional and lay observers alike the unwitting impression that "schizophrenia is a lifelong brain disease." Ironically, schizophrenia can become a lifelong brain disease because of drug treatment.

Though the neuroleptic treatment of presumably schizophrenic persons is generally considered helpful in at least some limited ways, and at least in comparison to milder, less damaging drugs, even this assumption lacks adequate evidence. In an analysis of more than 1,300 studies of neuroleptic effectiveness, Keck, Cohen, Baldessarini, and McElroy (1989) ascertained that only 5 provided sufficient information about the time course of antipsychotic effects to permit an analysis of treatment effects with acutely disturbed patients, namely, the type of patients thought to benefit the most clearly from neuroleptic treatment. Even these 5 studies had severe methodological limitations, such as a failure to provide blind ratings, and only 2 study reports specified diagnostic criteria. Furthermore, the results themselves suggested a peculiar lack of correspondence between the reported improvement and the duration of neuroleptic treatment: "short studies observed moderate improvement within hours or days, but longer studies observed little improvement in the first few days and marked improvement only over weeks of treatment." (Keck *et al.*, 1989, p. 1291). Finally, even when these 5 studies are taken at face value, nothing more "antipsychotic" is suggested in such treatment than could be achieved by administering sedatives. The results of this analysis should cause a healthy scientific skepticism:

> Whatever the limitations of the available studies, one striking conclusion remains: there appears to be no body of controlled studies with replicable results that provides convincing documentation of the onset and characteristic time course of the antipsychotic effects of neuroleptic drugs given to patients with acute exacerbations or acute onset of psychosis. Rather, available studies are few and yield conflicting data on the subject. It is interesting that little is known about this same variable in stable, chronically psychotic patients as well. (Keck *et al.*, 1989, pp. 1291–1292)

Lest one wonder how the very extensive research on the neuroleptics could be so badly flawed, the reader is referred to *The Limits of Biological Treatments for Psychological Distress* (1989) edited by Seymour Fisher and Roger Greenberg, who concluded that, scientifically, none of the major therapeutic "findings" that guide biological psychiatry are secure.

Broad-scale, conclusive kinds of evidence now point to the neuroleptics as a cause rather than a cure of brain abnormalities. As part of his summary of such evidence Breggin (1990) observed:

> Overall, investigators who assume that schizophrenia is the cause of brain atrophy and persistent cognitive losses do not offer convincing evidence or rational justification. On the other hand, there is a very cogent reason to believe that the atrophy found on CT scans cannot be the product of schizophrenia. Brain atrophy is far more accurately and definitively evaluated on direct postmortem pathological evaluation than on CT scan. The actual pathology, if it exists, can more easily be identified and accurately measured by direct observation and microscopic studies. Yet no consistent finding of brain atrophy was made in hundreds of autopsy studies performed on schizophrenics prior to the use of neuroleptics. (p. 452[206])

One need not account for all findings of brain abnormalities in "schizophrenic" subjects to claim that the neuroleptic drugs are a major cause. As discussed by Antonio Puente in Chapter 8 of this book, and as concluded by other reviewers of the literature as well, the findings of brain abnormalities have little specificity for "schizophrenia," a condition that is, in any case, poorly defined in the vast majority of studies. Nor do these findings explain the disorder:

> One can learn from decades of neuropathological studies that no morphological abnormalities found in the brains of schizophrenics are specific to patients with the disorder, and that the derangements that have been reported represent both degenerative and nondegenerative changes that by themselves cannot explain the mental symptoms of this disorder. (Garza-Treviño, Volkow, Cancro, & Contreras, 1990, p. 972)

People called schizophrenic have generally been subject to a host of destructive psychological and somatic influences—including, but not limited to, extreme anxiety, poor nutrition, and alcohol and other drug use—that, quite understandably, can lead to many functional and structural deficits. One of the major, if not the most important, destructive influences, is neuroleptic drug use.

Given such heterogeneity of deficits in "schizophrenia," many of which are manifested as cognitive inabilities, it is not surprising that some clinicians (e.g.,

Flesher, 1990) are attempting cognitive habilitation to compensate for deficits that may be either functional or structural. That is, the treatment of choice, even for brain-damaged patients and including those with neuroleptic-induced damage, may be psychological.

Finally, I would add this note about the broader social context in which our national predilection for dependency on drugs is firmly fixed. We are a drug culture. But we steadfastly deny the innately harmful drug properties of our most damaging drugs by not labeling them harmful. Though cigarettes embody the number one drug in shortening lives, we permit advertising and sales that do not label nicotine as a drug. Similarly, though we may admit that alcohol is the number two substance-use problem in our culture, we usually say "alcohol and drugs" quite as if alcohol is not a drug. It is not difficult, then, to call prescription drugs by the rather euphemistic term *medications* quite as if they are not really drugs. Or the prescribed psychotropic drugs may be called *psychotherapeutic drugs*, as they are by some authors; this is a misnomer because the drugs do not do psychotherapy. We should remember that a drug by any other name is still a drug, and that we are denying the reality that drugs are damaging when we pretend that they are not drugs.

But psychiatry as a profession has come increasingly to depend on the physical disease model and drug treatment, which are supported by quite powerful commercial interests that take little heed of scientific caution or the real physical diseases caused by drug treatment. The leading psychiatric journals reflect an overwhelming commercial incentive system. For example, the 1990 *American Journal of Psychiatry* devoted two thirds (311.5) of its initial 469 pages (before the articles in each issue) to drug ads. Additional pages were devoted to ads for electroshock treatment devices.

Prevention

Prevention is a term fraught with complications, especially in the "mental health" field. Some users of the term have borrowed from but misused public health terminology. Instead of recognizing that prevention refers, on the one hand, to many kinds of interventions and, on the other hand, to diverse outcomes, these users equate method with outcome. Thus, in their usage, treatment is not preventive; it is merely "remedial." Also in their usage, interventions that reach out to great numbers of people are often presumed to be preventive.

But treatment that succeeds even in just slowing the development of a disorder relative to nonintervention, is an example of prevention because the "remedial method" has resulted in lessening a process that would otherwise cause greater morbidity. Likewise, a "preventive method" may have no prevention outcome. For example, "reaching out" to large groups of people may seem impressive numerically but may result in no prevention.

This confusion of method with outcome arises partly from an understandable eagerness to lower the incidence of disorder (the rate of occurrence of new cases of the disorder), and not just the prevalence rate (the percentage of the population that is afflicted with the disorder at a given time). The traditional lament is "There will never be enough therapists to treat all of the patients, so we must find ways to prevent the disorder by reaching everyone at risk." After all, epidemiologists are concerned with whole populations rather than individuals, and public health practice, based largely on the science of epidemiology, is most ambitious to lower the incidence and not just the prevalence of disease.

In essence, the realm of public health is population-based study and practice aimed at curtailing rates of disease in given populations, and evidence of prevention means demonstrating the lowering of disease rates for such whole populations.

Primary prevention, which aims to eliminate a disease or disorder before it can occur, is difficult to assess in the mental health field. Some physical diseases, such as syphilis or pellagra, cause psychotic states, in their advanced stages, so preventing syphilitic infection, for example, can be said to prevent mental disorder, which in this case is literally disease-based. But there are no clear demonstrations of primary prevention of the so-called functional psychoses such as schizophrenic disorders, probably for the reasons discussed later in this section.

Secondary prevention shortens the course of a disease or disorder by early identification and intervention, thereby lessening prevalence, but not necessarily incidence. Langsley (1985) provided an example from his work in very active conjoint family outpatient treatment, which focused on the family as a unit rather than just on the identified patient. This program averted hospitalization for 150 patients deemed by intake psychiatrists to be in need of immediate hospitalization. Replication of the original Denver study provided similar results in Sacramento County, California. Langsley suggested that the prompt treatment of acute schizophrenic episodes, which afflicted many of these patients, lessens the acute phase and aids in a prompt return to functioning.

Tertiary prevention reduces chronicity by preventing complications and by active rehabilitation. Typically the chronic mental patient, most often schizophrenic, has an extremely disrupted and disrupting life with myriad costs and complications. Containing these problems with various treatment and rehabilitative measures exemplifies tertiary prevention in the mental health field.

In the absence of well-documented examples of primary prevention in mental health, Langsley's point (1985) is probably valid: "It must be admitted that discussions about primary prevention of mental illness are more frequently associated with a high level of rhetoric than with the low level of fact that is appropriate" (p. 1886).

Primary prevention efforts by their very nature tend to involve—some would say intrude upon—individuals and groups who may be at high risk for some disease or disorder but are not actually afflicted and may not be asking for intervention. Thus, programs aimed at primary prevention often raise political and human right objections. Even programs like Head Start, which is often regarded as successful in preventing a myriad of social and personal "ills," may be found objectionable by taxpayers. Efforts to prevent the transmission of a disorder, which is a major category in primary prevention (Okin & Borus, 1989), are especially likely to incite protest. For example, genetic counseling to prevent the uninformed conception of children with a high risk of chromosomal abnormalities may be found objectionable on personal and perhaps even civil rights grounds, as one is dealing only with whole-population risk predictions that do not necessarily apply to individuals. And although genetic influences in schizophrenic disorders may have a significant causative role for the population as a whole, the proportion of the total variance or explanatory factors to be accounted for appears small.

As discussed earlier in this book, the disease concept, on which public health practice is based, is problematic itself when applied to mental disorders generally and to schizophrenic disorders particularly. The primary prevention of disease, which is the chief concern of public health, refers literally to preventing contact between the biological etiological agent and the human host and/or increasing the host's resistance so that new cases of the disease do not occur. This mission might have some applicability to schizophrenics if, for example, it were proved that the schizophrenic disorders have a viral etiology, as Torrey and Peterson (1976) proposed.

Prevention is fraught with political complications even when the goal is the prevention of a physical disease by means of well-established and effective methodology. Placing fluoride in public water supplies to prevent tooth decay has aroused intense controversy and protest for many years. Promoting condom use to prevent AIDS transmission has met enormous resistance in many quarters. In fact, one might find it difficult to cite any widespread primary-prevention effort for the public good that has not aroused violent opposition. Even such an unmitigated public health benefit as banning cigarette smoking has aroused storms of protest nearly everywhere it has been tried. Individuals—in great numbers—are sure to protest their individual rights if banned from virtually any practice even if exercising their rights causes harm not merely to them but to others. One might go so far as to say that the practical fundamental basis of public health practice is coercion of the (not so) few for the (presumed) good of the many.

Recognizing these conceptual, programmatic, and political complications means that, to engage effectively in the primary prevention of the schizophrenic disorders, we must establish definite causative links, including psychosocial variables; develop workable methods of intervention applicable to large populations; and find the political support to carry out these interventions. No wonder it is so difficult to start, let alone maintain, such programs.

Conceptually, one may design many kinds of interventions that are likely to have primary-prevention outcomes. Psychosocially, any approaches that promote good parenting and increase feelings of self-respect, competence, personal security, and positive belongingness are likely to prevent mental disorders generally and schizophrenic disorders particularly. Conversely, it would be helpful to eliminate influences that contribute to loneliness, alienation, and poor self-esteem.

In this light, good day-care centers for children of working parents, the Head Start program, and any educational systems that are sensitive to children's emotional as well as academic needs may have major primary-prevention benefits. And because late adolescence and early adulthood are the ages at which people are most vulnerable to actual schizophrenic breakdowns, high schools, colleges, and universities can play especially vital roles in prevention. Campus mental-health professionals, working together with deans, professors, and students themselves can provide an early identification and resolution of many potential schizophrenic breakdowns.

Admittedly, it is difficult to launch, maintain, and demonstrate the preventive efficacy of even the best nurturant educational and mental health programs. Although such programs may be highly effective, including economically, in the long run and certainly over the course of a generation, they appear too costly during the short terms of elective office holders. Yet the real costs of maintaining a huge nonproductive population of schizophrenic and other mentally impaired persons are staggering. Our failures to prepare young people for life have contributed to social disintegration in recent decades, manifested in higher rates of hopelessness, drug use, and youth suicide, and in our resorting to building ever more vast prison systems. These forms of social disintegration are particularly expressive of our neglect of schizophrenic persons, who not only constitute a large proportion of the homeless and who tend to be drug dependent, but who "have been shown to have a suicide rate 210 times the rate of the general population and an arrest rate that is 10 times higher" (Langsley, 1985, p. 1887).

Research on suicide in the schizophrenic disorders has confirmed clinical impressions of a different pattern of prodromal signs than that in otherwise similar populations (Breier & Astrachan, 1984; Nathn & Rousch, 1984). Unlike in most populations, suicides among the schizophrenic population are more likely to occur in the young and are less likely to correlate with stressful life events, the direct communication of suicidal intent, or even a history of prior suicide attempts. Furthermore, the suicide attempts of schizophrenic patients tend to be made with more lethal means than are used by nonschizophrenic psychiatric patients (Breier & Astrachan, 1984).

Thus, suicide in schizophrenic persons is often quite unexpected and seemingly abrupt. The resultant shock to observers and would-be predictors and preventers is compounded by the very high rate of suicide in this clinical population, which ends the lives of 10% (Miles, 1977) to 15% (Nyman & Jonsson, 1986) of schizophrenic persons, and which has been estimated to account for about 3,800 suicides a year in the United States (Miles, 1977).

The best predictor of schizophrenic patient suicide may be self-reported subjective distress (Cohen, Test, & Brown, 1990) rather than more "traditional" signs of risk, such as "objective" measures of life stress.

Although certainly controversial in their own right, treatment programs remain the most socially acceptable form of intervention, if only because they are addressed to identified cases of disorder and are not aimed at masses of people, who in the majority are not at high risk of schizophrenic disorder. Thus, it is important to assess the effects of treatment on prevention.

As noted previously, effective treatment does have preventive effects, at least for the individual, if the treatment at least limits the progress of a disease or disorder. In addition, such tertiary prevention for the affected individual may be primary prevention for others at risk if contact with an afflicted individual, who has not been successfully treated, would have resulted in their developing the disorder. Because schizophrenic parents may have a "pathogenic," if not a specifically schizophrenogenic, influence on their children, successful treatment of the parents may prevent the development or at least the furthering of disorder in the children.

Treatment approaches also generate knowledge about the nature of the schizophrenic disorders. Seeing "what works" and observing the treatment process may provide important clues to how the disorder originates. For example, a correct interpretation or highly accurate empathizing in psychotherapy often strikes a chord in the patient, who then immediately shows better contact with both inner and outer realities, as when the therapist makes it possible for the patient to address and to understand their bizarre efforts in having to avoid a previously terrifying topic. One realizes, then, how vital it is to instill a great sense of security in children so that they do not have to deny the existence and importance of such topics.

Summary

All treatment approaches, whether psychotherapeutic, psychosocial, or drug treatment, ought to follow certain principles: respect for the individual; a focus on the person's basic strengths and deficits; and a longitudinal and development emphasis. Respect requires an appreciation of the uniqueness of personalities and an ability to understand problems of negative transference and negative countertransference. The person's basic strengths must be assessed and facilitated in the general context of treatment as well as in its specific aims. Developmental deficits and negative symptoms should be focused on more than the positive symptoms, though the latter have usually been the main, if not the only, focus of treatment.

Psychotherapy and psychosocial approaches were discussed before drug treatment because they are relatively neglected forms of treatment for schizophrenic persons, and because they are of more basic importance in effecting developmental progress, rather than just reductionistic results. Both of these more basic approaches were essentially set aside after the advent in the 1950s of the phenothiazines, which promoted the adoption of management and dischargeability as outcome criteria. However, the effectiveness of psychotherapy was evidenced three or four decades ago and has also been demonstrated in the modern era, quite notably in the Michigan State Psychotherapy Project. Psychosocial approaches, including milieu therapy and family therapy, have also shown considerable merit, though they are not now prominent forms of treatment.

Drug treatment was discussed in terms of its "main effects" and its "side effects," the former including the reduction of disturbing positive symptoms, especially in acutely schizophrenic persons. When primary reliance is placed on these "antipsychotic" drugs, as it is in most modern practices, they produce skewed treatment results, have a great many harmful side effects *and* cause nervous system damage that is integrally connected with the "main effects." High percentages of patients in long-term drug treatment develop various serious and lasting physical and psychological deficits, such as tardive dyskinesia and tardive psycho[illegible] directly attributable to the drugs. In many, if not most cases, the more i[illegible] forms of damage may be (but seldom are) prevented by adhering to recom[illegible] forms of practice, including giving lower dosages, avoiding polypharmacy [illegible]oss-medicating), and providing "drug holidays" to allow reassessment. In addition, many patients who are not schizophrenic, according to reassessment, have been placed on these drugs. Altogether, the era of drug treatment for "schizophrenics" has represented a setback generally for developmental approaches, and the anticipated "miracles" of cure by drugs has not occurred.

Prevention was discussed as a term fraught with complications, particularly as used in the mental health field. Methods and outcome have often been mistakenly and carelessly equated. The public health model of primary, secondary, and tertiary prevention was presented. The only clear example of primary prevention of mental disorder is the prevention of infectious diseases such as syphilis, which otherwise eventuate in psychoses. The secondary prevention of the schizophrenic disorders, which lessens their prevalence but not necessarily their incidence, was exemplified by the results of a family treatment approach that obviated the need for hospitalization and enhanced functioning ability. Tertiary prevention, which limits chronicity, is usually associated with myriad treatment and rehabilitative approaches, but the method of approach does not always indicate the result. For example, "remedial" treatment that may result in tertiary prevention for a parent may be primary prevention for the child.

To effect the primary prevention of the schizophrenic disorders on a broad scale, it is necessary to find causal links, to devise political and financial support for largely psychosocial programs, and to demonstrate positive results. The rise in recent decades of drug dependency, homelessness, youth suicide, and imprisonment reflects neglect of the nurturant needs of children and youth, especially those who have become schizophrenic. Greater attention to relatively long-term development needs, including educational systems ranging from preschool through college, may continue to be unpopular politically, though vital to our well-being.

Genetic counseling and genetic engineering may be considered potentially preventive, but they, too, are controversial both scientifically and in terms of human rights.

Treatment approaches remain the most acceptable forms of intervention, in part because they are not as demanding of widespread social change. Treatment also generates knowledge of causation, which can be applied to other forms of intervention.

11

Legal and Legislative Considerations

> Law, in its generic sense, is a body of rules of action or conduct prescribed by controlling authority, and having binding legal force.
>
> *Black's Law Dictionary* (fifth edition, 1979)

The law that binds schizophrenic persons has seldom been prescribed or controlled by their authority. In this respect, schizophrenic persons have had, at least until the 1970s, less authority than many criminals, especially criminals of the white-collar variety, who may have powerful influences on both statutory and case law. Schizophrenic persons also have less authority to make and to carry out law than their families, or nearly anyone else in society. This chapter addresses legal and legislative considerations regarding severely mentally disturbed persons, with particular attention to those labeled schizophrenic and with emphasis on the sense and nonsense of the most relevant and important laws.

The Nonsense of Insanity

Disenfranchisement of the schizophrenic individual, his or her deprivation of rights and privileges as a free citizen, occurs legally when the individual is declared *insane*:

> The term is a social and legal term rather than a medical one, and indicates a condition which renders the affected person unfit to enjoy liberty of action because of the unreliability of his behavior with concomitant danger to himself and others. The term is more or less synonymous with mental illness or psychosis. In law, the term is used to denote that degree of mental illness which negates the individual's legal responsibility or capacity. (*Black's Law Dictionary*, 1979)

This definition of insanity contains an inherent contradiction. First, it defines insanity as a social and legal term *rather than* a medical one. And, second, it defines insanity as more-or-less synonymous with mental illness or psychosis, *which are medical terms*. Third, the legal term *insanity* is again defined in medical terms, this time according to the degree of mental illness. Thus, insanity is a legal term, with disenfranchisement consequences, that purports to be founded on the social consideration of danger to the person and others, but that is defined medically in terms of the degree of mental illness. As psychiatrist Bernard Rubin (1975) pointed out:

> Commitment of the mentally ill has always been closely associated with their purported dangerousness. In fact, the association has often been so close that to make these determinations separately has at times been difficult or impossible. In part this has been due to a combination of the notions that a "beast" is released in man by mental illness and that the doctor has a responsibility to exclude all possibilities of dangerousness before opting for release. Therefore the psychiatrist, rather than attempting to carefully assess dangerousness, usually takes a safe course—that is, commitment. (p. 855)

The dilemma presented by the legal definition of insanity, founded on its initial claim of independence from a medical definition, might be resolved if all three of the following basic conditions could be met: There must be a highly reliable definition, first, of *mental illness* and, second, of the *degree* of mental illness, and third, the presence and degree of mental illness must be highly related to *dangerousness* to oneself or others. As documented earlier in this book, none of these conditions is regularly met. Therefore, the very bases for disfranchisement of the "mentally ill" are often insubstantial and unreliable in actual practice. The combination of unreliabilities in satisfying these basic conditions readily produces decisions that have only the appearance and not the substance of valid determinations of insanity.

In essence, because most ordinary practice for the determination of insanity is based on highly unreliable assessment methods—even though they are carried out by legal and medical experts—in combination with the generally false assumption that "mental illness" is an excellent predictor of danger to oneself or others, the ostensible purpose of declaring persons insane is poorly served. But this ordinary practice determines social disfranchisement, on the one hand, and the criteria for social protection, on the other. The protection motive is not well served by the patient-defendants' "winning" an insanity plea, as the mental hospitalization that results may offer as little protection for society or for the patient as ordinary incarceration and it may offer even less protection.

The best actual predictors of danger to oneself or others are usually actual, readily observable behaviors, though in some instances evaluators may need to actively elicit evidence of covert plans. In any case, diagnosis of severe mental illness, including the schizophrenic disorders, inevitably includes more nondangerous than dangerous individuals. Rubin (1975) noted, "Even in the most careful, painstaking, laborious, and lengthy clinical approaches to the prediction of dangerousness, false positive evaluations may be at a minimum of 60 to 70 percent." (p. 856). Similarly, psychiatrist Thomas Gutheil (1989) noted, "Much empirical research suggests that clinicians have low levels of success in predicting dangerousness, in part because it is not really a clinical concept and bears only an erratic relationship to mental illness." (p. 2114). However, he added:

> The Supreme Court has come down strongly on the side of clinicians being able to predict dangerousness reliably. To claim that clinicians cannot do so, one decision notes, after all the years when clinicians appeared to be doing it through commitment, would be tantamount to asking the Court to disinvent the wheel. (p. 2115)

In this light, it is no wonder that psychiatrist Thomas Szasz could not only argue with some merit that the mental health enterprise is based on *The Myth of Mental Illness* (1961) but deconstruct the notion of insanity (Szasz, 1987) in rather devastating detail and highlight the pseudoscience in the notion of *schizophrenia* as an insanity plea. He suggested that, in the case of John Hinckley, Jr. (who shot President Reagan), it was largely the unsubstantiated assumption that Hinckley had a brain disease that resulted in his successful insanity defense. That assumption was made possible by saying that Hinckley was schizophrenic and that "schizophrenia" is a brain disease. Thus, Hinckley was not to be held responsible for his actions, whereas people not adjudged "insane" should be held responsible according to this system or belief. The presumption of brain disease serves greatly to make the schizophrenic disorders sound like purely medical problems and thus to invite medical opinion as ultimate authority. But, as so often happens, the question of whether Hinckley was insane became extremely controversial not only among medical authorities but among the lay public, a great proportion of whom were outraged at the outcome of his court case.

Involuntary Civil Commitment: The Dilemma of Coercive Care

Because of the tendency of the criteria for judging insanity to overpredict dangerousness, the judicial system tends to commit many individuals to mental institutions who are unlikely to perform dangerous acts or to threaten their own lives. Furthermore, as every mental health practitioner knows, forcing patients into treatment settings rarely results in beneficial treatment. When treatment is provided to such patients, the treatment itself is coercive and quite likely to be of the reductionist variety that attempts to reduce positive symptoms at the expense of the development of abilities to function adaptively and creatively. Civil commitment gets the doctor–patient relationship off to anything but a civil start. In these circumstances, patients may develop much more sophistication about how to beat or avoid the institution's system than about how to learn to live well, just as prison inmates find themselves in an ideal environment for learning criminal vocations.

Even the most idealistic proposals to reform the commitment laws founder on the very bases for having any such laws. On the one hand, civil commitment is designed to protect society from dangerous persons, and, on the other hand, it is designed to protect and even to help these persons by providing them with treatment. Society would like to be able to say; "Sure, we have segregated these persons so that they are no longer a threat to us, but we have also done them good."

As the legally appointed executors of the seemingly impossible standards in the commitment laws, psychiatrists are easily drawn into unresolvable dilemmas in terms of both disposition and treatment. First, the prediction of dangerousness is an extremely faulty and inexact science, and psychiatrists are thus presented with a disposition dilemma: On one hand, fear of releasing anyone who might be dangerous readily leads to an overprediction of dangerousness and results in restraining harmless persons. On the other hand, truly dangerous persons may be released. Second, there is again the treatment dilemma; coercive treatment is rarely, if ever, helpful.

Thus, Thomas Szasz, in his book *Psychiatric Slavery: When Confinement and Coercion Masquerade as Cure* (1977), had ample bases for his argument against involuntary civil commitment. Szasz wholly rejected the notion that so-called mental illness is a medical problem that can be solved by medical means. Further, he stated, "I view the care provided by compulsory mental treatment as potentially much more harmful than the metaphorical disease it is supposed to cure" (p. 126).

Given a Right to Treatment, What Is the Available Treatment?

For all practical purposes, the only ostensible justification for committing persons to mental institutions is that they will be able to benefit from treatment. Otherwise, why not confine dangerous persons in prisons, which provide greater protection for society, or in other sorts of institutions and living situations that offer protection to patients and the public alike? In theory, if the treatment offered in mental institutions includes effective modes, some of the patients will benefit and there will be some justification for commitment. In actuality, effective treatment is not available and the abominable conditions characteristic of most state hospitals led to the "right to treatment" movement which was essentially the first active attempt in modern times to establish patients' rights. Perlin (1986) noted that

> prior to 1972 the topic was one to which virtually no legal attention was paid. Courts had been willing to examine the civil rights of criminal suspects, consumers, and racial minorities, but matters involving the procedural and substantive rights of the mentally disabled rarely, if ever, were litigated. (p. 401)

By the mid-1970s, the historic Alabama "right-to-treatment" case of *Wyatt v. Stickney* (1971) had established a constitutional right to such standards of treatment as a humane psychological and physical environment, adequate numbers of qualified staff, and individualized treatment plans that would give involuntarily committed patients a reasonable opportunity to be cured or at least to improve their condition. Though this case set a precedent that was followed in many state and federal courts around the nation, obtaining actual compliance proved quite difficult. Compliance had not been clearly established by 1980 even within the state of Alabama. In the absence of adequate funding for treatment, it was difficult to approximate the mandated standards. A further legal issue arose: Could a hospital or its staff be held responsible for failure to meet the standards when it lacked the necessary funding to do so? This further dilemma, caused by tardy compliance by the state, was addressed eventually by appointing the governor of Alabama as receiver of the state's hospital system.

Delays in compliance, though serious and even critical for the effective translation of law into treatment realities, became compounded by an even more fundamental conflict. The question of what professional treatment was available became paramount. It was easy to prescribe ordinary humane physical and psychological environments that serve the simple requirements of daily living, and to enforce these standards without much help from mental health practitioners; for example the requirement arising from *Wyatt v. Stickney* that the hot water used for dishwashing be maintained thermostatically at 180 degrees (Perlin, 1986). However, the legal mandates said very little about what constituted an adequate individualized treatment plan; their lack of specification left the question up to the mental health practitioners, particularly psychiatrists.

Inevitably, the frequent absence of both adequate funding and professional treatment standards and specifications that were agreed on by patient plaintiffs and professionals alike produced further conflict. It is not surprising, then, that actual adjudicated cases were generally reduced to the plaintiffs having to accept "treatment" limited to the kinds that were already available, an outcome that begged the question of treatment availability. It was as if the treatment authorities said, "So you want different kinds of treatment. Well, we don't have or wish to have different kinds of treatment to offer you!" The courts then acquiesced: "Where professionally prescribed treatment differed from that urged by plaintiffs, the difference reflected a modification "to conform to the available treatment, rather than to appropriate treatment, for patient's condition" (Perlin, 1986, p. 404).

It is not surprising that patients and their attorneys were dissatisfied with the actual outcomes of right-to-treatment litigation; and the next major legal movement focused on trying at least to proscribe those treatments that were considered harmful.

The Right to Refuse Treatment: If You Cannot Win, Try Not to Lose

Inevitably, patients and their attorneys mounted class actions against being "treated" in ways that they felt were injurious and out of their control. Because the currently available modes of treatment consisted very largely—and some might say exclusively—of doing things to patients that were intrusive, coercive, and at least potentially if not actually harmful, these actions were rejections of virtually all psychiatric treatment. It was as if the patients gave this retort to the treatment authorities: "If you won't treat us as we would like to be treated, then we refuse treatment!" In this sense "the right to refuse treatment" is a misleading designation. Many patients, probably the vast majority, wanted treatment provided that it was good treatment. But in the absence of alternatives to drugs and seclusion and because these treatments were often forced on patients, the patients and their attorneys wanted to have at least the power of refusal.

The "right-to-refuse" litigation, and the accompanying record-setting amount of discussion and literature, is clearly the most significant development yet in mental health law. No other issue more clearly elucidates the fundamental dilemmas involving the conflicting interests of patients, the mental health authorities, and the society at large: "It is no exaggeration to say that no other issue is more important to all participants; no other issue dredges up so many hidden conflicts; nowhere else are “turf” issues of such significance” (Perlin, 1986, p. 405).

Two major litigation actions were mounted in the late 1970s. The first, *Rennie v. Klein* (1978), resulted in the Third Circuit Court’s essentially affirming a District Court of New Jersey decision that involuntarily committed patients can retain a qualified constitutional right, based on the 14th Amendment’s “liberty” section in the due process clause, to refuse antipsychotic drugs that may induce permanently disabling side effects. But the protections that were afforded by this instance of case law were not very great even in terms of the court’s decision, much less in terms of implementation.

Reminiscent of the extreme tardiness and ineffectiveness with which the State of Alabama had implemented the “right-to-treatment” provisions mandated by the court, New Jersey effectively withstood compliance with patients’ mandated “right to refuse treatment.” As attorney Alexander Brooks (1987) noted:

> The district court in *Rennie* rejected a set of procedures that was hurriedly prepared and disseminated by the State of New Jersey under the immediate pressure of the *Rennie* litigation. Those new procedures were ignored by hospital medical directors, some of whom were unaware of their existence. (p. 358).

The second case, *Rogers v. Okin* (1979) and its continuance as *Mills v. Rogers* (1982), seemingly held more promise for establishing the right of patients to refuse antipsychotic drugs in other than emergency situations and to restrict the use of enforced seclusion. Seven patients were represented by attorneys from Greater Boston Legal Services. As a major expert witness in this case, I was able to read many accounts of treatment of these patients at the Boston State Hospital, and, in one case, I was able to meet a plaintiff:

> Mr. W., a black man in his 20s, was described as about 6 feet tall and weighing 200 pounds, but at the time of the initial court hearings, when interviewed, he appeared to be about 5 feet 10 inches tall and 180 pounds; it would seem that his size had been overestimated. True to staff description, however, he was well built.
>
> On entering the hospital ward, Mr. W. appeared upset. He quickly asked if he could be of help, such as by assisting with the physical maintenance of the ward. After being denied a helpful role, he appeared frustrated and overturned a Ping Pong table. He also objected to what he perceived as harsh treatment toward another patient. Following these behaviors and without his being provocative in any other way, he was placed in seclusion. Altogether, he was kept in seclusion for more than 60 days. He was given a variety of diagnoses, including paranoid schizophrenia and manic-depressive psychosis, and he was placed on a variety of neuroleptic drugs. The U.S. District Court found that he had been given overmedication and cross-medication, resulting in harmful side-effects without increasing the benefit, if any, of the intended effects. He also appeared to be damaged psychologically by the seemingly abusive nature and duration of his forced seclusion in what appeared to be nonemergency circumstances.

Though there was clearly demonstrable harm to the patients in *Rogers v. Okin*, including tardive dyskinesia, the plaintiff’s attorneys’ efforts to prove malpractice failed because the patient’s mental health care did not fall below the level of ordinary and acceptable practice. The court took into account the poor conditions at Boston State Hospital and agreed, as it were, with an American Psychiatric Association position statement that it would be unjust to hold the individual psychiatrists who were involved responsible for the hospital's deficiencies; the court decided that the doctors had acted in good faith and in concordance with accepted standards of medical care (Applebaum & Gutheil, 1980a).

The court's decision resulted in considerable limitation on the psychiatrists and other physicians, and on medical personnel generally, greatly reducing their latitude in forcibly administering drugs, and this limitation was upheld beyond the Federal District Court's initial restraining order. But the Court of Appeals for the First Circuit Court qualified and thereby lessened this limitation. Again, the treatment authorities were asked to determine the degree of the patient's dangerousness in the absence of forcible drug administration. If these authorities decided that a patient was or would be markedly dangerous, the authorities could continue to forcibly drug and/or forcibly seclude the patient. Thus the courts have continued to rely on psychiatrists' ability to determine dangerousness, which psychiatrists and other mental health practitioners are not well equipped to do.

But both committed and voluntary patients now have some effective rights to refuse antipsychotic drugs and seclusion as a result of a series of decisions beginning with *Rogers v. Okin*. Where these rights are enforced, psychiatrists who are attempting to administer drugs or seclusion may have to wait while independent psychiatrists are called in to help decide whether there is a safer and less restrictive alternative.

Though the U.S. Supreme Court had the opportunity to reject the ideas of a constitutional right to refuse treatment, it did not. Instead, the Supreme Court assumed that such a right did exist and remanded this case, then known as *Mills* in 1982, to the First Circuit Court for reference to state law. The Massachusetts Supreme Judicial Court observed expectations of "substantive rights" derived from state law relating to the 14th Amendment of the U.S. Constitution. In essence, patients' right to refuse drugs and seclusion in nonemergency situations was not denied but was assumed and even established by the conclusion of this very complicated judicial process, which spanned several years and involved various courts ranging from the state level to the U.S. Supreme Court.

Many psychiatrists, perhaps the majority, have found the decisions establishing the right to refuse treatment objectionable. Some have taken the position that drug treatment is unquestionably needed by schizophrenic patients and that refusal to take the drugs is itself a clear indication of mental incompetency. For example, E. Fuller Torrey (1983) stated, "People with schizophrenia have diseases of the brain; they cannot give informed consent. . . . Supporting this position is a study of chronic schizophrenic patients showing that only 27% of them understand that they needed medication" (Torrey, 1983, p. 191).

Contrary to many dire predictions about patients' fates in the era of the right to refuse treatment, the results have been rather benign. Psychiatrists Applebaum and Gutheil (1979) predicted that patients would be "rotting with their rights on" (p. 308). On the contrary, evidence cited below, which is based on empirical indices of trouble and deterioration, indicates that these dire predictions have failed to materialize. Ironically, and to their credit, these same psychiatrists, Applebaum and Gutheil (1980b), contributed data that tend to refute their own predictions; they reported that only 5 of 72 episodes of drug refusal at the Massachusetts Mental Health Center seriously impaired patient care. The feared epidemic of refusals in the wake of the *Rogers v. Okin* decision did not materialize despite patients' educating one another about the right of refusal. Furthermore, permitting what Applebaum and Gutheil called situational and stereotypical refusers (the majority of the refusers) to decline medication as a matter of clinical policy, and not as a "right," did not seriously impair their overall treatment but actually yielded some advantages in treatment efficacy:

> The need to negotiate with patients gave . . . doctors an opportunity to explore material which might otherwise have remained buried. All episodes ended quickly, even for delusional patients; emergency situations were rare and relatively smoothly handled under provisions allowing involuntary medication when danger to self or others was present. (Applebaum & Gutheil, 1980b, p. 345)
>
> Clinicians . . . may have to accept some limitations on their freedom to treat those patients declining therapy. As our study suggests, not only is permitting limited refusal generally innocuous, but some definite gains may accrue from the accompanying negotiations. Even among the class of long-term symptomatic refusers, prolonged refusal did not preclude subsequent positive response to medication. (p. 345)

Brooks (1987) summarized the findings of some other empirical studies. When refusals were upheld, little or no harm to the patient occurred, nor have a larger number of violent incidents occurred, nor suicide attempts, escapes, noncooperation, or need to restrain patients or place them in seclusion. Furthermore, refusers are discharged at about the same rate as consenters. In short, "there is no evidence that the delays cause patients to 'rot'" (Brooks, 1987, p. 370).

However, puzzled by the movement to establish a right to refuse because it came from a heretofore quite docile and unquestioning patient population, Applebaum (1982) stated:

> It is, in many respects, ironic that the issue of a right to refuse treatment has surfaced now. During a century and a half of widespread institutional care of the mentally ill in the United States, the power of physicians to prescribe most forms of treatment for committed patients went unchallenged. Generations of patients were thus routinely subjected to bleeding, purging, cold baths, and whirling chairs. When all these proved fruitless, they became the victims of callous neglect. The last 30 years, however, have seen a revolution in psychiatry's ability to treat the mentally ill, largely due to the use of effective new medications. (Applebaum, 1982, p. 46)

Apart from the question of whether drug treatment is truly the treatment of choice in the long run and whether alternative treatments such as psychotherapy should be offered, it is important to consider the evidence of the blatantly harmful effects of heavy drug administration and polypharmacy that characterized the pre-litigation years. Even ardent proponents of drug treatment who examined actual practices in comparison to recommend practices observed glaring discrepancies between recommended and actual practice in terms of drug overdoses and the use of too many different drugs for the same patient. Psychiatrist and psychopharmacologist Robert Sovner, who ran a Boston State Hospital unit that was not named in the suit, came to agree with the plaintiffs' arguments: "For every patient you can show me whose treatment is delayed by the need to have a court pass on his competency, I can show you more who were improperly medicated in the past and suffered needless side effects as a result" (quoted in Applebaum, 1982, p. 56). Similarly, as Brooks (1987 p. 352) noted, in the *Rennie* trial the medical director of a major New Jersey hospital, when queried under oath, estimated that 20%–40% of his patients suffered from tardive dyskinesia, whereas he had previously denied that any of his patients suffered from it. The New Jersey federal judge concluded that medications were being administered by State hospital staff in a "grossly irresponsible" manner.

How is one to interpret the contradictions between psychiatrists' predictions and the empirical findings? Some of the psychiatrists who protested the legal decisions, such as Applebaum and Gutheil, may have been thinking much more about their own evidently high levels of practice than about the common practices in the inadequately staffed and regulated mental hospitals of the type that became defendants in the *Rennie* and *Rogers* cases. The more exemplary institutions such as the Massachusetts Mental Health Center, would not only be less likely to have such refusal problems to begin with but would also be far more able to adapt to the new requirements by making good clinical sense of them and actually turning them to advantage.

The right-to-refuse cases continue to raise important questions about the actual effects of the "antipsychotic" medications:

> Until recently, little was known about these medications, even by the psychiatrists who used them routinely. Earlier beliefs turned out to be erroneous. We now know that the benefits of the medications are not always as clear-cut as they at first seemed. On the other hand, the harms caused by the medications, originally perceived as insignificant, are now regarded as serious indeed. (Brooks, 1987, p. 344)

Because the assessment and diagnosis of schizophrenia and related disorders are especially unreliable and inaccurate in ordinary practice, large numbers of nonschizophrenic individuals have been administered various "antipsychotic" drugs, often for many years and with irreversible damage, including tardive dyskinesia. Being forced to take such harmful drugs compounds their problems in many and various ways. The absence, in ordinary practice, of careful initial assessments, of reassessments, and of "drug holidays" that would make reassessment more meaningful often condemns patients to years of not only fruitless but harmful treatment. The most ardent proponents of drug treatment and the most ardent opponents alike have a stake in seeing that the ordinarily grossly inadequate assessment practices greatly improve.

The right-to-refuse-treatment cases brought into focus a doctrine of care called the *least restrictive alternative,* which holds that patients who purportedly need treatment according to the authorities should at least by protected from unnecessarily restrictive treatments. Clearly, forced seclusion and forced drugging are highly restrictive measures. Logically, protecting patients from unnecessarily restrictive treatment requires alternatives when treatment is mandated. But do patients who are involuntarily committed have any alternative other than restrictive treatment or no treatment?

As is well known, most modern psychiatric hospitals offer little treatment other than the somatic types that have inherently damaging consequences in addition to any beneficial effects they might have: usually drugs or, less often, electroshock or brain surgery that destroys brain tissue. The searching of the vast quantity of treatment records of the Boston State Hospital patients in *Rogers v. Okin*, for example, yielded no evidence of patients' receiving or being offered psychotherapy, nor was there any evidence of any kind of milieu therapy. Attorneys representing these and other patients were realistic, and apparently resigned, in choosing to plead for the right to refuse treatment rather than to insist on the provision of other treatments. Their intent drove forward two developments, one being an improvement in drug and seclusion practices, and the other—already under way—being the movement of patients out of hospitals.

Deinstitutionalization: From the Frying Pan into the Fire?

If one wants to protect the well-being and, indeed, the survival of the schizophrenic person, the proportion of hostile to caring attitudes in the environment is crucial. Most severely schizophrenic persons are very vulnerable to the hostile actions of others. Not only are many mental patients attacked on the streets in this era of deinstitutionalization, but many perish directly as a result, or their lives are greatly shortened by conditions of extreme poverty, neglect, and loss of any hope for the future.

Transferring mental patients from the undeniably harmful conditions of the vast majority of long-term mental hospitals to the conditions of the streets has merely exchanged one system of harm for another, as psychiatrist E. Fuller Torrey (1988) documented. He estimated that "There are at least twice as many seriously mentally ill individuals living on streets and in shelters as there are in public mental hospitals" (p. 6) and cited a "reasonably good consensus that approximately one-third of homeless individuals are seriously mentally ill" (p. 7).

Mental patients have not been better protected or helped to develop by being discharged to generally rejecting environments, and society as a whole has certainly not felt better protected: "Since 1961 it has become evident that the number of violent acts committed by mental patients has increased dramatically. The mental patients responsible for these acts have usually been diagnosed with schizophrenia" (Torrey, 1988, p. 17).

The laws that mandated deinstitutionalization were produced by a mix of incentives and political aims, together with the false assumption that the so-called antipsychotic drugs would—just by themselves perhaps—be an effective antidote to chronicity:

> The deinstitutionalization of patients stemmed from a variety of factors, such as the increasing use of effective antipsychotic drugs; concern for the civil rights of state hospital patients that led to landmark legal decisions ordering the provision of mental health treatment in least restrictive settings; and economic incentives (Pardes, Sirovatka & Pincus, 1986, p. 55). The politicians involved in promoting deinstitutionalization represented a coalition of strange bedfellows. Right wing conservatives interested in saving state's funds joined with activist civil libertarians interested in patient's rights. Both groups were supported by an indignant public. (Wolfe & Astrachan, 1986, p. 69)

Meanwhile, the original intent and understanding of the community mental health movement, which was provided impetus and federal funding by the 1963 Community Mental Health Centers Act advocated by President John F. Kennedy, had been undermined. Funding for the community care of the severely mentally ill, even when it was available for a few years after the act was passed, tended to be used for less disturbed populations. As this funding diminished after President Johnson's administration, recognition of the critical need for psychosocial developmental approaches with chronic patients lost its only feasible economic support after already having suffered a setback due to the dramatic, apparently miraculous advent of the antipsychotic drugs. Borus (1986) noted the simultaneity of this insightful recognition together with the advent of patient control by drugs as *both* became contributors to deinstitutionalization:

> [There was a] mid-century recognition by clinicians that many aspects of chronic patient's asocial, apathetic, and incompetent behaviors in state hospitals reflected the institutional expectation that they could not function more appropriately. Experimental manipulation of the state hospital social milieu in the 1940s and 1950s demonstrated that changing the structure of these institutions to provide patients with "ego stretching" experiences could stimulate them to function more independently without excessive violence and that many of these patients could learn sufficient social skills to function outside of the institutional setting.
>
> The advent of an effective pharmacology at mid-century . . . demonstrated that the psychotic behavior of patients with severe mental illness could be controlled pharmacologically and that long-term care in a hospital was not an essential ingredient in the treatment of mental illness. (p. 78)

By the time actual deinstitutionalization began in the 1960s, the crucial importance of psychosocial forms of treatment was easily denied, as it was assumed that the new "miracle" drugs were truly the answer to the problem of schizophrenic disorders. The harmful effects of the "antipsychotic" drugs were not obvious at first, especially with acute patients, and it was easy to cite gains in the reduction and manageability of the positive symptoms. Because the majority of the severely mentally ill had been diagnosed as schizophrenic and they seemed well contained by regimens of generally high drug dosages, the advent of these drugs was hailed as the third revolution in psychiatry. It took two decades just to begin to admit that the drugs are not a cure in any sense, that a reliance on the drugs skews treatment and may even promote chronicity, and that the drugs have a host of brain-damaging effects, such as tardive dyskinesia and tardive psychosis.

Whereas the severely mentally ill of the late 1950s through the 1970s were treated with drugs en masse, their young counterparts, beginning in the 1980s, greatly resisted treatment of any kind, generally avoiding contact with the would-be treaters, who essentially offer only drugs anyway. The new generation has learned to distrust the system.

When the severely mentally ill find a home, it is likely to be a nursing home or, in the case of the new generation especially, a penal institution (Borus 1986). This new generation of "severely mentally ill" people also constitutes a major segment, if not the majority, of the nation's vast homeless population. They are functionally inadequate to the demands of daily living. They do not hold jobs, or contribute to the welfare of the community, or establish stable families. They have not been offered much by society, and they do not offer much in return.

In conclusion, the harmful conditions of long-term mental hospitalization have been superseded by the possibly even more harmful conditions of deinstitutionalization. What began as a movement lauded by civil libertarians as a kind of modern-day removal of the chains of mental patients has proved to be a not-so-benign form of neglect producing massively destructive consequences for both the patients and society as a whole. The so-called severely mentally ill, and schizophrenic persons in particular, cannot simply be dismissed.

Summary

The severely "mentally ill," including "schizophrenics," have had little power to help determine what becomes of them in society and in the mental health system. The laws defining insanity, along with involuntary commitment, the establishment of the right to treatment and the right to refuse treatment, and deinstitutionalization, reflected the enormous difficulties in meeting both the needs of the patients and the needs of society as a whole.

Insanity is a legal concept designed to protect both the individual and society. Although it is purportedly independent of medical definition, it actually depends on psychiatric expertise to establish reliable and valid diagnoses, to indicate the degree of severity of "mental disease," and to predict the dangerousness of the "insane" person. But there is little evidence, in practice, that any of these functions can be performed very reliably or validly, and they are the target of extreme disagreement and controversy.

Involuntary commitment also presents great difficulties. Although society's need to be protected may be partially met, it is difficult to make coercive treatment effective. And because commitment depends on insanity proceedings, the very bases for involuntary commitment are dubious.

The right-to-treatment movement, begun in Alabama with *Wyatt v. Stickney* (1971), foundered in two principal ways: extreme delays and avoidances in complying with court decisions and the unavailability of effective treatments that would provide alternatives to the virtually exclusive use of somatic treatments, which were often administered coercively.

The right-to-refuse-treatment movement, marked by the New Jersey case of

Rennie v. Klein (1978) and the Massachusetts case of *Rogers v. Okin* (1979) and its continuance as *Mills v. Rogers* (1982), acted fairly effectively to provide safeguards against the indiscriminate nonemergency use of harmful coercive treatments such as drugs and seclusion. The courts upheld and enforced the original court decisions in the Massachusetts case particularly. Majority psychiatric opinion was adamantly against these decisions, predicting that patients would "rot with their rights on." But there is now ample evidence, in part from psychiatrists who were originally opposed to the decisions, that neither patients nor institutions have suffered from the enforcement of these decisions. The new safeguards sometimes delay treatment but provoke more meaningful dialogue with patients, who thereby achieve some long-overdue power to help determine their own care.

The right-to-refuse treatment movement was predicated on the seeming impossibility of developing better kinds of treatment such as psychotherapy and psychosocial treatment. Drug treatment has remained the principal and often the only treatment

The deinstitutionalization movement is also a concession to the seeming impossibility of developing more effective and humane treatment within psychiatric hospitals, especially the state hospitals, where the patients developed institutionalization syndromes and drug-induced damage on top of their original disorders. The bases for deinstitutionalization were formed in the 1950s, when the "antipsychotic" drugs were introduced, and the nascent strivings to develop psychotherapy and psychosocial approaches were replaced by management concerns emphasizing patients' tractability. The actual movement out of hospitals began in the 1960s, when "dischargeability" became a vaunted goal; since the 1970s, when the movement became massive, so have the numbers of homeless "mentally ill." Have the patients gone from the frying pan into the fire? The so-called severely mentally ill, including that enormous component called schizophrenic, continue to have little real power to determine their fate, while society has continued to neglect their care and to permit, perhaps to cause, further alienation.

References

Abrams, R., & Taylor, A. (1979). Differential EEG patterns in affective disorder and schizophrenia. *Archives of General Psychiatry, 36,* 1355–1358.

Acevedo, N., Gonzalez, M., Puente, A., & Whitaker, L. (1985). The measurement of schizophrenia conceptualization using a Spanish translation of the Whitaker Index of Schizophrenia. *Journal of Clinical Psychology, 41,* 157–161.

Acker, C. (1991). A schizophrenia drug withheld; Pa. won't pay to closely monitor. *Philadelphia Inquirer,* pp. 1A, 7A.

Alanen, Y.O., Räkköläinen, V., Laakso, J., Rasimus, R., & Kaljonen, A. (1986). *Towards need-specific treatment of schizophrenic psychoses.* New York: Springer-Verlag.

Albott, W. L., & Gilbert, L. (1973). Comparison of non-brain-damaged schizophrenic and brain-damaged non-schizophrenic males on the WIST. *Psychological Reports, 32,* 187–194.

Alexander, F. G., & Selesnick, S. T. (1966). *The history of psychiatry.* New York: Harper & Row.

American Psychiatric Association. (1968). *Diagnostic and statistical manual of mental disorders* (2nd ed.: DSM-II). Washington, DC: Author.

American Psychiatric Association. (1980). *Diagnostic and statistical manual of mental disorders* (3rd ed.); DSM-III). Washington, DC: Author.

American Psychiatric Association. (1987). *Diagnostic and statistical manual of mental disorders* (3rd ed., rev.; DSM-III-R). Washington, DC: Author.

Anastasi, A. (1988). *Psychological testing* (6th ed.). New York: Macmillan.

Andreasen, N. C. (1979a). Thought, language, and communication disorders: 1. Clinical assessment, definition of terms, and evaluation of their reliability. *Archives of General Psychiatry, 36,* 1315–1321.

Andreasen, N. C. (1979b). Thought, language, and communication disorders: 2. Diagnostic significance. *Archives of General Psychiatry, 36,* 1325–1330.

Andreasen, N. C. (1981). *Scale for the Assessment of Negative Symptoms (SANS).* Iowa City: University of Iowa.

Andreasen, N. C. (1982). Negative symptoms in schizophrenia: definition and reliability. *Archives of General Psychiatry, 39,* 784–788.

Andreasen, N. C. (1987). The diagnosis of schizophrenia. *Schizophrenia Bulletin, 13,* 9–22.

Andreasen, N. C. (1988). Evaluation of brain imaging technique in mental illness. *Annual Review of Medicine, 39,* 335–345.

Andreasen, N. C., & Flaum, M. A. (1990). Schizophrenia and related psychotic disorders. *Hospital and Community Psychiatry, 41*(9), 954–956.

Andreasen, N. C., & Olsen, S. (19820. Negative v. positive schizophrenia: Definition and validation. *Archives of General Psychiatry, 39,* 789–794.

Andreasen, N. C., Olsen, S. A., Dennert, J. W., & Smith, M. R. (1982). Ventricular enlargement in schizophrenia: Relationship to positive and negative symptoms. *American Journal of Psychiatry, 39,* 297–302.

Andreasen, N. C., Nasrallah, H. A., Dunn, V, Olson, S. C., Grove, W. M., Ehrhardt, J. C., Coffman, J. A., & Crossett, J. H. W. (1986). Structural abnormalities in the frontal system in schizophrenia: A magnetic resonance imaging study. *Archives of General Psychiatry, 43,* 136–144.

Applebaum, P. S. (1982). Can mental patients say no to drugs? *New York Times Magazine* (March 21), pp. 46, 51–56.

Applebaum, P. S., & Gutheil, T. G. (1979). "Rotting with their rights on": Constitutional theory and clinical reality in drug refusal by psychiatric in-patients. *Bulletin of the American Academy of Psychiatry and Law, 7,* 308–317.

Applebaum, P. S., & Gutheil, T. G. (1980a). The Boston State Hospital case: "Involuntary mind control," the Constitution, and the "Right to Rot." *American Journal of Psychiatry, 137*(6), 720–723.

Applebaum, P. S., & Gutheil, T. G. (1980b). Drug refusal: A study of psychiatric inpatients. *American Journal of Psychiatry, 137*(3), 340–346.

Arieti, S. (1974). *Interpretation of schizophrenia* (2nd ed.). New York: Basic Books.

Arieti, S. (1976). *Creativity: The magic synthesis.* New York: Basic Books.

Astrachan, B. M., Harrow, M., Adler, D., *et al.* (1972). New Haven Schizophrenia Index: A checklist for the diagnosis of schizophrenia. *British Journal of Psychiatry, 121,* 529.

Auden, W. H., & Kronenberger, L. (Eds.). (1981). *The Viking book of aphorisms.* New York: Penguin Books.

Autobiography of a schizophrenic girl. (1970). With analytic interpretation by Margaret Sechehaye. New York: Signet Books, New American Library.

Babigian, H. (1985). Schizophrenia: Epidemiology. In H. I. Kaplan & B. J. Saddock (Eds.), *Comprehensive textbook of psychiatry* (vol. 4, pp. 643–650). Baltimore: Williams & Wilkins.

Barbee, J. G., Clark, P. D., Crapanzano, M. S., Heintz, G. C., *et al.* (1989). Alcohol and substance abuse among schizophrenic patients presenting to an emergency psychiatric service. *Journal of Nervous and Mental Disease, 177*(7), 400–407.

Barrett, K., McCallum, W. C., & Pocock, P. V. (1986). Brain indicators of altered attention and information processing in schizophrenic patients. *British Journal of Psychiatry, 148,* 414–420.

Bassoe, P. (1945). Spain as the cradle of psychiatry. *American Journal of Psychiatry, 101,* 731–738.

Beck, A. T., Ward, C. H., Mendelson, M., Mock, J. E., & Ebaugh, J. K. (1962). Reliability of psychiatric diagnoses: 2. A study of consistency of clinical judgment and rating. *American Journal of Psychiatry, 119,* 351–357.

Bellak, L. (Ed.). (1979). *Disorders of the schizophrenic syndrome.* New York: Basic Books.

Berman, K. F. (1987). Cortical "stress tests" in schizophrenia: Regional cerebral blood flow studies. *Biological Psychiatry, 22,* 1304–1326.

Besson, J. A., Corrigan, F. M., Cherryman, G. R., & Smith, F. W. (1987). Nuclear magnetic resonance brain imaging in chronic schizophrenia. *British Journal of Psychiatry, 150,* 161–163.

Bettelheim, B. (1984). *Freud and man's soul.* New York: Vintage Books, Random House.

Bigler, E. D., Tucker, D. M., & Piran, N. (1979). Neuropsychological differentiation in a psychiatric late adolescent-young adult population: Preliminary report. *Clinical Neuropsychology, 1,* 9–14.

Bilder, R. M., & Goldberg, E. (1987). Motor perseverations in schizophrenia. *Archives of Clinical Neuropsychology, 2,* 195–214.

Bilett, J. L., Jones, N. F., & Whitaker, L. C. (1982). Exploring schizophrenic thinking in late adolescents. *Journal of Clinical Psychology, 38*(2), 232–243.

Black's law dictionary (5th ed.). (1979). St. Paul, MN: West.

Blatt, S. J. (1975). The validity of projective techniques and their research and clinical contribution. *Journal of Personality Assessment, 39,* 327–343.

Bleuler, E. (1920). *Lehrbruch der psychiatrie.* Berlin: Verlag von Julius Springer.

Bleuler, E. (1950). *Dementia praecox or the group of schizophrenics.* New York: International Universities Press. (Originally published 1911.)

Bleuler, E. (1951). Autistic thinking. In D. Rapaport (Ed.), *Organization and pathology of thought.* New York: Columbia University Press. (Originally published 1912.)

Bleuler, M. (1971). Schizophrenia. In R. Cancro (Ed.), *The schizophrenic syndrome.* London: Butterworth.

Bleuler, M. (1978). *The schizophrenic disorders: Long-term patient and family studies.* New Haven: Yale University Press.

Bleuler, M. (1979). My sixty years with schizophrenics. Foreword in L. Bellak (Ed.), *Disorders of the schizophrenic syndrome.* New York: Basic Books.

Bockhoven, J. S., & Solomon, H. C. (1975). Comparison of two five-year follow-up studies, 1947 to 1952 and 1967 to 1972. *American Journal of Psychiatry, 132,* 8.

Bolado, A. L. O., & Whitaker, L. C. (1990). Standardization of the Whitaker Index of Schizophrenic Thinking (WIST) in a Mexican population: A multivariable study. *Journal of Clinical Psychology, 46*(2), 140–147.

Borus, J. F. (1986). Chronic mental patients. In G. L. Klerman, M. M. Weisman, P. S. Applebaum, & L. H. Roth (Eds.), *Social, epidemiologic, and legal psychiatry,* in J. O. Cavenar (Gen. Ed.), *Psychiatry* (vol. 5, pp. 77–91. New York: Basic Books.

Bourman, A. (1936). *The tragedy of Nijinsky.* New York: McGraw-Hill.

Bourne, L. E., Jr., Justesen, D. R., Abraham, T., Beeker, C., Brauchi, J. T., Whitaker, L. C., & Yaroush, R. A. (1977). Limits to conceptual rule-learning by schizophrenic patients. *Journal of Clinical Psychology, 33*(2), 324–334.

Breggin, P. R. (1983). *Psychiatric drugs: Hazards to the brain.* New York: Springer.

Breggin, P. R. (1990). Brain damage, dementia and persistent cognitive dysfunction associated with neuroleptic drugs: Evidence, etiology, implications. *The Journal of Mind and Behavior, 11*(3,4) 425–463

Breggin, P. R. (1991). *Toxic psychiatry: Why therapy empathy and love must replace the drugs, electroshock, and biochemical theories of the "new psychiatry."* New York: St. Martin's Press.

Breier, A., & Astrachan, B. M. (1984). Characterization of schizophrenic patients who commit suicide. *American Journal of Psychiatry, 141,* 206–209.

Bridge, T. P., Kleinman, J. E., Karoum, F., & Wyatt, R. J. (1985). Postmortem central catecholamines and antemortem cognitive impairment in elderly schizophrenics and controls. *Journal of Neuropsychobiology, 14,* 57–61.

Brinnin, J. M. (1982). *Sextet: T. S. Eliot, Truman Capote & others.* London: André Deutsch.

Brockington, I. F., & Meltzer, H. Y. (1982). Documenting an episode of psychiatric illness: Need for multiple information sources, raters and narrative. *Schizophrenia Bulletin, 8*(3), 485–492.

Brooks, A. D. (1987). The right to refuse antipsychotic medications: Law and policy. *Rutgers Law Review, 39,* 339–376.

Buchsbaum, M. S. (1982). Cerebral glucography with positron tomography: Use in normal subjects and in patients with schizophrenia. *Archives of General Psychiatry, 39,* 251–259.

Buchsbaum, M. S., Wu, J. C., DeLisi, L. E., Holcomb, H. H., Hazlett, E., Cooper-Langston, K., & Kessler, R. (1987). Positron emission tomography studies of basal ganglia and somatosensory cortex neuroleptic drug effects: Differences between normal controls and schizophrenic patients. *Journal of Biological Psychiatry, 22,* 479–494.

Buckle, R. (1975). *Nijinsky.* New York: Avon Books.

Bush, C. T., Langford, M. W., Rosen, P., & Gott, W. (1990). Operation outreach: Intensive case management for severely psychiatrically disabled adults. *Hospital and Community Psychiatry, 41*(6), 647–649.

Cairns, R. B. (1986). Phenomena lost: Issues in the study of development. In J. Valsiner (Ed.), *The individual subject and scientific psychology.* New York: Plenum Press.

Cairns, U. (1986). Changes in patterns of mental illness over different hospital admissions. *Psychopathology, 17*(2), 98–104.

Cameron, N. (1963). *Personality development and psychopathology: A dynamic approach.* Boston: Houghton Mifflin.

Cameron, N., & Cameron, M. A. (1951). *Behavior pathology.* Boston: Houghton Mifflin.

Cardinal, M. (1983). *The words to say it: An autobiographical novel.* Cambridge, MA: Van Vactor & Goodheart.

Carpenter, W., Strauss, J., & Bartko, J. (1973). A flexible system for the diagnosis of schizophrenia: Report from the WHO international pilot study of schizophrenia. *Science, 162,* 1275–1277.

Carpenter, W. T., McGlashan, T. H., & Strauss, J. S. (1977). The treatment of acute schizophrenia without drugs: An investigation of some current assumptions. *American Journal of Psychiatry, 134,* 14–20.

Carpenter, W. T., & Strauss, J. S. (1979). Diagnostic issues in schizophrenia. In L. Bellak (Ed.), *Disorders of the schizophrenic syndrome.* New York: Basic Books.

Carpenter, W. T., Heinrichs, D. W., & Alphs, L. D. (1985). Treatment of negative symptoms. *Schizophrenia Bulletin, 11*(3), 440–452.

Cash, T. F. (1973). Methodological problems and progress in schizophrenia research. *Journal of Consulting and Clinical Psychology, 40,* 278–286.

Cernovsky, Z., Landmark, J., & Leslie, B. (1985). Social and anamnestic correlates of consensus in diagnosing schizophrenia. *Journal of Clinical Psychology, 41*(5), 614–619.

Chapman, L. J. (1975). Effects of phenothiazine withdrawal on proverb interpretation by chronic schizophrenics. *Journal of Abnormal Psychology, 84*(1), 24–29.

Chelune, G. J., Heaton, R. K., Lehman, R. A., & Robinson, A. (1979). Level versus pattern of neuropsychological performance among schizophrenic and diffusely brain-damaged patients. *Journal of Counsulting and Clinical Psychology, 47,* 155–163.

Chrzanowski, G. (1984). Book review of J. Cavenar & K. Brodie (Eds.), *Signs and symptoms in psychiatry. American Journal of Psychotherapy, 38,* 456–458.

Ciompi, L. (1980). Catamnesic long-term study on the course and life span of schizophrenics. *Schizophrenia Bulletin, 6,* 606–617.

Ciompi, L., & Muller, C. (1976). *Lebensweg und alter der schizophrenen: Eine katamnestische Langzeitstudie bis ins Senium.* Heidelberg: Springer.

Cohen, L. J., Test, M. A., & Brown, R. L. (1990). Suicide and schizophrenia: Data from a prospective community treatment study. *American Journal of Psychiatry, 147,* 602–607.

Cox, S. M., & Ludwig, A. M. (1979). Neurological soft signs and psychopathology: 1. Findings in schizophrenics. *Journal of Nervous and Mental Disease, 167,* 161–165.

Crow, T. J. (1980). Positive and negative schizophrenic symptoms and the role of dopamine: 2. *British Journal of Psychiatry, 137,* 383–386.

Crown, S. (1975). "On being sane in insane places": A comment from England. *Journal of Abnormal Psychology, 84*(5), 453–455.

Cumming, J., & Cumming, E. (1970). *Ego and milieu.* New York: Atherton Press.

Dawes, R. M., Faust, D., & Meehl, P. E. (1989). Clinical versus actuarial judgment. *Science, 243,* 1668–1674.

Deikman, A. J. (1971). Phenothiazines and the therapist's fear of identification. *Humanistic Psychology, 11,* 196–200.

Deikman, A. J. (1990). *The wrong way home: Uncovering the patterns of cult behavior in American society.* Boston: Beacon Press.

Deikman, A. J., & Whitaker, L. C. (1979). Humanizing a psychiatric ward: changing from drugs to psychotherapy. *Psychotherapy: Theory, Research and Practice, 16,*(2), 204–214.

DeMyer, W. E., Gilmor, R. L., Hendrie, H. C., Augustyn, G. R., & Jackson, R. K. (1988). Magnetic resonance brain images in schizophrenic and normal subjects: Influence of diagnosis and education. *Schizophrenia Bulletin, 14,* 21–27.

Donnelly, E. F. (1984). Neuropsychological impairment and associated intellectual functions in schizophrenic and other psychiatric patients. *Biological Psychiatry, 19,* 815–824.

Dorland's illustrated medical dictionary (27th ed.). (1988). (E. J. Taylor, Ed.) Philadelphia: W. B. Saunders.

Drake, R. E., Osher, F. C., & Wallach, M. A. (1989). Alcohol use and abuse in schizophrenia: A prospective community study. *Journal of Nervous and Mental Disease, 177*(7), 408–414.

Duffy, F. H. (1985). The BEAM method for neurophysiological diagnosis. Institute for Child Development Research Conference: Hope for a new neurology (1984, New York, New York). *Annals of the New York Academy of Sciences, 457,* 19–34.

Dymond, A. M., Coger, R. W., & Serafetinides, E. A. (1980). EEG banding and asymmetry in schizophrenic, alcoholic, and ambotic: An objective comparison. *Research in Psychology, Psychiatry, and Behavior, 5,* 113–122.

Edwards, J. (1973). Schizophrenia: Aspects of diagnosis. In A. Ridges & D. Eaves (Eds.), *Schizophrenia.* Liverpool: University of Liverpool Press.

Endicott, J., Nee, J., Fleiss, J., Cohen, J., Williams, J. B. W., & Simon, R. (1982). Diagnostic criteria for schizophrenia: reliabilities and agreement between systems. *Archives of General Psychiatry, 39,* 884–889.

Ewalt, J. R., & Farnsworth, D. L. (1963). *Textbook of psychiatry.* New York: McGraw-Hill.

Exner, J. E. (1974). *The Rorschach: A comprehensive system.* New York: Wiley.

Exner, J. E. (1980). But it's only an inkblot. *Journal of Personality Assessment, 44*(6), 563–577.

Exner, J. E. (1982). *The Rorschach: A comprehensive system* (vol. 3). New York: Wiley.

Exner, J. E. (1986). Some Rorschach data comparing schizophrenics with borderline and schizotypal personality disorders. *Journal of Personality Assessment, 50*(3), 455–471.

Exner, J. E. (1987). *1987 alumni newsletter.* Asheville, NC: Rorschach Workshops.

Exner, J. E. (1988). *1988 alumni newsletter.* Asheville, NC: Rorschach Workshops.

Fadiman, C. (Ed.). (1985). *The Little, Brown book of anecdotes.* Boston: Little, Brown.

Farber, I. E. (1975). Sane and insane: Constructions and misconstructions. *Journal of Abnormal Psychology, 84*(5), 589–620.

Faris, R. E., & Dunham, H. W. (1939). *Mental disorders in urban areas: An ecological study of schizophrenia and other psychoses.* Chicago: University of Chicago Press.

Farmer, A., Jackson, R., McGuffin, P., & Storey, P. (1987). Cerebral ventricular enlargement in chronic schizophrenia: Consistencies and contradictions. *British Journal of Psychiatry, 150,* 324–330.

Feighner, J., Robins, E., Guze, S., Woodruff R., Winokur, G., & Munoz, R. (1972). Diagnostic criteria for use in psychiatric research. *Archives of General Psychiatry, 26,* 57–63.

Fenichel, O. (1945). *The psychoanalytic theory of neurosis.* New York: Norton.

Fenton, W. S., Mosher, L. R., & Matthews, S. M. (1981). Diagnosis of schizophrenia: A critical review of current diagnostic systems. *Schizophrenia Bulletin, 7*(3), 452–476.

Fisher, S., & Greenberg, R. P. (Eds.). (1989). *The limits of biological treatments for psychological distress: Comparisons with psychotherapy and placebo.* Hillsdale, NJ: Erlbaum.

Fitzgibbons, D.J., & Shearn, C. R. (1972). Concepts of schizophrenia among mental health professionals: A factor-analytic study. *Journal of Consulting and Clinical Psychology, 38,* 288–295.

Flesher, S. (1990). Cognitive habilitation in schizophrenia: A theoretical review and model of treatment. *Neuropsychology Review, 1,* 223–246.

Flor-Henry, P., Koles, Z. J., & Tucker, D. M. (1982). Studies in EEG power and coherence (8–13 Hz) in depression, mania and schizophrenia compared to controls. *Advances in Biological Psychiatry, 9,* 1–7.

Foulds, G. A. (1955). The reliability of psychiatric, and the validity of psychological, diagnosis. *Journal of Mental Science, 101,* 851–862.

Freeland, J., & Puente, A. E. (1983). Relative efficacy of the Luria-Nebraska Neuropsychological Battery and the Wechsler Adult Intelligence Scale in discriminating schizophrenics with and without brain damage. *International Journal of Clinical Neuropsychology, 6,* 261–262.

Freud, S. (1950). *The question of lay analysis: An introduction to psychoanalysis.* New York: Norton. (Originally published 1926.)

Fromm, E. (1965). *Escape from freedom.* New York: Avon Books. (Originally published 1941.)

Garza-Treviño, E. S., Volkow, N. D., Cancro, R., & Contreras, S. (1990). Neurobiology of schizophrenic syndromes. *Hospital and Community Psychiatry, 41,* 971–980.

Gilbert, J. (1969). *Clinical psychological tests in psychiatric and medical practice.* Springfield, IL: Thomas.

Gill, M., Newman, R., & Redlich, F. C. (1954). *The initial interview in psychiatric practice.* New York: International Universities Press.

Ginsberg, G. L. (1985). Psychiatric interview. In H. I. Kaplan & B. J. Saddock (Eds.), *Comprehensive textbook of psychiatry* (4th ed., pp. 482–487). Baltimore: Williams & Wilkins.

Goetz, K. L., & Kammen, D. P. (1986). Computerized axial tomography scans and subtypes of schizophrenia: A review of the literature. *Journal of Nervous and Mental Disease, 174,* 31–41.

Goldberg, L. R. (1965). Diagnosticians vs. diagnostic signs: The diagnosis of psychosis vs. neurosis for the MMPI. *Psychological Monographs, 79* (9, whole No. 602).

Goldberg, T. E., Weinberger, D. R., Berman, K. R., Pliskin, N. H., & Podd, M. H. (1987). Further evidence for dementia of the prefrontal type in schizophrenia? A controlled study of teaching the Wisconsin Card Sorting Test. *Archives of General Psychiatry, 44,* 1008–1014.

Golden, C. J. (1981). Structural brain deficits in schizophrenia: Identification by computed tomographs and density measurements. *Archives of General Psychiatry, 38,* 1014–1017.

Golden, C. J., Purish, A., & Hammeke, T. (1980). Cerebral ventricular size and neuropsychological impairment in young chronic schizophrenics: Measurement by the Standardized Luria-Nebraska Neuropsychological Battery. *Archives of General Psychiatry, 37,* 619–623.

Goldstein, G. (1978). Cognitive and perceptual differences between schizophrenics and organics. *Schizophrenia Bulletin, 4,* 160–185.

Goldstein, G., & Halperin, K. M. (1977). Neuropsychological differences among subtypes of schizophrenia. *Journal of Abnormal Psychology, 86,* 34–40.

Goodwin, D. W., & Guze, S. B. (1979). *Psychiatric diagnosis* (2nd ed.). New York: Oxford University Press.

Graham, J. R. (1987). *The MMPI* (2nd ed.). New York, Oxford: Oxford University Press.

Graham, J. R. (1990). *MMPI-2: Assessing personality and psychopathology.* New York, Oxford: Oxford University Press.

Gralnick, A. (1986). Future of the chronic schizophrenic patient: Prediction and recommendations. *American Journal of Psychotherapy, 40*(3), 419–429.

Gray, A. L. (1975). Autonomic correlates of chronic schizophrenia: A reaction time paradigm. *Journal of Abnormal Psychology, 84,* 189–196.

Green, H. (1964). *I never promised you a rose garden.* New York: Signet Books, The New American Library.

Gruzelier, J. (1987). Hemispheric unbalances masquerading as paranoid and nonparanoid syndromes. *Schizophrenia Bulletin, 7,* 662–673.

Guelfi, G. P., Faustman, W. O., & Csernansky, J. G. (1989). Independence of positive and negative symptoms in a population of schizophrenic patients. *Journal of Nervous and Mental Disease, 177*(5), 285–290.

Guenther, W., & Breitling, D. (1985). Predominant sensorimotor area left hemisphere dysfunction in schizophrenia measured by brain electrical mapping. *Journal of Biological Psychiatry, 20,* 515–532.

Gunderson, J. G., Will, O. A., & Mosher, L. R. (Eds.). (1983). *Principles and practices of milieu therapy.* New York: Jacob Aronson.

Gutheil, T. G. (1989). Legal issues in psychiatry. In H. I. Kaplan & B. J. Saddock (Eds.), *Comprehensive textbook of psychiatry* (5th ed., vol. 1, pp. 2107–2124). Baltimore: Williams & Wilkins.

Haier, R. J. (1980). The diagnosis of schizophrenia: A review of recent developments. *Schizophrenia Bulletin, 6*(3), 417–428.

Harding, C. M., Brooks, G. W., Ashikagawa, T., Strauss, J. S., & Breier, A. (1987a). Aging and social functioning in once chronic schizophrenics 22–62 years after first admission: The Vermont story. In G. Hudgens & N. Miller (Eds.), *Schizophrenia, paranoia, and schizophreniform disorders in later life* (pp. 74–82). New York: Guilford Press.

Harding, C. M., Brooks, G. W., Ashikagawa, T., Strauss, J. S., & Breier, A. (1987b). The Vermont longitudinal study of persons with severe mental illness: 2. Long term term outcome of subjects who retrospectively met DSM-III criteria for schizophrenia. *American Journal of Psychiatry, 144,* 718–726.

Harding, C. M., Zubin, J., & Strauss, J. S. (1987c). Chronicity in schizophrenia: Fact, partial fact, or artifact? *Hospital and Community Psychiatry, 38,* 477–486.

Harrow, M. P., & Quinlan, D. (1977). Is disordered thinking unique to schizophrenia? *Archives of General Psychiatry, 34,* 15–21.

Harrow, M., Silverstein, M., & Marengo, J. (1983). Disordered thinking: Does it identify schizophrenia? *Archives of General Psychiatry, 40,* 765–771.

Hathaway, S. R., & McKinley, J. C. (1989). Update on the MMPI-2. *National Computer Systems Professional Development Services 1989 catalogue,* pp. 30–31, Minneapolis.

Heaton, R. K., Vogt, A. T., Hoehn, M. M., Lewis, J. A., Crowley, T. J., & Stallings, M. A. (1979). neuropsychological impairment with schizophrenia vs. acute and chronic cerebral lesions. *Journal of Clinical Psychology, 35,* 46–53.

Heinrichs, D. W., & Buchanan, R. W. (1988). Significance and meaning of neurological signs in schizophrenia. *American Journal of Psychiatry, 145,* 11–18.

Helmes, E., Landmark, J., & Kazarian, S. S. (1983) Interrater reliability of twelve diagnostic systems of schizophrenia. *Journal of Nervous and Mental Disease, 171,* 307–311.

Helzer, J. E., & Robins, L. N. (1988). The diagnostic interview schedule: its development, evolution, and use. *Social Psychiatry and Psychiatric Epidemiology, 23,* 6–16.

Hirschowitz, J., Casper, R., Garver, D., & Chang, S. (1980). Lithium response in good prognosis schizophrenia. *American Journal of Psychiatry, 137*(8), 916–920.

Holt, R. R. (1968). *Diagnostic psychological testing.* New York: International Universities Press. (Revised edition of book of same title by D. Rapaport, M. M. Gill, & R. R. Schafer. Original published 1984, by Yearbook Publishers, Chicago, Illinois.)

Holtzman, W. H. (1978). Holtzman inkblot technique. In B. B. Wolman (Ed.), *Clinical diagnosis of mental disorders.* New York: Plenum Press.

Holtzman, W. H. (1988). Beyond the Rorschach. *Journal of Personality Assessment, 52*(4), 578–609.

Holtzman, W. H., & Swartz, J. D. (1983). The Holtzman inkblot technique: A review of 25 years of research. *Zeitschrift für differentielle und diagnostische Psychologie, 4,* Heft 3, S. 241–259.

Holtzman, W. H., Thorpe, J., Swartz, J. D., & Herron, E. (1961). *Inkblot perception and personality.* Austin: University of Texas Press.

Horton, A. M. (1982). Differentiation between schizophrenic and brain damaged women: Clinical considerations. *Clinical Neuropsychology, 4,* 43–44.

Horton, A. M., Scott, M. L., & Golden, C. J. (1983). Discrimination of brain-damaged schizophrenics from nonbrain damaged schizophrenics: Value of the Wiggins MMPI Content Scales. *Clinical Neuropsychology, 5,* 21–22.

Howes, R. J. (1981). The Rorschach: Does it have a future? *Journal of Personality Assessment, 45*(4), 339–351.

Huber, G., Gross, G., & Schuettler, R. (1975). A long term followup study of schizophrenia: Psychiatric course of illness and prognosis. *Acta Psychiatrica Scandinavica, 52,* 49–57.

Huber, G., Gross, G., Schuettler, R., Linz, M. (1980). Longitudinal studies of schizophrenic patients. *Schizophrenic Bulletin, 6,* 592–605.

Iacono, W. G., Smith, G. N., Moreau, M., Beiser, M., Fleming, J. A. E., Lin, T. Y., & Flak, B. (1988). Ventricular and sulcal size at the onset of psychosis. *American Journal of Psychiatry, 145,* 820–824.

Illowsky, B. P., Julian, D. M., Bigelow, L. B., & Weinberger, D. R. (1988). Stability of CT scan findings in schizophrenia: Results of an 8 year follow-up study. *Journal of Neurology, Neurosurgery, and Psychiatry, 51,* 209–213.

International Classification of Diseases. (ICD-10). World Health Organization (WHO). (To be published, 1993).

Jampala, V. C., Sierles, F. S., & Taylor, M. A. (1988). The use of DMS-III in the United States: A case of not going by the book. *Comprehensive Psychiatry, 29*(1), 39–47.

Jung, C. G. (1936). The psychology of dementia praecox. *Nervous and Mental Disease Monograph No. 3,* New York: Nervous and Mental Disease Publishing Company. (Originally published, 1903.)

Kafka, F. (1946). *The trial.* New York: A. A. Knopf. (Originally published 1925.)

Kanba, S., Shima, S., Masuda, Y., Tsukumo, T., Kitamura, T., & Asai, M. (1987). Selective enlargement of the third ventricle found in chronic schizophrenia. *Psychiatry Research, 21,* 49–53.

Kane, J. M. (1989). Schizophrenia: Somatic treatment. In H. Kaplan & B. Saddock (Eds.), *Comprehensive textbook of psychiatry* (5th ed., vol. 1, pp. 777–792). Baltimore: Williams & Wilkins.

Karno, M., & Norquist, G. S. (1989). Schizophrenia: Epidemiology. In H. Kaplan & B. Saddock (Eds.), *Comprehensive textbook of psychiatry* (5th ed., vol. 1, pp. 4699–705). Baltimore: Williams & Wilkins.

Karon, B. P. (1978). Projective tests are valid. *American Psychologist, 33,* 764–765.

Karon, B. P. (1989). Psychotherapy versus medication for schizophrenia: Empirical comparisons. In S. Fisher & R. P. Greenberg (Eds.), *The limits of biological treatments for psychological distress* (pp. 106–149). Hillsdale, NJ: Erlbaum.

Karon, B. P., & VandenBos, G. R. (1975). Treatment costs of psychotherapy versus medication for schizophrenics. *Professional Psychology, 6,* 293–298.

Karon, B. P., & VandenBos, G. R. (1981). *Psychotherapy of schizophrenia: The treatment of choice.* New York, London: Jason Aronson.

Kathol, R., & Henn, F. (1983). Trycyclics—The most common agent in potential lethal overdoses. *Journal of Nervous and Mental Disease, 171,* 250–252.

Kay, S. R., Fiszbein, A., & Opler, L. A. (1987). The Positive and Negative Syndrome Scale (PANSS) for schizophrenia. *Schizophrenia Bulletin, 13*(2), 260–276.

Keck, P. E., Jr., Cohen, B. M., Baldessarini, R. J., & McElroy, S. L. (1989). Time course of antipsychotic effects of neuroleptic drugs. *American Journal of Psychiatry, 146,* 1289–1292.

Kelsoe, J. R., Cadet, J. L., Pickar, D., & Weinberger, D. R. (1988). Quantitative neuroanatomy in schizophrenia: A controlled magnetic resonance imaging study. *Archives of General Psychiatry, 45,* 533–541.

Kemali, D. (1985). Clinical and neuropsychological correlates of cerebral ventricular enlargement in schizophrenia. *Journal of Psychiatric Research, 19,* 587–596.

Kendall, R. E. (1975). *The role of diagnosis in psychiatry.* London: Blackwell.

Kiesler, C. A. (1982). Public and professional myths about mental hospitalization: An empirical reassessment of policy-related beliefs. *American Psychologist, 27,* 1323–1339.

Kishimoto, H., Kuwahara, H., Ohno, S., Takazu, O., Hama, Y., Sato, C., Ishii, T., Nomura, Y., Fujita, H., Miyauchi, T., Matsushita, M., Yokoi, S., & Iio, M. (1987). Three subtypes of chronic schizophrenia identified using ^{11}C-glucose positron emission tomography. *Journal of Psychiatric Research, 21,* 285–292.

Knight, R. P. (1952). Introduction. In E. Brody & F. Redlech (Eds.), *Psychotherapy with schizophrenics.* New York: International Universities Press.

Korcyzn, A. D., & Goldberg, G. J. (1976). Extrapyramidal effects of neuroleptics. *Journal of Neurology, Neurosurgery and Psychiatry, 39,* 866–869.

Kraepelin, E. (1971). *Dementia praecox and paraphrenia.* (R. M. Barclay, translator) Huntingdon, New York: Krieger. (Originally published 1919.)

Lambley, P. (1973). Rorschach scorer and schizophrenia: An evaluation of Weiner's clinical system of practice. *Journal of Personality Assessment, 37*(5), 420–423.

Landmark, J. (1982). A manual for the study of schizophrenia. *Acta Psychiatrica Scandinavica, Supplementum 298,* 65, 88 pages.

Landmark, J., Cernovsky, Z. Z., Merskey, H. & Leslie, B. (1986). Interrelationships of systems for diagnosing schizophrenia. *Comprehensive Psychiatry, 27*(4), 343–350.

Langell, M. E., Purisch, A. D., & Golden, C. J. (1987). Neuropsychological differences between paranoid and nonparanoid schizophrenics on the Luria-Nebraska Battery. *International Journal of Clinical Neuropsychology, 9,* 88–95.

Langfeldt, G. (1971). Schizophrenia—Diagnosis and prognosis. In R. Cancro (Ed.), *The schizophrenic syndrome.* London: Butterworth.

Langsley, D. G. (1985). Prevention in psychiatry: Primary, secondary, and tertiary. In H. I. Kaplan & B. J. Saddock (Eds.), *Comprehensive textbook of psychiatry* (4th ed., pp. 1885–1888). Baltimore: Williams & Wilkins.

Lawson, W. B., Waldman, I. N., & Weinberger, D. R. (1988). Schizophrenic dementia: Clinical and computed axial tomography correlates. *Journal of Nervous and Mental Disease, 176,* 207–212.

Leon, R. L., Bowden, C. L., & Faber, R. A. (1985). The psychiatric interview, history and mental status examination. In H. Kaplan & B. Saddock (Eds.), *Comprehensive textbook of psychiatry* (4th ed., pp. 449–462). Baltimore: Williams & Wilkins.

Leslie, B. A., Landmark, J., & Whitaker, L. C. (1984). the Whitaker Index of Schizophrenic Thinking

(WIST) and thirteen systems for diagnosing schizophrenia. *Journal of Clinical Psychology, 40,* 636–648.

Lewis, A. (1967). Schizophrenia. In P. B. Beeson & D. McDermott (Eds.), *Cecil Loeb textbook of medicine* (12th ed.) Philadelphia: W. B. Saunders.

Lewis, G., Golden, C. J., Purisch, A., & Hammeke, T. A. (1979). The effects of chronicity of disorder and length of hospitalization on the standardized version of Luria's Neuropsychological Battery in a schizophrenic population. *Clinical Neuropsychology, 1,* 13–18.

Lewis, R. F., Nelson, R. W., & Eggertsen, C. (1979). Neuropsychological test performances of paranoid schizophrenic and brain-damaged patients. *Journal of Clinical Psychology, 35,* 54–59.

Lewontin, R. C., Rose, S., & Kamin, L. J. (1984). *Not in our genes.* New York: Pantheon.

Liberman, R. P. (1985). Schizophrenia: Psychosocial treatment. In H. I. Kaplan & B. J. Saddock (Eds.), *Comprehensive textbook of psychiatry* (4th ed., pp. 724–734). Baltimore: Williams & Wilkins.

Lidz, T. (1987). Editorial book review: The effective treatment of schizophrenic patients. *Journal of Nervous and Mental Disease, 175(8),* 447–449.

Lidz, T., & Fleck, S. (1985). *Schizophrenia and the family* (rev. ed.). New York: International Universities Press.

Lipkowitz, M. H., & Idupuganti, S. (1983). Diagnosing schizophrenia in 1980: A survey of U.S. psychiatrists. *American Journal of Psychiatry, 140,* 52–55.

Lipkowitz, M. H., & Idupuganti, S. (1985). Diagnosing schizophrenia in 1982: The effect of DSM-III. *American Journal of Psychiatry, 142,* 634–637.

Losonczy, M. F., Song, I. S., Mohs, R. C., Small, N., Davidson, M., Johns, C., & Davis, K. (1986). Correlates of lateral ventricular size in chronic schizophrenia: 1. Behavioral and treatment response measures. *American Journal of Psychiatry, 143,* 976–981.

Luchins, D. J., Lewine, R. R., & Meltzer, H. Y. (1984). Lateral ventricular size, psychopathology, and medication response in the psychoses. *Biological Psychiatry, 19,* 29–44.

Luria, A. R. (1973). *The working brain.* New York: Basic Books.

Malec, J. (1978). Neuropsychological assessment of schizophrenia versus brain damage: A review. *Journal of Nervous and Mental Disease, 166,* 507–516.

Marengo, J. T., & Harrow, M. (1987). Schizophrenic thought disorder at follow-up: A persistent or episodic course? *Archives of General Psychiatry, 44,* 651–659.

Martin, R. M. (1968). The stimulus barrier and the autonomy of the ego. *Psychological Review, 75*(6), 478–493.

Mason, B. J., Cohen, J. B., & Exner, J. E. (1985). Schizophrenic, depressive, and non-patient personality organizations described by Rorschach factor structures. *Journal of Personality Assessment, 49*(3), 295–305.

Matarazzo, J. D. (1990). Psychological assessment versus psychological testing: Validation from Binet to the school, clinic, and courtroom. *American Psychologist, 45*(9), 999–1017.

Mathew, R. J., Partain, C. L., Prakash, R., Kulkarni, M. V., Logan, T. P., & Wilson, W. H. (1985). A study in the septum pellucidum and corpus callosum in schizophrenia with MR imaging. *Acta Psychiatrica Scandinavica, 72,* 414–421.

Mathew, R. J., Wilson, W. H., Tant, S. R., Robinson, L., & Prakash, R. (1988). Abnormal resting regional cerebral blood flow patterns and their correlates in schizophrenia. *Archives of General Psychiatry, 45,* 542–549.

Medvedev, Z. A., & Medvedev, R. A. (1979). *A question of madness: Repression by psychiatry in the Soviet Union.* New York: Norton.

Meehl, P. E. (1954). *Clinical versus statistical prediction.* Minneapolis: University of Minnesota Press.

Meehl, P. E. (1972). Specific genetic etiology, psychodynamics, and therapeutic nihilism. *International Journal of Mental Health, 1*(1), 10–27.

Meehl, P. E. (1977). Construct validity in psychological tests. *Psychodiagnosis: Selected papers of Paul E. Meehl.* New York: Norton.

Menninger, K., Mayman, M., & Pruyser, P. W. (1962). *A manual for psychiatric case study* (2nd ed.). New York: Grune & Stratton.

Menninger, K., Mayman, M., & Pruyser, P. W. (1963). *The vital balance: The life process in mental health and illness.* New York: Viking Press.

Messick, S. (1980). Test validity and the ethics of assessment. *American Psychologist, 35,* 1012–1027.

Miles, C. P. (1977). Conditions predisposing to suicide: A review. *Journal of Nervous and Mental Disorders, 164,* 231–246.

Millon, T. (1975). Reflections on Rosenhan's "On being sane in insane places." *Journal of Abnormal Psychology, 84*(5), 456–461.

Mills v. Rogers (1982). 457 U.S. 302–303.

Mindell, B. (1988). The MD-therapist connection. *American Medical News* (February 12) pp. 13–17.

Mosely, E. C. (1963). Psychodiagnosis on the basis of the Holtzman Inkblot Technique. *Journal of Projective Techniques, 27,* 86–91.

Moses, J., Cardellina, J. P., & Thompson, L. L. (1983). Discrimination of brain damage for chronic psychosis by the Luria-Nebraska Neuropsychological Battery: A closer look. *Journal of Consulting and Clinical Psychology, 51,* 441–449.

Munetz, M. R., & Schultz, S. C. (1986). Minimization and overreaction to tardive dyskinesia. *Schizophrenia Bulletin, 12*(2), 168–172.

Nasrallah, H. A., McCalley-Whitters, M., & Jacoby, C. G. (1972). Cortical atrophy in schizophrenia and mania: A comparative CT study. *Journal of Clinical Psychiatry, 43,* 439–441.

Nasrallah, H. A., Tippin, J., & McCalley-Whitters, M. (1983). Neurological soft signs in manic patients: A comparison with schizophrenic and control groups. *Journal of Affective Disorders, 5,* 45–50.

Nasrallah, H. A., Andreasen, N. C., Coffman, J. A., Olson, S. C., Dunn, V. D., Ehrhardt, J. C., & Chapman, S. M. (1986). A controlled magnetic resonance imaging study of corpus callosum thickness in schizophrenia. *Journal of Biological Psychiatry, 21,* 274–282.

Nathan, R. G., & Rousch, A. F. (1984). Which patients commit suicide? Letters to the editor. *American Journal of Psychiatry, 141,* 1017.

National Household Survey on Drug Abuse (1982). U.S. Department of Health and Human Services, Public Health Service, Alcohol, Drug Abuse, and Mental Health Administration.

Neale, J. M., & Oltmanns, T. F. (1980). *Schizophrenia.* New York: Wiley.

Newmark, C. S., Raft, T., Toomey, T., Hunter, W., & Hazzaglia, J. (1975). Diagnosis of schizophrenia: Pathognomonic signs or symptom clusters. *Comprehensive Psychiatry, 16,* 155–163.

Nijinska, B. (1981). *Early memoirs.* New York: Holt, Rinehart & Winston.

Nijinsky, R. (Ed.). (1968). *The diary of Vaslav Nijinsky.* Berkeley: University of California Press. (Originally published 1936.)

Nijinsky, R. (1972). *Nijinsky.* New York: Pocket Books, Simon & Schuster.

Nyman, A. K., & Jonsson, H. (1986). Patterns of self-destructive behavior in schizophrenia. *Acta Psychiatria Scandinavica, 73,* 252–262.

Obiols, J. E., Bachs, J. S., & Masana, J. (1986). Event-related potentials in young chronic schizophrenics. *Biological Psychiatry, 21,* 856–859.

Okin, R. L., & Borus, J. F. (1989). Primary, secondary, and tertiary prevention of mental disorders. In H. Kaplan & B. Saddock (Eds.), *Comprehensive textbook of psychiatry* (vol. 5, pp. 2067–2071). Baltimore: Williams & Wilkins.

Olfson, M. (1990). Assertive community treatment: An evaluation of the experimental evidence. *Hospital and Community Psychiatry, 41*(6), 634–641.

Pakkenberg, B. (1987). Post-mortem study of chronic schizophrenic brains. *British Journal of Psychiatry, 151,* 744–752.

Pancoast, D. L., & Archer, R. P. (1989). Original adult MMPI norms in normal samples: A review with implications for future developments. *Journal of Personality Assessment, 53*(2), 376–395.

Pardes, H., Sirovatka, P., & Pincus, H. A. (1986). Federal and state roles in mental health. In G. L. Klerman, M. M. Weissman, P. S. Applebaum, & L. H. Roth (Eds.), *Social, epidemiologic, and legal psychiatry* (vol. 5, pp. 45–62), in J. O. Cavenar (Gen. Ed.), *Psychiatry.* New York: Basic Books.

Perlin, M. L. (1986). Patients' rights. In G. L. Klerman, M. M. Weisman, P. S. Applebaum, & L. H. Roth (Eds.), *Social, epidemiologic, and legal psychiatry* (vol. 5, pp. 401–422), in J. O. Cavenar (Gen. Ed.), *Psychiatry.* New York: Basic Books.

Pfefferbaum, A., Zipursky, R. B., Lim, K. O., Zatz, L. M., Stahl, S. M., & Jernigan, T. (1988). Computed tomographic evidence for generalized sulcal and ventricular enlargement in schizophrenia. *Archives of General Psychiatry, 45,* 633–640.

Pishkin, V., Lovallo, W. R., Lenk, R. G., & Bourne, L. E., Jr. (1977). Schizophrenic cognitive dysfunction: A deficit in rule transfer. *Journal of Clinical Psychology, 36,* 79–89.

Puente, A. E., & Heidelberg-Sanders, C. (1981). Differentiation of schizophrenics with and without brain damage using the Whitaker Index of Schizophrenic Thinking. *Journal of Clinical Psychology, 37,* 464–461.

Puente, A. E., Heidelberg-Sanders, C., & Lund, W. (1982a). Detection of brain-damage in schizophrenics as measured by the Whitaker Index of Schizophrenic Thinking and the Luria-Nebraska Neuropsychological Battery. *Perceptual and Motor Skills, 54,* 495–499.

Puente, A. E., Heidelberg-Sanders, C., & Lund, N. (1982b). Discrimination of schizophrenics with and without brain damage using the Luria-Nebraska Neuropsychological Battery. *International Journal of Neuroscience, 16,* 59–62.

Puente, A. E., Rodenbough, J., & Horton, A. M. (1989). Relative efficacy of the ScO, P-O, P-N, and Sc MMPI scales in differentiating brain-damaged, brain-damaged schizophrenic, schizophrenic, and somatoform disorder in an outpatient setting. *Journal of Clinical Psychology, 45,* 99–105.

Purcell, K. (1965). The Thematic Apperception Test and antisocial behavior. In B. Murstein (ed.), *Handbook of projective techniques* (pp. 547–560). New York: Basic Books.

Purisch, A. D., Golden, C. J., & Hammeke, T. A. (1978). Discrimination of schizophrenic and brain-injured patients by a standardized version of Luria's Neuropsychological Tests. *Journal of Consulting and Clinical Psychology, 46,* 1266–1273.

Purisch, A. D., Golden, C. J., & Hammeke, T. A. (1979). Discrimination of schizophrenic and brain injured patients by a standardized version of Luria's neuropsychological tests. *Clinical Neuropsychology, 1,* 53–59.

Quinlan, D. M., Harrow, M., Tucker, G., & Carlson, K. (1972). Varieties of "disordered" thinking on the Rorschach: Findings in schizophrenic and non-schizophrenic patients. *Journal of Abnormal Psychology, 79*(1), 47–53.

Rado, S., & Daniel, G. E. (1956). *Changing concepts of psychoanalytic medicine.* New York: Grune.

Ragin, A. B., & Oltmanns, T. F. (1983). Predictability as an index of impaired verbal communication in schizophrenic and affective disorders. *British Journal of Psychiatry, 143,* 578–583.

Rapaport, D. (1951a). The autonomy of the ego. *Bulletin of the Menninger Clinic, 15,* 113–123.

Rapaport, D. (1951b). *Organization and pathology of thought.* New York: Columbia University Press.

Rapaport, D. (1958). The theory of ego autonomy: A generalization. *Bulletin of the Menninger Clinic, 22,* 13–35.

Rapaport, D., Gill, M., & Schafer, R. (1946). *Diagnostic psychological testing* (vol. 2). Chicago: Yearbook Publishers.

Raz, S., Raz, N., Weinberger, D. R., Boronow, J., Pickar, D., Bigler, E. D., & Turkheimer, E. (1987). Morphological brain abnormalities in schizophrenia determined by computed tomography: A problem of measurement? *Journal of Psychiatry Research, 22,* 91–98.

Rennie v. Klein (1978). 462 *F.Supp.* 1131 (DNJ) 1978), Suppl. 476 *F.Supp.* 1294 9DNJ 1979), mod. 653 F.2nd 836 (3 Cir. 1981), vacated and remanded 458 U.S. 1119 (1982), on remand 720 F.2nd 266 (3 Cir. 1983).

Reveley, M. A., Reveley, A. M., & Baldy, R. (1987). Left cerebral hemisphere hypodensity in discordant schizophrenic twins: A controlled study. *Archives of General Psychiatry, 44,* 624–632.

Rockford, J. M., Swartzburg, Chowdhrey, S. M., & Goldstein, L. (1976). Some quantitative EEG correlates of psychopathology. *Research Communications in Psychology, Psychiatry, and Behavior, 1,* 211–226.

Rogers v. Okin. (1979). 478 *F.Supp* 1342 (D.Mass. 1979), mod. 634 F.2d 650 (1 Cir. 1980), vacated and remanded *sub nom Mills v. Rogers,* 457 U.S. 291 (1982), on remand 738 F.2nd 1 (1 Cir. 1984).

Rorschach, H. (1951). *Psychodiagnostics text* (5th ed.). New York: Grune & Stratton. (Originally published 1921.)

Rosenhan, D. L. (1973). On being sane in insane places. *Science, 179,* 250–258.

Rosenhan, D. L. (1975). The contextual nature of psychiatric diagnosis. *Journal of Abnormal Psychology, 84*(5), 462–474.

Rubin, B. (1975). Psychiatry and the law. In S. Arieti (Ed.), *American handbook of psychiatry* (2nd ed. vol. 5, pp. 853–898). New York: Basic Books.

Saccuzzo, D. P., Braff, D. L., Sprock, J., & Sudik, N. (1984). The schizophrenia spectrum: a study of the relationship among the Rorschach, MMPI, and visual backward masking. *Journal of Clinical Psychology, 40*(6), 1288–1294.

Sandifer, M. G., Pettus, C., & Quade, D. (1964). A study of psychiatric diagnosis. *Journal of Nervous and Mental Disease, 139,* 350–356.

Sargent, H. D., & Mayman, M. (1959). Clinical psychology. In S. Arieti (Ed.), *American handbook of psychiatry* (Vol. 2, pp. 1711–1732). New York: Basic Books.

Saugestad, L. F., & Odergaard, O. (1983). Persistent discrepancy in international diagnostic practice since 1970. *Acta Psychiatrica Scandinavica, 68,* 501.

Schlesinger, H. J., & Holzman, P. (1970). The therapeutic aspects of the hospital milieu. *Bulletin of the Menninger Clinic, 34*(1), 1–11.

Schmidt, H. O., & Fonda, C. P. (1956). The reliability of psychiatric diagnosis: A new look. *Journal of Abnormal and Social Psychology, 52,* 262–267.

Schneider, K. (1959). *Clinical psychopathology.* New York: Grune & Stratton.

Schulz, C. G. (1985). Schizophrenia: Individual psychotherapy. In H. I. Kaplan & B. J. Saddock (Eds.), *Comprehensive textbook of psychiatry* (vol. 4, pp. 734–746). Baltimore: Williams & Wilkins.

Schwartz, M. S., & Ewert, J. C. (1969). A study of Weiner's deviant temps Rorschach signs for the psychodiagnosis of schizophrenia. *Journal of Clinical Psychology, 25*(3), 308–309.

Scott, D. F., & Schwartz, M. S. (1975). EEG features of depressive and schizophrenic states. *American Journal of Psychiatry, 126,* 408–413.

Searles, H. F. (1965). *Collected papers on schizophrenia and related subjects.* New York: International Universities Press.

Seeman, M. (1985). Clinical and demographic correlates of neuroleptic responses. *Canadian Journal of Psychiatry, 30*(4), 243–245.

Selye, H. (1974). *Stress without distress.* New York: Harper & Row.

Shagass, C., Roemer, R. A., & Straumanis, J. J. (1983). EEG activation levels in psychiatric disorders. *Advances in Biological Psychiatry, 13,* 36–46.

Shagass, C., Roemer, R. A., Straumanis, J. J., & Josiassen, R. C. (1984). Psychiatric diagnostic discrimination with combinations of quantitative EEG variables. *British Journal of Psychiatry, 144,* 581–592.

Shearn, C. R., & Whitaker, L. C. (1969). Selecting subjects in studies of schizophrenia. *Schizophrenia, 1*(1), 4–8.

Sheehan, S. (1983). *Is there no place on earth for me?* New York: Vintage Books.

Sillitti, J. (1982). MMPI-derived indicators of organic brain dysfunction. *Journal of Clinical Psychology, 38,* 601–605.

Silverstein, A. (1988). An Aristotelian resolution of the idiographic versus nomothetic tension. *American Psychologist, 43*(6), 425–430.

Simpson, G. B., Bourne, L. E., Justesen, D. R., & Rhodes, R. J. (1979). Schizophrenia and paranoid thinking in conceptual performance. *Bulletin of the Psychonomic Society, 13*(2), 97–100.

Simpson, G. M., & May, P. R. (1985). Schizophrenia: somatic treatment. In H. I. Kaplan & B. J. Saddock (Eds.), *Comprehensive textbook of psychiatry* (4th ed., pp. 713–724). Baltimore: Williams & Wilkins.

Smith, R. C., Baumgartner, R., Ravichandran, G. K., & Largen, J. (1987). Cortical atrophy and white matter density in the brains of schizophrenics and clinical response to neuroleptics. *Acta Psychiatrica Scandinavica, 75,* 11–19.

Spitzer, R. L. (1975). On pseudoscience in science, logic in remission, and psychiatric diagnosis: A critique of Rosenhan's "On being sane in insane places." *Journal of Abnormal Psychology, 84*(5), 442–452.

Spitzer, R. L., & Fleiss, J. L. (1974). A re-analysis of the reliability of psychiatric diagnosis. *British Journal of Psychiatry, 125,* 341–347.
Spitzer, R. L., Cohen, J., Fleiss, J. L., & Endicott, J. (1967). Quantification of agreement in psychiatric diagnosis: A new approach. *Archives of General Psychiatry, 17,* 82–87.
Starr, P. (1982). *The social transformation of American medicine: The rise of a sovereign profession and the making of a vast industry.* New York: Basic Books.
Stevenson, I. (1974). The psychiatric interview. In S. Arieti (Ed.), *American handbook of psychiatry* (2nd ed.). New York: Basic Books.
Stevenson, I., & Sheppe, W. M. (1974). The psychiatric examination. In S. Arieti (Ed.), *American handbook of psychiatry* (2nd ed.). New York: Basic Books.
Strauss, J. S. (1969). Hallucinations and delusions as points on continua function: rating scale evidence. *Archives of General Psychiatry, 21,* 581–586.
Strauss, J., & Carpenter, W. (1981). *Schizophrenia.* New York: Plenum Press.
Strauss, J. S., Böker, W., & Brenner, H. D. (1987). *Psychosocial treatment of schizophrenia: Multidimensional concepts, psychological, family, and self-help perspectives.* Toronto: Hans Huber.
Sullivan, H. S. (1954). *The psychiatric interview.* New York: Norton.
Sullivan, H. S. (1962). *Schizophrenia as a human process.* New York: Norton.
Szasz, T. S. (1961). *The myth of mental illness.* New York: Harper.
Szasz, T. S. (1976). *Schizophrenia: The sacred symbol of psychiatry.* New York: Basic Books.
Szasz, T. S. (1977). *Psychiatric slavery:* When confinement and coercion masquerade as cure. New York: Free Press.
Szasz, T. S. (1987). *Insanity: The idea and its consequences.* New York: Wiley.
Talbott, J. A., Goldman, H. H., & Ross, L. (1987). Schizophrenia: An economic perspective. *Psychiatric Annals, 17*(9), 577–579.
Taube, C. A., Morlock, L., Burns, B. J., & Santos, A. B. (1990). New directions in research on assertive community treatment. *Hospital and Community Psychiatry, 41*(6), 642–647.
Taylor, M. A., Redfield, J., & Abrams, R. (1981). Neuropsychological dysfunction in schizophrenia and affective disease. *Journal of Biological Psychiatry, 16,* 467–478.
Thorne, L. (1977). Inside Russia's psychiatric jails. *New York Times Magazine* (June 12), pp. 26, 27, 30, 60, 62, 64, 66, 68, 70, 71.
Torrey, E. F. (1979). Epidemiology. In L. Bellak (Ed.), *Disorders of the schizophrenic syndrome* (pp. 25–44). New York: Basic Books.
Torrey, E. F. (1980). Neurological abnormalities in schizophrenic patients. *Journal of Biological Psychiatry, 15,* 381–388.
Torrey, E. F. (1983). *Surviving schizophrenia: A family manual.* New York: Harper & Row.
Torrey, E. F. (1988). *Nowhere to go: The tragic odyssey of the homeless mentally ill.* New York: Harper & Row.
Torrey, E. F., & Peterson, M. R. (1976). The viral hypothesis of schizophrenia. *Schizophrenia Bulletin, 2,* 136–146.
Trifiletti, R. J. (1982). Differentiating brain damage from schizophrenia: A further test of Russell's MMPI key. *Journal of Clinical Psychology, 38,* 39–44.
Turner, S. W., Toone, B. K., & Brett-Jones, J. R. (1986). Computerized tomographic scan changes in early schizophrenia—preliminary findings. *Journal of Psychological Medicine, 16,* 219–225.
Tyrer, P., & Mackay, A. (1986). Schizophrenia: No longer a functional psychosis. *Trends in Neurosciences, 9,* 537–438.
Valsiner, J. (1986). *The individual subject and scientific psychology.* New York: Plenum Press.
Volkow, N. D., Brodie, J. D., Wolf, A. P., Angrist, B., Russell, J., & Cancro, R. (1986). Brain metabolism in patients with schizophrenia before and after acute neuroleptic administration. *Journal of Neurology, Neurosurgery, and Psychiatry, 49,* 1199–1202.
Von Domarus, E. (1944). The specific laws of logic in schizophrenia. In J. S. Kasanin (Ed.), *Language and thought in schizophrenia: Collected papers.* Berkeley: University of California Press.

Vonnegut, M. (1975). *The Eden express: A personal account of schizophrenia.* New York: Praeger.

Watson, C. G. (1984). The Schizophrenia-Organicity (Sc-O) and Psychiatric-Organic (P-O) MMPI Scales: A review. *Journal of Clinical Psychology, 40,* 1008–1023.

Wechsler, D. (1981). *WAIS-R Manual: Wechsler Adult Intelligence Scale—Revised.* New York: Psychological Corporation, Harcourt Brace Jovanovich.

Weiden, P. J., Mann, J. J., Haas, G., Mattson, M., & Frances, A. (1987). Clinical nonrecognition of neuroleptic-induced movement disorders: A cautionary study. *American Journal of Psychiatry, 144*(9), 1148–1153.

Weinberger, D. R. (1987). Implications of normal brain development for the pathogenesis of schizophrenia. *Archives of General Psychiatry, 44,* 660–669.

Weinberger, D. R., Berman, K. R., & Zec, R. F. (1986). Physiologic dysfunction of dorsolateral prefrontal cortex in schizophrenia: 1. Regional cerebral blood flow evidence. *Archives of General Psychiatry, 43,* 114–124.

Weinberger, D. R., Cannon-Spoor, E., Potkin, S. G., & Wyatt, R. J. (1980). Poor premorbid adjustment and CT scan abnormalities in chronic schizophrenia. *American Journal of Psychiatry, 137,* 1410–1413.

Weinberger, D. R., Torrey, E. F., Neophytides, A. N., & Wyatt, R. J. (1979). Lateral cerebral ventricular enlargement in chronic schizophrenia. *Archives of General Psychiatry, 36,* 735–739.

Weiner, B. (1975). "On being sane in insane places": A process (attributional) analysis and critique. *Journal of Abnormal Psychology, 84*(5), 433–441.

Weiner, I. B. (1966). *Psychodiagnosis in schizophrenia.* New York: Wiley.

Weiner, I. B. (1991). Editor's note: Interscorer agreement in Rorschach research. *Journal of Personality Assessment, 56,* 1.

Whitaker, L. C. (1965). The Rorschach and Holtzman as measures of pathognomic verbalization. *Journal of Consulting Psychology, 29,* 181–183.

Whitaker, L. C. (1973). *Whitaker Index of Schizophrenic Thinking (WIST): Manual.* Los Angeles: Western Psychological Services.

Whitaker, L. C. (1980). *Objective measurement of schizophrenic thinking: A practical and theoretical guide to the Whitaker Index of Schizophrenic Thinking.* Los Angeles: Western Psychological Services.

Whitaker, L. C. (1987). Macho and morbidity: The emotional need vs. fear dilemma in men. *Journal of College Student Psychotherapy, 1*(4), 33–47.

Whitaker, L. C. (1989). Myths and heroes: Visions of the future. *Journal of College Student Psychotherapy, 4*(2), 13–33.

Whitaker, L. C., & Deikman, A. J. (1980). Psychotherapy of severe depression. *Psychotherapy: Theory, Research and Practice, 17,* 85–93.

Wolfe, H. L., & Astrachan, B. M. (1986). Community mental health services. In G. L. Klerman, M. M. Weissman, P. S. Applebaum, & L. H. Roth (Eds.), *Social, epidemiologic, and legal psychiatry* (Vol. 5, pp. 63–76), in J. O. Cavenar (Gen. Ed.), *Psychiatry.* New York: Basic Books.

Wong, D. F., Wagner, H. N., Tune, L. E., Dannals, R. F., Pearlson, G. D., Links, J. M., Tamminga, C. A., Broussolle, E. P., Ravert, H. T., Wilson, A. A., Thomas-Young, J. K., Malat, J., Williams, J. A., O'Tuama, L. A., Snyder, S. H., Kuhar, M. J., & Gjedde, A. (1986). Positron emission tomography reveals elevated D_2 dopamine receptors in drug-naive schizophrenics. *Science, 234,* 1558–1563.

Taylor, M., & Abrams, R. (1977). Catatonea. *Archives of General Psychiatry, 34,* 1223–1225.

Wood, B. T., & Short, M. P. (1985). Neurological dimensions of psychiatry. *Journal of Biological Psychiatry, 20,* 192–198.

Woodbury, M. (1964). Milieu, symptoms and schizophrenia: The seven year history and evolution of a psychiatric ward; *Psychiatric research report 19. American Psychiatric Association,* 20–36.

Wyatt, J. R., Kirch, D. G., & DeLisi, L. E. (1989). Schizophrenia: Biological, endocrine, and immunological studies. In H. Kaplan & B. Saddock (Eds.), *Comprehensive textbook of psychiatry.* (5th ed.). (Vol. 1, pp. 717–732). Baltimore: Williams & Wilkins.

Wyatt v. Stickney (1971). 325 *F.Supp.* 781 MD Ala. 1971), 334 *F.Supp.* 1341 (MD Ala. 1971), 344 *F. Supp.*

373 (MD A 1972), 344 *F.Supp.* 387 (MD Ala 1974), aff'd *sub nom Wyatt v. Aderholt,* 503 F.2nd 1305 (5 Cir. 1974).

Wysocki, J. J., & Sweet, J. J. (1985). Identification of brain-damaged, schizophrenic, and normal medical patients using a brief neuropsychological screening battery. *International Journal of Clinical Neuropsychology, 7,* 40–44.

Yaroush, R. (1982). Application of the Whitaker Index of Schizophrenic Thinking to a non-English population. *Journal of Clinical Psychology, 38,* 244–252.

Yates, W. R., Jacoby, C. G., & Andreasen, N. C. (1987). Cerebellar atrophy in schizophrenia and affective disorder. *American Journal of Psychiatry, 144,* 465–467.

Yusin, A., Nihira, K., & Mortashed, C. (1974). Major and minor criteria in schizophrenia. *American Journal of Psychiatry, 131,* 688–692.

Zigler, E. & Glick, M. (1988). Is paranoid schizophrenia really camouflaged depression? *American Psychologist, 43,* 284–290.

Zigler, E., & Levine, J. (1983). Hallucinations and delusions: A developmental approach. *Journal of Nervous and Mental Disease, 171,* 141–146.

Zubin, J. (1987). Possible implications of the vulnerability hypothesis for the psychosocial management of schizophrenia. In J. S. Strauss, W. Böker, & H. D. Brenner (Eds.), *Psychosocial treatment of schizophrenia: Multidimensional concepts, psychological, family, and self-help perspective* (pp. 30–47). Toronto, Lewiston, New York, Bern, Stuttgart: Hans Huber.

Index